ArtScroll Series®

Rabbi Nosson Scherman / Rabbi Meir Zlotowitz

General Editors

From the Maggidim

by **Yaakov Ariel**

Adapted from the Hebrew "L'Haggid"
by **Libby Lazewnik**

Published by
Mesorah Publications, ltd

OF YESTERYEAR

RABBI BENZION YADLER

RABBI SHOLOM SCHWADRON

RABBI SHABSI YUDELEVITZ

RABBI YAAKOV GALINSKY

SHEMOS ✦ VAYIKRA

FIRST EDITION
First Impression … January 2009

Published and Distributed by
MESORAH PUBLICATIONS, LTD.
4401 Second Avenue / Brooklyn, N.Y 11232

Distributed in Europe by
LEHMANNS
Unit E, Viking Business Park
Rolling Mill Road
Jarow, Tyne & Wear, NE32 3DP
England

Distributed in Australia and New Zealand
by **GOLDS WORLDS OF JUDAICA**
3-13 William Street
Balaclava, Melbourne 3183
Victoria, Australia

Distributed in Israel by
SIFRIATI / A. GITLER — BOOKS
6 Hayarkon Street
Bnei Brak 51127

Distributed in South Africa by
KOLLEL BOOKSHOP
Ivy Common
105 William Road
Norwood 2192, Johannesburg, South Africa

ARTSCROLL SERIES®
FROM THE MAGGIDIM OF YESTERYEAR
VOLUME 2 — SHEMOS / VAYIKRA
© *Copyright 2009, by* MESORAH PUBLICATIONS, Ltd.
4401 Second Avenue / Brooklyn, N.Y. 11232 / (718) 921-9000 / www.artscroll.com

ISBN 10: 1-4226-0884-0 / ISBN 13: 978-1-4226-0884-5

Typography by CompuScribe at ArtScroll Studios, Ltd.

Printed in the United States of America by Noble Book Press Corp.
Bound by Sefercraft, Quality Bookbinders, Ltd., Brooklyn N.Y. 11232

❧ TABLE OF CONTENTS

FROM THE
MAGGIDIM
OF
YESTERYEAR

INTRODUCTION

To Speak ... and to Weep

Reverently, we entered the room of the aged *gaon hatzaddik* R' Yaakov Galinsky, *shlita*. In a low voice, but with his characteristic good humor, he told us the following.

"I know that you do not have the capability to transmit my *derashos* in writing in their original form and with their original intention — but do not let this trouble you. I don't care. Years ago, I heard from my rebbi in yeshivah that this project is a worthwhile one — needed to arouse the nation. He cited proof from the Gemara (*Yoma* 23a): 'R' Tzaddok stood on the steps of the hall and cried, "Our brothers, O House of Israel, listen! Behold it says, '*If a corpse will be found on the land ... your elders and judges shall go out*' to perform the mitzvah of *eglah arufah*[1] for atonement. As for us, upon whom does the responsibility fall to bring an *eglah arufah*? Does the responsibility fall upon the residents of the city of Jerusalem, or upon the *Kohanim* who guard the Temple courtyards?" Upon hearing this, all the people burst out crying ...'

---

1. *Eglah arufah* — lit. decapitated calf. If the body of a murder victim is discovered outside a town in Eretz Yisrael and his murderer is not known, the elders of the Sanhedrin must measure the distance to the surrounding towns to determine the town closest to the corpse. The elders of that town must then bring a female calf that was never worked and decapitate it in an untilled valley, in accordance with the procedure outlined in *Deuteronomy* 21:1-9.

"The Gemara asks, 'Does Jerusalem even bring an *eglah arufah*?! Rather, in order to increase the weeping …' Therefore, when anyone is aroused there is a purpose — and that will be my reward.

"*Rabbosai*, we in this orphaned generation no longer understand the purity of weeping, the depths of crying, and the wonder of how far a tear can reach.

"Jewish weeping, when the eyes blaze and the face shines with purity, has disappeared from our landscape. Soul-scorching tears, weeping filled with a longing that spills from an overflowing Jewish heart — all these have diminished, lost with the dwindling of the generations.

"Not long ago, there were still *maggidim* to cry for us. These *maggidim* traveled from city to city, offering words of *mussar* and fear of heaven, and were heard wailing in a loud voice: 'Wake up! Rouse yourselves! Destructive angels will accompany the wicked, so why not cry? And with the fine reward lying in wait for the righteous, how can we not cry with joy?' The *maggidim* would spread their hands over their audiences in the towns and villages, and break down in tears. There were individuals who joined them, swaying and crying, one pure teardrop after another.

"In those days, angels waited at the shul doors. They would enter respectfully to collect the tears. From the broad tables and from the thick-beamed *shtenders* they would gather the teardrops. Sometimes they had to bend to the ground to pick up an exceptionally large drop still cascading down: the tear of a woman in the women's section, or a wagoneer in whom fear of heaven burned strong. The angels would pick up each and every tear, wrap it in Divine grasses, and bear it in reverence to heaven. And these tears served as protection against many troubles and harsh decrees. Today, however, there are hardly any *maggidim* left. There is no one to cry, and to rouse the nation to cry. The wellspring of tears has dried up."

On a different occasion, we heard the following from R' Yaakov Galinsky, *shlita*. The greater the people were, he said, the more acute was their hearing, and the more their eyes would see and weep.

It says in *Mesillas Yesharim (perek beis)*: "This is what the *Navi* cried out when he said, *'Pay heed to your ways.'*" We may inquire regarding this. Who doesn't possess a *Navi Yirmiyahu* in his home? Have any of us ever heard the outcry of a *Navi*? The *Mesillas Yesharim*, apparently, did ... When the heart is different, one's hearing becomes more acute.

And who were greater than our holy *Tannaim*, for whom a fleeting glance at a certain verse in the *Navi* would set the tears flowing. "When R' Yonasan would reach this verse, he would weep" (*Yoma* 9b). The same is said of R' Huna (*Chagigah* 4b). The Gemara lists about ten other *Tannaim* and *Amoraim* who wept. They merely glanced at this verse and broke down in tears ...

The generations are dwindling.

May it be Hashem's will that this book *"From the Maggidim of Yesteryear"* will give its readers a taste of those old-time *maggidim*: the tears that are hidden between the lines, the *mussar* lesson tucked into the seemingly casual rhetoric. If even one tear sparkles in the eye of one reader who has never experienced that kind of tear before, that will be our reward.

ספר שמות

SEFER SHEMOS

פרשת שמות
Parashas Shemos

The Wagoneer's Warning

R' Shabsi Yudelevitz

abbosai, you must surely have heard of R' Yonasan Eibeshitz, author of the *Sefer HaTumim* and a *gaon* in his time, one of the Jewish leaders who saved Ashkenazic Jewry from the grasp of the Catholic Church.

R' Yonasan Eibeshitz told of a pious Jewish wagon driver who triumphed over a wicked priest.

During that period in Prague, a rabidly anti-Semitic priest joined the royal court, with the sole purpose of filling the king's heart with hatred for the Jews. From time to time he would enter into heated debate with R' Yonasan Eibeshitz. The embers of anti-Semitism that always burned in the hearts of gentile kings would be fanned into flame through these debates. We can imagine the degree to which the Jews' situation was dependent on these debates.

R' Yonasan Eibeshitz was granted special *siyata d'Shemaya* — Divine assistance. Hashem had graced him with a sharp intellect, a logical mind capable of responding forcefully to his enemies. In his debates with that rabid priest, R' Yonasan inevitably emerged the winner.

Then came the day when yet another such debate ended in R' Yonasan's favor. The priest stood up and announced to the king: "In principle, truth is on my side and the Christian faith is superior to any other. It is merely R' Eibeshitz's educated mind and sharp tongue that oppose me. He possesses not the truth, but a finely honed skill in the art of eloquent debate. I can prove my point. If a simple Jew were to be brought before me to engage in an ordinary debate, we would see which faith is the correct one."

It was decided that the first simple Jew to pass the royal palace would be summoned inside to engage in a question-and-answer session with the priest.

Before long, a horse-drawn wagon passed the palace, driven by a Jewish wagoneer. He wore shabby clothes and wielded an oversized whip.

On the king's orders, he was brought into the palace. His name and place of origin were presented to the king. The priest was given permission to open the debate.

"I have a deal to offer you," began the priest. "From this day forward, the king of Austria will authorize a wagoneer's position for you in the royal courtyard. Your wage will be considerable, and you will never again need to beg favors from people. You and your poverty-stricken family will be able to live near the palace at the king's expense, where you will enjoy the privileges of full citizenship. In addition, we will care for your immortal soul, and the souls of your family; you will go to heaven and enjoy eternal reward.

"In return, all you have to do is to allow me to sprinkle a bit of water on you, and to pronounce several words, as per Christian practice."

As the priest concluded his speech, the wagon driver's face flushed. Fearfully he gripped his whip as he shook his head negatively back and forth. Finally, he managed to blurt out his answer, forceful and curt: "No! No! No!"

The priest, who had been certain that such a destitute person would be eager to accept the deal, was taken aback. Quickly he asked, "Very well, my son. We will not force you, or your family, to do something against your will. But please explain to me the reasoning behind your decision. Why do you object to this fantastic opportunity?"

R' Yonasan Eibeshitz was among those present in the great hall. He prayed fervently that Hashem might instill wisdom in the heart of that Jew. As the wagon driver's eyes flitted from the priest to the king, it was clear that he was afraid to answer and was weighing whether to say anything at all. The king urged, "Do not be afraid. Speak freely. No harm will befall you."

Mustering his courage, the wagoneer responded:

"When you offered me this deal, I remembered my departed father, who would guide my every step. My father was a wagon driver, too — an honest and upright man. Before his death, he commanded me to live as a God-fearing Jew, to distance myself from evil and to do good, and to fulfill the will of the Creator. Also, he taught me the way of the world: how to conduct a negotiation. Among other things, he warned me, 'Do not become involved with a horse trader who tries to get you to trade your horse for a better one. Even if he is prepared to add money to sweeten the deal, don't do it. It will be a deceptive deal. He is not interested in giving you a horse plus money in the exchange. The horse might seem fine, but it will undoubtedly be suffering from some hidden disease, or it had been stolen, or has some other flaw that will only be uncovered at a later date. And if a trader comes to you and offers you another horse without any additional payment on his side, do not agree to that, either. In this case, too, he must have some deceitful agenda in mind. Why else would he wish to trade horses with no benefit to himself?'

" 'However,' said my father, 'if a man comes to you and says, "*Reb Yid*, take my horse in exchange for your own, but you must add a certain sum of money to sweeten the deal," this is an honest trade. That trader has upright intentions. In that case, examine the horse and if it suits you, be prepared to conclude the bargain.'

"You, sir," the wagon driver continued to the priest, "offered me a deal that includes all the good of this world, plus eternal life in the next. You ask for nothing in exchange from me. Therefore, the deal seems to me to be flawed. There's something rotten in it ... And that is why I say, 'No!' I decline your offer."

The king smiled. He ordered one of his servants to give the wagon driver a valuable gift and send him on his way in peace. The priest was pained. After a few minutes, he requested that R' Yonasan Eibeshitz be called up. In deep chagrin, he admitted, "You have bested me, Rabbi of Prague — again!"

Rabbosai, the young Jews in Egypt tried to become involved in Egyptian life. "And the land was filled with them" (as will be cited in the following *derashah* by R' Yaakov Galinsky). What did they get out of it? Nothing. It was a rotten deal … a sickly horse.

How many sick horses people buy! The Satan offers a plethora of fine horses for free … How clever he is! He sells stolen or ailing horses, which people purchase and later regret. They don't know about the old wagoneer's warning.

May Hashem help us, in the merit of all the *tzaddikim*, so that we never, heaven forbid, fall in with sickly or evil merchandise. And may we soon see the comfort of Zion.

וַיָּמָת יוֹסֵף וְכָל־אֶחָיו וְכֹל הַדּוֹר הַהוּא: וּבְנֵי יִשְׂרָאֵל פָּרוּ וַיִּשְׁרְצוּ וַיִּרְבּוּ וַיַּעַצְמוּ בִּמְאֹד מְאֹד וַתִּמָּלֵא הָאָרֶץ אֹתָם.

"Yosef died, and all his brothers and that entire generation. The Children of Israel were fruitful, teemed, increased, and became strong — very, very much so; and the land became filled with them" (Shemos 1:6-7).

JUST WORK WITH YOUR HANDS!

R' Yaakov Galinsky

Y ou are mistaken!" R' Yaakov Galinsky pounded his *shtender* with uncharacteristic force. "I returned from abroad yesterday, where I heard a *derashah* by a certain rabbi who explained the way things were in Egypt. He described what the enslavement in Egypt was like. And he was wrong! He was wrong because he placed primary emphasis on the physical enslavement of the Jewish people."

Was the primary enslavement in Egypt backbreaking labor? No! Let me explain in the words of the Kotzker Rebbe with regard to the verse, "*Yagia kapecha ki sochel, ashrecha v'tov lach* — *When you eat the labor of your hands you are praiseworthy, and it is well with you*" (*Tehillim* 128:2). This is what the Kotzker Rebbe said:

"If you labor with your hands you are praiseworthy, and it is well with you."

What does he mean? If only the hands work hard, that's all right. But if the head works — when a person's mind is absorbed in merchandise and business affairs — then the "*ashrecha v'tov lach*" disappears ...

I remember something else profound that is said in the Kotzker Rebbe's name. A chassid once came to see the Kotzker, complaining that foreign thoughts intruded on his mind during *davening*. Replied the Rebbe: "Foreign thoughts?! Are these foreign thoughts? They are your true thoughts! Your mind is taken up with the marketplace, so you think about that and other empty things during *davening*. For you, the *Shemoneh Esrei* is the 'foreign thought' ...!"

How profoundly we should study the Kotzker's Rebbe's answer!

Rabbosai, the great trouble in Egypt was not only the backbreaking labor: the aching arms, legs, and backs. The enslavement in Egypt was this: Because of their labor, they became more and more involved with bricks and mortar, to the point that they reached the 49th level of impurity. Before the exodus from Egypt, the angels came and asked *Hakadosh Baruch Hu* why He chose to redeem the nation of Israel. "These [i.e., the Egyptians] are idol worshipers, and these [i.e., the Israelites] are idol worshipers." To this extent were the Jewish people enslaved to Egypt.

☞ When Did the Slavery Begin?

On the one hand, the *midrash* teaches us that as long as one of the brothers was still alive, slavery was not decreed on the Jewish nation. *"Yosef died, and all his brothers and that entire generation"* — only then did the subjugation begin. Our Sages seemed to indicate that the brothers' deaths created an opening for the Egyptian enslavement.

On the other hand, *Chazal* tell us elsewhere that the decrees began when the Jews opted to leave the confines of Goshen for other locations. When "the land became filled with them" and conditions became too crowded in the land of Goshen, they went to buy new villas throughout Egypt, to the north and to the south. And suddenly, slavery came upon them.

This is the answer. Each one is bound up in the other. R' Yaakov Galinsky raises his voice and his right hand:

So long as the older generation existed — so long as there were still elders around, Yaakov Avinu's offspring — the Jewish nation remained on their high level and did not mingle with the gentiles. They maintained their privacy, and this constituted a lifeline for them in the Egyptian exile. They lived in the land of Goshen, where the impurity had not yet spread too far because Goshen still belonged to Sara Imeinu (an earlier Pharaoh had given it to her as a gift). However, with the passing of the last of Yaakov Avinu's sons, slowly they began to enter the business and political world of Egypt. Some became bureaucrats while others followed different occupations. They even attained positions in Parliament: *"The land was filled with them."* But all of this did not profit them at all. In fact, the opposite held true: *"A new king arose over Egypt, who did not know of Yosef."* The decrees began.

The moment we have people who come to listen to a discourse on the subject of *tzniyus*, modesty, but who only listen, while continuing to conduct themselves by the standards of the street, then the gentiles are able to master us. The slavery begins …

(If one behaves that way because a neighbor does, and the neighbor does so because of his or her neighbor, who conducts himself that way because of yet another neighbor, that's slavery!)

Therefore, let us work on a personal escape from Egypt. I am confident that every person knows how to extricate himself from his own personal slavery. May Hashem put an end to our troubles, and may we soon merit *techiyas hameisim* and the coming of the *Mashiach*, speedily in our days.

וַיֵּלֶךְ אִישׁ מִבֵּית לֵוִי וַיִּקַּח אֶת־בַּת־לֵוִי.

"A man went from the House of Levi and he took a daughter of Levi"(Shemos 2:1).

Where did he go? R' Yehudah bar Zevina says that he went on his daughter's suggestion ... Amram was the gadol hador. When Pharaoh decreed, "Every son that will be born — into the River shall you throw him!" [Amram] said, "We are toiling in vain." He got up and divorced his wife. Whereupon everyone else got up and divorced their wives. Said his daughter: "Father ... Pharaoh only decreed against the males ... His wicked decree may come to fruition and it may not. You are a tzaddik — your decrees must certainly come to fruition" (Sotah 12).

WHAT DID FIVE-YEAR-OLD MIRIAM SAY?

R' Yaakov Galinsky

*A*mram was the *gadol hador*" — the nation's leader in Egypt. When Pharaoh decreed, "Every son that will be born — into the River shall you throw him!" Amram then rose and divorced his wife. Thereupon everyone else did the same. For Amram said to himself: *We will build families, and Pharaoh will destroy them. What's the use?* That was why he divorced his wife, and all of Israel followed his example. This is *emunas chachamim* — a display of faith in the wisdom of our Torah Sages.

A person's greatness is evidenced by his listening to and paying attention to others, even if they are of lesser stature than he. *Chazal* tell us that Amram, the *gadol hador*, listened to the wise words that his daughter spoke. And in the merit of those words, our Sages say, Amram took back his wife, and Moshe Rabbeinu was born.

What was Miriam's wisdom? And what lesson can we glean from what she said?

Let's take a look.

First of all, never despair. Don't fall apart when times are hard. Pharaoh's decree can be nullified in a moment. "Pharaoh's wicked decree may come to fruition and it may not. You are a *tzaddik*, your decrees must certainly come to fruition," Miriam said. Jews do not fly into a tizzy over difficulties and suffering, and this is their praise!

Miriam taught us not to take it to heart, and certainly not to despair.

"In the merit of righteous women, our forefathers were redeemed from Egypt." *Chazal* tell us that the women were aware of the threatening decrees. They witnessed the government snatching children and slaughtering them. They saw decree piled upon decree and yet, they did not lose hope. Ignoring the king's decrees, they brought water for drinking and inside the water were fish for eating. From these, they prepared tasty dishes and built families. "What do I care what Pharaoh has decreed? I must do the job that has been given to me. I will make my effort, and Hashem will do His part." And so many children were born: "*They ... increased and became strong — very, very much so!*" These children were miraculously saved, and thronged together from the fields after they were saved. This is the message we learn from those righteous Jewish women in whose merit we were saved from Egypt: not to allow yourselves to be broken.

The Alshich comments on the words, *"V'achalta es shelal oyve-cha — You will consume your enemy's booty."* The letters of *"oyvecha"* are the initials of *"ein ye'ush b'olam klal — there is no despair in the world."* Despair is our greatest enemy.

* * *

☞ A Slap on the Mouth

In a separate *derashah* on *Parashas Shemos* and the Jews' suffering in Egypt, R' Yaakov declared in a loud voice filled with fervor:

The Gemara says, "Nevuchadnetzar, king of Babylonia, wished to sing Hashem's praises more than David Hamelech. Thus, *Chazal* say, "An angel came and slapped him on the mouth" to silence him. "R' Yitzchak said, had the angel not come and smacked him on the mouth, he wished to cast into the shade all the songs and praises that David said in *Sefer Tehillim"* (*Sanhedrin* 92b).

The commentaries ask: What gave the angel the right to prevent someone from praising Hashem more than David Hamelech did? After all, we live in a world of *bechirah* — of free choice. The Rambam says that every person is granted the possibility of even being like Moshe Rabbeinu. How and why was Nevuchadnetzar prevented from singing his praises?

The answer can be found in the words, "An angel came and slapped him on the mouth."

Nevuchadnetzar ruled the entire world. He lacked for nothing. Therefore, it was as though the angel came to him and said, "You are filled with contentment and every good thing, and it is your desire to praise *HaKadosh Baruch Hu*. Very nice — you deserve a good reward for that (for others did not even do that much). However, you have not yet earned the merit of praising Hashem as David Hamelech did. 'An angel came and slapped him on the mouth.' Now, after you've been struck a blow, let us see whether you are capable of singing Hashem's praises ..."

David Hamelech sang to Hashem under all sorts of circumstances. "*Of kindness and justice do I sing*" (*Tehillim* 101:1). Rashi explains: "When you perform a kindness for me, I will say, '*Baruch hatov u'meitiv*' ('Blessed is He Who bestows good'), and when You mete out justice to me I will sing, '*Baruch Dayan ha'emes*' ('Blessed is the true Judge'). Either way, I will sing to You, Hashem." Such is the power of a Jew! Jews do not fall apart under a situation; on the contrary, they sing Hashem's praises with all their hearts!

Nevuchadnetzar could not perform this feat: to sing amid suffering. So the angel silenced him ...

(We will see the second thing that Miriam taught in the following *derashah*.)

"*His daughter told him: 'Father, your decree is harsher than Pharaoh's, for Pharaoh only decreed on the males, but you have decreed on both males and females. Pharaoh decreed only in this world, but you — in this world and the next. For the wicked Pharaoh, it is an open question whether or not his decree will come to fruition. But you are a tzaddik; certainly your decrees will come to fruition'* ... *He got up and took back his wife, and everyone got up and took back their wives*" (*Sotah* 12a).

A DIN TORAH IN ADAM HARISHON'S HOUSE

R' Yaakov Galinsky

*I*don't know where Adam Harishon lived, but a *midrash* on *parashas Bereishis* tells us that his grandchildren came together in a *din Torah*, before Adam Harishon. Perhaps they knocked on the door of his house, his yeshivah, or some other place.

"And Lemech said to his wives, 'Adah and Tzillah, hear my voice; wives of Lemech, give ear to my speech: Have I slain a man by my wound and a child by my bruise? If Kayin suffered vengeance at seven generations, then Lemech at 77!"

What happened here?

Adah and Tzillah, Lemech's wives, came to a joint decision: to no longer live with him. They told him, "You are a sixth-generation descendant of Kayin, who killed Hevel, his brother. As we know, Hashem promised Kayin that he would be patient with him for seven generations (and no more). Therefore, if we give birth to children, they will be the seventh generation and will not survive. A flood will come and destroy them, or some other catastrophe. In that case, why should we bear children for naught?" That is what they said. Lemech gave all sorts of answers, which they didn't accept. So Lemech suggested, "Let us go to a *din Torah* with our grandfather. Our great-grandfather — Adam Harishon." They came.

The grandfather listened carefully to both arguments, neither of which was at all simple. On the surface, the women had a very valid complaint.

Adam Harishon told them: "You are to do your job without making calculations. Carry out Hashem's commandments, and Hashem will do His part." In other words, a person should not exert himself to figure out Hashem's plan. If his job is to bring children into the world, there's no room for rationalizations and calculations.

If you pay attention, you will notice something interesting. In those years, a "generation" was not a span of 20 or 30 years. A single generation was spread over many long years. For example, there were 10 generations between Adam Harishon and Noach, spanning a total of 1,000 years. People lived for hundreds of years and every generation was long lived. However, this does not apply to the generations that emerged from Kayin. Following him there were six generations, son after son born with exceptional speed over a very brief period: just 130 years! This gave Adah and Tzillah food for thought. They believed, justifiably, that *HaKadosh Baruch Hu* wished, as it were, to hasten the debt that Kayin owed him, to arrive at the seventh generation and then destroy his descendants. "Why, then, should we bear children for naught?" they protested.

But Adam Harishon rendered his verdict: They were not to make calculations, but to carry out the task that Hashem had given them to do.

Adah and Tzillah asked Adam: "In that case, why haven't you, Grandfather, brought children into the world for the past 130 years, ever since the birth of Kayin?" Adam listened to them [and returned to his wife], after which Sheis was born: "*Adam knew his wife again, and she bore a son and named him Sheis, because "God has provided me another child in place of Hevel ..."*

Have you ever thought about what happened to that seventh generation after Kayin?

Look at what the Ramban has to say, and you will see that children — son after son — did not survive from Kayin. The "generations" ended. But a remnant of him does remain. Not a lot; just one daughter named Naamah. "*And Tzillah, too — she bore Tuval-kayin, who sharpened all cutting implements of copper and iron. And the sister of Tuval-kayin was Naamah.*"

Who was Naamah? She became Noach's wife. We are all descended from Kayin's seed! For Naamah was the seventh generation — and she was the one who survived in the Ark. "*And from these the whole world was spread out ...*"

Had Adah and Tzillah followed through on their own thought processes, there would be no remnant of them in the world. Instead, they listened to Adam Harishon's advice — "You do your job and Hashem will do His" — and they benefited from it.

Miriam's strength was this very wisdom that Adam Harishon taught. "Let us do what we are bidden to do, and Hashem will do His part." She was only a little girl when she merited so much. What did she tell her father? "Father, let us do our part, even if Pharaoh has decreed that all the children must be killed. Hashem will take care of the rest ..." Amram listened to her — and Moshe Rabbeinu was born.

Ever since Adam taught his descendants this marvelous lesson, righteous women have known the secret. The righteous wives in

Egypt knew that they mustn't make calculations. They understood that it was incumbent upon them to carry out their own mission. It was then that the hidden power in their actions stood revealed. They refused to despair. "Why should we care what Pharaoh has decreed? I must do the job I've been given to do, and Hashem will do His part." And so, many, many children were born: *"The Children of Israel ... increased and became strong — very, very much so!"*

There are those who think, *I have no abilities, no influence in the home. What can I do? Can I fight everything?* This is a mistake! It is a very great error. Let us heed the advice of Adam HaRishon, and persevere.

☞ The Yetzer Hara's Sermons

If I were to tell you that a woman can become a *Rosh Yeshivah*, you'd laugh at me and probably ask, "What happened to Rabbi Galinsky? Can a woman be a *Rosh Yeshivah*?!" I'd tell them what *Chazal* have to say on the subject.

Rachel married R' Akiva when he was an unlearned man. She sent him off to "*kollel*" to learn for 24 years. When he returned home, accompanied by 42,000 students, Rachel wished to approach him. Some of the students barred her way. Said R' Akiva to them: "Allow her to pass! All of my Torah, and all of yours, belongs to her. She is the *Rosh Yeshivah*, not I ..."

Do you hear? A woman *can* be a *Rosh Yeshivah*! And how did she achieve that? By doing her job!

Take a look in the *midrash hagadol* and see the kind of suffering that R' Akiva endured. Until the age of 40 he learned nothing, and at 40 he joined the first grade in *cheder*. That couldn't have been easy for him ... He would describe to his wife the pain and ridicule that were his daily portion, and Rachel would comfort him and encourage his flagging spirits. She told him, "*Lefum tzarah agra*" — your reward will be consonant with your pain. You suffer, you endure, and you grow! Who made R' Akiva into a *gadol?* His wife. Rachel knew that when a person does the job that he's been given to do, *HaKadosh Baruch Hu* does His part.

On the one hand, the *yetzer hara* constantly draws us into arrogance. At the same time, it imbues us with a deep sense of our own inferiority: "What can I do? Am I capable of influencing my husband? Can I educate my children properly? We live in different times, when children do not listen and husbands pay no attention. What can I do to influence the spirituality of my home?"

These are the *yetzer hara's* sermons.

⌐ He Sat and Cried

R' Chanina ben Dosa was extremely destitute. He didn't have the money to buy an animal to be offered in Jerusalem on Yom Tov. All his neighbors brought offerings — sheep and goats — but he was exempt because he didn't have a penny in his pocket. Still, he thought to himself: *While it is true that I am exempt because I have no money with which to buy an offering, I do have the ability to take a large stone from a nearby hill and to chisel it nicely. Once the stone's been cut it will be worth money, which I will donate to the Beis HaMikdash. I do have abilities and possibilities ...* Such were the thoughts of R' Chanina ben Dosa.

And so he did. He left the city and chiseled a stone. When he had completed the work he asked himself, *Who will carry this heavy stone to Jerusalem?* He searched and found a group of porters. "How much will you charge me to carry this stone to Jerusalem?" he asked. "Fifty *sela'im* (a hefty sum)," they replied. But he had no money. Had he possessed 50 *sela'im*, he would have used it to buy offerings and to stand before Hashem in the Beis HaMikdash. He sat down on the stone and wept.

That much he could do. He could cry. "*Ribono Shel Olam*, I am not neglecting my obligations. I did everything that I could do. You did not give me money, but I took advantage of every other opportunity that came my way. (After all, a person is not asked to do more than that!)" So R' Chanina ben Dosa wept.

Five angels came along, in the form of men, and asked, "*Reb Yid*, why are you crying? What happened? Are you in pain?" He told them his story. "Listen," said the angels, "we are on the way to Jerusalem ourselves. We could take your stone along for the nominal sum of five *zuzim* — but only on one condition. We want you to come with us, to help us."

Together they heaved and lifted that stone, and ... R' Chanina ben Dosa found himself on his way to the holy city of Jerusalem. A miracle!

On his arrival, when he turned to pay the "men," there was no sign of them. In the words of *Chazal* (*Koheles Rabbah*): "If you see a man who is diligent in his work, he will stand before kings (*melachim*) or angels (*malachim*). It happened with R' Chanina ben Dosa ... etc." Amazing!

R' Chanina ben Dosa might have given up. He had no money, and no possibility of a loan. That, it would seem, was that ... Instead, the holy *Tanna* decided to do the maximum that he could, drawing from a powerful desire to fulfill the mitzvah. He knew the secret: When man does his part, Hashem does His! In this way, he was unimaginably successful. And after R' Chanina's passing from this world, the *mishnah* in *Sotah* tells us, "From the time that R' Chanina ben Dosa died, there have been no more people of deeds" (*Sotah* 49a and see *Tosafos, Chagigah* 14a).

* * *

⌐ We Are Soldiers

In the 1950's, when the Jewish Agency was doing its utmost to prevent Yemenite immigrants to Israel from registering for religious education, a group of us yeshivah *bachurim* traveled to Rosh Ha'ayin to conduct a registration drive for *frum* schools. How we were beaten! And cursed and reviled. Those in charge goaded the *olim* (immigrants) into berating us: "Robbers! Thieves!" Pain and disappointment, blows and curses were our lot. The situation seemed as far from success as anything could possibly be.

Incidentally, on one of these trips, as we boarded the bus for the return trip to Bnei Brak, an elderly Yemenite man sat beside us. Seeing that we wore beards and *peyos*, he spread his hands and said, "Precious Jews, I am crying — crying and saying, 'For our sins, we were exiled to our land …'"

The pain was enormous in those days, and despair encroached everywhere. What could we do? We were a tiny band pitted against a cruel and well-funded operation.

Immediately upon our return, we went to see the Chazon Ish. We were broken and shattered. "We don't even care about being beaten, as much as we do about the spiritual holocaust that we witnessed in those camps," we complained to him. "During World War II, we suffered from the Germans who murdered our bodies. Now, before our very eyes, thousands of pious, innocent God-fearing Jewish souls are being slaughtered!"

The Chazon Ish looked at us. Understanding the pain that engulfed us, an expression of sorrow crossed his face. He was silent. Then he turned to us and said, "We are soldiers. We will carry out the mission we have been appointed to do, and you will see how *HaKadosh Baruch Hu* repays us for it."

We left the room in silence.

Time passed: days, and then years. Today, everyone can see the payment for that dedication. The individuals that we did manage to rescue from the claws of assimilation are founding Torah institutions and attracting students from the Mideastern communities.

The *ba'alei teshuvah* are multiplying without end. "*There is a reward for your actions, and your children will return to their borders.*"

The pain and agony that was the portion of the Jews in Egypt led them to despair, but the righteous women of that generation encouraged their husbands and gave them strength: "We are soldiers. We will carry out our mission and we will witness wonders!"

☞ Extending a Hand

Another woman who demonstrated what it is possible to achieve was Pharaoh's daughter. "*Pharaoh's daughter went down to bathe in the river.*" Discovering Moshe Rabbeinu's basket 400 *amah* from the bank of the Nile, she longed to rescue him. What chance did she have to achieve this, given the length of her arm? But she did not leave her arm dangling uselessly at her side. Rather, she did everything that it was possible for her to do: "*She stretched out her hand*"! This was her only chance. And then the miracle happened: "R' Huna says that her arm stretched 400 *amah*."

She could have said, "What can my arm do?" But she didn't say that. And that's when the miracles started happening.

A Divine voice, as it were, is constantly speaking to a person: "Demonstrate, at least, that you really, really want it. Stretch out your hand!" "Make an opening for Me like the eye of a needle, and I will create an opening for you as wide as a hall!" Move! Advance! Do not stand still in frozen despair! We must know that *HaKadosh Baruch Hu*, Who is found everywhere on heaven and earth, is available to help us at any hour of the day or night. Anyone who comes to purify himself is offered Divine assistance.

Let us do our part, and Hashem will be at our side to help us toward spiritual satisfaction and success.

"She called his name Moshe" (Shemos 2:10).

From here we learn the reward of those who perform acts of lovingkindness. Despite the fact that Moshe had several names, the only name by which he was called in the entire Torah was Moshe, the name given to him by Bitya, Pharaoh's daughter. Even HaKadosh Baruch Hu did not call him by any other name" (Shemos Rabbah 1:3).

Ten Names!

R' Shabsi Yudelevitz

Seven names, ten names, twenty names ... What is all this business about names?

Secondly, why did Heaven really invest so much importance in the name "Moshe," given to him by *bas* Pharaoh? R' Shabsi begins his *derashah* with this question, and proceeds to tell a story:

Rabbi Marcus Lehman, of Germany, was the author of numerous works of fiction. R' Lehman was a great *talmid chacham* and the leader of a vibrant community in Germany, who wrote books with the intention of saving German Jewish youth. In one of his books (not known today), he related a story that had happened to him.

As rabbi of a large community, he had an appointment to meet with the king at a certain time on a certain date. The appointment had been arranged in advance in cooperation with other community leaders, who were also slated to attend the meeting under R' Lehman's leadership.

In those days, of course, there were no private automobiles. The community heads would have to travel by train. Horses and wagons would bring them to the train station. The community leaders agreed to meet at the station and together board the last train departing for the capital city.

☞ *I'm Sorry, Reb Yid*

The appointed day arrived. R' Lehman waited impatiently at home for the wagon driver who was supposed to take him to the train station. Suddenly, a Jew came pounding on his door, asking to speak to the *rav*. The rebbetzin said, "I'm sorry, *Reb Yid*, but that's impossible. The *rav* is traveling to the capital city and is very pressed for time."

The Jew began to plead loudly. "But I only need two minutes! It's a matter of life and death!"

Hearing this, the *rav* called out to him to come in. The man entered.

"Rebbe — *baruch Hashem*! I've heard you deliver more than 15 *derashos* in my life, and I can recite each of them by heart. But seeing as the rebbe's time is short, I'll say only one of them. It's etched in my memory ..."

R' Lehman was taken aback. "I'm on my way to see the king. It's already 8:15, the trip takes more than half an hour, and the last train leaves at 9 o'clock. Please tell me what you need, and let us conclude quickly! Do I have time to hear *derashos* right now?"

"No, Rebbe. This is a matter of life and death. I need ..."

"Well?"

"Can I say half a *derashah*?"

"Please forget about the *derashos*. Is this really a question of *pikuach nefesh*? I've already explained, my dear man, that the wagon is due to arrive at any moment and I am in a great hurry!"

"All right, dear Rebbe. I'll tell it over briefly."

"No!"

"Okay, I understand. I'll tell the *derashah* another time."

"Well, what do you want (*Ribono Shel Olam!*)?

"A grandson was born to me, and I very much want — having heard so many of the *rav's derashos* …"

"You're back with the *derashos?* Leave the *derashos* alone!"

"I wanted to honor the *rav* with serving as the *sandak*."

The wagon pulled up outside the house and the driver raced to the house, signaling to R' Lehman to come outside as he was in a hurry to depart.

"Good-bye," said the *rav*, and stood up.

"But, excuse me, rebbe, one minute! In the end, they told me that it would be better if I'd be the *sandak* myself."

"So, what is it you want?"

"Well, the baby died."

"So where is the *pikuach nefesh?* Do you want me to bring him back to life, like Elisha Hanavi? Shall I make him rise from the grave?! I must run, the wagon is here and I have exactly half an hour. Who knows if I'll catch the train …"

"Rebbe! Rebbe! Just another minute, please! Yesterday, another grandson was born to me, *baruch Hashem*."

"*Mazal tov!* And what do you want?"

"I have a question: Shall I be the *sandak* again, with no fear that the baby will die, heaven forbid, or shall I give the honor to somebody else?"

R' Lehman thought he would go out of his wits. "Give it to someone else!" he pronounced, and raced toward the wagon in distress, thinking, *Who knows if the meeting will even take place now? The whole trip is at risk!*

The man ran after him and tugged at his coat. R' Lehman was beside himself. (*There are community matters at stake, and this nudnik won't leave me alone …*)

"Rebbe! One more question. Rebbe can't just drive off and leave me like this."

"*Nu???*"

"I forgot to ask: What name shall we give the child?"

R' Lehman's patience was at an end. "What do I care? Shimon, Zalman, Getzel, Berel, Shmerel, Dan, Yosef, Yaakov — what's the difference what name you give him?" He turned at once to the driver and said, "Please whip the horses. Hurry! Perhaps there will be a *kefitzas haderech* ..." In a turmoil, he mumbled, "Hashem, please help me, for the sake of the *klal*!"

The wagon reached the train station just as the second whistle was blowing, announcing the train's departure ...

"I thought that my soul was departing," R' Lehman related. "What would I tell the king? What mortification!" The other community leaders who were to have accompanied him streamed from the platform to greet him, wringing their hands in pain and frustration: "What have you done to us? How will we show our faces to the king?"

"What can I say?" R' Lehman said, greatly agitated. "A man grabbed me, shouting about *pikuach nefesh*, and I couldn't get rid of him." They sat down at the side of the station and looked around in despair.

An hour or more passed, and they were already on their way home, when the bitter news came that the train had crashed and most of its passengers had been killed.

"Hodu l'Hashem ki tov, ki l'olam chasdo!" ("Give thanks to Hashem for He is good; His kindness endures forever!")

"I was certain," said R' Lehman said. "For 12 years, I was convinced in my heart that that man had been none other than Eliyahu Hanavi. Was anything else possible?

"But listen. When nearly 13 years had gone by, an old man came to my house. The moment I saw his face, I stood up to welcome him and to fulfill what *Chazal* say about Eliyahu Hanavi: 'Fortunate is he who greets him with *shalom* and returns his greeting with *shalom*' ... But I very quickly saw that he was really only an ordinary Jew.

"I sat down beside him and said, '*Reb Yid*, now you can repeat as many *derashos* as you like. I have time. I don't have to travel to see the king ...'

"The old man seated himself comfortably and said, 'Rebbe, I don't have the strength to repeat *derashos*. But I'd like to tell you that I took your advice. I didn't serve as the *sandak* myself, and *baruch Hashem* the boy is alive. You saved me, Rebbe, and you saved the child from death!' "

R' Lehman thought to himself, *He thinks that I saved him — but I happen to know that he saved me ... What an amazing world. Hashem can bring about anything at all.*

"And now," the old man announced, "the rebbe must be present at the boy's *aliyah* to the Torah, at the *simchas bar mitzvah* that will take place this Shabbos."

"How could I not come?" R' Lehman said.

"That Shabbos, the rebbetzin and I were guests in that old man's house, and we rejoiced in his company. Then suddenly, during the Torah reading, when it was the bar mitzvah boy's turn to come up to the Torah, the *gabbai* announced, "*Ya'amod hachasan*: Shimon Zalman Getzel Berel Shmerel Dan Yosef Yaakov ..." Everyone smiled.

And later: "*Mi shebeirach avoseinu, hu yevareich es hachasan*: Shimon Zalman Getzel Berel Shmerel etc." The "*mi shebeirach*" took half an hour ...

"What's this?" one of those present asked with a smile. "When they learn *mishnayos* for him after 120 years, will they learn a full month of *mishnayos* to spell out all his names ...!"

I whispered to the boy's father, "My dear man, tell me the secret. Why so many names?"

"May the rebbe live and be well! That was the rebbe's marvelous idea, before the rebbe boarded the wagon ..."

That's the story.

Rabbosai, are these considered names, like the "ten names" we have heard about? No! Those are just an ordinary list of names, by a simple man who misunderstood and made a mistake. But the names listed in the Torah, those names highlight the person's essential character. When we say, for example, that we went to "America," that one name is sufficient. There is no need for further explanations. Similarly, if you say "sky," everyone knows what the word means.

But when the Torah wants us to understand the nature of the man called Moshe Rabbeinu, one name is insufficient. The Torah needs 10! Another name, and another … 10 names. Why? Because each of Moshe's names constituted a history unto itself. Ten histories — 10 worlds … 10 names!

When Moshe was born, the house was filled with light: "*She saw that he was good ('ki tov')*." Our Sages say that when the baby Moshe was born, the whole world was filled with light. We see this hinted in the words, "*Elokim saw that the light was good ('ki tov')*" [*Yalkut Shimoni*]. This was a singular historical event. At that time, he was given the name "Tovia" (*Midrash Rabbah Vayikra* 1:3). That's one name. When Moshe brought the Torah down from heaven, he was named "Yarad," and his sister Miriam bestowed on him the name "Yekusiel." Each name is a wonder all on its own; each name, another monumental piece of Moshe Rabbeinu's history.

⌐ Moshe! Moshe!

When Yocheved, saw the house fill with light from the newborn baby, she, too, gave him the name "Tov." The mother quickly hid him, but after three months this was no longer possible. It was about this period that *Shir HaShirim* tells us: "*Seize for us the Egyptian foxes, even the small foxes who spoiled Israel's vineyards …*" The Egyptians would carry in an Egyptian baby and make him cry, so that the Jewish baby would hear him and cry along with him. In this manner, they would uncover the fugitive infants. It was because of this that Yocheved realized she could no longer conceal Moshe. So she made a basket for him and placed him among the reeds on the riverbank. The basket began to float on the water. And that's when the miracles happened.

The Ponevezher *Rav* traveled to distant corners of the United States, collecting funds for his yeshivah. One Shabbos, which happened to be *parashas Shemos*, he was hosted by a community of totally ignorant Jews. Immediately with the onset of Shabbos, he realized that he mustn't speak of deep things in his *derashah*. They were simple people who would not understand. Therefore, he decided to tell them the simple story of the *parashah*, verse after verse. In this way, they would merit hearing *divrei Torah*.

And so he did. Using details gleaned from the Gemara and *midrash*, he described how Yocheved, the mother, hid little Moshe, and he told of the fateful moments that the baby spent bobbing on the waters of the Nile River. The people listened with obvious enjoyment. When he was finished, he was approached by a prosperous Jew who knew that the *Rav* had come to town on a fundraising mission for the Ponevezher Yeshivah in Israel. "Rabbi! I love sports. I know every type of sport in the world but this one, that you do when you're only three months old, is one I've never heard of before. Do you really teach this kind of thing in your yeshivah? If you do — or at least train them to be like that Moshe you told us about — I'll give you a nice sum to build another building on the yeshivah campus …"

Well, to each his own view of Moshe Rabbeinu. If you want to call him a sportsman …

To return to the subject at hand, "*His sister stationed herself at a distance to know what would be done with him*"(2:4). Miriam saw how one child after another was being hurled into the river. *Master of the Universe, promise us that the Egyptians will not take this basket. Oh, please, don't let them come any nearer. Don't let them see the basket floating on the water,* she thought to herself.

"*Pharaoh's daughter went down to bathe by the River*"(2:5). Oh, no! Who knew what would happen next? Pharaoh's daughter would finish him off …

Then she stretched out her hand! Hashem! In just another minute, Moshe would be no more … *Gevald!*

But — no. She picked up the basket and opened it. She saw the child, picked him up, and kissed him. "*She took pity on him*"(2:6).

After that, things moved quickly until the child was taken to be nursed by his own mother. Later, Pharaoh's daughter took him back. *"The boy grew up and she brought him to the daughter of Pharaoh and he was a son to her. She called his name Moshe, as she said, 'For I drew him from the water'"* (2:10). At that moment, he was given a new name: Moshe. Later, when he performed wonders and took the *Bnei Yisrael* out of Egypt, he was given an additional name.

But the Torah's name for him is specifically the one he was given by Pharaoh's daughter. Of all his names, "I do not call him anything but the name he was called by Bitya, daughter of Pharaoh." This is the name that *HaKadosh Baruch Hu* established in His Torah: Moshe.

Why? Let me tell you.

☞ *"He Was a Son to Her"*

I knew Jews who had merited to see the awesome *gaon*, the *Maharil* Diskin. They told me that once, toward evening, he went out to get some fresh air for his health. On his way, he looked up at a large tree growing at the side of the road. "It's really big. It has [a certain quantity] of leaves," he said, and lowered his gaze. It is said that he gave the number of leaves as in the thousands …

His students hurried to the home of R' Shmuel Salant, another great *gaon*, and asked him, "Rebbe, is there any way of checking the number of leaves in order to authenticate what our rebbe said? How can we do it without cutting down the tree?"

R' Shmuel Salant replied, "Pluck several scores of leaves from the tree and count them. The next time he passes by that tree, ask him again how many leaves the tree has."

And so they did. The *Maharil* Diskin replied with a different number — the first number, less the quantity that they had removed … Such was the awesome mind of the *Maharil* Diskin, one of the last *geonim* of the generation.

During that same period, in the *Maharil's* lifetime, there lived in Jerusalem an orphan who had no home. In those difficult times, children who were out on the streets would be taken away by either gentiles or (monied) heretics and were soon lost to Yiddishkeit. R' Yehoshua Leib Diskin hastened to take this particular orphan into his home — and later others — whom he raised and educated. In time, he founded an institution known as the "Diskin Orphanage." His students and friends later refurbished and expanded the building, which stands at the entrance to Jerusalem to this day.

The *Maharil* Diskin told his students that one of the orphans living in his home would regularly burst into tears whenever the rebbetzin washed him and scrubbed his hair. He would cry and cry, the tears of an orphan child.

"I asked him, 'Dear child, why do you wail so? What hurts you when you're being washed?'

"In tears, the boy replied, 'Rebbe, rebbe, when the rebbetzin washes me, I remember my Mama. I once had a mother, and she used to wash my hair, too. And Mama — Mama would give me a kiss after scrubbing my hair. Ever since my mother died, there's no one who kisses me like she used to …'" Hot tears poured down R' Yehoshua Leib's face. From that day, the rebbetzin would kiss that orphan whenever she washed his hair. And still, she was no substitute for his Mama.

Pharaoh's daughter, in contrast, succeeded to the extent that the Torah testifies: "*He was a son to her!*" Literally, like a son. The *midrash* says, "From here, you learn the reward of those who perform deeds of lovingkindness." Despite the fact that he had many names, he was not called anything in the Torah except the name that Pharaoh's daughter gave him, because what she did was an act of pure lovingkindness.

"*He was a son to her*" — to that degree! This is what the Torah wishes to draw to our attention: the reward for those who perform *chesed*. That's why he was called Moshe.

"She opened [the basket] and saw him, the child, and behold! a youth was crying" (Shemos 2:6).

He is called a youth and a child in the same verse. According to R' Yehudah, this tells us that he was a child but his voice was that of a youth. R' Nechemiah protests: In that case, you've made Moshe Rabbeinu a "ba'al mum" (i.e., the possessor of a defect that would disqualify him for singing with the other Leviim in the Beis HaMikdash). Rather, we learn that his mother made him a "chuppas ne'urim" — a symbolic wedding canopy — in his basket, saying, "Lest I do not merit seeing him under his own chuppah" (Midrash Rabbah).

A WEDDING CANOPY IN HIS YOUTH

R' Shabsi Yudelevitz

Oy, the heart of a compassionate mother. A mother's heart. His mother put him into the basket and placed a canopy over his head, "Lest I do not merit his own *chuppah*."

Let me tell you a story.

In a certain large city in Austria, a meeting was held to discuss the construction of a large shul. An announcement was made, to the effect that anyone willing to donate gold to equal the weight of the cornerstone would be honored with laying the cornerstone for the new building. In addition, the *rav* of the city — a *gaon, mekubal,* and outstanding *tzaddik* — promised that he who donated the cornerstone could request a blessing and a guarantee for anything that his heart desired.

Among those gathered to perform this happy mitzvah was a certain Jew (I think he was a doctor) who agreed to donate gold in the weight of the cornerstone — an enormous sum. He was honored with laying the cornerstone. At the end of the ceremony, he lost no time in going directly to the holy *rav's* home to request the *berachah* and the guarantee.

"What is your wish?" asked the *rav*.

"Rebbe, I have more than enough money, both silver and gold — but no children at all. I would like the *rav* to promise me a child …"

"Oho." The *rav* was shaken. "You've asked a difficult one, my son. If you want a child, you will have to wait three days." As the *rav* spoke, his eyes were fixed on heaven.

Three days later, the man was summoned back to the *rav's* presence. "All right, I can make you the promise," the *rav* said. "But it will come at a very steep price. If you really want a child, you will lose all your money. And secondly, even before the child is born, you will die."

"I agree! I undertake all of it. The main thing is the child. It's all worthwhile," the man replied resolutely.

The *rav* looked him in the eye and added, "There is a third condition. After the child is delivered, the mother will die, too."

"I am not the one who can make that decision. I will have to ask my wife."

An hour later, he returned, with his wife's consent. Both of them had agreed to the terms. Self-sacrifice.

The rebbe blessed them and gave them his promise.

After that, things started happening in swift succession.

The couple learned that they were indeed expecting a child. Just weeks later, the man began to incur serious losses. His business concerns deteriorated, and within a short time he had lost most of his property in failed enterprises. As time passed, the situation grew even graver, until he was left destitute. About a month before the birth he fell ill and he passed away.

His wife, once so prosperous, was left without a penny. Ashamed to remain in the city, she gathered together what meager belongings were left to her and moved to another town.

When her time was very near, she set out with the intention of reaching a nearby village to give birth there. The trip was a hard one, with cold wind and rains that soon turned to heavy snow. A tremendous weakness engulfed her. She thought she was going to freeze to death. Suddenly, in the distance, she saw a light from the village. Mustering the remnants of her strength, she walked to the house at the edge of the village. It was the home of the baker who, apart from baking for a living, was a great *tzaddik*.

The woman knocked on the door of the courtyard. The household roused itself to welcome her and to prepare a bed so she could rest. Before many hours had passed, she was embracing her son. The house was filled with light.

The mother kissed her son, hugging him with all her might. She broke down in tears of intense emotion at this first meeting with the child born to her after so many years. Who can imagine her feeling? These were also tears of parting ...

Two days later, the baker's wife gave birth as well: to a baby girl.

The mother of the boy said to her hostess, "Let us make a *chuppas ne'urim* — a canopy of youth — over their cradle. We will make a *shidduch*." And so they did.

On the day after the baby's *bris*, the mother of the boy passed away. A quorum of 10 men accompanied her to the cemetery.

The little boy remained in the baker's house, and the baker's wife raised him with devotion for many years. Who was this child? It was the Maharsha!

His mother's name was Rachel, but the Maharsha was known by the initials: Shmuel Aidlish, or Shmuel ben Aidel. His name, and the name of the work he authored, is etched in the Gemara for all time in the name of his *adoptive* mother, Aidel!

When he grew up and became the Maharsha, his renown spread to the nearby cities. Many people wished to take him for a son-in-law. But he consistently declined. "No," he would say. "A *chuppah* was made for me when I was in my cradle. I will marry the baker's daughter. Her mother raised me and I was as a son to her. I owe them my life."

He is known by his mother's name: Maharsha.

Do you understand? *HaKadosh Baruch Hu* said, "Out of the 10 names that you possess, I will not call you anything but Moshe, the name you were given by Bitya bas Pharaoh" — the adoptive mother who raised him!

⌒ *The Dream*

Let me tell you a little bit about the Maharsha.

They say that the Maharsha had long hair which he tied to a rope that dangled from the ceiling when he learned Torah at night. Whenever he fell asleep and his head fell forward with fatigue, he would feel the pain of the rope tugging at his hair and he would wake up to continue his learning. They also say that once, when a student remarked in the midst of a *shiur* that he wanted to sleep, the Maharsha said, "If you were to grow tired and fall asleep here, that's one thing. But to get up and go to bed, how could you?"

It is known that there were some who opposed the Maharsha in his native city. The *shamash* of the shul in that city was a great *tzaddik*. After midnight each night, his custom was to close the shul and to circle the *bimah* seven times, reciting the *Sefer Tehillim* seven times as he did so. One night, he fell into a deep sleep. Along came a man and woke him. He was a tall and very distinguished-looking individual. Once again the *shamash* fell asleep, and again someone woke him up, asking, "Where is R' Shmuel ben R' Yehudah *Halevi* (the Maharsha's name)?" This man's face glowed like sapphires.

"First," said the *shamash*, "tell me who you are and what is your name?"

"I am Eliyahu Hanavi."

"And who was the first man I saw?"

"That was the holy Shaul, king of Israel."

"And what is your business here?"

"In the heavenly court, a certain judgment is being determined with regard to Shaul and David Hamelech. The verdict must be rendered by a great scholar from this world: the Maharsha. That is why we have come to him."

Then Eliyahu Hanavi added, "Take heed of his honor, for he is exceedingly great. His Torah and his righteousness are important in heaven! But do not tell what you have seen, for on the day you reveal what your eyes have seen, you will die."

The *shamash* could not restrain himself. Several days later, he climbed to the *bimah* in the center of the shul and announced in a ringing voice, "There are those who oppose the Maharsha. There are those among us who sow the seeds of conflict over this *tzaddik*. But you should know that an incident occurred, and in it I was told that the Maharsha in our generation is the one who renders verdicts in heaven. I've decided to tell you this despite the fact that I am forfeiting my life with this revelation. That will be your sign that this story is true: when I leave this world in the very near future." And so it happened.

Harav Shmuel Aidlish — son of Aidel. "*He was a son to her*" …

וַיֵּצֵא בַּיּוֹם הַשֵּׁנִי וְהִנֵּה שְׁנֵי־אֲנָשִׁים עִבְרִים נִצִּים וַיֹּאמֶר לָרָשָׁע לָמָּה תַכֶּה רֵעֶךָ: וַיֹּאמֶר מִי שָׂמְךָ לְאִישׁ שַׂר וְשֹׁפֵט עָלֵינוּ הַלְהָרְגֵנִי אַתָּה אֹמֵר כַּאֲשֶׁר הָרַגְתָּ אֶת־הַמִּצְרִי וַיִּירָא מֹשֶׁה וַיֹּאמַר אָכֵן נוֹדַע הַדָּבָר: וַיִּשְׁמַע פַּרְעֹה אֶת־הַדָּבָר הַזֶּה וַיְבַקֵּשׁ לַהֲרֹג אֶת־מֹשֶׁה.

"He went out the next day and behold! two Hebrew men were fighting. He said to the wicked one, 'Why would you strike your fellow?' He replied, 'Who appointed you as a dignitary, a ruler, and a judge over us? Do you propose to murder me, as you murdered the Egyptian?' … Pharaoh heard about this matter and sought to kill Moshe" (Shemos 2:13-15).

WHEN THE LEADERSHIP RESORT TO BLOWS

R' Sholom Schwadron

*W*ho were the "two Hebrew men fighting"? Rashi tells us that they were Dasan and Aviram. It was always those two rascals who went out to war together — against Moshe Rabbeinu. Together.

These two later told Moshe, *"You have made our very scent abhorrent in the eyes of Pharaoh"* (5:21). Similarly, during Korach's controversy, *"Dasan and Aviram went out erect at the entrance of their tents"* (*Bamidbar* 16:27). The pair were also in unison in leaving their *mon* out till morning. Yet here, they are suddenly seen struggling with each other — coming to actual blows! "Why," Moshe asks, "would you strike your fellow?" What happened to them? Are they friends or enemies?

Yes, yes — and yes again! This is how their leaders appear. By outward appearances, one might think that they are united. Indeed, they do unite: to cause damage to others. Among themselves, however, they engage in quarrels — until they raise their fists to start fighting ...

A question is asked: The *mishnah* in *Maseches Avos* says, "What kind of conflict is for the sake of heaven? The conflict between the House of Shammai and the House of Hillel. Which conflict is not for the sake of heaven? The conflict of Korach and his assembly." It should have said, "The conflict between Korach and Moshe Rabbeinu," not "Korach and his assembly." A very good question.

Various answers are given. A wonderful one is provided by one of the great Chassidishe rebbes: The participants in the conflict went out, together, to take on Moshe. At the same time, however, they fought among themselves about their leadership. "The conflict of Korach and his assembly" — who would be the leader ...

The same thing happens with Dasan and Aviram. Left alone, the Torah tells us, *"Wicked one, why do you strike your fellow?"* Immediately afterward, they united in their haste to inform on Moshe to Pharaoh ... How surprising. As Rashi says on the *pasuk*, *"Pharaoh heard about this matter and sought to kill Moshe,"* they informed on him!

⌐ A Slap in the Face!

Let's talk a little more about our friends, Dasan and Aviram.

"*He went out on the second day, and behold! two Hebrew men were fighting*"(2:13). Rashi explains: It was Dasan and Aviram who left over the *mon.*" We face a profound question here. Apparently, this is Dasan and Aviram's identity card. But was this their greatest crime? After all, they were involved in every public crime and controversy: the *mon,* Korach's conflict, fighting with each other, accusing Moshe of fouling the Hebrews' scent with Pharaoh (i.e., causing their lot to worsen), and so on. Why does Rashi point only to the act of leaving over the *mon?*

In everything that Dasan and Aviram did, one might infer their innocence — view it with a positive slant, stand up in their defense, and understand what motivated their bad actions: concern for *Klal Yisrael,* for example.

At the end of our *parashah,* when they told Moshe and Aharon, "*May Hashem look upon you and judge, for you have made our very scent abhorrent in the eyes of Pharaoh and the eyes of his servants, to place a sword in their hands to murder us!*" (5:21) we might believe that they were not completely wicked. After all, they were only pained at the Hebrews' suffering from Pharaoh's sadistic measures. Similarly, when they informed on Moshe for killing the Egyptian, they may have been worried about incurring pogroms and vengeance over the Egyptian's murder. In short, their intentions may have been for the good of the Jewish nation. This rule holds true for the other episodes as well.

However, when Moshe told them, "*Do not leave [any of the mon] over till the morning*" and they left the *mon* — why did they do it? Was this out of concern for the Jewish nation? No. It was private affair involving their personal interests. When an individual defies Moshe Rabbeinu's command in order to make certain of tomorrow's breakfast — "What if there's no *mon* for me tomorrow?" — he is concerned only with himself. Faith in *HaKadosh Baruch Hu* and in Moshe, his servant, is lacking.

(This also explains the fistfight between the two. Let there be even the faintest suspicion that someone is trying to take something away from you — even if he's a good friend — and you lose your wits and do anything you can to prevent him ... even to the point of coming to blows.) In short, as *Chazal* tell us, "They were always wicked!" It is from the episode with the *mon* that we learn about all the others.

In the affair of Korach, they were not concerned for the greater good. When they came out to rail at Moshe, *"You have made our very scent abhorrent in the eyes of Pharaoh,"* they were thinking only of themselves. When they informed on Moshe, it was for their own benefit. The "I" was at the forefront. They were not concerned with *Klal Yisrael.*

These are the world's leaders, in every generation. (They kick up their split hooves, as if to say, "I'm pure." See *Vayikra Rabbah* 13, where it discusses that the pig has split hooves. What does this resemble? Just as a pig shows its hooves as if to say, "See how pure I am," the kingdom of Edom acts in arrogance and thievery and corruption while putting on the appearance of doing good. [There is a story of a certain ruler who would put robbers and adulterers and practitioners of sorcery to death, while boasting that he had perpetrated all three of those very same misdeeds in a single night.] They put on a show of caring for the public ...)

In contrast to this, the leaders of *Am Yisrael* were concerned with others, more than with themselves. "He focuses his eyes and heart to be distressed over them" (Rashi, on Moshe Rabbeinu, in the verse, *"And he saw their burdens."*) And in the *Midrash Rabbah*, *Chazal* tell us that Moshe would cry and say, "I have pity on you ..." and would lend his shoulder to help each and every one." Genuine *tzaddikim* really cared for the public. They guided their flocks without any thought of personal gain.

This reminds me of a brief story concerning a certain *talmid chacham* who is still alive in our time.

When the Jews of the Diaspora began to ascend to Jerusalem and settled there to engage in Torah study, the state of their livelihood was as bad as could be. Destitution and hunger were the order of the day. To help remedy the situation, *kollels* were founded: the Hungarian Kollel, the Polish Kollel, the Galician Kollel, and so on. The administration of these *kollels* received regular monthly support and various loans for the members of the Old *Yishuv*. Those with special needs quietly received a few extra pennies in addition to the monthly stipend.

Every Thursday, various clerks sat in their offices to oversee the distribution of the loans. On Friday these offices were generally closed, as expenditures for Shabbos had already been budgeted the day before, on Thursday. There were, however some exceptional cases; therefore, the office of the Galician Kollel in the Old City was open to the public on Fridays as well.

A God-fearing Jew was in charge of the office of the Galician Kollel. (His name has slipped my mind at the moment, but 30 years ago, when I first told this story in my Friday-night *derashah* in the Zichron Moshe shul, I mentioned his name and someone in the audience became so agitated that he began to feel unwell. They poured water over him, and what happened? It turned out that he was a grandson of that righteous *gabbai*, and he had been overcome upon hearing the story.)

R' Shmuel Pepperman, the *shochet*, lived one floor below the *kollel* office, and he told me the following story.

"One Friday, I heard someone shouting. I hurried upstairs to the *kollel*, and saw what was happening: A young Yerushalmi yeshivah man had come to request a loan. The *gabbai* told him, '*Reb Yid*, weren't you here yesterday, and they gave you money?' The man, not knowing how to answer, began shouting and cursing and screaming. 'Why don't you take care of me? You're stingy and wicked!' and more in this vein. The *gabbai* tried to explain, 'Our coffers are nearly empty. There are literally only a few pennies left, which are designated for the needy who have not yet come in for a loan. You already received a loan yesterday.'

"The man was not appeased, and continued shouting bitterly. Finally, in the heat of the moment, he raised his hand and slapped the *gabbai's* face."

What would we have done?

Today, when there is such a thing as a telephone, we would certainly call the police at once. Or, if not the police, then we'd summon someone else in a position of authority to throw the man out, through the door or the window ... But listen to what happened. The *gabbai* who had received the slap called over the *shamash* who was sitting in the next room, and whispered urgently, "Reb Yankel, listen, the money's almost gone. Hurry out to the city street and somehow scrape together a loan of half a napoleon (a respectable amount of money that a person could live on for about half a year)."

About five minutes later, the *shamash* returned with the money in hand. The *gabbai* handed the half-napoleon to the man, who was seated at one side of the room. "Here, go and take care of your needs."

The man, who had by this time recovered his wits, began to apologize for his outburst. "I didn't know, I didn't think about what I was doing, I went out of my mind," etc. But the *gabbai* consoled him, "It's all right, nothing happened ... Calm down, don't take it to heart ..." And he sent him off with honor.

R' Shmuel the *shochet* asked him, "What is this? How did you come to have so much patience — and even went so far as to repay bad with good? How did you do it? Where did you find the strength?"

That righteous *gabbai* stood up and said emotionally, "R' Shmuel! What is it that you don't understand? He was already here yesterday and he knew very well that I remembered giving him a loan. If, despite this, he screamed and cursed like that — and even went so far as to slap my cheek — his situation must be extremely grave. Therefore, on the contrary, I was obligated to help him ..."

Tears of emotion trickled from R' Shmuel's eyes. They ran down his cheeks and fell onto the doorstep of the Galician Kollel. Who is like Your nation, Israel!

Rabbosai, that's what a Jewish leader looks like. These were honorable leaders: leaders who dedicated their lives to loving their fellow Jew.

* * *

BREIF VIGNETTES ON THE PARASHAH FROM THE MAGGIDIM

WE DON'T WANT TO!

R' Sholom Schwadron

*I*n general, there is no such thing as "I can't." Rather, it's "I don't want to ..." Because if you really want something, it's possible! I, for example, smoked cigarettes for a long time. But I really wanted to stop — and I stopped.

It is said in the name of the Ba'al Shem Tov that he taught this to his disciples: If a person listens carefully to what is said around him in his daily life, he will be able to discern what heaven is trying to tell him ... what he needs to hear.

His disciples decided to take note of what was going on around them, and to try to understand the significance of what people said in their hearing.

One day, an elderly villager passed their house. He was a "fix-it" man. Knocking on their door, he asked, "Do you have anything that needs repairing?"

"We have nothing that needs fixing," the students replied.

As the villager raised his voice in rebuke, the students pricked up their ears: "You have nothing that needs fixing? There is certainly something that needs to be fixed, but the fact is that you don't want to fix it. Right now, you're not interesting in making repairs. In that case, don't say, 'We have nothing that needs fixing.' Say, 'We don't *want* to fix anything.'"

The Ba'al Shem Tov's disciples received heaven's message joyously. Wonder of wonders!

Many times, a person thinks, or wants to think, that there is nothing that needs fixing. There is! It's just that we don't want to repair [it] ...

If we do want it, we'll receive help from above. Bitya bas Pharaoh stretched out her hand — and a miracle occurred. Why? Because she wanted. Truly wanted. And so, she merited Hashem's help. If one wants to make repairs, he will succeed.

וַיִּפֶן כֹּה וָכֹה וַיַּרְא כִּי אֵין אִישׁ וַיַּךְ אֶת־הַמִּצְרִי וַיִּטְמְנֵהוּ בַּחוֹל.

"He smote the Egyptian and hid him in the sand" (Shemos 2:12).

HIDDEN MEANINGS

R' Shabsi Yudelevitz

How did Moshe kill the wicked Egyptian? "R' Avisar says that he struck him with his fist. And there are those who say that he used a cement trowel … Rabbanan say: He spoke the Name [of Hashem] and killed him, as it says, *'Are you saying to kill me, as you killed the Egyptian?'* "

Our Sages discovered that the *"Shem Hameforash"* with which Moshe killed the Egyptian is hidden in the verse, *"V'ahavta es Hashem Elokecha b'chol levavecha u'vechol nafshecha"* (*"And you shall love Hashem, your God, with all your heart and with all your soul"*).

When R' Akiva's skin was being scraped with metal combs, he called out the *Kerias Shema*: "*Shema Yisrael, Hashem Elokeinu, Hashem Echad!*" With this, he was accepting upon himself the yoke of heaven. His students asked, "Rebbe, why stop here?" In other words, why do you stop here, and do not continue with *"V'ahavta es Hashem Elokecha, etc."* with its awesome hidden meanings, and bring about the executioner's death?

R' Akiva answered, "All of my life I have been distressed, wondering when this verse will come to hand so that I may fulfill it …"

וַיֹּאמֶר הַשְׁלִיכֵהוּ אַרְצָה וַיַּשְׁלִכֵהוּ אַרְצָה וַיְהִי לְנָחָשׁ וַיָּנָס מֹשֶׁה
מִפָּנָיו: וַיֹּאמֶר ה׳ אֶל־מֹשֶׁה שְׁלַח יָדְךָ וֶאֱחֹז בִּזְנָבוֹ וַיִּשְׁלַח יָדוֹ
וַיַּחֲזֶק־בּוֹ וַיְהִי לְמַטֶּה בְּכַפּוֹ.

*"He said, 'Cast it on the ground,' and he cast it on the ground
and it became a snake. Moshe fled from it. Hashem said to
Moshe, 'Stretch out your hand and grasp its tail.' He stretched
out his hand and grasped it tightly, and it became a staff in his
palm" (Shemos 4:3-4).*

GRASP THE SNAKE AND EMERGE VICTORIOUS

R' Yaakov Galinsky

I heard a fine *derush* on this *pasuk,* said in the name of R' Meir
Shapiro:

Every child is like the staff in Moshe's hand: the staff of
Hashem. He has the potential for flourishing growth. As long as
Moshe Rabbeinu is holding him, that illustrious educator will have
an influence over him. A Jewish child can develop to the point
where it would be possible to perform miracles and wonders with
him. *"With which you shall perform the signs."*

On the other hand, should the child fall to the ground (at the
moment that Moshe Rabbeinu lets him go), he turns into a snake.
And what a snake! To the point where others will run to escape
him. *"Moshe fled from it."*

And lest you say, "What can we do? He's moved out of my sphere
of influence. He's already turned into a snake. There's no more
hope" — no! Do not despair, *HaKadosh Baruch Hu* says to Moshe.
Grab him again. *"Stretch out your hand and grasp its tail."* Talk to him,
influence him.

At the moment when he is grasping the snake, it becomes once
again a staff of Hashem.

וַיָּמָת יוֹסֵף וְכָל־אֶחָיו וְכֹל הַדּוֹר הַהוּא: וּבְנֵי יִשְׂרָאֵל פָּרוּ וַיִּשְׁרְצוּ
וַיִּרְבּוּ וַיַּעַצְמוּ בִּמְאֹד מְאֹד וַתִּמָּלֵא הָאָרֶץ אֹתָם: וַיָּקָם מֶלֶךְ־חָדָשׁ
עַל־מִצְרָיִם אֲשֶׁר לֹא־יָדַע אֶת־יוֹסֵף.

"Yosef died, and all his brothers and that entire generation. The Children of Israel were fruitful, teemed, increased, and became strong — very, very much so ... A new king arose in Egypt who did not know of Yosef" (Shemos 1:6-8).

THE THRONE!

R' Sholom Schwadron

*I*t's very hard for us to understand this matter in human terms. How did such a turnabout take place? Pharaoh was a friend who regarded Yosef with great esteem and accorded him authority, announcing, *"There is no one as smart as you!"* Yosef proceeded to treat Pharaoh with unlimited loyalty and beneficence. And suddenly, the man lost his sanity, exhibiting an extraordinary degree of cruelty, even to the point of bathing in the blood of Jewish children. (There is a difference of opinion among our Sages as to whether he was actually a new king, or the old one with new decrees; we are addressing the second opinion.) Is there any logic to this sequence of events?

The question redoubles in force after we read what the *midrash* has to say. *Chazal* tell us, *"A new king arose in Egypt"* who issued harsh new decrees. In other words, he stepped off the throne and afterward rose to power again. What happened?

His ministers informed Pharaoh that Parliament had decided to impose forced labor on the Jewish nation. Pharaoh was shaken: "You fools! Are you not ashamed to repay good with evil? Their grandfather, Yosef, saved us all!" In response, "They removed him from his throne." Today, they'd call this a vote of no confidence. We don't need a king like you. Go home.

Pharaoh tried to maintain his resolve in his home, but it didn't last long. Three months later, he "broke." Humbly, he came and said, "All right. I agree." And then, on his reestablished throne, not only did he join the others, he became worse than they were! He became far more cruel than they. He led the wicked pack. He had been a man of integrity, to the point where he gave up his throne, but that same man of integrity did not stand up to the test and executed an about-face. He deteriorated sharply, falling much lower than the others.

There is a big difference between a light aircraft that plunges to the depths, and a huge jumbo jet. A large plane that has risen very high in the air will fall many times faster and harder ... The same law applies to human beings. A person of small intellect who chooses to walk a crooked path does not do much damage. But when a man of towering intellect abandons the straight path, his corruption is far worse!

Why, in fact, did Pharaoh fail to pass the test? Why did he lose his way and stumble so badly despite his intellect? How did it happen, and why?

Earlier, in *Parashas Mikeitz*, he was prepared to sacrifice everything — except for his throne. *"Only by the throne shall I outrank you."* In the end, that throne mastered him. "They removed him from his throne." He truly did try to stand firm, but three months later he found himself incapable.

The throne! To lose the throne ...

וַיִּקַּח מֹשֶׁה אֶת־אִשְׁתּוֹ וְאֶת־בָּנָיו וַיַּרְכִּבֵם עַל־הַחֲמֹר וַיָּשָׁב אַרְצָה מִצְרָיִם וַיִּקַּח מֹשֶׁה אֶת־מַטֵּה הָאֱלֹקִים בְּיָדוֹ.

"So Moshe took his wife and sons, mounted them on the donkey, and returned to the land of Egypt; and Moshe took the staff of God in his hand" (Shemos 4:20).

THE DONKEY THAT MOSHE RODE

R' Yaakov Galinsky

*T*he donkey — introduced with the definitive "the." Which donkey was it? The *midrash* explains that it was the same donkey that Avraham Avinu rode on his way to sacrifice his son Yitzchak. *The* donkey.

The *midrash* continues that that same donkey (considerably advanced in years) will bear the Redeemer, *Mashiach tzidkeinu*, speedily in our days. A long-lived donkey. This is how we understand the *midrash*. However, deeper things are hinted at here.

Chazal are giving us a hint, *rabbosai*, that Moshe Rabbeinu did not seek new donkeys … He was very happy with the old one, so why seek something new? And this is how we will be redeemed …

Ai, ai, it's a different world today. These days, we don't ride on donkeys at all; we ride in Volvos. No! If it was good enough for Moshe Rabbeinu, an elderly donkey is good enough for us to be redeemed …

There are those who sit back in their easy chairs and think: "We've got to suit the Torah to the times. Times change; we need something up to date in the Torah." They have their facts reversed. The Torah is eternal, for all generations. They are the ones who must suit themselves to the Torah.

This reminds me of the story of the wagon driver.

A wagon driver was commissioned to transport glass vessels from the village to the city, at the height of a harsh winter. The owner of the vessels was traveling to the city as well, but he would be taking the train while sending his merchandise by wagon through villages and forests.

Apparently, the wagon driver fell asleep for a few moments. He was only human. The wagon overturned about a kilometer before the entrance to the city and all the glass was smashed into millions of pieces.

When the owner arrived in the city and met up with the wagon driver, he found himself confronting a wagon full of broken glass. Furious, he shouted, "I hired you. You are a *shomer sachar* (in the category of a paid watchman). This is a crime. How could you have fallen asleep? Let's go to the *beis din*."

Together, they went to see the *rav*. The *rav* opened a *Shulchan Aruch* to *Choshen Mishpat* and told the wagon driver, "*Reb Yid*, you're liable by law. You are obligated to pay him."

The wagon driver became enraged. He removed the "kasket" (hat) from his head, climbed onto the table, and began to ask forcefully, "Rebbe, may I ask where his honor is taking this verdict that obligates me?"

"Yes. It says so here, in the *Shulchan Aruch* — the *Choshen Mishpat* section. You said you want a *din Torah*, not a compromise," the *rav* replied.

"Your honor, forgive me, but how does *Choshen Mishpat* know that I owe the money? How does it know that I work in the wagon line, and how is *Choshen Mishpat* so sure that a poor driver like myself is obligated to pay?"

"The *Shulchan Aruch* derived this from the words of the *Tur*," explained the *rav*.

"And where does the *Tur* have the knowledge to find me liable?"

"From the Rambam."

"O.K., your honor. From where does the Rambam get this fateful decision that obligates me to pay?"

The *rav* understood that he was embroiled with a nuisance of a litigant who possessed little understanding, but he had no choice but to continue: "The Rambam took it from the Rif, and the Rif from the Gemara, and the Gemara from the *mishnayos*," he answered briefly, anticipating future questions ...

"*Mishnayos?*" the wagon driver asked, in pain and surprise.

"Don't you know what *mishnayos* is? It was given on *Har Sinai* — the Oral Torah."

"Your honor, you're making a little mistake."

"What do you mean?"

"In what month was the Torah given? Everyone knows that it was in the month of Sivan — in the height of summer. There was no mud in the streets, no snow, no freezing cold. But today, we're in the month of Teves ..." the wagon driver complained. "Today isn't what it used to be."

This, *rabbosai*, is our tragedy. "Different times."

◠ One Gigantic Prison

About two years ago, in the month of Nisan when I was in Jerusalem, I met with a representative of the Israeli penal system, who asked if I would be of assistance.

"What? You're interested in having me go live in jail, too?" I kibitzed. "How can I possibly help you?"

"No, no, R' Yaakov. Listen. You are no doubt aware of the overcrowding in the prisons. (In other words, they have no room to house new inmates ...) Recently, we've been promised a budget to build another two prisons: one in the south and another near the center of the country. However, the finance committee has delayed authorizing the budget. There are some religious people serving on the finance committee. (Perhaps he thought I was the chairman?) Could you slip them something under the table, to help facilitate matters ...?"

I explained to him that I had nothing to do with financial matters and that he had unfortunately come to the wrong address. Before we parted, I added, "I can't help you out financially — but if you want to listen, you can at least come out of this with a good story."

"By all means, rabbi." He sat down.

Listen to this story. In the Galil, there was a winding road filled with potholes and cracks on the asphalt surface that caused, sadly, numerous injuries and deaths. The distance from the highway to the nearest hospital in Chadera was considerable, and the severely injured usually did not survive the trip.

A special committee was convened to discuss ways and means of making things easier for the injured and trying to prevent lives from being lost en route to the hospital. After discussing the matter at length, the committee finally decided to make a special effort to raise funds for constructing a large new hospital near the old highway. An intelligent decision, no?

Once the decision had been reached, one of the participants stood up: "May I ask a question?"

He was given the floor.

"Building the hospital will cost the government a fortune. With the same money, we could repair the old road, or even construct a new highway, thus avoiding all the injuries in the first place ..."

"I don't understand the analogy," the prison representative told me.

"You're looking to build new prisons," I scolded. "With the same money, you have a simple option: to educate your youth so that there would be no need for them to go to jail at all. Now, that's something that I could help you with ..."

He thought a moment, then asked, "Just a second. Who taught you this kind of clever reasoning?"

"I don't know who taught me but anyone with an ounce of sense in his head would say what you just heard." With that, we parted ways.

Ribono Shel Olam! In previous generations, when we lived in Poland or Hungary, did we ever hear of Jewish murderers? May

Hashem have mercy. I delivered a talk in the Ramla prison. I cried out from the bitter depths of my heart. I told them that I had asked the warden what to speak to the prisoners about, and he returned a surprising answer: "There's no problem finding something to speak about. Any topic you choose will be fine. Does the problem lie with the 5 percent of the population that's behind bars? The real problem is with the 95 percent who haven't arrived here. Those are the ones you need to talk to. They're the ones who should be brought into this place. The pain is over the 95 percent who are not here. If I had the funds, I'd build a roof over the entire country — one gigantic prison."

How is such a situation created? I will tell you what I said then, in that prison.

The Jewish nation has been detached from the old. They want something new. It's all "Times are different" now, as that wagon driver claimed. They have tried to educate our youth by the light of gentile concepts. As *Chazal* say, "When [Israel] rises, they rise to the sky ... And when they fall, they fall into the depths." There are no compromises with the people of Israel: It's either up or down. So many of the young have reached the depths and are tasting the bitter brew that their parents cooked up for them. "*Fathers ate unripe grapes, and the children's teeth were blunted.*" The children are not to blame.

It says in the *pasuk*: "*He smelled the fragrance of his clothes and blessed him.*" Before Yitzchak Avinu blessed Yaakov Avinu, he smelled the fragrance of Yaakov's clothes, and then rendered the blessing.

Our Sages say: "Do not say '*begadav*' ('his clothes'), but rather, '*bogdav*' ('his betrayers')." That is, even those descendants of Yaakov Avinu who will betray the Torah in the future will do *teshuvah* and send a pleasant fragrance up to Hashem. "*And he blessed him.*" In other words, I told those prisoners, you who are sitting in jail, having supposedly betrayed us, it was your fragrance that he smelled, and he blessed you! Who blessed you, my dear brothers? Yitzchak Avinu.

Chazal, in the *Midrash Rabbah* on this verse, offer an illustration in the form of a story of a traitor who repented and sent forth a pleasant fragrance to Hashem:

When the enemies of Israel marched in to destroy the Beis HaMikdash, a certain Jew by the name of Yosef Meshisa mingled with them. They needed a cooperative Jew to guide them through the winding streets to the Beis HaMikdash. They didn't know the way, so they found a nice Jew called Yosef Mashita to help them out. He marched along with them.

When they reached the proximity of the Beis HaMikdash, they suddenly panicked. What if a punishment from God were to befall them the moment they entered? They stood frozen, afraid to enter. What was their solution? They asked Yosef Mashita, the Jew, to go in first and remove a vessel from the Beis HaMikdash. Afterward, if all went well, they would follow him inside to steal the rest of the vessels. (After all, it would be a pity to burn the Beis HaMikdash along with all of its contents and precious vessels.) To help him gather his courage, they promised him that whatever vessel he might carry out would be his. He was a clever Jew, and when he went in, he came out with the Menorah, worth a fortune.

The wicked enemy, seeing what he had carried out for himself, taunted him cruelly, saying, "An ordinary man would have no use for a vessel like that. Go back in, and whatever you take out will be yours."

He refused.

"What's the matter with you, Yosef?" they asked in surprise.

"Nothing's the matter, but I won't go back in," he replied. "It's bad enough that I angered my God once. I won't anger Him a second time."

They subjected him to unimaginably cruel torture, but he remained firm in his refusal until he gave up his life. As the gentiles tortured him for those long, long minutes, he screamed repeatedly, "Oy, oy, woe is me that I have angered my Creator."

These are the traitors that Yitzchak Avinu smelled and then blessed Yaakov. My dear brothers, you are capable of sanctifying Heaven's Name a great deal, and many blessings will be heaped upon your heads. That's what I said, there within those prison walls.

☙ "This Madness Is My Concern"

Somehow, a youth from Ramat Gan, a student in a secular high school, fell under my influence. I don't know exactly how he was influenced, but I was told that he had decided to spend one year learning in yeshivah. His home was "traditional," as it is called these days.

I was out of the country at the time. When I returned to Israel, my wife told me, "Someone from Ramat Gan has been calling every day and asking if R' Galinsky is back yet. He left his phone number. Call him and find out why it's so urgent that he speak to you."

I hastened to make the call. I quickly realized that I was speaking to the father of that *bachur*. "Mr. Galinsky," he said in a complaining way. "Tell me, please, what you want from our lives. My son came home from yeshivah and wants *shemurah* matzah, made with a hand-grinder. What nonsense! I don't know the difference between a hand-grinder and a foot-grinder. For years we've been holding a Seder on Pesach night, and we've bought our *matzos*. Suddenly, he's coming with new ideas. 'Hand ground.' I don't mind the money involved. I mind the nonsense of it all."

I told him, "Sir, it says in the Gemara (*Sotah* 49b) that before the *Mashiach* comes, a son will do battle with his father. Tell me, what would you rather your son brought home — a gentile wife, or *shemurah* matzah, hand ground ...?"

"Oy, R' Galinsky, don't confuse me. I knew you'd be difficult to talk to. Good-bye." The line went dead.

Rabbosai! In the past, there was someone to talk to. Today, unfortunately, they understand nothing. Hand-ground, foot-ground — they all fall into the category of *"she'eino yodei'a lishol"* ("those who do not know how to ask"). They've searched out new ways and see where those ways have led.

I encouraged those prisoners, and I cried along with them, saying, "*Ribono Shel Olam! Rabbosai*, it's not you who should be sitting in jail, but those who educated you. Let *them* sit here! They're the ones who really led you to this place. You are not to blame."

Let's conclude this *derashah* with what we began.

The Jewish nation does not seek out new ways. There is no need to burden the prison system. Since the exodus from Egypt, at the start of our redemption, we learned that there is no seeking sustenance in new behaviors. We are content to walk the same long road that our forefathers walked. The way they behaved is the way we will behave. We will ride the same donkey that Avraham Avinu used on his way to sacrifice Yitzchak. And in this way, we will be redeemed.

Amen — may it be Your will!

פרשת וארא
PARASHAS VA'EIRA

לָכֵן אֱמֹר לִבְנֵי־יִשְׂרָאֵל אֲנִי ה' וְהוֹצֵאתִי אֶתְכֶם מִתַּחַת סִבְלֹת מִצְרַיִם וְהִצַּלְתִּי אֶתְכֶם מֵעֲבֹדָתָם וְגָאַלְתִּי אֶתְכֶם בִּזְרוֹעַ נְטוּיָה וּבִשְׁפָטִים גְּדֹלִים: וְלָקַחְתִּי אֶתְכֶם לִי לְעָם וְהָיִיתִי לָכֶם לֵאלֹקִים וִידַעְתֶּם כִּי אֲנִי ה' אֱלֹקֵיכֶם.

"Therefore, say to the Children of Israel: 'I am Hashem, and I shall take you out from under the burdens of Egypt; I shall rescue you from their service; I shall redeem you with an outstretched arm and with great judgments. I shall take you to Me for a people and I shall be a God to you; and you shall know that I am Hashem your God'" (Shemos 6:6-7).

THE EGYPTIAN EXILE
AND A WOODEN BOX FROM SIBERIA

R' Sholom Schwadron

When I was in America, I was asked to speak in a magnificent shul, where only slightly over one-half of the congregants in attendance were mitzvah observant. A number of them were already assimilated, r"l.

The custom of the place was that, before delivering a talk, the topic had to by approved by the shul president that same morning. The honored president troubled himself to call me over and we went into one of the side rooms in the shul building, where he asked, "What does our esteemed speaker intend to talk about today?"

"About Shabbos observance," I said.

"Shabbos? How can you deliver a sermon on that topic, when so many of the worshipers drive here in their cars on Shabbos? No! Choose another topic."

"Family purity," I suggested.

"When I authorize a talk of this kind, we are always careful not to distress members of the shul. There are many here who are very distant from mitzvah observance. It's not worth your while to speak about things like that."

"Well, then, I'll speak about education," I said.

"Absolutely not! The local public school educates most of our congregants' children, while only a few attend the Jewish school. Why speak to no purpose? They won't listen to you. It's a waste of your time and energy."

I became angry. "Then what *can* I talk about in a shul like this?"

"Talk about *Yiddishkeit*," he replied.

I walked out. Talk about *Yiddishkeit*! Not about education, or about Shabbos, but about *Yiddishkeit*!

We know that in the world at large there are those who go to their house of worship now and then, while in their daily lives they continue to rob and murder just as before ... but Jews?!

When I left that shul president, I understood the words of the *parashas hashavua*: "I shall take you out from under the burdens of Egypt."

"*Therefore, say to the Children of Israel: 'I am Hashem, and I shall take you out from under the burdens of Egypt; I shall rescue you from their service; I shall redeem you with an outstretched arm and with great judgments. I shall take you to Me for a people and I shall be a God to you; and you shall know that I am Hashem your God ...'*"

Rabbosai, anyone with a modicum of understanding knows that the four expressions of redemption mentioned in this verse are not merely four synonyms in Hebrew, but refer to four types of redemption from the Egyptian slavery.

Just as four aspects of redemption, *geulah*, exist in a physical sense, there are also four nuances of spiritual redemption.

"*I shall take you out from under the burdens of Egypt*" refers to one spiritual aspect, while "*I shall rescue you from their service*" is another aspect of *geulah*. "*I shall redeem you with an outstretched arm and with great judgments*" refers to the exodus from Egypt and the parting of the Reed Sea, of which it is said, "A maidservant saw [more miracles] on the Sea [than did the prophet Yechezkel]!" Lastly, "*I shall take you to Me for a people*" is an additional stage of *geulah*: the giving of the Torah. So teach our Sages.

The reason we plummeted into four cycles of exile was because we had entered four kinds of spiritual exile. With our leaving Egypt, we merited having Hashem redeem us from these spiritual exiles, until we arrived at Sinai and received the Torah.

☞ *The First Redemption*

The first spiritual exile to be mentioned is "the burdens of Egypt": "*And I shall take you out from under the burdens of Egypt.*" To what does this refer? The word used for "burdens" is "*sivlos*": "*sivlos Mitzrayim.*" "*Sivlos*" is "*savlanus*" — patience. In other words, spiritual patience. Patience in *ruchniyus*.

There is a joke that it is permissible for us to hear and to repeat. A certain Jew once announced that he had learned the *sefer* "*Mesillas Yesharim*" very thoroughly from cover to cover, and had reviewed it two or three times.

"So what did you learn from the *Mesillas Yesharim*?" his friends asked.

"I learned one thing: the *middah* of '*savlanus*' — patience. The *Mesillas Yesharim* spoke to me, it shouted at me, and I armed myself with patience. I demonstrated that I have patience."

Hashem promised: I will take you out of that *savlanus* — that type of patience!

Among the gentiles we find a plethora of this kind of patience. The gentile can step out of his house of worship, where he just finished praying and listening to a thundering sermon, and go on to do just as he pleases. He may continue to rob, steal, kill, etc. In his house of worship he is like a different man for a short while, and on his leaving it, he returns to his usual life. On the surface he seems to be enjoying the best of both this world and the next.

Unfortunately, a bit of this kind of patience has infiltrated us during our exile among the gentiles. This is a negative kind of patience: apathy.

My dear brothers. We've already related, several times, the Chofetz Chaim's parable about the person who prays to *HaKadosh Baruch Hu*, "Have mercy on us and open our hearts to understand, to be wise, to learn, and to teach, etc. I very much want to learn and to understand what I learn — oh, how much I want it!" But when he finishes *davening* he doesn't open a Gemara or *mishnayos*. He just says, "Good-bye," kisses the *mezuzah* on the shul door, and disappears. He doesn't open a *sefer* until the next day when, once again, he pleads for Hashem to give him understanding in his Torah study! *Nu?* Open a *mishnayos* already! But, no — he has patience. "There's plenty of time. What's the rush? A little patience."

It was about this that Hashem said, "*And I shall take you out from under the burdens of Egypt.*" Out of that patience and apathy. This is the first redemption.

☞ The Second Redemption

After the first *geulah*, Hashem promised us further, "*I shall rescue you from their service.*" I will save you from their service of foreign gods — their *avodah zarah*.

Does their "service" — *avodah zarah* — have anything to do with us? Is there anyone today who serves foreign gods?! After all, the Torah is eternal and *Chazal* have said, "Draw it and take it for yourselves" — that is, draw your hands away from *avodah zarah!* Do we have any connection to their *avodah zarah* today?

It says in *Koheles* (10:1), *"Dead flies putrefy the perfumer's oil."*

⮑ An Animal at the Table / A Foreign God

As a disciple of the Dubno Maggid wrote: The *yetzer hara* (comparable to a fly) has many soldiers. "Dead flies" is written in the plural; they putrefy the perfumer's oil — that is, they direct a person toward desires that lead to rot. For example, gluttony, the desire for food, has gotten out of hand in our generation. It's reached the point where people aren't even embarrassed anymore! I'm not saying that we see a great deal, but the little that we do witness of the desire for food sears the eyes. I sometimes attend weddings where I myself feel embarrassed. Hardly has the *kesubah* been read when, in the hall downstairs, people are grabbing seats and clinking forks. They're not bad people. They've written a check, given a gift. But they can't resist e-a-t-i-n-g. They eat and eat!

Others, who've managed to control themselves until after the *chuppah*, or even a bit afterward, still make sure to tip over their chairs beforehand (as though to indicate, "This place is taken!"). And later, when they sit down at the table? Everything is kosher; there are fifteen *hechsherim* attesting to that. *Glatt*-kosher gluttony. And these people at home do not lack bread to eat, and meat to repletion. *Gevaldig*.

I am focusing on this particular drive because other drives are even more reprehensible and we ought not to deal with them. Also, when it comes to gluttony our own eyes can witness the humiliating spectacle, the sight of all ten fingers digging into the food.

They say that the Ba'al HaTanya once took along a student who was close to him to visit a certain individual, in order to ask for a donation for an important mitzvah. On their arrival, they found the man busy eating meat.

"Do you see anything?" the Ba'al HaTanya asked his student. "No," the student said.

The *rav* took out a handkerchief and passed it over his student's eyes. Suddenly, the student actually saw an animal seated at the table, eating.

"What's going on?" the student asked in astonishment.

The Ba'al HaTanya explained, "Because he is engaged so devotedly in his eating, the spirit of the animal has entered him until with spiritual vision he appears in this grip of the animal — to the point where he and the beast are one."

I am not coming here to criticize everyone. However, those who do devote themselves to the business of eating, from where does it derive, if not from the gentiles and the exile? The foreign god that resides within the body — the drive to eat — has grown in them until physicality has become their *avodah zarah*. The Gemara says (*Shabbos* 105b): "Do not have a foreign god within you. What is a foreign god inside a person's body? This is the *yetzer hara*." That is one fly — one that putrefies.

⌒ The Gutter Cleaner of Grodno

But there is a different fly: one that puffs itself up in arrogance. Sometimes it engages in matters of honor and pride in a delicate way; many other times, however, there is no delicacy at all. Arrogance works the same way: sometimes crudely, and at others, more delicately. For example, he longs for a certain position, to the point where he becomes ill over it. "I want that job!" And if someone were to belittle his *kavod*, his honor, he would be beside himself. "Flies of death."

They say in the name of R' Chaim Volozhiner (and *chassidim* tell this story about one of their rebbes), that a certain rebbe went to the *"shvitz"* (a sauna) to take a sweatbath for his health. As is known, the bathhouse custom is to have one's body beaten in order to get the blood circulating, to cleanse the skin of impurities, and so on. The man who did the beating received several pennies from the rebbe and began striking him. But the rebbe was not pleased because the blows were painful. He reacted with a movement that expressed his dissatisfaction. Offended, the beater grew angry. "For 40 years I've had the job of beating people's backs, and you're not satisfied? Are you going to teach me where to strike?"

Leaving the bathhouse, the rebbe taught, "Here is an example of '*kavod*.'" To each his own brand of honor.

And we? We, too, have our brand of honor.

One of my friends, a student in the Grodno yeshivah before the war, was one of its finest and most diligent students. For some reason, however, he refrained from participating in the Torah discussions taking place in the yeshivah. When the other yeshivah *bachurim* argued and debated in the heat of their learning, trying to delve into the meaning of a Gemara or Rashi or *Tosafos*, as a rule he did not join in.

Then, one day, he accompanied the *Mashgiach* on a walk. The *Mashgiach* mentioned that he had noticed that when the other students roiled and seethed, this student would sit and learn on his own, not participating. "Why is that?" asked the *Mashgiach*. "Why do you stay apart?"

The *bachur*, mischievous by nature, offered a "clever" response. With a small smile, he said, "My abilities are not weak, as the *Mashgiach* knows. If I were to participate in the arguments and win, I'm fearful of *ga'avah* (arrogance)."

The *Mashgiach* did not respond.

They walked on, and a few steps later came upon Grodno's "gutter cleaner." In those days, there was no indoor plumbing. Every house had a pit dug in its yard, and a "gutter cleaner" would pass by periodically, transferring the sewage into his pails and onto his wagon, which he would then transport to the large dump outside the city limits. This was his livelihood.

Grodno's gutter cleaner, passing them in his wagon now, was a particularly haughty individual. When he drove through the streets of Grodno, the expression on his face hinted at an arrogant nature.

The *Mashgiach* turned to the *bachur*. "Are you worried that you will acquire arrogance from the study of Torah? Is it Torah study that brings one to arrogance? Look at him. What is that gutter cleaner thinking about as he sits up there on his high perch with the sewage in his wagon? He is probably thinking, *I am holding this whole town on my shoulders. If not for me and my strength, all of Grodno's citizens would choke from the stench.* Understand? He, too, is a prideful person."

In summary, there is the "putrefaction" of ordinary desire, and there is "puffed-up" pride and arrogance. The gentiles have this in great measure. As for us, *HaKadosh Baruch Hu* promised: "*I shall rescue you from their service.*"

⌇ The Third and Fourth Redemptions

Afterward came the third *geulah*: "*I shall redeem you with an outstretched arm and with great judgments.*" This refers to the miracles that occurred at the parting of the Reed Sea. The mind boggles at the extent of the wonders and the *Shechinah's* revelation, which we are told was witnessed even by a simple maidservant! They stepped out of the physicality of Egypt, were redeemed, and witnessed Hashem's outstretched arm and mighty judgments.

Later still came the fourth redemption: "*I shall take you to Me for a people.*" At *Matan Torah* — the giving of the Torah — the nation attained higher levels and were rescued from physicality, for "I created the *yetzer hara*; I created an antidote for it."

⌐ A Finger from Siberia

After we became Hashem's nation —"*I shall take you to Me for a people*" — we were closely attached to Him; even those most far away are never truly lost. The day will come when, "*the lost ones will come from the land of Ashur and the remote ones from the land of Egypt, and they will prostrate themselves to Hashem on the holy Mount in Jerusalem*" (Yeshaya 27:13). Even in our own generation, thousands have returned to their Father in heaven.

Let me tell you what two members of the *Chevrah Kaddisha* told me this week. It's an extraordinary story that falls under the rubric of "*I shall take you to Me for a people*."

A new immigrant to Israel from Russia entered the offices of the *Chevrah Kaddisha* in a state of obvious agitation. Sitting down, he found it hard to begin speaking. They gave him a drink of water, after which he wept for a while and then began to speak.

He said that for more than two years he had been a prisoner in Siberia, where he had been forced to perform backbreaking labor. This past week he had finally been released, and permission was granted for him to move to Israel since his sentence had been served. His joy was boundless.

Before he left the Siberian prison camp — literally, in his final hour — he was summoned by the Jewish woman who had been serving as the camp doctor for many years.

In tears, she said, "It seems that I'll be here for the rest of my life, and it is reasonable to assume that I will not merit a Jewish burial. They will bury me along with the other camp prisoners, most of whom are non-Jews. I've been told that you will shortly be crossing to the other side of the Iron Curtain and leaving Russia to go to Israel. I'd like to give you something."

She went into an adjacent room. There, she cut off a finger from her left hand. Returning with the finger, she cried aloud, "At least my finger can be buried on the Mount of Olives in Jerusalem!"

When the man reached this point in his story, he took out a wooden box covered in cloth, on which the woman's name and that of her father were written in ink.

The members of the *Chevrah Kaddisha* broke down and cried. And cried.

I don't know if she did the right thing. But she certainly did it — along with the tears and intentions — as a Jewish woman very far from Judaism and lost in remote Siberia. She possessed the exalted inner feeling of a Jewish daughter, out there in the wilds of Siberia!

Where did it come from? From *Matan Torah*. From "*I shall take you to Me for a people*." That holiness bursts forth and awakens in many different forms and guises, even out there beyond the dark mountains.

May Hashem help all of us to nurture the spark of repentance. And may we arrive at the fifth redemption — the *geulah sheleimah* — *bimheirah b'yameinu*.

וְגָאַלְתִּי אֶתְכֶם בִּזְרוֹעַ נְטוּיָה וּבִשְׁפָטִים גְּדֹלִים: וְלָקַחְתִּי אֶתְכֶם לִי לְעָם וְהָיִיתִי לָכֶם לֵאלֹקִים וִידַעְתֶּם כִּי אֲנִי ה׳ אֱלֹקֵיכֶם.

"*I shall redeem you with an outstretched arm and with great judgments. I shall take you to Me for a people and I shall be a God to you; and you shall know that I am Hashem your God.*" (Shemos 6:6-7).

DON'T BECOME INTOXICATED

R' Sholom Schwadron

*I*t's sad, but this really happened. It happened to me. Learn from this story how things look without the fourth *geulah*, without "*I shall take you to Me for a people*" (e.g., *Matan Torah*).

Fifty or more years ago, when we were young *bachurim*, we would go out in pairs near sunset on Friday to the Bucharim neighborhood and its environs, to encourage the shops to close. "Shabbos, Shabbos!" we told the shopkeepers. "It's time to lock your store. Go home and get dressed in honor of the Shabbos!"

There was one barber who always gave us a hard time. Every Friday his shop was crowded, and closing was a slow affair. Usually, until he shut his doors it was already very late, and by the time we returned to yeshivah (Yeshivas Chevron) we were unable to find an Ashkenazi shul that had not yet begun to *daven Ma'ariv*. (The Sephardim began their service even earlier.) Ten or so of us *bachurim* would gather to *daven* on our own.

Oy, how many people that man shaved with a razor, *r"l*. How many transgressions took place in that barber shop. After all, both the one who does the shaving and the one who is shaved are transgressing five prohibitions! The barber himself transgressed the additional prohibition of *"Do not place a stumbling block before a blind man"* — six prohibitions in all. But what could we do? He was a great boor. As he closed up shop, he would kiss the *mezuzah* three times! Neither more nor less. Don't smile, that's exactly what he did.

And then came a period of six or seven weeks when the shop was closed, locked up completely. We didn't know what had happened. Had someone died in his family, or had the barber fallen ill? Then, one Friday, we saw that the shop was open again. The barber had returned to work.

Because we'd always spoken to him in a friendly way (according to the dictum of "the left hand pushes away while the right hand draws close"), we were able to ask with interest, "What happened?"

"Don't ask," he responded with feeling.

"I was very ill. But a miracle happened: Hashem healed me. Let me tell you something. As I lay sick in bed, I made a vow that if Hashem cured me, I would travel to Meiron to R' Shimon bar Yochai and I would shave my beard at his grave." Do you understand? Another five prohibitions! We held our heads in our hands and moaned.

A person who does not see will sink into the pit and expect to be rewarded for doing so. He fulfilled his vow in its entirety.

Since we have mentioned the five prohibitions involved in shaving with a razor, I'll tell you another story. As a youth, I didn't grow my beard. I would remove the hair on my face with a depilatory foam, not an electric shaver. One evening, I went to *daven* in a shul in the Beis Yisrael neighborhood and met someone I knew. It was clear to see on his face that he shaved with a razor, may Hashem have mercy. I'd met him several times before, and he'd look the same. Mustering my courage, I rebuked him, "*Reb Yid*, how can you do such a thing?!"

He looked at me. "What are you talking about? You don't have a beard and I don't have a beard. Scissors or razor, what difference does it make? Leave me alone. It's all the same thing." It pained me to see how even a permissible beard-cutting could serve to lead someone to stumble.

Nevertheless, what is clear is that only with, "*I shall take you to Me for a people*" — with Torah — can we be redeemed. Without Torah we remain ignorant. We may pray three times a day, yet still stumble. We don't know the difference between scissors and a razor, between a shaver and foam. Or else we visit R' Shimon bar Yochai in order to shave with a razor in front of his grave. We err and sink into the retribution of *Gehinnom, r"l.*

⌐ Between Cups

The *mishnah* says that one is permitted to drink additional wine between the four cups of wine at the Seder except for the interval between the third and fourth cups. The *Talmud Yerushalmi* comments on this distinction:

If one drinks wine between the first and second cups, he will not become drunk, because wine that is consumed before eating or with a meal does not intoxicate. The third cup, however, is drunk after the meal is finished, which may result in intoxication. Therefore, wine must not be drunk after it.

I've found a profound allusion in this idea.

The cups correspond to the four terms used to describe the *ge-ulah*, the redemption, both physically and spiritually (as we've elaborated upon in the previous section). Hashem redeemed us from the suffering of Egypt and rescued us from its idol worship. Afterward, He also showed us His outstretched arm and mighty judgments. Along with the exodus from Egypt came a revelation of the *Shechinah*. "A maidservant on the Sea saw what Yechezkel ben Buzi did not see!" One might feel intoxicated, saying, "Well, we've arrived! We've achieved so much! We've been rescued from Egypt; we are walking with Aharon HaKohen and Moshe Rab-beinu, surrounded by Clouds of Glory and eating *mon*. We've been fully redeemed."

But we tell him, "No! Don't get drunk here, for the *geulah* still lies before you: the fourth cup. "*I shall take you to Me for a people*" — *Matan Torah*. Only then will you "*know that I am Hashem, your God.*" Without receiving the Torah, exile still surrounds us.

The *Talmud Yerushalmi* alludes to this: "It is forbidden to drink wine between the third and fourth cups." In other words, we are not to place a separation between the third and fourth redemp-tions! Why? Because the foundation is Torah. Without Torah, there is nothing.

☞ "At the Merrymaking for a Chasan and Kallah"

Do we grasp what that maidservant saw on the Sea? Let me tell you an awesome story from the Gemara (*Chagigah* 14b).

"R' Yochanan ben Zakkai would ride a donkey and go along the road, and R' Elazar ben Arach would lead the donkey." The student served his rebbi by leading the donkey on which his rebbi rode and, at the same time, learned Torah from him. Wonderful.

The student, R' Elazar ben Arach, asked R' Yochanan ben Zak-kai, "Rebbi, teach me one portion of the *Ma'aseh HaMerkavah*." He wanted his rebbi to teach him one piece of the Hidden Torah.

R' Yochanan ben Zakkai replied, "I've taught you that one does not teach these secrets except to a unique individual who understands what is told to him in the form of a hint."

Said the student, "Rebbi, permit me to recite before you what I've already learned about the secrets of the Torah, and I will demonstrate that I can understand a hint. Then I will merit hearing more from you."

R' Yochanan gave him permission to speak.

The Gemara tells us that R' Yochanan ben Zakkai immediately got off the donkey, wrapped himself in his cloak, and sat on a stone, beneath an olive tree. [R' Elazar] said, "Rebbi, why have you gotten off the donkey?" [R' Yochanan] said, "Is it possible that you will speak about the Ma'aseh HaMerkavah, as the Shechinah is among us and the attending angels accompany us, and I ride a donkey?!"

At once, R' Elazar ben Arach began speaking about the Ma'aseh HaMerkavah. As he spoke, fire descended from the heavens and roused all the trees in the field. The trees began to sing [to Hashem]. Which song did they sing? "Praise Hashem from the earth, sea giants and all watery depths ... fruitful trees and all cedars ... Halleluyah!" One angel answered from the fire, saying, "Hen, hen Ma'aseh HaMerkavah."

R' Yochanan ben Zakkai stood up, kissed [R' Elazar] on the head, and said, "Blessed is Hashem, God of Israel, Who gave a son to Avraham Avinu who knows how to understand and to delve and to study the Ma'aseh HaMerkavah. There are those who speak well but do not fulfill [what they speak about], and those who fulfill well but do not speak well. And you — you speak well and fulfill well. How fortunate is your lot, Avraham Avinu, that Elazar ben Arach descended from your loins!"

We're not done yet. When they related this episode to other Tannaim, this is what happened. "R' Yehoshua and R' Yose HaKohen went along the road and said, 'Let us, too, speak about the Ma'aseh HaMerkavah.'" R' Yehoshua began to speak, and although it was a day in the summer month of Tammuz, the sky became wreathed in clouds and a rainbow of sorts was seen among the clouds, and the attendant angels gathered together to listen, like people who gather together to see the merrymaking for a bride and groom." (For the continuation, see *Chagigah* 14b.)

R' Elazar ben Arach was a student of R' Yochanan ben Zakkai, who received Torah from the six pairs of great teachers mentioned at the beginning of *Pirkei Avos*. Each of those pairs were greater than R' Yochanan ben Zakkai. Among them was Shimon Hatzaddik, one of the last of the *Anshei Knesses Hagedolah*. Included in their number were also several prophets (before prophecy ended). How awesome was their greatness! These prophets received Torah from the prophets who came before them — until Yechezkel ben Buzi Hakohen, of whom it is said, "*I will see visions of God.*" And yet, *Chazal* tell us that, at the time of the splitting of the Reed Sea, the Jewish nation saw things that "even Yechezkel ben Buzi did not see." In other words, these were the momentous moments that Hashem had promised us, "*I shall redeem you with an outstretched arm and mighty judgments.*"

And yet, as we began by saying, we had not yet attained the level of "I shall take you to Me for a people" — *Matan Torah*. Only then will you "*know that I am Hashem!*" Why? Because Torah is the foundation. We — ourselves and our children — must learn it and learn it. Therefore, the *Yerushalmi* hints, there is no drinking between the third and fourth cups so that we do not become intoxicated, heaven forbid, with the first three redemptions, and remain without the fourth one. Do not insert anything between the cups and do not be satisfied until you have received the Torah!

⌒ Bare Feet

I'm sure you've heard of R' Yechezkel Abramsky. He was a *rav* in London and afterward here in Jerusalem. A very great man. I heard this story directly from him.

R' Yechezkel Abramsky was exiled to Siberia. He had committed some sort of "crime": learning Torah with his students, delivering *shiurim* under the Bolshevik regime.

They sent him to Siberia for a number of years (I don't recall the exact number) to perform backbreaking labor, r"l. As is known, many of those sentenced this way never completed their sentence. Most gave up their lives there in icy Siberia.

"On the first morning of my stay in the prison camp," says R' Abramsky, "we went outside." The cold was horrific — 50 or 60 below zero. We, the laborers, were told to remove our shoes and then our socks. We were to run 30 kilometers on the snow — in our bare feet. We stood there, barefoot, waiting for the signal from the commander to start running."

(R' Yechezkel would always talk to *HaKadosh Baruch Hu* the way a son speaks to his father: "*Tatteh*, Abba." That was his practice, consonant with his level of faith in "Hashem is before me always.")

"As I stood there on the snow for those few minutes," R' Yechezkel said, "I spoke to *HaKadosh Baruch Hu*. 'Father in heaven, You said in Your Torah, "Everything is in Heaven's hands except for chills and colds." (That is, a person is obligated to safeguard himself against becoming ill from the cold.) But here, as You know, I cannot safeguard myself. So I am asking you, Father, protect me from the cold as well.'"

R' Yechezkel turned to me and asked, "Do you hear, R' Sholom?" Then he continued, "And during my entire stay in Siberia, I never caught a cold — not even once!"

He went on, embellishing his story with additional details:

"I was in Siberia for a long time. On the morning of *erev Yom Kippur*, a certain officer approached me and said, 'You can go free. Go wherever you please.' He handed me a railroad ticket so that I could travel to my home, hundreds of kilometers away.

"I gathered the few rags I still had in my possession, for by then I had neither shoes nor socks: nothing. I took the few rags and began walking toward the train station, to wait for a train that would pass that way.

"I'd been sitting there a long time when, suddenly, I saw the head of that camp coming toward me. He looked around to make sure he was unobserved, and then bent over and whispered, 'Are you a rabbi?'

"He looked around again, then asked, 'Show me the card they gave you.'

"Terrified, heart pounding, I wondered if he was going to take away the ticket. Well, what good would it do to be frightened? I took out the white ticket. He took it, glanced at it, and said, 'Rabbi, do you know what? If you travel with this ticket, you will certainly die on the way and they will toss your body out the window into one of the fields. They gave you a ticket for an unheated car. You'd never survive the cold.' "

Do you understand? During that period, tremendous efforts were made, along with many pleading letters and threatening ones from all over the world, to free R' Abramsky from his Siberian prison. It was hard for the Communists to refuse, so they played this little trick. Later, they would be able to innocently claim, "We released him. What could we do? He died on the way."

"The camp commander looked around for a third time, and then removed a different ticket from behind his coat lapel. 'Take this ticket and hide it in your pocket. It's a ticket for a heated compartment. This way, you'll arrive home safely.'

"As R' Yechezkel took the ticket, the director added, 'I am a Jew. I am also a Jew. I beg your forgiveness for the work I made you do and the trouble I caused you.' " R' Yechezkel Abramsky later said that the man had indeed been very wicked and had caused him great distress. (Perhaps, on that *erev Yom Kippur*, a spark of repentance ignited in the man. After all, he was still a Jew!)

"I climbed aboard the train," said R' Abramsky, "into a heated compartment. *Oy*, R' Sholom. On the way I saw a number of people hurled out of the windows. They had frozen to death. But I arrived safely, *baruch Hashem*. It was nearly evening when the train stopped at a station that was near a remote Russian village where a small number of Jews lived. I got off and went there in my rags. I did not have time to eat anything before the fast because the sun had already set. I went in as I was, to the village shul, and fasted on Yom Kippur.

"The next day, I continued on my way and traveled home."

You still haven't heard the main part (R' Sholom chants).

R' Yechezkel went on to tell me about other adventures he had undergone, with the government trying to kill him in various ways and Hashem performing wonders for him until he finally left Russia.

"On my way to Lithuania," R' Yechezkel continued, "I arrived in Odessa, where I boarded a train bound for Warsaw. It was there that I met R' Elchanan Wasserman, a student of the Chofetz Chaim. Of course, we kissed and embraced each other, joyous over my rescue and redemption. Then R' Elchanon said to me, 'Is it true that you left the prison camp on the morning of *erev Yom Kippur?*'

"I was stunned.

" 'Yes,' I replied. In astonishment, I asked, 'But how does the esteemed Rav know that? Even my family doesn't know that I'd been released.'

" 'You're asking me how I knew? I'll tell you,' R' Elchanan answered. 'At about 10 o'clock that morning, on *erev Yom Kippur*, the Chofetz Chaim and I left the shul where we had *davened Shacharis*. Suddenly, as we walked along the lane that led away from the shul, the Chofetz Chaim stopped walking and said, '*Nu*, the Bolsheviks didn't win! They've taken R' Abramsky out of Siberia!' "

Do you hear that? Who received the first telegram about R' Yechezkel Abramsky's release? The Chofetz Chaim. Who sent the telegram, and how? The Torah! It came from, "*I shall take you to Me as a people, and I shall be a God to you*." As *Chazal* tell us, "*HaKadosh Baruch Hu* saw the light of the Creation and the world did not merit it. And he saved it for the *tzaddikim* in the Torah."

וַיְדַבֵּר מֹשֶׁה כֵּן אֶל־בְּנֵי יִשְׂרָאֵל וְלֹא שָׁמְעוּ אֶל־מֹשֶׁה מִקֹּצֶר רוּחַ וּמֵעֲבֹדָה קָשָׁה.

"So Moshe spoke accordingly to the Children of Israel; but they did not heed Moshe, because of shortness of breath and hard work" (Shemos 6:9).

COUNTING BUSES

R' Yaakov Galinsky

*T*he following is a well-known true story about the Chofetz Chaim.

One morning many years ago, when the Chofetz Chaim was a young man, he walked into a shul in his town and saw the people laughing, their faces wreathed in smiles. This didn't interest him until he noticed that they were looking at a certain person, who was obviously the source of the amusement.

What's so funny? he wondered. He looked again — and saw. Now he understood what was happening.

The previous evening, someone had angered Avremel the *Meshuggener*, the name by which the town's "Fool" was known. The incident had taken place between *Minchah* and *Ma'ariv*, when that "someone" had provided everyone in shul with a pinch of tobacco; everyone, that is, except for Avremel. Avremel, justifiably angry, had shouted, "Do you think I can't get my hands on some tobacco? I'll show you!" Furious, he stomped out of shul and made his way to the town of Ishashok, which was not too far from Radin.

Avremel walked a long way until he reached Ishashok, where he knocked on the door of one of his friends and asked for *"ah shmeck taback."* Holding the pinch of tobacco tightly between his two fingers, he immediately started back on the return journey to

Radin. He had walked all night. Just minutes before, at the end of Shacharis, he had stumbled into the shul exhausted and covered with mud, crowing happily, "Here! I have some!" And he showed everyone the grains of tobacco clamped between his fingers.

Typically, the children who were present began to tease him. They tried to snatch the tobacco from between his fingers, and he did his best to evade them. Round and round the *bimah* the children chased him, laughing, "The *meshuggener* walked kilometers just to get a sniff of tobacco — a '*shmeck taback*.' "

Hearing this, the Chofetz Chaim thought a moment, and then said sadly, "And us? What about us?"

The congregants did not grasp his meaning.

Suddenly, Avremel approached the Chofetz Chaim, waving his hands in the air in an attitude of victory. "See? I've brought a '*shmeck taback!*' " A moment later, the Chofetz Chaim began to read from the Gemara (*Chagigah* 13a).

"But behold! from the earth until the first heaven is a 500 year journey; and the thickness of a heaven is a 500 year journey; and so it is between each of the heavens. Above them are the holy *chayos*: The feet of the *chayos* are equivalent to [all of the above mentioned spans]; the ankles of the *chayos* are equivalent to all of them; the lower parts of the legs of the *chayos* are equivalent to all of them; the middle parts of the legs of the *chayos* are equivalent to all of them; the upper parts of the legs of the *chayos* are equivalent to all of them; the torsos of the *chayos* are equivalent to all of them; the necks of the *chayos* are equivalent to all of them; the heads of the *chayos* are equivalent to all of them; [and] the horns of the *chayos* are equivalent to all of them." (In other words, there is a distance of tens of thousands of kilometers from heaven to earth.)

The Chofetz Chaim raised his voice, as a tear trickled from his eye. "Avremel walked 28 kilometers and at least received a '*shmeck taback*' for his efforts. He became covered in dirt and dust solely to bring back something we find amusing. But how many people who have come such a long way — the distance from heaven to earth — don't even bring a pinch of tobacco with them?

"The souls of Israel were carved from beneath the Throne of Glory. The soul sets out on its way and spends some 70-odd years here before making the return trip. Arriving back in Heaven, the soul is asked, 'What have you brought with you?' And that soul displays a finger, with a tiny pinch of tobacco ... the Gemara *shiur* that it attended just once a month ... They laugh at him there, too ..." Another tear stole down the Chofetz Chaim's cheek.

On another occasion, the Chofetz Chaim touched on a verse in *Koheles* (4:1): "*I returned and contemplated all the acts of oppression that are committed beneath the sun: Behold! Tears of the oppressed with none to comfort them, and their oppressors have the power — with none to comfort them.*" Who has no one to comfort them? Those who have brought with them from this world only a few *tefillos* and *berachos* and *mishnayos*. In the future, they will bang their heads on the wall in regret — unable to be comforted.

The story of Avremel's walk to Ishashok and the Chofetz Chaim's reaction to it illustrate the power of thought to touch the heartstrings. Why are we laughing? Whom are we mocking? Avremel the *Meshugenner* is not the only one. He is only an example and a representative.

People think that the job of speakers such as myself is to give *mussar* to our fellow man — to deliver fiery sermons — to cry out in a tearful voice. No! This is a mistake. An individual is most expert at scolding himself. All he needs, as the Ponevezher Rav, once told me, is someone to awaken him from his torpor. Asleep, a person cannot take stock of himself. But if he wakes from his slumber he will be able to make a reckoning of his gains and losses, and the losses will prompt an uprising against the *yetzer hara*.

⤳ The Labor Intensifies

Pharaoh was afraid of an uprising. He knew that the Jews were a difficult people with whom to do battle. Moreoever, he knew that they were even capable of staging a rebellion. "*Behold! the people, the Children of Israel, are more numerous and stronger than we.*" Therefore, he invested continually in a single plan: "*Let the work be heavier upon the men.*" Explains the *Mesillas Yesharim*: "He intended not to give them any respite at all, so that they would not turn their minds to devising a plan against him. He tried to detach them from any contemplation through the constancy of endless work. And so the *yetzer hara* plots against people." (*Mesillas Yesharim, perek beis*).

Rabbosai, is there anything in the world more valuable than time? The *yetzer hara* steals our lives away; it robs us of our time. It does not grant us the leisure to take stock, to think: "Why am I not learning? Why do I get angry over little nothings and walk around so tension filled all the time?" If a person would only devote a bit of thought to his situation, everything would look different. This was Pharaoh's cleverness: He kept them too busy to take proper care of themselves.

And if you ever do want to wake up, the *yetzer hara* hastens to give you a sleeping pill. When thieves wish to steal the contents of a house, what do they do? They enter through a window and spray a form of sleep-inducing drug on the members of the household. While the family is enjoying its lovely dreams, the thieves — along with the dreams — are busy emptying out the house.

⌁ Youth, Prime of Life, and the Old-Age Home

"*R' Dosa ben Horkinas says: Morning sleep, midday wine, children's chatter, and sitting at gatherings of the ignorant remove a person from the world*" (*Avos* 3:14). The day is divided into morning, afternoon, and evening — like life itself. There is a time for *Shacharis*: the days of one's youth. Afterward comes an age, comparable to noon, and still later, the age of evening.

Along comes R' Dosa ben Horkinas and says, "*Bachurim* like yourselves (this talk was delivered to yeshivah *bachurim*) are still *davening* the *Shacharis* of your lives. What tactics does the *yetzer hara* use on you? 'Morning sleep'! He says, 'Don't hurry, kid. You've got your whole life ahead of you. You've got plenty of time. Don't learn. Go ahead and sleep a little longer.' When I was a child, they used to say, 'You'll be a *gaon* half a year later!'

"*There's no need to hurry right away*, one thinks. *I'll start a couple of months from now. Life is ahead of me, I'm still young.* The *yetzer hara* gives you a couple of sleeping pills as the sun comes up: 'Morning sleep'!

"Then noon rolls around. A person begins to scratch his head, thinking, *Oy, the morning years have passed. Where did they go so fast?* The *yetzer hara* becomes frightened: 'He's starting to lift his head and look around. He's getting organized.' So he hurries off to buy some wine: 'Midday wine.' The *yetzer hara* gives him delicious wine and other sweet, tasty things: 'Live it up! Have a drink!' He drowns him in sweetness.

"Of course, he drops several sleeping pills into the wine goblet, so our fellow keeps on sleeping.

"What becomes of this individual? '*Children's chatter and sitting at gatherings of the ignorant.*'

"R' Sholom Schwadron once told me about the time he went to an old-age home to *daven Minchah*. No sooner had R' Sholom entered the gates when he heard two old men (who were sitting in the courtyard sunning themselves) arguing. One of them said, 'Forty-two!' while the other shouted, 'Forty-three!' A minute passed, and then the argument broke out again, the first old man saying, 'Forty-three!' and the second countering with a furious, 'Forty-four!' And so on, through forty-five and forty-six.

"R' Sholom approached them. 'Tell me,' he said. 'What's the argument about? Are you having a *din Torah* about something?'

" 'No.' They declined to tell him any more.

"He stood at the side of the courtyard, watching and listening until he realized that all they were arguing about was the number of buses that had passed in the past five minutes. They were sitting and counting the buses as they passed the building. While one of the two counted a total of only 42 buses, the other was convinced that the total was really 43 ... Their voices grew louder and shriller, with the first old man stubbornly insisting, 'Forty-eight,' while the other furiously countered, 'Forty-nine!'

"R' Sholom walked into the shul that was part of the old-age home, where he saw elderly men sitting with magnifying glasses, learning from big Gemaras and splendid *mishnayos*. Tears stood in his eyes.

"Later, R' Sholom delivered an emotional sermon in Zichron Moshe. 'We've all seen people who took advantage of their mornings and their afternoons and so are able to fill their evenings as well. But if they sleep through the morning and drink wine and "have fun" at midday, what is left of them? "The chatter of children." How many buses have passed?'

"And so they leave this world, returning home with a pinch of tobacco between their fingers."

☞ Shlomo's Wisdom

At the start of *Sefer Koheles*, Shlomo Hamelech mentions the word "*hevel*" seven times. "R' Yehoshua ben Levi said: 'The seven '*hevels*' in *Koheles* correspond to the seven worlds that a person experiences in his lifetime. From the time he leaves his mother's womb until he is about a year old, everyone hugs and kisses him. At 2 and 3 he is like a pig, digging and burrowing and putting whatever he finds into his mouth. By the age of 10 he prances like a goat, etc." (See *Midrash Rabbah* at the start of *Koheles*.)

Life is divided into seven parts. The 70 years of life are divided into decades, with every 10 years constituting one part. And about them all Shlomo Hamelech declared, "*Hakol hevel!*" ("All is futile!") He touches on this concept of futility seven times in all.

This presents us with two questions. First: Why seven times? Let

Shlomo make his point once, to encompass all of life: Futility of futilities, all is futile! The Vilna Gaon asks a second question: What is Shlomo saying that is so novel? If you ask any elderly person to look back at his life, even if he is not as wise as Shlomo, he will ask, "Why did I work so hard? What have I accomplished? So many years ... Why did I force myself to run around so much in my life? After all, it's all *hevel*."

In that case, why did the wisest of men have to tell us that all the 70 years of a lifetime are *hevel*? Even unintelligent old men, with a backward look, can say the same.

The Vilna Gaon provides an answer, concealed in the first question.

Shlomo Hamelech used the term "*hevel*" seven times. Therein lies his great wisdom.

To use the term once to refer to an entire lifetime is no great feat. The wisdom comes with saying it seven times — that is, at the age of 20, at 30, at 40, at every age and stage of life: the dreams of 20, the ambitions of 30, the ideas of 40, — and to apply "*hevel havalim*" to them all. This is the difficult part, and something that most people in the world are far from understanding. They succeed in achieving this wisdom only once, at the age of 70.

My dear brothers! A 2-year-old child sees everything in his life as a marble. If you steal his marble — take away his property — he cries as bitterly as if his entire house were up in flames.

Later, when he grows up and reaches the age of 10, he turns around and laughs at his 2-year-old brother: "What's he crying about? They only took away his marble." And what does that 10-year-old cry about? His bicycle.

At 15, he'll laugh at his younger brother for crying over a bicycle. He himself is happy with his new motorbike which, if broken or stolen, will induce tears of fury in that 15-year-old.

With every stage of life, the marble changes form. It rolls right along with one's age.

At 30, he will look back on his 20-year-old aspirations with disdain. At 40, he doesn't understand why the 30-year-old is so absorbed with yet another fantasy, such as a new job. Isn't life really all about status and respect?

Were he a wise person, he would perform a simple calculation: If, at 10, I laugh at a 5-year-old and at 15 I laugh at a 10-year-old, then at 20 I will certainly laugh at a 15-year-old, and so on. In that case, why should someone else laugh at me? I'll laugh at myself instead. I'll become clever, and tell my *yetzer hara*, "Don't addle my wits with marbles and bicycles and motorbikes. Let me learn Torah and behave the way I'm supposed to, and that's that!"

This is wisdom.

A wise person will understand at an early age, but even someone older can learn to extrapolate the future from the past. Seeing the way he scoffs today at his former self, he can learn the lesson we've described above. By the age of 20 or 30 he can comprehend that all is vain. *Reb Yid*, be wise! You are still here in the world, and you have the power to achieve and to accomplish.

A man's greatest distress comes when, after a long, difficult journey, he arrives at his destination to find the place locked and bolted. "I traveled all this way for nothing," he sighs. That's why we pray every day, "*Lema'an lo niga larik v'lo neled labehalah* — So that we will not struggle in vain or produce for futility." We labor arduously in so many areas of life, and in the end we sometimes see that we've toiled in vain. Someone has kept us busy all along with truly marginal chores.

The *yetzer hara* has a vast supply of sleeping pills in his arsenal. Take care that he does not put you to sleep in the morning or at midday, or allow you to leave the world empty-handed.

May Hashem help us to wake up in the morning, at noon — or at the very least, in the evening hours!

פרשת בא ⬿
PARASHAS BO

INTRODUCTION: ON YOUR CHILDREN

R' Yaakov Galinsky

*T*he verse says, "*Each woman shall request from her neighbor and from the one who lives in her house silver vessels, golden vessels, and garments.*" (*Shemos* 3:22) The commentaries ask a question. Every child knows that it was in the merit of their not changing their names, clothing and language that they were redeemed from Egypt. How can the Torah tell us that they borrowed clothing from the gentiles?

However, if you take a second look at the verse, it says, "*A woman will borrow .... vessels of silver and vessels of gold and clothing — on your sons and daughters.*" An Egyptian woman's dress is short, and a Jewish woman would have thrown it away. But it wasn't the Jewish women themselves who wore the clothing; they dressed their children in the adults' clothing. "*You will put them on your sons and daughters.*" For those small children, the garments were long enough.

"In the merit of righteous women, our forefathers were redeemed from Egypt."

"R' Huna said in the name of Bar Kapara: Because of four things, Israel was redeemed from Egypt. They did not change their names or their language, and they did not speak *lashon hara*, and none of them were promiscuous. They did not change their names: Reuven and Shimon came in — and Reuven and Shimon went out. They did not call Yehudah 'Rupa,' nor Reuven 'Luliani,' nor Yosef 'Lastis,' nor Binyamin 'Alexandri.' They did not change their language: '*Ki pi hamedaber eleichem* — For my mouth is speaking to you' — that is, in *lashon hakodesh*. They did not speak *lashon hara*, as it says (*Shemos* 11:2), '*Please speak in the ears of the people*' [instructing them to borrow vessels and clothes from the Egyptians]. We find that they possessed this knowledge for twelve months, yet no Jew spoke slightingly to the Egyptians about any other Jew. And there was no promiscuity among them: We know this because there was only one woman who fell into this category and she is mentioned by name, (*Vayikra* 24:11) [as an unusual case]: '*And his mother's name was Shlomis bas Divri of the tribe of Dan*' (*Vayikra Rabbah* 32)."

"MOTHER, HELP ME!"

R' Benzion Yadler

R' Benzion Yadler had wonderful things to say about *lashon hakodesh* — the Hebrew tongue. "They did not change their language."

It was in the year 5674. A group of us — *rabbanim* from Jerusalem — were traveling together to visit the settlements of Eretz Yisrael. Participating in the trip were R' Yosef Chaim Sonnenfeld, R' Avraham Yitzchak Kook, chief rabbi of Yaffo, R' Yonasan Binyamin Horowitz, and R' Yaakov Moshe Charlop. The trip traversed the Upper Galil and the Lower Galil to strengthen the spiritual fabric of the peoples' lives and to arouse the residents to religious observance. This was in the early days of the renewed settlement of the Land. Unfortunately, we witnessed what was happening in these Galil settlements: *chilul Shabbos*, forbidden foods, and a lack of modesty, *r"l*.

On the day we returned from this tour, I set in motion some urgent rescue activities. I knew that there was much for us to do. We made contact and were helped with a great deal of *siyata Dishmaya* (Divine assistance). Let me tell you about a specific incident. I sent a letter to Mr. Ushiskin, director of the *Keren Kayemet L'Yisrael*. I requested a meeting regarding the settlements of Israel, which he supervised.

Several days passed before I received a positive response, confirming a meeting on a certain date. However, a condition was specified: "The meeting will be conducted in Hebrew only." (The battle over Modern Hebrew was then at its height: This was the language of choice by the secular Shabbos-desecrators.) I gave my consent to the meeting.

At the start of our talk, I said, "Mr. Ushiskin, let me tell you a story that took place in Russia:

"A poor young Jewish couple were married and began their life together. The language spoken in their home was Yiddish, the tongue with which they had both been raised as children.

"The husband tried his hand at business and was successful. Two years later, he was a wealthy man. He continued expanding his operations and became more and more involved in life in the greater Russian community. On the heels of his success and his involvement with the general population, he began speaking Russian to his friends and acquaintances. At home, too, the couple relinquished their mother tongue and began to converse in Russian. Another year passed. By this time they'd become so accustomed to their new lives that they were embarrassed to utter a word of Yiddish.

"And then came the day of the birth of their first child.

"The husband urgently summoned a doctor to his wife's bedside. The doctor came at once, but passively stood by without assisting in the birth.

"The woman cried out with the pain of labor. The Russian doctor was unmoved.

"The husband was going out of his mind. 'Doctor!' he exclaimed. 'Why don't you try to ease my wife's suffering?'

"Calmly, the doctor explained, 'Don't worry. The moment the actual birth begins, I will render all the assistance that I can. But that time has not yet arrived.'

"The woman continued to groan with pain, and the doctor continued to wait. Again, he said decidedly, 'There is nothing to be done. It is not yet time for the birth.'

"Suddenly, the woman began screaming, 'Oy, *Mama, helf mir!* (Mama, help me!) *Oy, Mama! Oy, Mama, helf mir!*'

"The doctor hurried to assist in the baby's birth. 'Yes, yes, the birth pangs have come. It is time.' He went on to explain: 'Now that she is calling out in her mother tongue, these cries are from the heart. The pain is very intense and so she is calling out from the depths of her heart. This is a sign that the time for the birth has arrived.'

"Mr. Ushiskin! I, too, will speak in the Yiddish language so that what I say will come from the heart ..." Then I went on to speak (in Yiddish now, of course): "Do you believe in the Creator of the world?"

" 'Yes,' he replied politely.

"Do you believe in the words of our Sages, 'Know before whom you are destined to render an accounting'? Are you aware that you, too, Mr. Ushiskin, will be called upon to give a reckoning of all your deeds, both good and bad?"

" 'Yes, yes,' he answered.

"I have recently returned from a joint rabbinical tour through the settlements of the Galil. Everywhere I stayed, the hostess would caution me, 'Rabbi, that fork and knife are not for you; the plates are not kosher for you.' Is this the kind of settlement that a believing man such as yourself wants to establish?!"

" 'Personally, I also refrain from eating in other people's kitchens,' said the administrator, 'and I've even rebuked them a number of times. But what can I do when they don't listen to me about keeping their kitchens kosher and observing the Shabbos?' "

I had an answer for him. "In the contracts that the *Keren Kayemet* writes for the sale of land, the first paragraph should address Shabbos observance. After all, your organization is providing them with money, tracts of land, mules for plowing, and so on. If the contract is written that way, they'll think twice before desecrating the Land." I continued to speak emotionally, asking Ushiskin how he would answer for himself on the Judgment Day. "Why did you bring about so much evil in your lifetime? You caused the destruction of faith in the settlements of Eretz Yisrael, through *chilul Shabbos*, the raising and eating of rabbits, settlements where boys and girls mingle, and where there is no shul or *mikveh*. Woe unto you, Ushiskin, for it is because of this that we were exiled from our Land, as is written in the Torah, '*Let not the Land spit you out for having contaminated it*' (*Vayikra* 18:28). As I've told you, I've traveled the length and breadth of this land and seen with my own eyes that you have caused Israel to stumble over prohibitions that are punishable by *sekilah* (stoning) and by *kares* (excision), *r"l*. I have come to you now to rebuke you for this, in order to fulfill my obligation of offering rebuke. You have been warned! I have done my part, and I hope that you will do yours."

Baruch Hashem, I had some impact. From that time on, the *Keren Kayemet* began to include, in its sales contracts disbursing land, a clause about Shabbos observance. True, the clause was a superficial one and was not enforced, but I saw a merit in it, for at least the Shabbos day would be remembered in our settlements.

Here ends the *maggid* R' Ben Zion's story. As was his way, he told it in thunder and tears, not in Hebrew but in the "mother tongue," the language spoken throughout the Jewish Disapora in those days. But Ushiskin had answered him in Hebrew. Why? Because Ushiskin's heart was not pained. Ushiskin had a different kind of labor pangs. He envisioned the birth of the new generation, the kind of wild children we see today. Now, nearly a century later, everyone can see the bottomless pit where those children are walking: the grandchildren of the men and women who founded those *moshavim* and *kibbutzim*.

☙ Nonsense!

I heard this story, continues the Yerushalmi *maggid*, from *Harav hagaon* R' Yitzchak Shlomo Blau.

The man who was the chief force behind the modern usage of the Hebrew language came to see *Hagaon* R' Shmuel Salant. I do not wish to mention his well-known name.

Entering R' Salant's home, he proceeded to speak at length in praise of his language — *Ivrit* — which is largely *lashon hakodesh*. He then went on to complain to the chief rabbi of Jerusalem, asking why the city's Talmud Torah schools did not teach in *Ivrit*.

R' Shmuel Salant answered wisely. "The choicest of drinks is wine. We use wine for every holy ritual: for *Kiddush*, *Havdalah*, the Grace after Meals, at a *bris milah*, and at weddings. But isn't this of interest? Just let a person who publicly desecrates the Shabbos touch the wine, and it immediately becomes prohibited. If there is no other wine available, we make *Kiddush* and *Havdalah* over some-thing else, but not over the prohibited wine."

The same thing applies to *Ivrit*, explained R' Shmuel. "Even if it is true, as you say, that it contains elements of *lashon hakodesh*, once it is used by those of you who desecrate the Shabbos and perform other transgressions, it becomes prohibited for us to speak it."

Hearing this clever answer, the visitor became enraged and declared insolently, "I never thought I'd hear such nonsense ('*shtusim*') from you, Rabbi." Whereupon R' Shmuel replied, "I never knew that you, sir, do not know how to speak *Ivrit* — saying '*shtusim*' instead of '*shtuyot*.' "

The man took his leave in a rage, and later poured out his vitriol in a newspaper called "*Ha'or*" (though my father, R' Yitzchak Ze'ev, used to call it "*Hachoshech*") on R' Shmuel Salant and other Torah figures of Jerusalem.

This episode took place on the eighth day of Sivan in the year 5663. On the twentieth day of Sivan, the *Beis Din Tzedek* (the "*Badatz*") declared a public fast day with regard to the pogroms in Russia. A large crowd gathered in the big shul in the *Churvas* R' Yehudah Hachassid, in accordance with instructions issued by R' Shmuel and the *Badatz* not to *daven* in small *minyanim* but rather to come together to pray. Before the *tefillah*, I was asked to deliver a *derashah*.

I began by touching on the words of *Chazal* (*Chagigah* 14a): "Yeshayahu cursed Israel with eighteen curses, and his anger did not abate until he told them, '*They will domineer, the youngster over the elder and the base over the respectable*' (*Yeshayahu* 3:5). With this reference, I started my speech by criticizing what had been written in the above mentioned newspaper against *hagaon* R' Shmuel Salant and other Torah leaders. I threw his criticism back in his face, giving him a double portion for his despicable actions.

SECRETS THAT THEY KNOW AT THE U.N.

R' Yaakov Galinsky

Y ou have gathered together here, on 5th of Iyar,[1] to hear *divrei Torah*. "A gathering of *tzaddikim* is good for them and good for the world." *Baruch Hashem*, you have designated this as a day of Torah for yourselves. In appreciation, you will hear a terrific question in conjunction with *Parashas Bo*.

The Gemara (*Avodah Zarah* 2a) says, "In the future, *HaKadosh Baruch Hu* will hold a *sefer Torah* and say, 'Whoever has engaged in Torah, come and get your reward!' " The pronouncement will be issued: Your salaries are being paid today! You've learned so much,

---

1.The 5th day of the Hebrew month Iyar is the day set aside to be celebrated as a secular holiday in commemoration of the establishment of the State of Israel. It is known as *Yom Ha'atzma'ut*.

and the time has come to receive payment. "Today to do them, and tomorrow to receive the reward for them."

Chazal say that the nations of the world will throng in ahead of the Jews. They will come en masse, each one shoving the other aside in his eagerness to enter first. Hashem will tell them to organize themselves and not enter in a jumbled mass. So the nation of Rome will go in first.

"Well, what do you want?"

"We heard on the radio that they're giving out rewards for learning Torah today. That's why we've come!"

"What were you involved in? Which Gemara: *Shabbos*, *Eruvin*, or *Pesachim*?"

"No! We didn't learn Torah. We paved roads and built bridges. but we did all of this so that the Jewish people might involve themselves in Torah."

Then *HaKadosh Baruch Hu* will say to them, "You fools! Did you really do all that for the sake of the Jews? Is that why you worked so hard? You did it for yourselves!" And they will be evicted.

The kingdom of Persia will be next in line. "Why have you come here?" asks the Gemara. "Didn't you see what just happened to Rome?"

"No — we're altogether different. Rome may have built buildings, but they also destroyed the Beis HaMikdash. We, on the other hand, helped to build the Second Beis HaMikdash."

"O.K., come in. What do you want?"

"We want our payment!"

"What did you learn?"

"Well, we didn't learn, exactly. But we fought wars so that Israel might sit and involve themselves in Torah!"

HaKadosh Baruch Hu will answer them, "You fought wars? Fools, were you the ones who made war? It is by My will that wars are fought or not. Victory depends on Me!"

So ends the Gemara.

There are several questions in understanding this Gemara. First of all, where were the Jews when it was announced that those who had toiled in Torah should come get their reward? Why didn't they, too, hurry in? Those precious Jews — instead of going to Teveryah on the 5th of Iyar to make a picnic — came here to learn Torah instead! They deserve a reward.

Second question: Do the nations think that it's possible to trick Hashem? After all, they are speaking before the King of the world!

And, third: Why did Hashem call them "fools"? Why not "liars"? And if He did not call them liars, it must mean that what they said was not a lie, but only nonsense. This is hard to understand. What's going on here?

⌐ The Blind Man from Pressburg

Elsewhere, the Gemara tells us that if a person loses a coin, and a poor man, without a cent with which to buy himself a morsel of bread, finds it and puts it in his pocket (for a coin has no identifying marks that will enable him to find the owner), and then goes into a store and buys bread to nourish himself — the act is credited to the man who lost the coin as if he performed the *mitzvah* of giving *tzedakah*. Through him, a hungry Jew was able to be revitalized.

In the future, the world will see amazing things. Many people, at different times in history, have made their plans and devised formulas with different aims in mind; to what purpose? For the "last stop" on the train: the Jews' benefit. Sometimes they merely constructed bridges to serve their own needs, skyscrapers for their own honor. At other times, in contrast, they paved roads for the specific purpose of hounding the Jews, r"l. And witness the marvel: The results were the opposite of those that were intended!

Like the man who lost the coin, they will hasten to demand their reward. They will push and shove forward for their payment. Therefore, they are not liars. They are telling the truth. They did build bridges and fight wars, and thereby brought about benefit to the

Jews, "so that the Jews might sit and involve themselves in Torah." But they are fools because "what you did was to serve your own needs," as the Gemara points out.

David Hamelech, in *Tehillim* (117:1-2), says, "*Praise Hashem, all nations; praise Him, all the states! For His kindness has overwhelmed us ...*" Have you ever paid attention to what you're saying with these words? (One can say something for many years and not know what he is saying. We mumble the prayer and are done with it. As the *Yerushalmi* says, a person ought to thank his head, because while he's "dreaming" during *Shemoneh Esrei* and he reaches "*Modim*," his head bows down on its own. The head knows when to bow automatically!) In *Hallel*, we cry, "*Praise Hashem!*" We go over to Saddam Hussein, for example, and ask him, "Why haven't you said *Hallel*? '*Praise Hashem, all nations!*' We say the same to all the countries of the world: '*Praise him, all the states!*'" It is as though David Hamelech walks into the U.N. building and requests, "Silence! Everyone, please stand." Everyone rises to his feet. "Recite *Hallel*!" he commands.

"What happened?" they ask.

"'*His kindness has overwhelmed us.*'"

HaKadosh Baruch Hu has performed great acts of lovingkindness for us [Note: this speech was given at the conclusion of the Gulf War]. For example, 39 missiles fell here in Eretz Yisrael, and *baruch Hashem* we are able to gather together here today for a day of Torah, healthy and whole. A single missile fell on an American army base, and 40 people were killed. So please, say *Hallel*!

But — the gentiles reciting *Hallel*?!

The Chasam Sofer explains this with a story that took place in his large city of Pressburg.

A certain blind man who lived in Pressburg was very wealthy. Distrustful of humanity — including banks — he kept his money at home. When he had to leave the house, he would put his money into his pocket and leave. Naturally, all the thieves in town strained their brains for ways to relieve him of his fortune. Nowadays, thieves do not face a huge problem when it comes to getting the money. They merely exchange *"Lo signov"* ("Thou shall not steal") for *"Lo sirtzach"* ("Thou shall not kill"), and things fall into place. In those days, however, thieves were less sophisticated. Did someone who happened to have money deserve to be killed?

So what did they do? How to get at the money? A band of thieves joined together and came up with an idea. The blind man routinely visited the grocery store once a week, on Tuesdays. On that shopping excursion he would purchase enough food to last all week. The thieves came up with a simple plan: He always walked the same route, because he could not see. Let us dig a hole in the middle of the way, they thought. He will fall into the pit; and of course we'd have to run over and rescue him. That's only human kindness, right? They would come to his aid and raise him from the pit; at the same time, of course, relieving him of the money in his pockets. Afterward the quarrels would ensue among themselves over how to divide up the loot. Does a greater share go to the one who dug the hole, or the one who came up with the idea, or the one who took the money, and so on?

In short, the thieves dug their hole, then stood and waited tensely for several hours until the moment came. The blind man emerged from his house and began to walk slowly along. Of course, he suspected nothing amiss. They held their breaths in excitement and rubbed their hands with pleasure. Just a few more steps, and they would have all the money they wanted for beer.

The blind man continued walking, coming closer. And then, quite suddenly, when he was nearly at the pit, he decided for some reason to retrace his steps, return home, and postpone his shopping trip. Perhaps he had left something at home and went back for it; the reason is unknown. What is clear is that he returned home and did not go out again that day. The thieves were beside themselves with frustration.

Who, asks the Chasam Sofer, should say *Hallel* here: the blind man or the thieves? The blind man had no idea that a trap had been laid for him. The thieves, on the other hand, were in a position to marvel over the miracle that had spared the blind man, who returned home with his health and his fortune intact.

This is what David Hamelech is calling out in the U.N.: You, nations of the world, know how many plots you have woven in your palaces to ensnare the Jewish nation — and what came of them all? You ought to know. "*Praise Hashem!*"

Morai v'rabbosai, the *midrash* asks about the words, "*To the One Who performs great wonders alone.*" What is the meaning of "alone"? Are there other things that He does *not* perform alone? For instance, "*Who spreads out the earth upon the waters*" — is there anyone here in the audience who helps *HaKadosh Baruch Hu* in this feat?

The *midrash* explains.

There was once a man who usually went to bed at 10 p.m. He has his rest and wakes at 5:30, before dawn, to *daven Vasikin*. One midnight, as he slept, a snake came into the room in which he was sleeping and moved about the room until 5 a.m., after which it left and disappeared. The man, rising at 5:30, says "*Modeh ani*," washes his hands, and dresses. Does anyone know of the miracle that has occurred here, apart from Hashem? Only when he reaches the *Olam Ha'emes*, the World of Truth, will he be told the story of the snake and the miracle that happened to him. Therefore, "*To the One Who performs great wonders alone*" — only Hashem knows about them! This is how our Sages explain it.

Who, apart from Pharaoh and his closest advisers, knew the details of their plans — plans that failed to such an extent that Pharaoh's own daughter paid the woman (his own mother) who nursed the Hebrew nation's savior? Pharaoh, ruler of the world, tried to turn over the world in order to prevent that savior from being born — and in the end? The savior was reared in his own palace.

Say *Hallel!* Praise Hashem! This is what *Klal Yisrael* says to the gentile. You witness the miracles more than we do. We sit here in Eretz Yisrael and have no idea what's being plotted in Iran or Iraq.

When it is possible for us to gather together on the 5th of Iyar to learn Torah, both Rome and Persia will step forward to receive their reward. So will those who established *Yom Ha'atzma'ut* (the

Israeli Independence Day). They will come before the Throne of Glory and say, "Pay us, because Jews made a Torah-study day on the 5th of Iyar. True, we meant the day for a different purpose, but see what good things came from it!" And "He Who sits in heaven will laugh"; "Did you establish a holiday from work so that Jews might sit and learn Torah?!"

Hashem has many ways of protecting us and helping us to learn Torah and receive great reward. All we have to do is think about our purpose in our world, and to carry it out.

And Hashem will help us.

יָדֹעַ תֵּדַע כִּי־גֵר יִהְיֶה זַרְעֲךָ בְּאֶרֶץ לֹא לָהֶם וַעֲבָדוּם וְעִנּוּ אֹתָם אַרְבַּע מֵאוֹת שָׁנָה: וְגַם אֶת־הַגּוֹי אֲשֶׁר יַעֲבֹדוּ דָּן אָנֹכִי וְאַחֲרֵי־כֵן יֵצְאוּ בִּרְכֻשׁ גָּדוֹל.

"Know with certainty that your offspring shall be aliens in a land not their own — and they will serve them, and they will oppress them — four hundred years. But also the nation that they will serve, I shall judge, and afterward they will leave with great wealth" (Bereishis 15:13).

THE SOLDIER'S PATIENCE RAN OUT

R' Yaakov Galinsky

*W*ith just a few words — *"But the nation that they will serve, I shall judge"* — many wonders and miracles were performed. The exodus from Egypt, and the parting of the Reed Sea, and leaving with great wealth.

R' Saadia Gaon remarked: Many prophets have prophesied again and again about the coming of the *Mashiach*, not in a few words but in full chapters. Ah, the things they have described! If a single verse provided so much wealth and hope, how much more so these numerous prophecies.

Says the *navi*: *"For but a brief moment have I forsaken you, and with abundant mercy will I gather you in"* (*Yeshayahu* 54:7). Based on R' Saadia Gaon's perspective, the commentaries say: "If thousands of years of *galus* are 'a brief moment,' as in *'For but a brief moment have I forsaken you,'* what amazing wonders, salvations, and consolations will there be when the day of *'with abundant mercy will I gather you in'* arrives!"

However, *morai v'rabbosai*, we lack patience. Know that *Klal Yisrael* has always armed itself with patience and the end result has been pleasant and good.

Our Sages say, *"Strength and majesty are her raiment, she joyfully awaits the last day (Mishlei 31:25)."* Who laughed on that last day: Moshe or Pharaoh? Avraham or Nimrod? Nevuchadnetzar or Chananiah, Mishael, and Azaryah? In other words, he laughs best who laughs last. This epigram originated in these words of *Chazal.*

Waiting patiently. The Jewish nation is predicated on ordeals, pockmarked with problems, coated with suffering, and the Jew inclines his head and says, "I do not understand what Hashem is doing, but the way He runs things is good for me (for, were I able to understand, there would be no challenges in the world). But tomorrow, in the end, I will understand and rejoice. *"She joyfully awaits the last day."*

Chazal tell a story about a man who loaded his entire fortune onto a ship, including his personal bag, his wallet, and his papers. He went ashore for a short time, and his foot was pierced by a nail. As he sat on the ground to remove the nail, the ship sailed away.

He broke down in tears. "How bitter is my fate!"

The next day, he learned that the ship, with everyone on board, had sunk in the ocean. He lifted his hands heavenward and cried, "I thank You, Hashem, for You were angry with me!" (*Yeshayahu* 12:1). R' Yosef comments, " 'I thank You, Hashem, for You were angry with me. Your wrath has subsided and You have comforted me.' To what does this refer? To two men who set out on business.

One of them stepped on a thorn and began to wail and curse. Later, he heard that his friend's ship sank in the sea. He began to thank and praise [Hashem]. Therefore, it says, 'Your wrath has subsided and You have comforted me' " (*Niddah* 31a).

☞ You and I Are Guests

"*Fortunate is he who waits for Him.*" Our job is to wait. We must not become overly preoccupied with the here and now. (Smiling) I heard that there are people, Kabbalists, who can predict what will happen tomorrow or the next day. Perhaps there are individuals nowadays who know what will happen, but they are certainly keeping quiet about it. Those who *think* they know actually know nothing for the future is veiled.

Don't get excited over the here and now. The Chofetz Chaim tells a parable about a man who spent one Shabbos as a visitor in the city's biggest shul. At the conclusion of the Torah reading, he exploded, railing at the *gabbai*: "What's the matter with you? You seem incapable of distributing the *aliyos* with discernment: either according to the seating plan of those in the shul, or at least alphabetically! I think you've lost your mind. You gave the first *aliyah* to a *Kohen* sitting on the eastern wall. For "*Levi*" you called up a guest. You gave the fourth *aliyah* to a person sitting in the third row, and so on, in complete confusion: one from the second row, one from the fifth, here and there with no order whatsoever! Where is your head, and where are your good *middos*?" He began to stalk out of the shul, still grumbling.

The *gabbai* smiled and called after him, "Reb Yid! You weren't with us last week, and next week you'll be *davening* in a faraway shul in your own city. So why strain your mind with useless questions? Last week, we had a *chasan* as well as someone making a *bris*. Both of them received an *aliyah*. Next week, and the week after that, two guests are due to visit, guests whose families have asked that they receive *aliyos* in their stead. Therefore, this week I gave *aliyos* to others. And that's only a part of the overall plan that I must arrange every Shabbos: each week in accordance with changing circumstances. Also, there is an ultimate goal: to ensure that every congregant receives an *aliyah* at least once every six months, without taking anything away from anyone else. Do you understand? On the contrary, were I to distribute *aliyos* by seating order, that would give rise to a great many quarrels. *Reb Yid,*" he concluded, "when you started to complain to me, the *gabbai,* I immediately realized that you lack even a modicum of understanding about what it takes to manage communal affairs."

The Chofetz Chaim went on to say, "A person comes to this world for 70 or 80 years. He knows nothing about what came before him or what will come after: neither the merits or debts of his ancestors nor the future of his descendants. He is shortsighted, entering a long, complex process in midstream. And he complains: 'I don't understand what's going on here!' Remember that you are, after all, only a visitor."

So let us not become agitated over the present. Let us wait, and merit "*she joyfully awaits the last day.*"

☞ The Gentile on Seder Night

The three greatest gifts were given through suffering. "*HaKadosh Baruch Hu* gave three gifts to Israel, and did not give them except through suffering: Torah, the World to Come, and Eretz Yisrael" (*Berachos* 5a). When we are suffering, it is worth our while to arm ourselves with patience, as in the story that R' Sholom and R' Shepsel (*sheyichyeh*) often told.

A group of soldiers, both Jews and Germans, shared living quarters on an army base somewhere in Germany. One day, a gentile soldier whispered to a Jewish one, "I envy you. When you feel hungry, you go into the nearby town on a Friday night and there, in the synagogue, your fellow Jews invite you home for a meal. You return to the base satisfied and happy." (And what other sort of happiness did those soldiers have, but a good meal?)

The Jew replied, "What's the problem? The Jews will be glad to host you as well. In our army uniforms and hats, we very much resemble one another, and we both speak German. Therefore, act like me and they'll think you're a Jew. Follow me to shul and pretend to pray, and after the service someone will certainly invite you over, for we Jews never leave a guest behind without a place to eat.

"The festival of Passover falls in just two days' time. Everyone looks for guests then, as it says, 'Any who are hungry, come and eat.' Come to shul with me. Don't worry, just do as I tell you so that you don't make any mistakes. By the end of the evening you'll be stuffed and satisfied. Just follow these instructions:

"On Seder night, we don't eat right away. We recite the Haggadah and tell stories and afterward we eat. When they bring potatoes (*karpas*) to the table, even though you're hungry do not take a full portion, but only a little bit. Hold yourself back. All through the time that the words are being spoken, look around carefully and watch what everyone else around the table is doing, because apart from saying things they'll also be doing all sorts of things. Do just as they do. O.K.?"

On the first night of Yom Tov, they went to shul together. The Jew managed to *daven* a little, relying on memories from his childhood home. The gentile soldier tried to sway his body while moving his lips, mumbling in German. When the singing of "*Adon Olam*" was over, he was approached by one of the Jews in the shul. "Where are you having the Seder?"

"I have no place."

"Then come home with me!"

The gentile followed him happily. By this time he was hungry, having eaten nothing since morning.

They entered the house. Before long, all were gathered around the festive table and had begun pouring the first cup of wine. At "*Kadesh*" the gentile soldier drank down the first cup, like the others.

What was a single glass of wine to a German solider? He was used to four or five glasses of whiskey in a row. He very much wanted to ask for another glassful, but remembered his Jewish friend's instructions: "Be patient."

The potatoes were brought out. Everyone was given a scrap on the tip of his fork (less than a "*kezayis*"). Slightly addled by the wine, and really hungry now, he began to grow angry. Such a small piece of potato? What was going on here? *I haven't eaten since morning. They give out wine without food, and then barely any food at all!* he grumbled to himself. However, seeing a second cup of wine being poured, he calmed himself. Without looking around to see what the others were doing, he made the mistake of gulping down his cup of wine right then. "That's all right," the others told him. "Don't feel uncomfortable. We'll pour another cup, as we're not ready to drink yet."

Everyone began singing and reciting the Haggadah. On and on they went. Apparently, their host was one of those who set a leisurely pace. The gentile tried to mumble along; he dozed off and then awoke, dozed and woke, until his taut nerves began to scream. *I'll teach him a lesson, that Jewish friend of mine. He was just making a fool out of me, sending me here on a Jewish fast day!*

By the time "Maggid" was finished and the second cup was drunk, the gentile was ravenous. *Where's the meat and fish that rascal promised me?*

Matzos appeared next. They washed their hands, took a "*kezayis*," and then another one. The gentile nearly broke his teeth. For his part, he would have gladly risen to his feet and escaped in a fury. He muttered to himself in German, *They talk and talk, and after two hours all I get is a thin piece of tasteless bread!* Being hungry, he swallowed the matzah, and asked for more. He was given some. Suddenly, "Maror!" was announced, and something was distributed around the table: white horseradish. *Ah! Salvation has come*, he thought, and began eating. Everything went black in front of his eyes. *What's going on here?* And then to top it off, he was given a sandwich of matzah and horseradish. His patience disintegrated and he began to scream: "Phew, it's hot! It's bitter. Wicked Jews!" He got up from the table and left the house in a rage.

Back at the army camp, he lay down on his bed thinking, *I'll pay that guy back!* Sleepless, he waited for his Jewish friend to return, which he did long after midnight. The gentile got up and greeted him with curses. "I'll get you for this ..."

"What happened? Tell me. Don't be angry."

Still cursing, the gentile told the whole story of his sorry evening.

"When did you get up and go?" asked the Jew.

"When they gave out a bitter herb, and then matzah again, with the bitter herb inside. I went out of my mind, because I knew that you'd tricked me. You laughed at me. You should be ashamed of yourself!"

"You fool! If you managed to hold out till the *maror*, all you had to do was wait five minutes longer and they would have been up to 'Shulchan Arech.' You would have been served a meal with every good thing: fish, soup, meat, delicacies. All you needed was a pinch more patience."

Rabbosai! That gentile could not know the secret of the Jews: that, in the end, we reach the "Shulchan Arech." Who laughed on the last day — Moshe or Pharaoh? He laughs best who laughs last.

The Jews plead with Hashem: We have reached the "*maror.*" Please spread for us, soon, the festive table that awaits us in the future to come.

⮡ Rich and Poor

Let us conclude with a question from the Dubno Maggid: We are always asking Hashem for the redemption and the coming of *Mashiach*. The Gemara says that one of the *Tannaim* (*Sanhedrin* 98b) asked, "Let him come and I not be there to see him." The terrible suffering that will take place before the coming of the *Mashiach* will be very difficult to endure. That's why he asked not to live through that period.

The question remains: Why did that *Tanna* ask not to see the period of the *Mashiach*, while we request the opposite? We constantly beseech to be present at the coming of the *Mashiach*: "*May our eyes behold Your return to Zion in compassion.*"

There are various simple answers to this, but the Dubno Maggid, as was his wont, wove a parable:

There was a custom in many cities for the poor to attend weddings, for they were sure to receive abundant food to eat. These days, weddings no longer have a "poor man's table," for everyone has what to eat; once, there were people who were truly poor. In short, when a big wedding was held in the city, the poor flocked to it at an early hour. If the *chuppah* was scheduled for early evening, they would arrive in the afternoon. They would sit and wait.

One evening the guests arrived at a wedding, among them prominent *rabbanim*. Suddenly, all the *rabbanim* began to leave the hall (to greet the *chasan* and *kallah*). The poor men did not understand why everyone was leaving. One of them told the others, "Look, they're all leaving. Let us also go and come back later. It's a pity to sit here for hours doing nothing."

The old-timers explained his mistake. "Those are the rich and the rabbis. Without them, the *chuppah* will not be held. Therefore, when it's time for the *chuppah* to begin, someone will call for them and fetch them back in a taxi. But we poor, who will bring us back? No, we'd better sit here and wait right here until the *chuppah* starts."

The *Tannaim* and *Amoraim* and our holy *Chazal*, says the Dubno Maggid, can afford to say, "Let him come and I not be there to see him," because when he does come, those great men will be immediately brought back. However, we unfortunates, so poor in good deeds — if we are not alive in the world at that time, if we are not there — who will bring us?

Rabbosai. Let us ask together: *Ribbono Shel Olam,* You have given us a big "*kezayis*" of *maror*. We have received what we deserved.

Give us at least a "*Shulchan Arech.*" May we merit living and seeing and inheriting good and blessing in *Mashiach's* day and the life of the World to Come.

וַיֹּאמֶר ה׳ אֶל־מֹשֶׁה בֹּא אֶל־פַּרְעֹה כִּי־אֲנִי הִכְבַּדְתִּי אֶת־לִבּוֹ וְאֶת־
לֵב עֲבָדָיו לְמַעַן שִׁתִי אֹתֹתַי אֵלֶּה בְּקִרְבּוֹ. וּלְמַעַן תְּסַפֵּר בְּאָזְנֵי
בִנְךָ וּבֶן־בִּנְךָ אֵת אֲשֶׁר הִתְעַלַּלְתִּי בְּמִצְרַיִם וְאֶת־אֹתֹתַי אֲשֶׁר־
שַׂמְתִּי בָם וִידַעְתֶּם כִּי־אֲנִי ה׳.

"Hashem said to Moshe: 'Come to Pharaoh, for I have made his heart and the heart of his servants stubborn so that I can put these signs of Mine in his midst; and so that you may relate in the ears of your son and your son's sons ...'" (Shemos 10:1-2).

A WORLD OF FANTASY

R' Sholom Schwadron

*M*y father-in-law, *zt"l*, once returned home from abroad and his ship docked at the port of Yaffo. He related a shocking spectacle that he saw there. Perhaps his story will shed some light on the *pasuk* from our *parashah*: "Hashem said to Moshe: 'Come to Pharaoh, for I have made his heart ... stubborn.'" The word used here for stubborn is "*kaved*" — literally, heavy. What do these words mean to convey?

We can understand a heavy hand, or a heavy foot that is hard to lift because of its weight. But what is a "heavy heart"? How can a heart become heavy? My rebbi once explained this concept, R' Sholom said as he launched his talk to his Chevron Yeshivah students in his home in Sha'arei Chesed.

Another question. If it was clear that Pharaoh's heart was heavy and hard as a stone, and that he was sure to refuse to send the Israelites out at any price, then why all the requests and warnings? Why not skip the preamble and just pummel him with the plagues?

It must be emphasized that the Torah does not say, "I took away his heart," but rather, "I have hardened his heart." That is, he still has a heart, but it has become heavy — oh, how heavy!

Have you ever seen small children breaking things? Why do they do it? By nature, they were born with a bad nature: "The nature of a person's heart is bad from his youth (*Bereishis* 8:21)." They come into this world with a *yetzer hara*, and on the day of their bar mitzvah the *yetzer tov* is introduced. He is then a young boy of 13 — neither sickly nor weak, but young. There is a vast difference between a recently born child and a youth of 13, and that's why we have challenges in life. With a little effort, we can overcome these challenges. But it certainly requires effort! For example, someone who needs to pick up a heavy stone can do so, but it may require some effort. So, too, is a person's heart. That's what the Torah means when it says, "I have hardened his heart": It requires effort to move it, as though it were a heavy object.

Let us cite a few examples of times when a person is called upon to exert effort. One of them is what my father-in-law saw in Yaffo more than half a century ago.

At that time, hashish was widespread only among the Arabs. Between Tel Aviv and Yaffo there was a restaurant in which Arabs would sit and smoke their hubble-bubbles, or opium pipes. Inside these pipes were coals, with leaves of hashish on top of them. My father-in-law, *zt"l*, knew nothing of these things. He merely passed that restaurant on his return from a trip abroad, and when he arrived home in Sha'arei Chesed he told the following story, clearly shocked.

"I went through Yaffo and saw a restaurant filled with Arabs. They were eating and smoking. Suddenly, one Arab climbed onto a bench and cried, 'Oho! I'm a king! I'm a king!' Whereupon all the other diners stood up and prostrated themselves on the floor. After a few moments, he stood up again and cried hoarsely, 'I am a king!' Everyone shook with awe, and bowed to the ground once more. He said he was a king, and they all bowed. What happened to them?"

They were smoking their hubble-bubbles. and living in a fantasy world.

In his imagination, that man was a king, and they all responded. (The listeners laugh.) We are really laughing at ourselves for this is how our world appears to us.

In *Parashas Vayishlach*, we spoke of Yaakov Avinu's struggle with the angel, in which Yaakov asked him to reveal the secret of why and how most of the world's population were drawn after it. "*Mashach abirim b'kocho* — He will sweep away the powerful with his might" (*Iyov* 24:22). He sweeps up the strong and draws them after him; how? What weapon does he have at his disposal?

The angel said to him: All my strength is this: "Why do you ask for my name?" In other words, don't ask questions. Live in your fantasy world. The power of hashish.

The *yetzer hara* doesn't need to spend money buying illicit opium. He has more than enough of it in his own pocket, and he gives everyone as much as he wants. Dream of a trip to Cyprus, and then of buying a new car, top-of-the-line in every way ... Fantasize that you are a king. Dream that you are incomparable, that you buy yourself a magnificent new house. Fantasize about anything and everything, until old age overtakes you (if you merit it) and you are buried away in an old-age home. What is left of you then?

So what can we do against these fantasies?

First of all, know that they are fantasies!

Rabbosai, we could have offered new thoughts today about *Parashas Bo* and the exodus from Egypt. But heaven must know that it's worth our while to touch on this topic.

When I was in London more than 30 years ago, my hosts expressed a desire to show me the sights of London. "R' Sholom," they said, "we have a royal palace, with soldiers on guard wearing red uniforms and bearskin hats. We also have a museum."

"What's in the museum?" I asked.

This is what they told me. A certain woman created figures of every king that ever was — from Pharaoh to King George V — and fashioned them out of wax. I don't know all the details, but the short version is that she built this fantasy of how they appeared during their lifetimes: the hats they wore, the swords on their hips, the thrones on which they sat. There are about 250 figures in all: kings, officers, and noblemen.

I went to that museum. I saw three kings and then said that I'd had enough. We left. And because I had to deliver a talk to the yeshivah, I had an interesting thought about the words of the Gemara.

> *Shlomo Hamelech said (Koheles 9:14-15): "There was a small town with only a few inhabitants; and a mighty king came upon it and surrounded it, and built great seige works over it. Present in the city was a poor wise man who by his wisdom saved the town. Yet no one remembered that poor man."*

Chazal explain:

"A *small town*" — This is the body, a puny human being.

"*With only a few inhabitants*" — These are the 248 limbs.

"A *mighty king came upon it*" — This is the *yetzer hara.*

"*And surrounded it*" — These are sins. The *yetzer hara*, that mighty king, came to the small town and surrounded it with fortifications.

"*Present in the city was a poor wise man who by his wisdom saved the town*" — This is the *yetzer tov*, poor and pitiful, who saved the "city" from the *yetzer hara.*

"*Yet no one remembered the poor man*" — The Gemara tells us: At the moment that the *yetzer hara* comes to a person, the person does not remember the *yetzer tov.*

The following questions emerge.

1) If the town is small, why does the mighty king need to conquer it? Let him send a few dozen soldiers to capture it without any need for tanks and planes.

2) If they came in great numbers and with fearsome weapons, how did the poor wise man manage to save the town with his wisdom? Can a poor man really overpower a mighty army?

3) And if that poor wise man was actually such an incredible commander that he was able to rescue his entire city — that is, he killed off the *yetzer hara* — why doesn't anyone remember him?

And a fourth question: How does the *yetzer hara* come back if he had already been conquered and killed by that poor wise man?

The answer to these questions occurred to me at that moment in London, and it is truly sweet. David Hamelech likened the Torah to gold and honey: *"more pleasant than gold and great wealth, and sweeter than honey."* Mere gold alone, or honey alone, was not enough for him. Gold, however precious, cannot be eaten. Someone with gold in hand can nevertheless die of hunger. But one may use gold to buy bread and food. And what is the sweetest kind of food? Honey. The Torah possesses both of these things at once: the preciousness and the sweetness. Listen, and you will hear something very sweet indeed.

She created a wax museum. And because people enjoy being entertained these days — everyone likes a good laugh — at the museum entrance stands a life-size English policeman in full uniform. When you go over to him to ask for directions, he won't answer you. Why? Because he is likewise made of wax. The museum is wax, both inside and out. Now we can begin to understand.

"A small town" is the body, and the "few inhabitants" are the limbs. A "mighty king" came along: the *yetzer hara*. But what is the nature of that great king, the *yetzer hara*?

Wax! Fantasies!

He wears a crown on his head. The crown is made of wax, as is his sword. And the king himself is likewise made of wax. The *yetzer hara's* policemen are wax, with cheeks painted red and a menacing wax sword in hand. Terrifying! He weaves fantasies for people and frightens them: *"He built great siege works over them."* Fantasy tanks, planes, and bombs. Soldiers? Wax. Rifles? Wax.

I remember from the wartime — I don't know if it is still there today — there was an open field opposite Jerusalem's police head-quarters. In this field, large plywood airplanes had been erected. From a distance they gave the appearance of genuine planes. The goal was to fool approaching enemy aircraft into dropping their bombs on this make-believe airfield. The Israelis wanted to dupe the enemy with a fantasy: a trick right out of the *yetzer hara's* bag.

And because the fantasies are so lifelike, we cannot discern the truth and we are terrified.

What does that poor fellow do? The wise man knows that it's all made of wax. He has no sword, for he has no need of one — nor of tanks or planes. All he has in his pocket is a small box of matches. He throws a lit match onto the wax-king's hat, and everything is destroyed. No more hat! No more gleaming medals! No more king! He never really existed. Amazing.

The trouble is that later, when the *yetzer hara* returns with a new fantasy, one forgets that the weaponry is really made of wax. Once again the world looks real and frightening to him. Listen, and I will tell you to what this may be compared.

We have to get up at 7 a.m. and go to shul. "*A prayer of the afflicted man when he swoons, and pours forth his supplications before Hashem*" (*Tehillim* 102:1). Prayer! Wonder of wonders. Well, along comes the *yetzer hara* and says, "What?! Is it 7 o'clock already? *Oy*, everything hurts. I think I have pneumonia. It's so cold. How can I get up now?" And he turns over and goes back to sleep.

His *yetzer tov*, on the other hand, tells him, "Fantasies! What are you talking about: pneumonia? If you'd only stand on your feet and take a few steps, it'll all go away." Yes, yes, I saw it for myself just this morning: When I woke up, I ached all over. Then, after I'd taken a few steps away from the bed, the pains disappeared. "Strengthen yourself like a lion for the service of the Creator!"

All is well. *Baruch Hashem*, he strengthens himself and under-stands that his aches and pains are fantasies made of wax. He shakes off the remnants of sleep, says, "*Modeh ani*," gets out of bed, calls his *yetzer hara* a rascal and a liar, and goes to shul. Afterward, perhaps, he stays on to learn or sets aside time for Torah study. In other words, his whole day goes very well, and nothing at all is really wrong with him. He is hale and hearty.

And the next morning?

Back come the planes. His body groans, "*Oy*, I have an ulcer. How can I get out of bed?" Fortifications, tanks, planes, and bombs.

Ribbono Shel Olam! Only yesterday, he saw for himself that it was all fantasy! But, no, he doesn't remember. He goes on sleeping, thinking to himself, *Today is not like yesterday. Today, I really can't do it.*

Don't forget! Remember that it's all fantasy. Toss a burning match, and it'll all go up in smoke.

"*For Pharaoh's heart was heavy.*" He was afflicted with the plagues, and for a few moments he understood. "Hashem is righteous and I and my people are wicked." But when the plague passed he returned to his former intransigence and refused to let the Jewish people go. Just yesterday, Pharaoh, you saw that you were being rightfully punished. Why are you being obstinate again?! Because when the heart is hard, one fantasizes to himself that all will be well, that he will be saved from the plagues. And so he will be afflicted with further plagues, and on and on.

וְהָיָה לְאוֹת עַל־יָדְכָה וּלְטוֹטָפֹת בֵּין עֵינֶיךָ כִּי בְּחֹזֶק יָד הוֹצִיאָנוּ ה' מִמִּצְרָיִם.

"And it shall be a sign upon your arm, and an ornament between your eyes, because with a powerful arm Hashem has taken us out of Egypt" (Shemos 13:16).

THE WALLS OF HIS HOME TESTIFY

R' Shabsi Yudelevitz

I once stayed in a remote neighborhood in America," began R' Shabsi Yudelevitz in his weekly *derashah* (at a shul in Jerusalem's Bucharim section).

"And if you were to say, who stands witness for me? The walls of a person's home testify about him on the Day of Judgment" (*Chagigah* 16a).

The walls. The ceiling stands witness! Our holy books state that if a person eats non-kosher meat, the very plate and spoon come forward on the Day of Judgment to testify against him. As it is written in "*Nega'im,*" if a person commits a sin in the concealment of his room, the wall will inexplicitly sprout a blemish. That's the way it will be on that future day: The walls of our homes will sport all sorts of stains and blemishes, in accordance with the transgressions that were committed in that place.

Let me tell you a story. I was once in a remote neighborhood in America and it snowed heavily. As I sat in shul and learned, the *gabbai* approached me and requested, "Rabbi, perhaps you can learn with my son before his bar mitzvah? Learn something with him." I consented.

I began to learn with the boy. Among other things, I told him, "Listen to me, my child. If you put on a *tallis* and *tefillin* only on the day of your bar mitzvah, and the next day you hide them away in your home, the next time you wear a *tallis* will be at your own funeral, on the way to the cemetery. Then you won't be called a 'bar mitzvah,' but a '*bar aveirah.*' My dear child, if you wish to be a true 'bar mitzvah,' put on the *tallis* and *tefillin* every day, and observe the other Jewish laws." The bar mitzvah was scheduled to be celebrated about a week later.

One evening, as I walked into the shul I noticed that the *gabbai*, the bar mitzvah boy's father, did not greet me. I went over to him and asked, "Mr. Jack, are you angry at me?"

"Yes. Of course!"

"What have I done to you, Mr. Jack?"

"My son asked me a question that embarrassed me very much."

"Do you think I told him to ask you that question?"

"You didn't tell him to ask, but it's more than enough that he asked! My son asked, 'Daddy, when are you going to have a bar mitzvah?' A degrading question!"

I told the *gabbai*, "The boy, in his innocence, is correct, because he has never seen you putting on *tefillin*. Painfully, he thinks to himself: 'If my father is not yet a bar mitzvah, how can I ever be one?' "

I was invited to the bar mitzvah celebration. On that night, I sat at a table on the dais and was asked to speak. In front of all the assembled guests I said to the bar mitzvah boy: "Know this! If you do not put on *tefillin*, everything will bear witness against you. 'The walls of a person's home testify about him.' If you do not put on *tefillin*, even the forks and spoons now lying on the table will testify against you. A person who eats non-kosher meat will have his plate and spoon serve as witnesses against him. In this case, too: Either the *tefillin* themselves will testify, or other things will."

The Americans didn't want to believe what I was saying. One of them seated on the dais said, "No! Rabbi, that's not right. A spoon has no mouth and can't testify!"

I raised my voice angrily. "Yes — they *will* testify! Our Sages say so, and you tell me not?" But he insisted, "No! No!"

A golden ladle lay on the table. Picking it up, I said, "My friend, tomorrow I will put *tefillin* on the bar mitzvah boy. As we have said, one is obligated to put on *tefillin* every day. If not," I turned to address the bar mitzvah boy, "this big spoon will testify about you, to say whether or not you put on *tefillin*." Furiously, I put the spoon into my pocket and ended my speech.

The guests at the bar mitzvah thought that, in my anger, I was punishing them by taking the ladle.

The next morning, after I put *tefillin* on the boy for the first time in his life, the *shamash* of the shul came and whispered in my ear, "Rabbi, yesterday, when you got angry during your speech, you put the big spoon into your pocket. First of all, you should know that it's a valuable piece, made of pure gold. Secondly, it is an inheritance that has been passed down from generation to generation. And third, it's part of a set (and if a set is missing a spoon, it's like a person missing a foot). That's no ordinary ladle!" He spoke in great agitation.

"Listen," I said. "Go tell the *gabbai*, who owns the ladle, not to worry. I'll return it to him at the right time. Meanwhile, with his permission, I would like to keep it with me. Tell him that I did not take it by mistake or without forethought. But because I promised the bar mitzvah boy that this spoon will one day testify about his wearing *tefillin*, I took it so that I can ask it, tomorrow and the next day, whether or not he put on his *tefillin*!"

The *gabbai*, hearing this message, though that I was mocking him.

Another night passed. The next afternoon, the *shamash* whispered sarcastically to me, "Well, what did the spoon say? Did he put on *tefillin* or not?"

"The ladle has already started crying. It said, 'Here it is, the very first day after his bar mitzvah, and already he didn't put on *tefillin*.' That big spoon is crying, and it's screaming, 'The first day after his bar mitzvah and he's not wearing his *tefillin*!'" That's what I answered him.

Shaken by my words, the *shamash* departed. Half an hour later, the father and son came to me: "Rabbi, you're suspecting my son for no reason."

"Sir, I don't suspect. The ladle is speaking. If you want, I'll ask it again." I went into an inner room, then emerged and announced, "The ladle said again, 'The boy did not put on *tefillin*.' And it cried."

"So we're liars?"

"Don't be angry with me. I'm not saying anything; it's the spoon that's talking. Do you want me to ask it to tell me about other transgressions taking place in your home?"

"No, no! We don't want that. But give back the ladle. It's mine, not yours," the father demanded.

"All right, no problem. I'll give it back. But first, I want the boy to put on *tefillin* in front of everyone, and you will see that the ladle will testify before you all. And you will also see that it not only has a mouth, but also feet. Come into the shul and let it testify."

It was decided that, at 7 o'clock the next morning, the bar mitzvah boy would come to *Shacharis*, put on *tallis* and *tefillin*, and everyone would see the big spoon arrive. We may imagine that half the worshipers in that shul didn't sleep all night from sheer suspense. How would the ladle get there? Would it jump or roll, or would they actually see frightening little feet? How?

The next morning the shul was packed. Everyone trembled as though standing in front of *Har Sinai*. The bar mitzvah boy climbed onto the *bimah* so that everyone present could see the ladle arrive.

He took out his *tallis*, made the blessing the way I'd taught him, and wrapped himself in it. At that moment, everyone heard the sound of a small explosion: a boom. What had caused it? The boy stooped down, and saw, along with everyone else, the ladle lying on the floor. It happened so quickly that no one had a chance to see where it had come from. But they all heard the noise of its arrival: *Boom*.

"Amazing!" many of the people cried out in astonishment. I left the shul, and they begged my forgiveness for shaming me. "Rabbi, we admit it. It has a mouth and feet."

Before my departure, the rabbi of that shul came over to me and asked in an undertone, "R' Shabsi, which kabbalistic names did you employ?"

"Heaven forbid! Is one permitted to use such names for just anything?"

"So how did you do it?"

"The matter is very simple," I whispered. "On Sunday, I was the one who put the boy's *tefillin* on him. Who arranged the *tefillin* for him? It was also me. Who put the *tallis* and *tefillin* in their bag afterward? I did. When I put the *tallis* into the bag, I placed the ladle among the folds of the *tallis*. There it stayed. The next morning, when the *shamash* asked me where the ladle was, I immediately understood the situation. Had the boy put on his *tefillin*, he would have found the missing spoon. That's why I told them that I was certain he had not put on *tefillin*. And now, as he was putting on his *tallis* in front of everyone, the ladle fell out of the *tallis* and fell to the ground." That's all.

Rabbosai. Chazal say, "The stones of a person's home and the walls of a person's home testify about him on the Day of Judgment." If I can manage a feat like that, then the all-knowing *HaKadosh Baruch Hu*, as it were, can certainly do so! And he promises that the walls of a person's home will testify as to what he has done in his inner rooms. He commits a sin, thinking that the door is shut, the windows are sealed, and the shutters are closed. He is hidden from all eyes. "No one will come forth as a witness against you!"

But he is mistaken. "The stones of a person's house and the walls of a person's home testify about him on the Judgment Day!"

אָז יָשִׁיר־מֹשֶׁה וּבְנֵי יִשְׂרָאֵל אֶת־הַשִּׁירָה הַזֹּאת לַה׳ וַיֹּאמְרוּ לֵאמֹר אָשִׁירָה לַה׳ כִּי־גָאֹה גָּאָה סוּס וְרֹכְבוֹ רָמָה בַיָּם.

"Then Moshe and the Children of Israel chose to sing this song to Hashem, and they said the following: 'I shall sing to Hashem for He is exalted above the arrogant, having hurled horse with its rider into the sea'" (Shemos 15:1).

A CHILD'S GOOD QUESTION

R' Sholom Schwadron

R' Chaim Shmulevitz, the *Rosh Yeshivah* of Mir, once sat at the Seder with his young son — age 5, or perhaps 7 — on his lap. In fulfillment of the *mitzvah* of "*v'higadeta l'bincha — You shall tell it to your son*" — the father related the story of *yetzias Mitzrayim* (the exodus from Egypt) with all its attendant wonders and miracles.

Before sleep could overtake the child, R' Chaim described the Ten Plagues: Blood, Frogs, Lice, etc., until he reached *Kerias Yam Suf* — the parting of the Red Sea. What did he tell his son? He told him what he had heard from his own father, and his father from his father before him, and so on down the line, reaching back to the generation of the Exodus: that the *Bnei Yisrael* literally walked in the midst of the Sea on dry land, and picked fruit. Anyone who wanted to pick an orange just reached up a hand and plucked one, and if you were thirsty, you just took a drink of water. *Yetziyas Mitzrayim* and *Kerias Yam Suf!* "*The water was like a wall to their right and to their left.*" The floor of the Sea was completely dry, with the water standing high on either side.

The father, R' Chaim Shmulevitz, noted that his son did not seem particularly moved by this description. The boy was young, but he had the ability to understand. R' Chaim asked, "Did you hear?"

"Yes, I heard."

"And did you understand?"

"Yes, I understood everything."

"*Nu?!*" asked R' Chaim, as though to ask incredulously, *How can you not be moved?*

The boy lifted his eyes bashfully. "I'm not really sure what Father wants. Hashem created the world, He made the sea and the dry land. So what's so amazing if He can turn water into dry land and dry land into water? What's the big deal? Father, I don't understand!"

Yes, a logical child: If you know that Hashem created both dry land and the sea, you know that He has no problem switching the two. The boy was right!

In that case, we may ask, what really is the special excitement attached to the parting of the Sea?

⌐ See How Beloved You Are!

HaKadosh Baruch Hu, Creator of the world, runs it according to natural law at all times. The world proceeds in constant and unchanging step with nature. When does Hashem decide to effect a change? When we merit one. When He wishes to show that you, the Children of Israel, are above nature! That's what Hashem showed us in the exodus from Egypt. Hashem took the Sea from one place and moved it to another for their sake. *"He Who passes His children between the walls of the Reed Sea"*...

As we see in the Gemara (*Yoma* 21b), when those who came up to Jerusalem for the festivals gathered together, the *Lechem Hapanim* would be taken out for them to see: the steam still rising from the loaves, which were as warm as when they had been removed from the oven, freshly baked, seven days earlier. It was a miracle that aroused wonder. Why, the Gemara asks, was the bread shown to them? It explains, "See how beloved you are before Hashem!" See how much Hashem loves you, and how He nullifies the laws of His creation in the *Beis HaMikdash*. This is the salient point, too, in the parting of the Reed Sea.

The little boy was right. The One Who created the sea could do with it as He pleased. We are moved not by the fact that Hashem can produce miracles — that's obvious — but by the fact that Hashem shows these miracles to us to demonstrate His love for the people of Israel. And primarily, so that someone who does not possess the understanding of that young Shmulevitz boy will be able to grasp, after seeing the miracles and the changes wrought in nature, that *Hashem Hu HaElokim* — Hashem is *Elokim* — and that there is none other apart from Him.

☞ How Do Bananas Grow?

In truth, the whole world is a riddle, a miracle, and a wonder, but people do not discern the miraculous. It is only when Hashem suddenly shows them a change in the laws of nature that they distinguish something wondrous. Up until that moment, custom and familiarity render them blind.

When I was a boy of 14, someone came over to me and asked, "The Gemara says that, in the future, trees will grow loaves of bread. How can that be?" He looked at me as if to say, "Let's see how you answer *that* one!"

I replied, "Let me ask *you* something. How it is that, nowadays, trees grow bananas? Do you understand how that works? You put a seed into the ground, the seed then proceeds to decay completely and then, after it has decayed, something suddenly starts growing there! Out of the surface of the soil pokes a thin branch, which grows and flourishes until small green bananas sprout all over. After a certain period of time, we have branches filled with large bananas! How? How? How? In the same way that you understand how bananas grow today, that's how you'll understand how loaves of bread can grow. Had it been bread that grew today and not bananas, you would not have been asking me questions about bread because you would be accustomed to seeing bread growing on trees. It would be bananas that would make you ask in amazement, 'How is it possible that, in the future, bananas will grow on trees? They're curved like shofars, each one a light color with a thick peel that divides into several layers, and so on. How? How can one believe that such strange things will ever grow?' "

Things that we are not used to seeing look like miracles. But the truth is: it's all miracles! Dry land is a miracle, and so is the sea. May Hashem enlighten our eyes to see His wonders.

פרשת בשלח ⟵
PARASHAS BESHALACH

ה׳ אִישׁ מִלְחָמָה ה׳ שְׁמוֹ. מַרְכְּבֹת פַּרְעֹה וְחֵילוֹ יָרָה בַיָּם וּמִבְחַר שָׁלִשָׁיו טֻבְּעוּ בְיַם־סוּף.

"Hashem is Master of war, through His Name Hashem. Pharaoh's chariots and army He threw into the sea; and the pick of his officers were mired in the Sea of Reeds" (Shemos 15:3-4).

SIXTY THOUSAND GRAVES

R' Shabsi Yudelevitz

After the Six-Day War, a soldier came to me and said, "R' Shabsi, I'd like you to speak to the soldiers — to strengthen them in *yiras Shamayim*."

I tried to disregard the request, to no avail. He pressed me repeatedly. Finally, I consented.

On my way to the army base, I speculated to myself that perhaps I'd find a few dozen soldiers gathered to hear me speak. But when I entered the place I was shocked: thousands of soldiers were waiting!

They sat in their uniforms, proud of their military might after such a victory. The I.D.F. was filled with self-congratulation during that period. I nearly turned back, but I had no choice. I walked in.

I sat down in the place that had been designated for me. Naturally, I was preoccupied with my thoughts in advance of my talk, but at the same time I listened with half an ear to a speech given by a senior commanding officer. He spoke smugly about various military matters, giving me time to prepare my *derashah*.

Suddenly, as he was winding down his speech, the commander straightened his back, stood silently for a moment, then lifted a hand, turned to me, and said, "As everyone knows, the Israeli Air Force was a full participant in our recent military triumph. They took part on all fronts. Our engineering corps also performed devotedly in the most responsible of positions. Our infantry put their lives on the line and promoted our success in battle. In short, our great victory came about as a result of the contributions of our troops on the ground, in the air, and on the sea. And now, honored soldiers, a rabbi from Jerusalem has come here — perhaps from Meah Shearim or some other yeshivah — to present to you the part that yeshivah students contributed to our victory."

Those thousands of troops applauded loudly as the officer ended his speech. "If you please, rabbi," he said cynically, to another round of vigorous applause.

I stood up on the dais and began to speak, inwardly trembling.

"Honored soldiers, a question has been asked. What did we contribute to the victory? What percentage did the yeshivah boys render to the triumph? I will begin with a short answer that goes to the heart of this question, after which we will turn to other topics.

"As you and I both know, the military leadership had a gloomy forecast for this war. Before it began, they spoke in terms of 60,000 casualties, *r"l* — to the point where a decision was made to designate large parks in various cities to be used as temporary burial sites at the height of the war.

"With such numbers of dead — may it never happen — who would have seen to the burials? The yeshivah boys. They are the ones who would have been recruited to serve as a devoted 'Chevrah Kaddisha' in this holy mitzvah. In that case, the esteemed commander who just addressed you would have stood here and announced that the yeshivah students contributed mightily to the war effort.

"However, honored soldiers, HaKadosh Baruch Hu, not wanting us to lose time from our Torah study, decreed in the Heavenly Court to pass on the 60,000 corpses. He decreed that the merit of our Torah study would protect them. In that case, I am here to let you know that we, the yeshivah population, contributed 60,000 men. We also donated city parks in Tel Aviv and Jerusalem. Did you really want to be in those graves? Do you mind that Hashem granted life to tens of thousands of soldiers, and that in place of temporary graves there are lush, green parks? Stand up and thank Hashem!"

Thunderous applause filled the hall. I did not return to my seat, but decided instead to give it to them "in the teeth," to help them understand that with the arrogance of "kochi v'otzem yadi" ("my power and the strength of my own hand") it is possible to lose out on miracles. Had the army triumphed? The Six-Day War witnessed miracles that were decidedly strange. Who had anything to boast about? It is Hashem, as it were, Who decides the fate of all battles. "Hashem is Master of war." In other words, He alone conducts all wars and He orchestrates victory.

The Gemara (Avodah Zarah 2b) relates that in the future the gentile nations will step forward to demand their just reward, claiming, "We waged many wars, and we did it all just for Israel, so that they might involve themselves in Torah." And HaKadosh Baruch Hu will respond, "I made the wars, as it says, 'Hashem is Master of war!' "

Wars do not fall under man's dominion; people are only dragged into them. Wars are not the exclusive business of the military, which thinks it can start one whenever it decides. Soldiers must not lift their noses into the air in arrogance. "Hashem is Master of war, *through His Name Hashem. Pharaoh's chariots and army He threw into the sea; and the pick of his officers were mired in the Sea of Reeds."*

Let us conclude with Rashi's comment, which highlights one of the differences between a flesh-and-blood general and Hashem, Master of war: "Hashem, even when waging war and exacting vengeance on His enemies, continues to show compassion for His creations and to provide sustenance for everyone in the world, not like earthly kings who, when engaged in war, turn their attention away from all other interests and lack the ability to attend to other matters."

The merit of the *bnei hayeshivah* is our hope. Were it not for Torah, the Arabs would long since have hurled us into the sea. May we speedily have salvation with the redemption of Zion, and the building of Jerusalem, *amen*; let it be Your will!

***

(There is an additional *derashah* on topics related to the *Kerias Yam Suf* and *emunah* in *Parashas Tzav*.)

"[The *mon*] that was left in the field disintegrated and became rivulets, and the rams and deer would drink from it, and the peoples of the world would trap them and taste the flavor of the *mon* in them, and they would know the praise of Israel" *(Mechilta Rashi)*.

HE FLED THE ISRAELITE CAMP

R' Yaakov Galinsky

I saw a story in one of the *midrashim*," says R' Yaakov Galinsky.

When the *Bnei Yisrael* were in the desert there was a young man, a bit reckless, who got up one day and decided to flee the Israelites' camp.

The young man walked in the desert for long hours, and naturally thirst became a problem. He was thirsty and hungry. He quickened his pace and began to run, until he arrived at the camp of the Ammonites.

When he reached the people of Ammon, he wanted to enter a restaurant to satisfy his hunger, but he thought to himself, *I am a Jew. How can I eat from the gentiles' treif kitchen?* He had an idea. Going over to the waiter, he said, "My dear sir, give me a piece of venison, for I am very hungry." Why venison? Because deer are kosher. Though the deer had not been slaughtered according to the dictates of Jewish law, he thought to himself, *It's only half a sin — that's not so terrible. It's kosher meat, just not properly shechted.*

(Apparently, that young man belonged to a half-and-half political party. You should know that there are such parties: ones that have decided that the correct route is to observe half the Torah. Can one be a zealot? They consider it zealotry to have the meat be kosher as well as properly slaughtered. One of the two is enough!)

So the waiter served him a portion of grilled venison. The meat was very tasty. The young man ate and was satisfied.

When he was done, he decided, *I'll hurry back to my friends in the Israelite camp and show them that there are places outside of that camp where one can enjoy oneself. There's no need to remain constrained by the Clouds of Glory.* In other words, there was also the possibility of life in the camp of the Ammonites.

He left the restaurant and walked all the way back. It was toward evening when he reached the camp. The hour was already well advanced toward dusk — between *Minchah* and *Ma'ariv*. As you know, that is a time when a lot of people assemble together. The young man entered the courtyard of the shul, gathered a group of friends around him, and began to enthusiastically fill them in: "Gentlemen, it is possible to enjoy life. There's no need to limit ourselves to this camp," and so on. Suddenly, Moshe Rabbeinu, appeared. His arrival was greeted with a respectful silence.

"What's going on?" Moshe Rabbeinu asked. "What is this gathering? There are no elections taking place today. What has happened to make you all assemble in a group like this?"

Silence. Finally, the young man himself began to explain: "R' Moshe, every day you say, 'Ashreichem Yisrael — fortunate is your lot, Israel!' Well, this afternoon I was in the Ammonite camp, and I've brought back some leftover meat that I ate there. R' Moshe, it was so delicious! You have no idea what a good meal I had at that Ammonite restaurant. Here's the meat." He took a piece of meat out of his pocket and held it up. "Delicious!"

"Tell me, please," requested Moshe Rabbeinu, "just what made the meat taste so good. What special ingredient is hidden in this venison that you ate? Or is this deer different from the world's other deer?"

"What difference does it make? The meat tasted good, that's all!"

"Nevertheless, explain it to me, please."

The young man fell silent, not knowing how to respond.

"Then let me tell you," Moshe Rabbeinu told the young man. "Listen well. It says in the Torah, 'The sun was hot and it melted.' The *mon* didn't last long, because once it had all been collected, the sun rose and melted into water everything that remained. Where did all that water flow? It gathered into mighty streams moving toward the Jordan River. Some of the water was absorbed into the desert sand and made its way to nearby rivers. The deer from which you ate swam in the Jordan and quenched its thirst in that very water near the camp of Ammon. That's why the meat was so tasty.

"In that case, you did something foolish. You exerted so much effort in order to receive the *mon* in a roundabout way — through the sand and the water that streamed into the Jordan, and from there into the deer's innards — when you had the original thing right here, pure and delicious: the *mon* that falls from heaven!"

☞ The Old South African Doctor

Let me tell you something I heard from a Jewish doctor who moved here from South Africa, where he studied the art of massage therapy. The professor who taught him was an elderly gentile who was familiar with *Tanach*. Before moving to Eretz Yisrael, the doctor wanted to take leave of his teacher. He went to see him in his office and told him that he had decided to move to the Middle East, to Eretz Yisrael, where he would treat Jews as a Jew. The professor beamed at him and said, "I am happy that you are making such a wise move. Go in peace, and you will undoubtedly earn a respectable living over there for I saw in the Bible that Jews are a stiff-necked people, so they must be in need of a great deal of massage." That's the way the gentiles understand the Torah!

Rabbosai, after the giving of the Torah, if there is anything in the world it is the crumbs left by the Torah. They have laws from the Torah, Shabbos from the Torah, and so on. They do not know *Tanach*, but try to seize a bit for themselves here and there. They don't understand.

People are looking for substitutes for the original good. They travel far to get some grilled venison in the Ammonite camp. Today, on 5 Iyar, the people are out making picnics and barbeques, imagining that happiness will come from the sand and the meat. Apparently, they've been told that this is the way the gentiles celebrate their own Independence Day. You, on the other hand, have come to the *beis midrash* to hear Torah *shiurim*. *Ashreichem!*

☞ Between Light and Darkness

As we all know, one of the great kindnesses that Hashem did for us is found in the verse at the end of *Parashas Kedoshim*: "*I will separate you from the nations, to be Mine!*" The people of Israel are elevated and separated from all other nations. We have an eternal bond with *HaKadosh Baruch Hu* and there is a very high and thick dividing wall between us and the nations of the world.

Each week, on *Motza'ei Shabbos*, we say, "*Who separates between holy and secular, between light and darkness, between Israel and the nations.*" Just as everyone understands the difference between light and darkness — there is no need for outstanding intelligence to know that light and darkness are different from each other, and that they cannot coexist in the same place — in the same way, "*Who separates ... between Israel and the nations*"!

Neither Jewish celebrations nor Jewish mourning are like those of the gentiles. Look at Achashverosh's palace and see how the gentiles make merry; then compare this to a Jewish celebration. When a Jew throws a party or celebration he speaks words of wisdom and immerses himself in Torah thoughts. He sings *zemiros* and praises Hashem. What does the gentile do? What does he speak about? Nonsense: grown people behaving like children, old men comporting themselves like fools. "*As the king's heart was filled with wine, he requested to bring Vashti.*" These are their parties. We, on the other hand, do not practice this kind of merrymaking. "*I will separate you from nations.*"

"*When Yirmiyahu told Israel, 'Why do you not involve yourselves with Torah?' they told him, 'If we involve ourselves with Torah, how will we earn a living?' Immediately, he took out the jar of mon and told them ... *" (Midrash Tanchuma).

HOW MANY BLIND PEOPLE ARE THERE IN THE WORLD?

R' Sholom Schwadron

A malevolent *letz* (joker) was walking down the street when he ran into a group of men who were unfortunately blind. It was difficult for the blind men to navigate the street, and they clung to one another, taking slow steps one at a time.

R' Sholom related this parable in one of his *derashos* in the Zichron Moshe shul.

The *letz* went over to the blind man who walked at the head of the group, and said loudly, "*Reb Yid*, take these $10 and divide it even among yourselves: one dollar per person." In truth, however, he did not give the blind man anything. What will happen now, may Hashem have mercy, when the other poor blind men ask their leader to give them what is coming to them and he says, "I have nothing"?

The blind men, being unable to see, were quick to accuse him. They were convinced that he had been given $10 and had put the entire sum into his own pocket. In distress, the blind leader told the others, "I didn't get anything. Maybe he gave the money to the man standing right behind me."

The man behind him assured the others that he had not received any money. "It looks like the man in front got it all, and he's stealing from us!" Each of the blind men began to suspect and accuse the man next to him. "You took money that belongs to all of us. You are a thief!"

"But I have nothing," the accused men cried. "I didn't receive any money for myself, nor did I take any money of yours!" But no one believed anyone else. The quarrel escalated, with each blind man convinced that the next one had received money meant for them all and kept it for himself.

This is the way most of the people in the world look: just like those blind men. The Dubno Maggid once described it this way:

A person thinks that his neighbor earns a nice living. *My neighbor is getting a plentiful livelihood from heaven, and not only that, he is receiving it at my expense!* The man feels as though the neighbor was taking money away from him. But what is the truth? Both of them are destitute. Neither has a thing. Reuven has debts and failing business affairs, while Shimon is a poor man who behaves like a rich one. Each suspects the other without reason. Decades of quarrels and envy ensue between two unfortunate poor men, each of whom is persuaded that the other has been blessed with riches.

➢ He Will Toil Beneath the Sun

Listen to a marvelous explanation from the Dubno Maggid.

Shlomo Hamelech, in *Koheles*, wrote, *"What profit does man have for all his labor which he will toil beneath the sun?"* In other words, what is left to him after all his life's work in this world?

The language is puzzling. It should have said, "all the labor which he *has* toiled" — in the past tense — rather than "which he *will* toil," in the future tense. After all, we are talking about profit, about what is left to him in his last days on earth, at the end of a lifetime of labor. Why, then, does *Koheles* use the term, "all the labor which he *will* toil"?

The Dubno Maggid has an explanation, which he offers via a parable that is sweeter than honey:

A bookseller is sitting in his bookshop, with many years of work behind him. He has run this store for 40 years. He is approaching 60, the beginning of old age.

When he has a free moment, he sits and thinks, *What is left in my hand after these 40 years of work? I bought myself a house, not especially big. I married off my three children, and I have a little money left over, as they say, for my golden years. That's my entire profit. No more. Doesn't this hurt? Forty years of work and effort — and these are the results.*

He continues to ponder sadly. *Every night, on my way home from shul, I pass my neighbor's garage across the street. He's owned that garage for many years now. All day, every day, customers flock to his garage. He makes enormous amounts of money!* Envy burns in his heart: *He has doubtless invested a fortune in the bank: perhaps half a million, I'd think. After all, he's been working here for more than 20 years without pause, and his place is always full to the end of the day.* Pain engulfs the bookseller. *What do I have to show for all the years I've sat in this store? I'm not complaining to Hashem, heaven forbid. Baruch Hashem, I earn a respectable living. But after so many years, I'm left without anything serious in hand. It hurts."*

And what does his neighbor, the garage owner, think? Listen.

He, too, sits down one night with the members of his household. Heaving a sigh, he begins to discuss a topic he's already broached a number of times before.

"*Oy*, my hands! My hands are approaching the age when they will begin to shake. Unfortunately, I am forced to work these aging hands hard. True, I'm making a very nice profit, and I've managed to save up a considerable sum, but what is my life except lying under cars? Fifty times a day I have to lie flat on my back, with my clothes and hands black and oily. The work is exhausting. It's happened more than once that my hand has been injured till it bled. Also, I am sometimes forced to act deceitfully, to lie to people a little: replacing an old screw, patching things up quickly, and the like. That's the way it's been for 20 years, morning to night. See our neighbor, the bookseller, walking down the street like a human being, dressed nicely and neatly? He has peace of mind; he earns his living in a respectable way, working a few hours a day and then returning home, while I, here in the garage, have no rest. I must work late into the night to complete the repairs. It's hard," he ends with a heavy sigh.

What are we to conclude? The bookseller is convinced that his work is unprofitable, while his neighbor's job is. Conversely, the "happy" garage owner is certain that his heavy work doesn't pay, and he envies the bookseller. The common denominator is a shared conviction that one's own lot is no good, while his neighbor's is very good indeed: My toil has no profit, while *his* yields a very high return.

Gevaldig! The wisest of all men, Shlomo Hamelech, reveals the secret of life: Your belief that your neighbor's work is profitable is *hevel havalim* — futile. "*What profit does a man's neighbor have for all his labor which he will toil beneath the sun?*" Both are right. The bookseller is right in thinking that this own work isn't worth much — and so is the mechanic. There is no profit in any of it.

What is not *hevel*? "*Fear God and keep His mitzvos, for that is all of man.*"

☞ Don't Dream of Future Gold

We can explain further (chants R' Sholom).

"Which he will toil" is expressed in the future tense. Many people think that, though they may not be making a profit right now, in the future — oh! in the future! — in the years to come, there will be profit for their labors. These people are making a mistake. *"What profit does man have for all his labor which he will toil beneath the sun?"*

We leave the world empty-handed, except for a *tallis*. Above the sun, there is profit. What is meant by "above the sun"? Involving oneself with Torah. That's what will stay with him. Only that! As the *Targum* on *Koheles* says, "What is left in a person's hand after he dies, of all the work that he troubled himself over beneath the sun in this world — except for his involvement in Torah, and to receive a good reward and payment in the World to Come, before the Master of the Universe?"

R' Shimon ben Yochai's students asked him: Why did the manna not come down for the Israelites once a year? He said to them: I will devise for you a parable. To what is the matter similar? To a king of flesh and blood who has one son. [The king] would allocate his sustenance once a year, [the son] would not visit his father but once a year. [The king] arose and allocated sustenance daily and he would visit his father daily. So too the Israelites: One who had four or five children would worry and say, "Perhaps the manna will not fall tomorrow, and it will be found all of them will die of starvation. As a result, all [the Israelites] would direct their hearts to their Father in heaven (Yoma 76a).

HATING THE MASHGIACH?

R' Yaakov Galinsky

I once had the privilege of sitting at a wedding not far from the *mashgiach* and *tzaddik*, R' Yechezkel Levenstein. Wishing to gladden the *chasan*, I turned to the *mashgiach* and remarked out loud, "The *rav* thinks that it is only today, in our generation, that there are those who hate *mashgichim*. No; way back in the generation that received the Torah, the *dor hamidbar*, they already hated *mashgichim*. How do we know this? In reference to the *mon*, it says, "Our soul is disgusted with the insubstantial food." Why did they feel that way about the *mon*? Because it served as a *mashgiach*. The *mon* gave them *mussar*."

In my reverence toward him, I did not expound at length, but I will explain to you why the *mon* was a *mashgiach* and why the Jews hated it.

R' Yaakov Galinsky, for example, is of course a *tzaddik* (he says – tongue in cheek), so the *mon* comes right to his door. But it is difficult for a person to constantly remain on the same spiritual level. Inadvertently, I do a small sin. The next day, no *mon*. I'll have to walk 2,000 *amah* to find it. What will people say? "That speaker gives everyone *mussar*, and he himself is a sinner!" Filled with shame, I close the door and tell my wife, "I'm fasting today." And since a good wife does her husband's bidding, she, too, refrains from opening the door. She fasts along with me. We use that day to do complete *teshuvah*, so that tomorrow I can have the *mon* delivered right to my door again.

Rabbosai, there is a question implicit in the words, "*He afflicted you and let you hunger, then He fed you the mon ...*" They were able to eat their fill of the *mon* — "*And you shall eat, and you shall be satisfied, and you shall bless.*" So why the "hunger" for *mon*?

I have an answer, based on what we have said.

"*V'ha'mon k'zera gad hu.*" *Chazal* tell us that "*k'zera gad*" refers to the fact that the *mon* "*maggid*" — tells — about the sins of Israel. It served as an X-ray of a person's *yiras Shamayim* (fear of heaven). Day by day, the *mon* examined a person to see whether or not he had transgressed. If he had, he was often forced to remain hungry out of shame: "*He afflicted you and let you hunger ...*"

With a smile, I turned to the *mashgiach*, R' Yechezkel: "That's why they said, '*Our souls are disgusted with this insubstantial bread.*' It was because the *mon* was such a great *mashgiach*. 'Leave us alone!' they shouted at the *mon*. Do we have to hear *mussar* even when we're eating? Let us eat in peace — don't bother us so much!' They had a hard time with the *mon*, because it's not easy listening to *mussar*."

The *mashgiach* said to me, "R' Yaakov, you're right."

◉ Directing Their Hearts

Apart from serving as a *mashgiach*, the *mon* had another function.

R' Shimon bar Yochai's students asked him the following question: "Why was it not enough to have the *mon* fall once a year?" They could have set aside a container of *mon*, to last from Rosh Hashanah to Rosh Hashanah, and then they could be at ease. If Hashem wanted to show the *Bnei Yisrael* the great miracle of the falling *mon*, would it not have been sufficient to see the *mon* fall from the sky 40 times (that is, once a year) on *erev Rosh Hashanah*? Why did they have to wait for the *mon* to fall each and every day, 14,000 times during their sojourn in the wilderness? (*Yoma* 76a).

Was this merely a question of understanding the Torah in an academic way, or did the query find expression in practical halachic terms as well? Why else should R' Shimon bar Yochai's students care what had happened in the desert 2,000 years earlier?

Let me tell you.

There is a well-known dispute between R' Shimon bar Yochai and R' Yishmael regarding a person's obligation to make an effort ("*hishtadlus*") to earn a living. The Torah says, "... *that you may gather in your grain, your wine, and your oil.*" R' Yishmael explains that the Torah intends to convey the following concept. We are commanded, "This *sefer Torah* shall not leave your mouth," meaning that a person should not stop learning Torah. In addition, the Torah teaches in the above verse that there is a need to gather in one's grain, to tend one's vines, and squeeze oil from his olives so that he will not require any person's support. The Rambam, ruling like R' Yishmael, defines the halachic guidelines for a Jew to follow in order to fulfill both these injunctions. There are 12 hours a day at a person's disposal. Three of those hours may be used for working, and the remaining nine for Torah study. That is the halachah, in the opinion of R' Yishmael.

R' Shimon bar Yochai disagrees. R' Shimon asks, "If a person plows at plowing time and plants at planting time and harvests at harvest time, what will become of Torah?" In other words, if one lives as R' Yishmael suggests, working three hours a day and learning nine, the Torah will be endangered! If there is a possible minute to learn, one must utilize it to learn. The holy *Tannaim* followed R' Shimon's pattern: R' Akiva and his colleagues did not put off their learning, even for prayer.

According to your system, asked R' Shimon's students, if every second is to be used for Torah study, then the descent of the *mon* constituted a danger for the Jews. As we know, the *mon's* delivery was no simple matter. *Tzaddikim* found their portion at their door, but the less righteous were forced to walk up to 2,000 *amah* to find theirs — and the wicked, 12 *mil.* There were no identity cards labeling one a *tzaddik*, a *rasha,* or something in between. The situation changed every day. In short, collecting the *mon* was a time-consuming operation. And in that case, R' Shimon's students wondered, wouldn't it have been better if it fell just once a year, so that they might use the rest of the time for Torah study?

Their rebbi, R' Shimon bar Yochai, offered the following response. "Let me tell you a parable to which this can be compared. A mortal king had one son. He provided for his sustenance once a year, and the son did not see his father's face except for one time a year. Then he started providing the son's sustenance daily, and the son saw his father's face every day. So it was with Israel, too: Someone who had four or five children would worry and say, 'Lest the *mon* not fall tomorrow and we'll all die of starvation!' So they would all incline their hearts to their Father in heaven."

The *mon's* delivery had a very important purpose. The Israelites walked through the desert, surrounded by a sea of sand and desolation. Each night, their food supply ran out and not even a morsel of bread remained to them. When they woke up, they recited the "*Shema*" and lifted their eyes heavenward. Who knew what would happen that day? Perhaps the *mon* would stop falling; with no other way to obtain a morsel of food, they would perish in the wilderness. So they directed their hearts to their Father in heaven and prayed to Him knowing that He provides sustenance to all living things. Moshe Rabbeinu established the Grace after Meals: "*He gives nourishment to all flesh, for His kindness is eternal. And through His great goodness, we have never lacked, and may we never lack nourishment for all eternity.*"

This is a purpose of incomparable significance, and one that is crucial to the success of Torah study, even if the work of gathering the *mon* interrupted their study for a short time. It was worthwhile, if only to direct their hearts heavenward!

"The flavor of all things could be tasted in the mon — their flavor and texture" (Yoma 75a).

A 1987 Car

☞ The Kindness of the Dor Hamidbar

R' Yaakov Galinsky

S omeone once asked me, "R' Yaakov, perhaps you know and can tell me what kind of *chesed* was done by the people in the *dor hamidbar* — the generation in the wilderness? How did they fulfill the mitzvah of *gemilus chasadim*?"

They all ate *mon* in the same measure. No one went hungry. They did not need doctors, so no medical clinics were opened in the desert. And there wasn't much work for a *Chevrah Kaddisha* either.

So how did they perform acts of *chesed*? Jews love making a *gemach*. Without *chesed*, life hardly functions. The children of Avraham, Yitzchak, and Yaakov are "*baishanim, rachmanim,* and *gomlei chasadim*" — bashful, compassionate, and doers of acts of lovingkindness." An interesting question.

I answered him. "*Reb Yid*, I've heard that question before. And I've also heard an answer ..."

The Gemara says that any flavor that a person wanted to taste in the *mon* was the flavor he tasted: each one according to his thoughts. The poor, who were accustomed to eating bread and water, thought, *Here's bread and water,* and that was what they tasted: dry bread and water. The wealthy, on the other hand, habituated to meat or fish, thought of meat or fish, and that's what they had.

A rich man decided to do a favor for a poor one. "Listen," he said to the poor man. "Let me teach you something. When you eat the *mon*, why think about dry, dark bread? Think about bread that is not dry, or about a bit of fish and the like. Then your *mon* will taste differently." By teaching the poor man this concept and showing him new ways to think, the rich man did an act of kindness.

These are the kindnesses that the Jews did with one another in the desert. They taught concepts and revealed new perceptions, particularly in the spiritual realm.

Rabbosai, the biggest *chesed* one can do for a Jew is to teach him concepts such as *emunah* (faith), *bitachon* (trust in Hashem), "Everything that Hashem does is for a person's benefit," "Nobody can touch what Hashem has alloted to his friend," and so on. Concepts! This is unparalleled *gemilus chasadim*.

⌒ Do Not Seek in Strange Fields

We have been implanted with eternal life through such an incredibly rich Torah that can carry us to the most exalted levels. Why do fools seek out the ideas of others? Will a person acquire his basic attitudes for life from the street? We are obligated, therefore, to extend this *chesed* to other Jews: to teach them concepts!

This applies to religious Jews, as well. A certain respectable member of the community was giving me a lift to Haifa in his '87 automobile (when this speech was delivered, that was the latest model). He drove along peacefully and we chatted a bit. Suddenly, he became agitated.

"What happened?" I asked. "Is something wrong?"

"What nerve! See that '78? It just passed me — an '87. What chutzpah!"

"R' Avraham!" I said in surprise. "R' Avraham, what's the matter with you? Is a man's worth measured by the car he drives? '*Avinu Malkeinu*, we have no king but our car.'?"

He smiled at this sadly. After a few moments of silence, a pained expression crossed his face. "R' Yaakov," he said, "what shall I do? I've lost my bearings, my concepts. My idea of success is another thousand *shekels*, another new car. And my notion of failure is measured by the gentile's yardstick. *Hashem yerachem* (May Hashem have mercy)." He had become deeply conscious of his dismal situation.

☞ *Living for Others*

I was once walking down Rechov Rashi, in Bnei Brak. A resident of the block was redoing the front of his house uisng special, costly marble slabs. A wise Jew, passing by, stopped to watch the men at work. Suddenly, he began to offer them all sorts of advice and suggestions. "I think it will look beautiful if you paint the top part a pale blue, and I'll find it especially nice if you put a square slab of marble down here at the bottom, and add another colored slab ..."

"Why are you becoming involved in a building that isn't yours?" the householder demanded, approaching in a huff. "Everyone has his own taste in beauty. Don't disturb the workmen!"

The Jew smiled and said, "Why are you sinking so much money into this project, if not for the sake of the people who pass your house each day? In that case, I am interested in expressing my opinion as to what would strike me as most pleasing."

Rabbosai, we live for other people — to look important in people's eyes. People who are here today and in the grave tomorrow, who cannot help me either in my hour of sorrow or of joy. These are non-Jewish concepts.

"I must have wall-to-wall carpeting," insists a housewife. Nonsense! Why does she need a carpet at all? Because her neighbor has one. And why did the neighbor buy one? Because she suspected that the first woman was intending to buy one, and she wanted to pre-empt her.

Someone once told me, "Believe me, R' Yaakov, for my part, I could walk around in a sack. I only bought an expensive suit for others. And what happens? I walk around in my new suit, and no one even says 'Thank you'!"

A person lives for the sake of others — and the others just laugh at him.

We have lost hold of our exalted human principles: a paradise of *chesed*, of good-heartedness, of strengthening Torah, and raising our children properly. The Torah provides all the necessary ingredients for our happiness: the vitamins and calories we need to live our lives. There is no need to seek substitutes in other places. What is not found in Torah? *"Study it well, for everything is in it."*

Yes, my dear brothers. Feel the pleasure of keeping the Torah and the sweetness of establishing regular times for Torah study. *"Better for me is the Torah of Your mouth than thousands in gold and silver."*

A CHELEMER MOUNTAIN IN EVERY GENERATION

R' Shabsi Yudelevitz

*T*he citizens of Chelm once needed to create a new cemetery. As the city had grown, its population had grown along with it, forcing them to designate land for a new cemetery at the edge of town. They searched, but did not find a suitable location for burying their dead. After more fruitless searching, the city elders conferred over the problem for seven days and seven nights, until a decision was made: to move the mountain that stood to the south of the city. The space thus freed would made a large burial ground that would last them for many years.

How do you move a mountain? Another meeting was held for an additional seven days and nights, until the wisest of them all declared, "We will all get up, every single man among us, and together push the mountain with our hands and feet. I am sure that our joint strength will bear fruit and that we will succeed in pushing that mountain a considerable distance away, to free up the space we need."

This sage suggestion was accepted by one and all, and on the following day posters were put up in the city streets: By decision of the City Council, every man was to cross the town limits to lend a hand in the joint effort of moving the mountain and obtaining land for a new cemetery.

On the morning of the appointed day, the area was filled with all the city's residents: boys and men, young and old together. They began to push the mountain, using their hands and feet to shove with all their might.

At the end of 10 minutes, the sweat was pouring from their faces and they were forced to take off their coats. After another quarter-hour's energetic pushing they were even hotter, and divested themselves of their shirts. Bare from the waist up, they pushed and shoved at that mountain!

As all of this work was going on, a gang of robbers passed by. Seeing what was happening, they hurried to fetch wagons and piled them with the perspiring Chelemers' clothing. Their work done, the robbers made their escape with the loot.

An hour later, one of the wise men of the city turned his head and looked back. To his surprise, the heap of clothing had disappeared.

"There are no clothes!" he shouted. All the other Chelemers turned to see. They stopped their heaving and pushing. "Where are our clothes? What happened?"

Then the wisest of them all cried, "Don't you see? It's a sign that we've succeeded. We've moved the mountain so far from the city that we can't even see our pile of clothes anymore!"

His fellow citizens applauded happily and began to sing and rejoice, drinking a toast and passing out pieces of cake.

Why am I telling you this story?

Yesterday I met a "clever" man who is not scrupulous in his *mitzvah* observance. I rebuked him as the Torah tells us to do. In self-justification, he offered various excuses that I've heard before: "Things are different today. It's impossible to be as observant as people once were. We've left the past behind," and so on. I continued to rebuke him, when he suddenly mentioned *Har Sinai*. "Life has become easier for us! We left a few of the stringencies about modest dress behind us, and things have become a little easier for me and my wife. We've left behind some of the things that our parents observed; we've freed ourselves. So we've moved over a bit from *Har Sinai*; that's not so terrible." At once, I was reminded of the story of the wise men of Chelm.

With a bitter smile, I said, "'We've moved away from *Har Sinai* and *Matan Torah*,' you tell me. Do you think that if you take off a Jew's clothes, if you remove the beauty of *tzeniyus* from your life, you've profited by the move? If the members of your household do not comport themselves according to Jewish values, and are dismissive of the *mitzvos*, have you really succeeded in distancing yourself from *Har Sinai*? Is it possible to move *Har Sinai* to another place? You are making a serious mistake. The mountain remains where it is. It is you who end up naked!"

"Yisro, priest of Midyan, heard ..." What was it that he heard, that led him to come and be part of the Jewish people? R' Yehoshua says he heard about the war with Amalek. R' Elazar Hamoda'i says he heard about *Matan Torah*. R' Eliezer says that he heard about *Kerias Yam Suf* and came.

THEY COULDN'T PLAY CARDS

R' Sholom Schwadron

A good part of this audience doesn't understand Yiddish. However, by way of introduction, I am obliged to begin with a story which contains a mixture of Yiddish. Anyone who may not understand, forgive me.

I walked into a big shul in Boro Park to deliver a speech. The shul president, as was his custom, went up to the *bimah* to introduce me. Being convinced that I had come for the purpose of raising funds for *tzedakah* — as did most of the speakers in that shul who had traveled a great distance — he ended his introduction with the words, "And I bless you, R' Schwadron from Yerushalayim: *zulst gut arois nemen!*" ("You should take a lot out!")

I stood up and began speaking immediately, not waiting a minute: "*Teirer brider* (my dear brothers), do not think that I've come here before you '*arois nemen*' (to take out). Rather, I've come '*arein geben*'! To give, and give powerfully. *Arein geben!*"

In our *derashah* in this shul today, too, I come with the same aim: *arein geben.*

There is a custom of beginning a speech with a bit of humor, as an *Amora* is described as doing in the Gemara (*Shabbos* 30b, and *Pesachim* 117a), to make the listening heart receptive. That *Amora* did so only at the onset, for after that everyone learned Torah with seriousness and reverence, as at the time of its giving. I am saying this in introduction because, as the *derashah* proceeds, we will describe the way person appears — something that will naturally arouse laughter. I ask, therefore, that we take care not to overdo the laughter, heaven forbid, so that we do not lose sight of the important point: the *mussar haskel* (the moral).

And so that we know, when all is said and done, that we are not laughing at others. We are laughing at ourselves.

* * *

☞ Was He the Only One Who Heard?

"*Yisro heard.*" The commentators ask whether he was the only one who heard the news that "*Hashem had taken His nation, Israel, out of Egypt.*" Didn't we already see, in *Parashas Beshalach*, that everyone heard? "*Peoples heard — they were agitated; convulsive terror gripped the dwellers of Philistia. Then the chieftains of Edom were confounded* (*Shemos* 15:14-15)."

The Gemara, in *Zevachim* (116a), asks further: What was the actual news that led Yisro to come? "*R' Yehoshua says he heard about the war with Amalek. R' Elazar Hamoda'i says he heard about *Matan Torah*. R' Eliezer says that he heard about *Kerias Yam Suf* and came.*"

R' Elazar Hamoda'i, who claims that Yisro heard about *Matan Torah*, elaborates: "When the Torah was given to Israel, His voice reached from one end of the world to the other, and all the kings of the idol-worshipers were seized with trembling in their palaces, and they said *shirah*, as it says, *'U'veheichalo kulo omer kavod'* (*'While in His Temple, all proclaim, Glory!'*). The nations trembled from the voice at *Har Sinai* at the giving of the Torah, and they said *shirah* to *HaKadosh Baruch Hu!*"

Well, *rabbosai*, what does one do when one is seized with trembling and reciting praises to Hashem?

One embraces the faith of Israel. One comes to the wilderness and looks into the Torah and those who received it.

But conversion is no simple thing. What do you think? Now they could no longer play cards, or watch TV, follow the soccer matches, or the like. Part of the "fear and trembling" that took hold of them came from panic at leaving everything behind — no easy matter. What to do? What did *they* do?

They all gathered before Bilaam the wicked and said, "What is that thunderous noise we heard? Perhaps another flood is coming to the world."

Bilaam the prophet, seeing their terror, soothed their fears: "*HaKadosh Baruch Hu* has already promised that he will never bring another flood to the world."

Still agitated, the leaders of the nations persisted: "Maybe He won't bring a flood of water, but one of fire!"

"Don't worry," Bilaam answered. "Hashem has already promised that He will not destroy the world."

"But we heard awesome sounds. Something is certainly happening in the world. Tell us what it is!"

"What were the sounds you heard?" he asked. "There is a good and desirable thing in His storehouses that has been placed near Him for 974 generations before He created the world. He wanted to give it to His children, as it says, *'Hashem will give His nation strength.'* "

Hearing this, the kings all cried, "May Hashem bless His nation with peace," and they all returned to their homes. In other words, they blessed the nation of Israel, who had received the Torah, and then dispersed to their separate corners of the globe.

What does R' Elazar Hamoda'i wish to relate with this anecdote? Does the Gemara simply tell stories? Certainly not. R' Elazar Hamoda'i offers this elaboration in order to explain what Yisro heard that the others did not, and why the Torah mentions only *his* hearing about it.

R' Elazar Hamoda'i explains that Yisro heard *Matan Torah*, as well as the ensuing dialogue among Bilaam and the leaders of the nations. He heard the nations realize that Hashem was perpetrating something great and awesome in His world, and how terrified they were as a result. But they did not seek out Moshe Rabbeinu, but rather the wicked Bilaam. Even after they were told that Hashem was giving Israel something desirable that He'd kept stored away up till then, the nations did not interest themselves in Torah, but returned to their homes. This is proof that their terror did not have its roots in fear of heaven; they were simply afraid for their own lives.

Very simply, they trembled lest a flood be on its way that would take away their ability to live — to eat sandwiches, steaks, or merely ice cream. And so, when Bilaam reassured them that nothing dangerous was happening, that Hashem was "just" giving His Torah to His people, Israel, and that they could go on living and eating as merrily as before — very good! They waved good-bye and were off to their homes. The convocation of multinational wise men heard what was happening, and their only conclusion was that it was worthwhile blessing the nation that was the recipient of the Torah.

Is that called "hearing" about *Matan Torah*?!

Yisro witnessed this amazing episode: the world's leaders hearing and at the same time not seeming to hear at all. They all got up and went home. He took a lesson from this: how a person can hear and not hear! He saw, and was shaken to the core. And then he deepened his own understanding, and listened the way one ought to listen: "*He heard and he came.*"

Hearing and not coming is not called hearing! My rebbi had a parable to describe this:

There was once a villager who had neither seen nor heard a locomotive in his life. One day, he went to the capital city and noticed, at the side of the road, long strips of gleaming metal, with wooden slats every meter or so along the way. Train tracks.

Enjoying the sight, he sat down on the slats to inspect them more closely. Suddenly, a train appeared in the distance. The conductor, appalled at seeing a person sitting on the tracks, quickly sounded the whistle as loudly as he could, blowing long and short blasts to attract the villager's attention.

The villager did lift his eyes. He saw something gigantic bearing down on him, and heard the blaring sounds issuing from it. Standing up, he began to dance. *This must be somebody's wedding day, and here comes the band*, he thought naively.

Passers-by shouted, "Help! Help him! He must be deaf!"

The truth? He was able to hear very well. But he did not know what it was that he was hearing. Alas, he heard an orchestra.

So it was with the "orchestra" of *Matan Torah*. "What was it that he heard — and came?" Yisro heard the way the others didn't really hear *Matan Torah*. He witnessed the way the other leaders heard the mighty sounds that echoed from one end of the world to the other but didn't understand. "*Yisro heard*" — how the others couldn't hear.

☞ "Rebbi Already Told Me"

The Alter of Slabodka was an outstanding educator who knew when to rebuke a student and when not to say a word. Once, he rebuked a student but the student did not rectify the behavior in question. Several weeks passed. When they next met, the Alter repeated his earlier rebuke, word for word, without any introduction or epilogue.

"But Rebbi already told me that," said the *bachur*. "I heard exactly the same words from him just a few weeks ago!"

The Alter looked at him and asked, "If you are walking down the middle of a main street in London, and 25 cars are all honking at you at once (back then, Israel did not boast such a broad street filled with cars), and you innocently turn your head around to look at them, lift a hand, and say politely, "Thanks, I heard you" — have you really heard?"

You haven't heard. Because if you heard, you'd get up on the sidewalk!

Yisro left all his foreign gods and came to the wilderness. *That's* how one listens!

☞ *"These Days, There's a Maggid!"*

An additional explanation of "Yisro heard."

In my younger days, I would ask myself, "*Maggid*? What kind of name is that? After all, it's Hashem Who is the '*Maggid*,' as it says, '*maggid l'adam mah sicho* — He tells a person what he spoke about ...' "

"Even a trivial conversation between husband and wife is told to a person at the hour of judgment!" There are tape recorders on the table and everything is recorded and stored up above. Afterward, Hashem tells a person what he spoke about. But a *darshan* is called a "*maggid*." As a young man and later as a married one, I would go out of the Ohel Torah *kollel* and hear the "news" from the others: "There's a *maggid* today."

A *tzaddik* had come to Meah Shearim: the Rav of Homeler (R' Elyashiv's father), who was also considered a "*maggid*." I heard him speak often. I remember hearing him deliver a *derashah* as follows:

In previous generations, when a youth emerged from hearing a *derashah* that had been told before an audience of *bachurim*, he understood that the *derashah* had been intended for him. That is, the words had been directed at him, to help correct his character traits and behaviors.

However, with the passage of time things began to change. When a *derashah* was over, Moishy would say to Yankel, "Ah, Yankel, the rebbe told it to you straight today, didn't he?" And Yankel would tell Moishy, "On the contrary, he gave it to *you* — right between the eyes!'"

Years passed, and things changed even more. They deteriorated further and further, until today, when they emerge from a *maggid's* talk they say angrily, "He meant *me?* Well, in that case, I'll show *him*."

Don't laugh.

In those days, when the *maggid* would chant his message to an audience, a man or woman would return home having heard something. Husband and wife would discuss how to improve themselves and their household. They would cry and acknowledge their faults — because the *maggid* had said so! They listened to words of rebuke. I will never forget how when I was still in yeshivah, for example, the *mashgiach* (R' Leib Chasman) read the words of the Gemara in *Nedarim* (9b) about a *nazir* who brought a guilt-offering to the *Beis HaMikdash* before Shimon Hatzaddik, and told the *Kohen Gadol:* "I was a shepherd for my father, and I went to fetch water from the spring. As I looked into my own reflection, my *yetzer* tried to distract me. I told it, 'Wicked one! Why are you so proud of a world that is not yours — of someone who is destined for worms' " As my rebbi quoted aloud from the Gemara, he suddenly cried, "Wicked one! Why are you so proud of a world that is not yours — of someone who is destined for worms? Wicked one!" Each of us was convinced that the *mashgiach* was shouting at him. *Rasha!* Wicked one! I thought he meant the words for Sholom Schwadron, while my neighbor thought that he was talking to him. That's the way it used to be. We listened, and we heard.

R' Aryeh Levin was not a "*maggid,*" but he would give a *shiur* between *Minchah* and *Ma'ariv* in the old "Knesset" neighborhood. Attending that *shiur* was a Jew who was apparently quick tempered by nature, with the result that the peace of his household was not as it should have been. Without her husband's knowledge the man's wife came to the home of R' Aryeh Levin, complaining about her husband and begging the *rav* to find an opportunity in his *shiur* to touch on a man's obligation to honor his wife. This is correct: One is obligated to honor his wife, as the Gemara says (*Yevamos* 62b), "[A man should] love his wife as himself and honor her more than himself."

R' Aryeh Levin did as she asked. In the course of one of his *shiurim*, he brought the topic around to the words of *Chazal* about loving one's wife as oneself and honoring her more than himself. He discussed the topic from every angle, until he was certain that his words had penetrated the man's heart at least a little bit. Then, as R' Aryeh was speaking on this subject — it was near the end of the *shiur*, before *Ma'ariv* — the *gaon* R' Isser Zalman Meltzer walked into the shul. He heard the way R' Aryeh elaborated to his audience on the teachings of *Chazal* regarding a man's obligation to treat the members of his household gently, with respect and compassion. The elderly *gaon* listened closely to every word R' Aryeh spoke.

After *Ma'ariv*, R' Isser Zalman walked up to R' Aryeh Levin and whispered, "*Yasher kochacha* (well done), R' Aryeh! You doubtless intended your words for me, as well. Therefore, I guarantee that from this day on I will treat my household with more respect and there will be an improvement in my behavior."

Rabbosai, that's the way things were in the generation before us and in earlier generations before that. Young people today, however, believe that they are O.K. and have nothing to correct.

(With a smile) "Earlier generations." My rebbi once said something profound, something one could talk about for hours, but he put the deep thought into several concise meaningful sentences. Here is what he said:

"How were things once? Wagons were hitched to horses. People sat in the wagons and the horses would take them to their destination. Today, we have progress. There are no wagons; instead, we have trains. Who conducts the train? Not horses, but people. And what do they transport in their trains? Horses!"

Progress!

This brings us to an additional understanding of Yisro's extraordinary level in "hearing" and coming. Yisro heard about the exodus from Egypt and understood that this awesome "*shmooze*" — the *shiur* of *yetziyas Mitzrayim*, the talk about the war with Amalek, and the *derashah* on *Matan Torah* — were being said directly to him. Not to someone else. *Gevaldig*!

⌒ A Third Perspective

Going out into the street, one sees degradation and corruption. We see the cynics of our generation. Every year, some 13,000 male youths and 8,000 girls are sent to prison. Why are those thousands of children sitting in jail? Is it because they put on *tefillin*? Is it because they kept Shabbos? They are there because they are guilty of robbery and theft and so on. Were things this way a generation ago? If a young man was caught performing transgressions and acts of cruelty, he would be one in thousands! How have we come to this situation? The answer is: *chinuch*. We must educate our children, not with "modern" ideas, but rather the way your father educated you and the way your grandfather raised your father.

But things are not like that today. "The world is different," people tell me. What do they mean by that? I'll explain it to you. Don't laugh; this is a true story.

I once delivered a talk to a group of soldiers — religious, of course — and one of the soldiers approached me afterward. Apologetically, he said, "R' Schwadron, you're right. You're absolutely right. But reality ..." In other words, we are living in a different reality, so that even if you are right, with reality as it is, what's a person to do? So claimed the soldier.

I thought to myself, *I've just lectured for an hour and a half, and he's still asking questions. Does he want me to speak for another five hours?* However, he seemed to be sincere.

"I turned and faced the soldier who had approached me with his question. Loudly, I asked, 'What reality are you talking about when you say, "But reality is different"? The reality of hashish? The reality of ... Which reality?'

"The main purpose of a person's life is to break his nature. That's what the Noam Elimelech said, and the Vilna Gaon, too. This is the work we are meant to do. And if a person does not break and correct his bad nature, *oy vey! Oy vey!* One's good nature, too, must be nurtured and made to flourish. That is a person's reality. Is it wise to leave nature alone and live like animals on all fours, because 'that's reality'?!"

To be a person: *that's* reality.

This brings us to a third perspective on Yisro's greatness in "hearing and coming." After hearing the lecture on *yetzias Mitzrayim* and breaking through the "reality" of the peoples of the world, he heard, and came to the true reality. In contrast, the international leaders — upon hearing that the world was not about to come to an end, but that Hashem was just giving His nation, Israel, the Torah — said, "May Hashem bless His people with peace," and returned home to their own reality: to sports, money, drugs, and guns.

⌐ An Animal from Sha'arei Chesed

Now let me tell you another story. The first time I stayed in Antwerp, I would eat lunch in the kosher restaurant run by a certain God-fearing Jew. One day — as opposed to every other day, when the eatery was filled at noon (in the mornings, people rush off to work; it is only for lunch that they can calmly go to a restaurant) — the place was empty.

Twenty minutes later, after I'd already washed my hands, a lone Jew came in. Following him was another Jew, both of them with sad faces and downcast eyes.

Something's happened, I thought with foreboding.

Being a bit of an alarmist by nature, I sat silently, in an inner turmoil of fear. As we all know, the situation in the Holy Land (this was in the year 5717/1957) up to this day is tense. For decades there has been no rest in Eretz Yisrael. Naturally, my thoughts turned in that direction. *Who knows what happened? Why are they so anxious and aren't saying a word to me?*

Suddenly, I heard a third person enter the restaurant, also with a slow step. He sat down and asked, "How many people do you think were at the funeral?"

I calmed down somewhat: A funeral is sad, but apparently no one I knew was threatened. Then I wondered, *Which gaon and tzaddik has passed away here in Belgium?* (This being my first visit to the country, I was not yet familiar with its Torah leaders.)

Another man came in and said out loud, "There must have been a million people at the funeral."

A million? I thought. *There aren't even half a million Jews in all of Antwerp. What happened?* Standing up, I walked tensely over to their table and asked, "Tell me what happened."

They evaded me with a slight smile. "R' Schwadron, this is not for you."

I was even more curious now. I begged them to tell me. And, finally, they did. This was the story they told. Listen!

Every country has its own particular sports craze: In England, it's horses. Horse races and festivals. The Queen owns expensive race-horses. Americans love football, and in Belgium, they hold bicycle races in the city streets. Belgian cities feature a special side lane for bikes.

What had happened in Belgium that day? A certain gentile, the bicycling champion for 16 consecutive years and consequently a very wealthy man, had decided to perform some remarkable stunt on his bike. In the middle of the stunt, he'd flipped over and cracked his skull ... And there was a funeral.

A quarter-million Belgians, a half-million, and some said a million people had attended the funeral. A number of Jews had also gone to witness the spectacle. I heard details of the event. I listened and was silent.

They looked at me again. Then I whispered to one of them, "In order to participate in such a funeral, does one have to come to Belgium? Back in Sha'arei Chesed, in Yerushalayim, a champion cat died. She climbed to the heights of the tallest tree in a quarter of the usual time — and she died. 'Go to the funeral!'" Those men laughed. (The audience laughs.) And you, who are now laughing so hard, do you think I came here to put on a show? It's simply worth your while to understand that such talents are not a man's pride. Any cat in any neighborhood in Yerushalayim can outdo that. The thing that lends honor to a human being is whether or not he conducted his life properly. Whether he acted with his thinking mind. Whether he recognized his Creator. Whether he kept the Torah and *mitzvos*. Such a person deserves our respect! But running and jumping — what do these things have to do with respecting someone?

May Hashem help us to hear and to come to shuls and houses of study to repair our *middos*.

I'll conclude this *derashah* on *Parashas Yisro* with something from the Chofetz Chaim, the final hammer-blow, which I usually say first thing whenever I find myself speaking in a new place. Let us carry this parable by the Chofetz Chaim around in our pockets wherever we go.

He's Gone Crazy!

Each time I repeat this parable by the Chofetz Chaim, I experience a gamut of new emotions. Each time, I am moved afresh.

In a certain town, as in many towns that boast a Jewish community, there lived a *talmid chacham*. He had beautiful *middos* and was wealthy and respectable as well — every good thing. He was named R' Baruch. The whole town, figuratively, rested on R' Baruch's shoulders. Anyone in need of advice came to him. Anyone in need of a loan or a donation knocked on his door.

And, again as in any town, there lived a poor Jew by the name of Shlomo Zalman.

Shlomo Zalman had a daughter who had reached marriageable age. As he had no dowry to bestow on her, she grew older, for without a dowry it was nearly impossible to find her a *shidduch*. Her parents thought and thought, and finally decided that they had no choice but to turn to R' Baruch. They called him up. (There were actually no telephones back then, and the Chofetz Chaim did not mention one, but we'll have them speak on the phone.)

One morning, the phone rang in R' Baruch's house. It was 7 a.m., right after the *vasikin Shacharis* service. "Hello?"

"Good morning, R' Baruch. How are you today, R' Baruch? How are your children, R' Baruch? How's the whole family?"

R' Baruch had already grasped the situation. At once, he asked, "R' Shlomo Zalman, do you perhaps need a loan?"

"Ah, yes, yes, you should be well, R' Baruch. May blessings shower upon your head! I have a daughter of marriageable age ..."

"That's perfectly all right. No need to apologize. Hashem gave me money, not for myself, but to do good things. So, how much do you need?"

"Three hundred rubles. I'll pay you back when my ship comes in." You all know what that means: when *Mashiach* comes! (Laughter) It's not I who says this, but Rashi (*Ezra* 2:3, see also the end of *Maseches Sotah*).

R' Baruch agreed happily: "All right, come down to my office at 12 o'clock today, when the customers have gone, and I'll give you a check and my best wishes." They hung up.

Before closing his office for lunch, R' Baruch wrapped up his affairs and finished with his clients, in order not to cause Shlomo Zalman any discomfort. At exactly 12 o'clock he was sitting and waiting. But Shlomo Zalman didn't come.

Nu, he probably got caught up in some distressful situation. As Chazal tell us (Bava Kamma 92a), "The poor get poorer," R' Baruch thought in distress. He waited another five minutes and then, when Shlomo Zalman didn't come, locked the office door and went out, thinking, *Usually, with a loan of this kind, people aren't late. Who knows what happened to him? Perhaps he broke a leg, heaven forbid. How could he not have come?!* He wondered.

At 7 a.m. next morning, the phone rang again. "Good morning, R' Baruch, good morning! How are you, R' Baruch? How's the family?"

"Ah! It's you, Shlomo Zalman! I waited for you impatiently yesterday. I'd prepared a check for you. What happened? Why didn't you come? Drop in at noon today and you can pick it up."

"All right. Thank you!" said Shlomo Zalman.

He'll certainly come today, R' Baruch thought confidently as he hung up the phone.

But 12 o'clock came and went that day, as well, with no sign of Shlomo Zalman. R' Baruch waited half an hour, but he didn't come. *What happened? Something going on with Shlomo Zalman,* he thought.

At 7 a.m. the next day: "Good morning, R' Baruch! How are you, R' Baruch? How are the children?"

He's gone crazy! R' Baruch muttered to himself, and quickly hung up. *Meshuggener.*

(Chanting) This, the Chofetz Chaim says, is how we look in shul. A person comes to shul at 7 o'clock each morning, and sings Hashem's praises. "*With an abundant love have You loved us, Hashem. With exceedingly great pity have You pitied us!*" Such good things. "Our Father! Our King! For the sake of our forefathers, who trusted in You." Pleading words roll off his tongue. "*Instill in our hearts to understand and to elucidate, to listen, learn, teach, safeguard, perform, and fulfill all the words of Your Torah's teachings with love!*" We beg Hashem to give us the privilege of learning, understanding, and fulfilling His precepts.

The angels up above become excited, waiting eagerly for the moment when the man will finish *davening* and will open a *Mishnayos*, Gemara, or *Chumash*, so that they may pour barrels of understanding over him. They stand poised with barrels of wisdom and intelligence.

Comes "*Ashrei*" and "*U'va l'Tzion*," and he kisses his *tefillin*. During the "*Shir shel Yom*" he folds his *tallis*. Then it's "Good-bye, good-bye!" and he's out the door. The angels wait; perhaps he will still return that day to study with a partner. Or maybe he will come in the evening to hear a *shiur*.

No! He doesn't come. Well, perhaps he broke a leg, heaven forbid.

The next day, at 7 a.m.: "*Have mercy upon us, instill in our hearts to understand and to elucidate, to listen, learn, teach, safeguard, perform, and fulfill all the words of Your Torah's teachings with love!*" To learn and also to teach, "*all the words of Your Torah's teachings with love!*" He asks this with all his heart, and the angels wait again. Let him only open a Gemara and barrels of wisdom will pour over him.

But after *davening*, he goes to work, to his shop, his office — and that's the end of that.

The next morning, again, sighs and pleadings and prayers: "*Instill in our hearts to understand and to elucidate, to listen...*"

"He's gone crazy!"

אַתֶּם רְאִיתֶם אֲשֶׁר עָשִׂיתִי לְמִצְרָיִם וָאֶשָּׂא אֶתְכֶם עַל־כַּנְפֵי נְשָׁרִים
וָאָבִא אֶתְכֶם אֵלָי. וְעַתָּה אִם־שָׁמוֹעַ תִּשְׁמְעוּ בְּקֹלִי וּשְׁמַרְתֶּם אֶת־
בְּרִיתִי וִהְיִיתֶם לִי סְגֻלָּה מִכָּל־הָעַמִּים כִּי־לִי כָּל־הָאָרֶץ .... אֵלֶּה
הַדְּבָרִים אֲשֶׁר תְּדַבֵּר אֶל־בְּנֵי יִשְׂרָאֵל.

"You have seen what I did to Egypt, and that I have borne you on the wings of eagles and brought you to Me." Hashem lifted us up — "I have borne you" — very high — "and brought you to Me"! "And now, if you hearken well to My voice and observe My convenant, you shall be to Me the most beloved treasure of all peoples, for Mine is the entire world ...These are the words that you shall speak to the Children of Israel." These words — neither less nor more — you shall say to the Children of Israel as an introduction to Matan Torah (Shemos 19:4-6).

ON THE WINGS OF EAGLES

*W*hat is the meaning of, "*im tishme'u b'koli*" — "*If you hearken to My voice*"? R' Sholom Schwadron asks: Which voice?

I once heard the following parable in the name of the Kotzker Rebbe:

A man was walking in a dense forest with his young son. The child strayed to the sides of the path from time to time, jumping and playing among the trees. The father said, "Be very careful not to wander too far away from me, because in this part of the forest it is very easy to lose your way, and then you will be lost."

"Father," the boy requested, "I'd like to walk around a little."

"I have an idea for you and for me," the father said. "Every minute or two, I'll call out to you. As long as you can still hear my voice, that will be proof that you haven't wandered too far. But the moment you can no longer hear my voice, know that you've moved too far into the woods and are about to get lost."

It occasionally happens that a Jew is walking down the street when he is suddenly struck by a marvelous idea in *yiras Shamayim*. Or else he simply begins to ask himself, *Did I daven with kavanah today? Did I recite the berachos the way I'm supposed to? Did I learn enough?* He has no idea why or from where these thoughts have popped into his head. The real reason is: It is the voice of *HaKadosh Baruch Hu*. "If you listen to My voice" — the voice of Hashem, as it were, knocks on the gates of his heart. "Return, wayward sons ..." "Return to Me and I will return to you!" When we hear this voice, we know that we have not yet strayed too far away. What profound thoughts are hidden in this parable of the Kotzker Rebbe!

If we listen to His voice and keep His *mitzvos*, we will merit being *"the most beloved treasure of all peoples."*

⌒ The Most Beloved Treasure

I must tell you a story. Let me preface it by saying that it is a true story, and that I heard it from a very great person. I don't think you knew him; you're young, and even most older people didn't know him. He lived in Batei Brodie. An awesome and wonderful story.

As a youth, in the World War I era, he lived in the city of Stuchin. The Russians drafted him in their war against the Germans. Along with a group of other *bachurim*, he was sent to a battlefront not far from the city.

In those days, soldiers would dig trenches. Their heads stuck up above the ground, which was covered with sandbags, and they would shoot from between the sandbags.

Our *bachur* was standing in a trench. Beside him was another Jew, no longer young, a man in his 40's. Bullets flew all around them. The enemy's fire whistled at them ceaselessly, and his fellow soldier fell mortally wounded. He begged the *bachur* to make sure he received a Jewish burial. The *bachur* promised with reverence.

A quarter of an hour later, the soldier died.

For long hours, the battle continued unabated. There was no lull on the horizon. The *bachur* began to fear for his own life. "If only there would be a temporary cease-fire, I would be able to bring him to the cemetery in Stuchin, which is relatively nearby. But the guns are still firing. The battle is raging. What shall I do?"

At a certain point, at the height of the turmoil and under danger of death, the *bachur* gathered his courage and made a decision: "I promised this man, and I will keep my word. I will bring him to a Jewish burial, come what may!"

Being physically strong, the *bachur* stood up, lifted the body, and slung it over his shoulder. Then he climbed out of the trench. Under the open sky, in full daylight, at the height of the battle, he began running toward the city, the corpse over his shoulder.

The *bachur* told me that on his way he passed near Cossack camps. It is almost impossible to overstate the danger of his running into one of their troops. But, for some reason, no one saw him. And so he ran with his burden, seeing but not being seen — engaged in a mitzvah!

He hastened along with devotion, vigorously and without stopping, for three kilometers, until he reached the city entrance. There he met a member of the *Chevrah Kaddisha* and handed over the body. His *mitzvah* completed, the *bachur* immediately retraced his steps and, again, he was not seen until, *baruch Hashem*, he was back in his trench as though nothing had happened. (His Russian superior officers did not dare move around among the living and the dead; only at night did they pass among the soldiers and distribute some food. Therefore, they never noticed his absence.)

In the end, the Russians who'd had control of Stuchin were conquered, and the Germans took over. The *bachur* was granted permission to return to the city. A few days later the conquering Germans sought him out and recruited him for their own war effort. His job? Tending the animals.

Because animals (for food) were a valuable commodity in wartime, they warned him as they assigned him the task: "If a single animal is missing, your life is over."

The *bachur* took his new responsibilities seriously: "During the day I was subject to the sword, and ice by night." Then, one morning, as he shepherded his flock in one of the huge pastures outside the city, he came upon a second opportunity to involve himself with the dead. A gunshot was heard in the distance, and he was able to discern a soldier falling. Seeing no one else in the vicinity, he realized that the soldier had just committed suicide. He began to race toward the fallen soldier, to try and save his life. He gave no thought to the animals in his charge; all he could think of was the soldier's life. Such devotion.

When he reached the soldier, he saw to his joy that the man was still breathing. Taking off his coat, he ripped it into strips which he used to bandage the injured man and try to stop the flow of blood. Nevertheless, he was not successful; only moments later, the soldier died.

While he was still at work trying to save the man, other soldiers arrived. They saw a fallen soldier, dead on the ground, and another soldier beside him. Hastily they surrounded our *bachur*, believing that he must have fired the shot that killed the soldier. They carted him off to prison. Within hours, he was taken before a military tribunal, which quickly sentenced him to death.

The court permitted him to make a speech in his own defense. Naturally, he pleaded for his life, claiming, "I only wanted to save him! I don't know him, I've never had a quarrel with him. I only saw someone fall and I ran over to save him."

His pleas were like a voice calling in the wilderness; opposing him, the military prosecutor placed on the courtroom table 18 "proofs" that he had indeed killed the man. You know how a lawyer can turn day into night and night into day. In short, he was sentenced to death. The sentence was to be carried out on the following day, at 12 noon. He would stand facing a row of soldiers and be shot. That's the way things are done in wartime, *r"l*.

In the 24 hours remaining to him, the *bachur* was confined to a small, dank cell. *Oy, oy*... We should never know what such a cell is like; you can't sit or take care of your needs, terrible torture, without the slightest possibility of falling asleep. But even without the cell he would never have dreamed of sleeping, just hours before he was to be taken out and shot.

In the middle of the night, he stood up in shock. It seemed to him, whether asleep or awake, that he saw the man he'd brought to Jewish burial two months earlier. The man asked him, "Why are you so afraid? Don't be afraid. Don't worry. In the merit of your effort to bring me to a Jewish burial, you will be saved. Even if you stand at the very gates of death, they will not kill you." Then he disappeared.

Was that my imagination or not? He didn't have much time to wonder. When it was close to 12 o'clock, they came to get him. He was dragged from the cell, his eyes were covered, and he was taken some distance to an open field near Stuchin.

They placed him by a wall, facing a row of soldiers.

When the hands of the clock pointed to 12 o'clock precisely, the officer in charge cried, "One!" He waited a second, then shouted, "Two!" But before he could cry, "Three!" from the distance came a soldier galloping on a horse and screaming at the top of his lungs. He waved a piece of paper in the air, shouting for them to wait!

The soldiers waited half a minute for him to reach them. When he was close enough, he showed them the paper and said, "Just a little while ago we buried that soldier. In his pocket we found a suicide note, addressed to his family. In the note, he wrote that he was knowingly taking his own life. Here's the paper."

Of course, they removed the blindfold from our *bachur's* eyes and set him free.

And instead of the harsh staccato of gunfire (R' Sholom ends his tale), the air seemed to fill with the eternal voice of the Jewish people, of the Jewish young men who observe the *mitzvos* with such devotion and self-sacrifice. *"You shall be to Me the most beloved treasure of all peoples, for Mine is the entire world ... Guardian of Israel, Guardian of the remnants of Israel who say, 'Shema Yisrael.' "*

⌒ The "Tenth" Is Saved

Let me tell you another story on the theme of *"You shall be to Me the most beloved treasure of all peoples."* I heard this story personally from the person to whom it happened, one Friday night after my *derashah* in the Zichron Moshe shul.

That night, more than 34 years ago, the subject of the *derashah* was "the loss of a *mitzvah* versus its reward." We said then that a person may think he's lost out by doing a *mitzvah*, but in the end he sees the reward for the act. And, sometimes, he has the privilege of receiving a rich reward even in this world.

After the *derashah*, a man came over to me and asked, "Maybe Russian?" That is, perhaps I was a Russian?

"No, I am not a Russian. I was born in Meah Shearim."

"But I am from Russia. I want to tell Rav Schwadron a story," he said.

Here is what he said.

"When Czar Nikolai — may his memory be blotted out! — was killed, I was living in Russia. Russia experienced half a year of *Gan Eden*, as it were." (The czar was a cruel murderer as well as anything else evil you can name. After him came the Socialists, under the leadership of Prime Minister Alexander Kerensky. Wonder of wonders, free enterprise flourished without limitation. People went crazy and made tremendous profits.) "I earned my living trading on the Exchange. From morning to night I bought and sold gold and pearls, and I did very well.

"One morning, I left the house at 8 a.m., after *Shacharis*, on my way to the Exchange. As I walked along with a small briefcase in my hand which held a considerable sum of money, I suddenly heard a voice calling me from behind: 'A tenth! A tenth!' This was not something we heard often in our neighborhood. *Nu*, a Jew was looking for a 'tenth.' I turned around and walked back, and he explained, 'Today's my father's *yahrtzeit*. Can you come into the shul to complete the *minyan*?' I agreed.

"I followed him into the courtyard. I went to the doorway and walked in, and there I was greeted by a shocking sight.

There were only four men there.

" 'A tenth?' I asked in surprise. 'You said I'm the tenth — but I'm only the fifth. I'm leaving!' "

" 'You can't go!' He stood by the door and pleaded. "When you'll have a *yahrtzeit*, you'll do the same thing.'

"Hearing this, I felt pity for him. I thought, *O.K., what can I do? I'm here already. I'll wait until there are 10 men so he can say Kaddish for his father.*'

"I sat at the edge of my seat, impatient. He went out to search for others. Apparently, he used the same ruse on them, for at the end of a quarter-hour ten men were gathered. In my innocence, I thought I'd be off to the Exchange in another minute. The man would recite *Kaddish* and I'd be on my way. But no ... He began to say, '*Hodu*'...

" '*Shacharis*?!' I asked.

" 'Yes! *Shacharis*!' he replied. I thought I'd explode.

"I got up to leave. Once again, he stood in the doorway and said, '*Reb Yid*, you're not leaving. It's my father's *yahrtzeit* today!' Giving up, I thought, *I'll be an hour late to the Exchange and I'll lose money — for the sake of doing a mitzvah for this Jew. That's that.* I sat back down.

"When *davening* was over, the man showered me with all sorts of blessings and thanks. Of course, now that I'd done the *mitzvah* I didn't regret it. I left the shul happy and lighthearted."

(I heard from my rebbi, R' Aharon Katzenelenbogen — says R' Sholom — that this is a well-known rule: Before doing a *mitzvah*, the *yetzer hara* comes into play. Afterwards, a man wouldn't sell that mitzvah for even 50,000 *shekels*!)

"Happy and satisfied, I walked toward the Exchange, briefcase in hand.

"When I came closer, about 100 meters before the entrance, a man ran up to me and whispered in agitation, 'Get away from here! They're killing people in the building! Murderers! Run!' That was the morning that the Communists took control. The first thing they did was enter the Exchange building. 'They've already killed 70 wealthy traders,' the man told me, and pushed me away. I turned and ran for my life.

"So I say to the Rav," he concluded his story, " 'the loss of a *mitzvah* versus its reward': I was half an hour late, so I lost money for doing a *mitzvah*, and what did I receive as a reward? My life! I received my life. And I've lived a long life to this day, right here in Zichron Moshe."

May Hashem help us to be His treasure among the nations, and let us perform *mitzvos* in abundance and in good health. And let us all merit life and peace, and a full repentance, and a full redemption speedily in our days — *Amen*, be strong and blessed!

פרשת משפטים
PARASHAS MISHPATIM

"Lifneihem" — before them, but not before non-Jews. Even if you know about a certain matter of law that [non-Jews] judge according to the same legal principle as the law of Israel, do not bring it to their courts, for one who brings legal matters of Israel before non-Jews desecrates the Name of God (Rashi on Shemos 21:1).

THE DOG IN THE MAHARIL'S HOUSE

R' Benzion Yadler

*T*he power of Jewish judges is very great. They merit tremendous *siyata d'Shemaya* (Heavenly assistance), as R' Benzion Yadler describes.

The holy *gaon*, the *Maharil* Diskin, once officiated at the divorce proceeding between a man and his wife. Suddenly, in the midst of writing the *get*, he stopped and announced his decision to leave the rest of the writing until the following day. The *gaon* did not explain his decision; he only asked that the woman's personal details be rechecked, and said that the divorce would be postponed until the next day. The other *dayanim* who were involved, and who were familiar with the case, were surprised but, in reverence, they did not protest.

On the following day, after further clarifications had been made, it was discovered that the woman was about to receive a false *get*. She had hired another man to pretend he was her husband and to hand her the *get*. This duplicity came to light, as we have said, in the midst of writing the divorce document and only a short time before it was to have been given.

When the *Maharil* returned home, the members of his household asked him, "The *rav* does not believe in miracles. Is there a greater miracle than this?"

Replied the *Maharil*, "Is it a miracle? It is wisdom, which *HaKadosh Baruch Hu* gave man so that he may extrapolate one thing from another."

That "divorcing" couple had brought with them a small dog, as was the style with modern folk at that time (as R' Yadler put it). Up until that day, they had never arrived at the *beis din* at the same time. That day, for the divorce ceremony, they had both come together.

"As the *get* was being written, I noticed that the dog was walking back and forth, from the woman to the man and from the man to the woman. It went back and forth several times. I was surprised to see how comfortable the dog was with both of them. They had told the court they'd been separated before the divorce, due to the quarrels between them. Therefore, the dog must have been living either with him or with her. How was it that it was moving easily from one to the other? The dog was accustomed to both of them. I understood from this that their story was a lie: that he was not her husband, and there was therefore no quarrel between them. I stopped writing the *get* until I could look into the matter again — and the deception was uncovered.

"With reference to this episode, I cite the words of *Chazal* in *Yevamos* 121a: 'Shmuel applied this to Rav: No harm shall befall a *tzaddik*.'"

➾ Three Napoleons

On another occasion, in discussing the wisdom of *dayanim* (judges), R' Benzion Yadler mentioned the *gaon* R' Shmuel Salant. This is the story he told:

My mother used to sell flour for baking Pesach matzos. There was a matzah-bakery owner in Jerusalem (who also dealt in dairy products) who owed her 20 *napoleons* and refused to pay. Even the *beis din* did not succeed in getting him to pay his debt.

My mother was forced to bring him to the *beis din* of R' Shmuel Salant. After hearing her claims, R' Shmuel turned to the man and asked forcefully, "Why don't you want to pay the 30 *napoleons* that you owe her for the flour?"

The man was unprepared for the question, or for the demanding tone R' Shmuel had adopted with him. He stammered, "I owe only 20! Why does the *rav* say 30?"

With these words, he admitted that he owed the 20 *napoleons*. At once, R' Shmuel said sternly, "I hereby give you until this time tomorrow to bring the money."

The next day, the man did not come at the appointed time. R' Shmuel sent a messenger with the following ultimatum: "You should know that I have never begun a case that I did not finish. If you do not bring the money, I will immediately send my *shamash* to announce throughout the city that your merchandise is prohibited to the public, and that you may not be included in any holy matter."

Hearing this, the baker turned up at once — money in hand.

וְאִם־אָמֹר יֹאמַר הָעֶבֶד אָהַבְתִּי אֶת־אֲדֹנִי אֶת־אִשְׁתִּי וְאֶת־בָּנָי לֹא אֵצֵא חָפְשִׁי. וְהִגִּישׁוֹ אֲדֹנָיו אֶל־הָאֱלֹקִים וְהִגִּישׁוֹ אֶל־הַדֶּלֶת אוֹ אֶל־הַמְּזוּזָה וְרָצַע אֲדֹנָיו אֶת־אָזְנוֹ בַּמַּרְצֵעַ וַעֲבָדוֹ לְעֹלָם.

"But if the bondsman shall say, 'I love my master, my wife, and my children — I shall not go free'; then his master shall bring him to court and shall bring him to the door or to the doorpost, and his master shall bore through his ear with the awl, and he shall serve him forever" (Shemos 21:5-6).

"I Was So Thirsty"

R' Yaakov Galinsky

The laziness in today's world is increasing. People are even becoming too lazy to calculate two plus two. Instead, they press buttons on a calculator to get the answer. Put your head to work! No. Today, we don't put our heads to work.

When I studied in the yeshivah of Novaradok, they told the story of a farmer who placed a sack of flour over his shoulder and made his way from the village to the city. On his way, he began to think about what he was doing. A farmer's profundity ...

Thoughts rolled about in his head:

"I need my feet in order to walk all this long way from the village to the city. I must have them.

"Hands, now — what do I need hands for?" He pondered, until he had the answer: "I also need my hands, because without my two hands, would I have been able to load this sack of flour onto my shoulder?

"My back — do I need that? Certainly. After all, the sack is lying over my shoulder and back.

"But my head ... That's something I don't understand. What do I need that for?!"

He continued walking along the way, and finally realized that he'd erred. "I made a mistake. Of course I need my head. If I didn't have a head, where would I put my hat?" Now all was clear. He understood why he had feet, hands, a back, and a head.

You're laughing, but I'm speaking seriously. Why do we need a head these days, if we don't use it? Only to wear a hat?! We are too lazy to think. There is a terrible laziness — in Torah study, too.

These days we have beautifully printed *sefarim* and sets of *Shas*. What don't we have nowadays? In the old days, when we sat in yeshivah, we had to work hard. Sometimes, after hours of study, we would suddenly discover a printing error. For example, the Zhitomir *Shas* would have one letter that we pored over for hours until it turned out that the author of the *sefer* on the *Acharonim* who had written those words had been using a Vilna *Shas*, and all the questions fell away. Today, we have galleys and proofs of all the various printings of the Talmud, and every other possibility that exists. I'm not complaining about that, but we *could* wonder and complain about why people don't exert their minds enough. In our generation, the mind is being diminished.

And not only is the mind being diminished, but so is inwardness as a whole. The heart, too, has been weakened as the external and the superficial rise to power. Where has the inner life gone? Where is our *yiras Shamayim* hiding?

We must make greater use of our hearts and minds if we want to be different from that farmer.

And now, *morai v'rabbosai*, let's talk a bit about the *parashah*. About the *pasuk*, "I love my master, my wife, and my children." About the heart of a bondsman.

☞ The Gentile on the Train

Chazal tell us (*Yoma* 35b) that when the poor, the wealthy, and the wicked are brought to judgment, the poor man will be asked,

"Why did you not engage in Torah study?" He will answer, "I was busy earning a living." So they will show him Hillel Hazaken, who was destitute. Lacking a coin with which to gain admission to the *beis midrash*, but loath to miss the *shiur*, he climbed up to the roof to listen from there. He could have learned at home, but he wished to grow in wisdom by listening to the *shiur* — to the point of genuine self-sacrifice. While we might ask ourselves, "What's so terrible about missing one *shiur*?" Hillel, apparently, thought otherwise. In short, the poor man will be shown Hillel Hazaken and will be asked, "Were you poorer than he was?" So the Gemara tells us.

The rich man, too, will be brought to judgment. "Why didn't you engage in Torah study?" he will be asked. And he will answer, "I was busy with my business affairs and could not set aside time for learning Torah." They will take him to see R' Elazar ben Charsum, of whom it is said that his father bequeathed him a thousand towns on dry land along with a thousand ships at sea. And every day, he would take a measure of flour on his back and go from city to city and from place to place to learn Torah. Once, his servants found him and tried to press him into service. He told them, "Please, let me go so I can go learn Torah!" They said, "By the life of R' Elazar ben Charsum, we won't let you go!" He had never even seen them, for he sat and learned Torah all day and night.

Then they will bring the wicked man in for judgment. "Why didn't you engage in Torah study?" He will excuse himself with a new argument: "I was burdened by my *yetzer hara*." A new notion. "The *yetzer hara* started up with me; he grabbed me and said, 'Sir, you have nowhere to run. You're caught!' What was I to do?" So says the wicked one. And do you think his words are groundless?

Akiva ben Mahalalel said, "Look at three things and you will not fall into the hands of sin." Why, one may ask, does he put it in these terms? Why not simply state, 'and you will not sin'? Why 'the hands of sin'? Does sin have hands?"

Yes, it does. R' Eliyahu Lopian explains in a profound way. Akiva ben Mahalalel does not assure us that if we look at three things we will never fall into sin. A person may, unfortunately, stumble into transgression. But Akiva ben Mahalalel is ready to guarantee one thing: If one looks at these three things, his sin will never have hands. Because sin has hands! "*Aveirah goreres aveirah* — one sin drags another in its wake." However, if one sets his mind to comtemplating three things — "Where did you come from, and where are you going, and before Whom are you destined to render judgment?" — then even if he does fall into sin, he will retain the strength to flee from sin. He will be able to run away from its groping hands.

Here is a story that I've told numerous times. When I was in Russia, we were taken from place to place. We boarded trains that traveled long distances. They were freight trains, which made falling asleep at night very difficult. Each car had three ledges, one on top of another, on which we were supposed to sleep. Some of the passengers climbed onto these to sleep, while others preferred to lie on the floor.

One night, I felt deeply exhausted and wanted to rest a little. But the moment I fell asleep, one of the gentiles began to shout from his perch on a ledge: "I'm so thirsty! I need a drink!" He shouted and shouted and wouldn't allow anyone to sleep. "Oh, I'm thirsty. I need a drink so badly!"

Seeing that he would give us no rest, I went over to the man and said, "Give me your kettle." He handed me the vessel, which I filled with water and handed back to him. Being so very thirsty, he proceeded to gulp down the whole thing like a wild beast.

I was satisfied that the episode was over. Silence reigned for a few minutes. I dozed off. Suddenly, the whole thing started up again. The gentile began talking to himself out loud: "Oh, how thirsty I was. Oh, how badly I needed a drink of water! I was so thirsty!..."

Here is an example of someone who is burdened by his *yetzer*. The problem is solved; why continue to wallow in it? Why keep the brain busy with nonsense? That's what we tell a person: O.K., you stumbled into sin. But why do you continue hanging around with it? Run away! Don't just stand there shouting, "*Oy*, I was thirsty!" "*Oy*, I drank!" Turn over a new and better leaf, and flee from yesterday's sin.

⌐ "I Love My Master"

When the police arrest any criminal, even a most accomplished one, the first thing they do is have him examined by a psychiatrist to see if he's sane, for if found to be mentally ill he is absolved from punishment. *Chazal* tell us (*Sotah* 3a), "No person does a sin unless a spirit of foolishness enters into him." In other words, our Sages are telling us that if a person sins, he's not quite sane. Do you hear that?

In that case, the question arises: Why can't every sinner absolve himself with the excuse, "I'm not normal! What does *HaKadosh Baruch Hu* expect from me?" How interesting to contemplate that, according to *Chazal*, so many abnormal people are walking around our cities.

The answer is as follows. When committing the first sin, a person is not a complete fool, but only subject to a spirit of foolishness that has entered into him. If he suffers a temporary nervous attack, when the attack passes what is he to do? Ask for help, from his parents, or his rebbi: "Get me to a doctor or give me some medicine." His father or rebbi may ask him, "What happened? What brought on the attack? What, exactly, led you to behave in such a crazy manner?" And he will answer, "I saw so-and-so" or, "I saw such and such." Then they'll administer some sort of tranquilizer (spiritual in nature) and the episode will pass.

However, *rabbosai*, if a person "commits a sin and repeats it" — if the spirit of foolishness that initially entered into him does not dissipate, but rather continues to animate his actions until he sinks further and further — then he becomes "abnormal" in a more complete way. "If a person commits a sin and repeats it, it becomes like something permissible to him." He has been seized by the hands of the sin and has become less than sane, ruining his health and running after foolishness day and night. Madness has ensnared him.

There is a tangible illustration of this in our *parashah*. "*I love my master, my wife, my children — I shall not go free.*" He committed a sin and repeated it, until servitude feels good to him. Have you ever

met someone who wanted to be a servant? Here is this poor fellow
— a "*nirtza*," a servant whose ear was pierced as a symbol of volun-
tary servitude — who has sunk firmly into the hands of sin!

Some individuals will be rebuked, an accusing finger pointed at
them: "You know how weak you are and in what sort of state. Why
didn't you call for help? Why didn't you try to change until now, as
you descended into the coils of *aveirah*? By now, you've reached a
state where you feel comfortable with degradation, like that servant
who was unwilling to leave the mud behind even when everyone
mocked him. His good sense deserted him, and he cried piteously,
"But I love my master!..."

The Gemara (*Yoma* 39a), says, "You shall not pollute yourseves
and become polluted by them." If a person pollutes himself a little,
he becomes greatly polluted. If he courts corruption in this world,
— he will be found corrupt in the World to Come. "*You shall make
yourselves holy and become holy.*" If a person courts holiness just a bit,
he is granted a great deal of holiness.

May Hashem help us not fall into the hands of sin.

כָּל־אַלְמָנָה וְיָתוֹם לֹא תְעַנּוּן. אִם־עַנֵּה תְעַנֶּה אֹתוֹ כִּי אִם־צָעֹק
יִצְעַק אֵלַי שָׁמֹעַ אֶשְׁמַע צַעֲקָתוֹ.

*"You shall not cause pain to any widow or orphan. If you
[dare to] cause him pain...! — for if he shall cry out to Me, I
shall surely hear his outcry"* (Shemos 22:21-22).

CAUTION!

R' Sholom Schwadron (*in a talk to yeshivah bachurim*)

R' Eliyahu Lopian told us a story that he heard from a student of R' Yisrael Salanter, *Hagaon* R' Naftali Amsterdam.

There came a period of time when R' Naftali noticed that R' Shmuel Salanter had changed his usual routine. He questioned his rebbi as to the meaning of this change (as R' Shmuel had always been very scrupulous to maintain his ways).

R' Shmuel replied that his wife had hired a widow as a live-in housekeeper. If he were to wake early to leave the house, the widow would be forced to rise as well, in order to lock the door after him from the inside. Therefore, he now refrained from rising at his usual early hour, in observance of the dictum, *"You shall not cause pain to any widow or orphan."* And R' Shmuel proceeded to enumerate several other ways in which he had altered his routine for fear of transgressing this prohibition in even the smallest way.

When he was done, he added, "And if you suggest, R' Naftali, that I fire her (respectably) so that I may benefit, that would mean that it is forbidden to allow a widow or orphan into a Jewish home, lest they be pained. How can we possibly say that?"

This is how great people exercise caution in every aspect of their behavior.

But let me tell you something. This is no fantasy, but an actual story that happened.

A certain young yeshivah man, who lived far away in a different city, once came to Yerushalayim for Succos. His wife's family lived there, and the wife had pleaded with her husband to come with her to spend the first days of Succos at her mother's house. The mother was a widow.

The husband, naturally, agreed to the plan.

They arrived in Yerushalayim on the afternoon of *erev Succos*. The first thing the young man did was go out to inspect the *succah*. To his dismay, he found that it was not built according to the requirements of the Chazon Ish. He didn't approve.

So upset was he that, had there been sufficient time, he would have returned to his own city. But it was late. *Yom Tov* was approaching.

What did he do? That night, the first of Succos, he went and ate in someone else's *succah*!

How did his widowed mother-in-law react? She cried. And the man's wife? She, too, wept bitterly. But he ate in a Chazon Ish-style *succah*.

Hagaon hatzaddik, R' Yisrael Fisher, related this episode with a bitter smile. " *'You shall not cause pain to any widow or orphan'* is not stated in the writings of the Chazon Ish (rather, this is a verse in the Torah itself), but a *succah is* mentioned by the Chazon Ish!" Do you hear? *Gevald.*

What, you may ask, is my complaint against that young man? After all, he was simply scrupulous about building a *succah* according to the guidelines set down by the Chazon Ish. His error was in not understanding that eating in a *succah* without these stringencies carries no danger of transgressing a Torah prohibition, while *"You shall not cause pain to any widow or orphan"* is a very serious matter. He simply didn't know.

This teaches an important lesson. If you don't know, don't be a stickler in rulings that impinge upon the serious and awesome area of causing pain to family members and widows. For example, a man walks into this yeshivah, goes over to a *bachur*, and says, "I have a question. I fried some fish in a pan, and when I was done I noticed that the pan had some pieces of meat in it as well. What must I do? May I eat the fish, or must I throw the whole thing out?"

Shamefaced, the *bachur* would answer, "I don't know. I'm not a *posek*. I'm not a *rav*."

In these terms, the young man in our story of the *succah* deserves to be beaten and mortified: "You know that you are neither a *rav* nor a *posek*, yet you take it upon yourself to rule that it's all right to cause pain to a widow? Why didn't you ask? Why didn't you harbor any doubts? Now see what a serious sin you've committed: a widow's tears, and your own wife's." (By the way, I've heard that the young man did regret what he'd done and expressed great remorse afterward.)

Sometimes, in the area of *lashon hara* or other matters dealing with interpersonal behavior, a question will arise. Am I permitted to speak *lashon hara* in this case? That's when a *bachur* may decide to become a *posek* and rule that it is permissible. Where did he see that? Where did he learn such a thing?

"*The fruit of a tzaddik is the tree of life.*" If it is not a tree of life, it is not Torah. And if one does not study *mussar*, the Torah will not be a tree of life. Yes, yes! I heard the following from my rebbi, and from R' Berel, who heard it from the Chofetz Chaim. Once, the Chofetz Chaim inquired about a certain yeshivah, "Do they learn *mussar* there?" When they answered, "No," he stated, "Then there's nothing to be hoped for from there." Neither more nor less.

"Do not pervert the judgment of your destitute person in his grievance"(23:6). Why does it say this? [Elsewhere,] it already says, "Do not glorify the poor person in his grievance (23:3)"... [Rather, this refers to the case of] a wicked man and a righteous one who stand before you in judgment. Do not say, "Because he is a rasha, I will turn the judgment away from him." Therefore, it says, "Do not pervert, etc." (Yalkut, remez 352).

To Pervert Ben-Gurion's Judgment

R' Sholom Schwadron

*A*s you all know, the Chofetz Chaim traveled extensively to sell his *sefarim*. I knew a person who claimed to have met the Chofetz Chaim about 100 years ago, during one of these trips.

They say that on one trip, when he was a middle-aged man, he stayed in a certain Polish town during the week. On *erev Shabbos*, he was in a quandary as to where to hide the purse containing his money. Finally, he decided to entrust the purse to the *rav* of the town.

That Shabbos, he stayed in the *rav's* house, handing the *rav* his money on *erev Shabbos* for safekeeping.

The Chofetz Chaim was already famed as a *tzaddik*. The *rav* of the town noted to himself that his guest had entrusted the money to him without witnesses, which is not a halachically sound move. "When he asks for the money back," the *rav* decided, "I will whisper, 'How did you come to do such a thing? You made a mistake with reference to an explicit Gemara!' "

The *rav* waited patiently. Shabbos came to an end, *Motza'ei Shabbos* passed, and it was Sunday morning. The *rav* understood that the Chofetz Chaim planned on resuming his journey and leaving the town. Indeed, after *Shacharis* and a bit of breakfast, the Chofetz Chaim thanked his host, showered him with blessings and praise, and was ready to part in peace.

The *rav* kept waiting for the Chofetz Chaim to ask for his money. But the Chofetz Chaim said nothing.

The *rav* watched his guest complete his packing, kiss the *mezuzah*, and leave the house. The *rav* accompanied him, keeping his mouth closed and wondering how all this would end.

The Chofetz Chaim crossed the yard and reached the street, where they would really part ways. He held out his hand in farewell. Unable to restrain himself any longer, the *rav* asked, "*Nu*, what about the money?"

"What money?"

"You gave me money ..."

Even before the *rav* could finish, the Chofetz Chaim said, "Because I entrusted it to you without witnesses, I relinquished my claim on the money."

Deeply struck by this, the *rav* said, "All right, it's true that there were no witnesses. I am impressed to see that you thought of doing what you did. But now, here's your money. Please, take it." He withdrew the purse from his coat and held it out to the Chofetz Chaim.

"No!" the Chofetz Chaim said. "I thought it over and gave the money up in retrospect. Not only if you would deny that I gave it to you, heaven forbid, but regardless."

"But here's the money!" protested the *rav*.

"I gave it up," the Chofetz Chaim insisted.

"Then I'm giving it to you as a gift."

"Heaven forbid! 'He who hates gifts shall live!' " With that, the Chofetz Chaim passed through the gate, without the money. Following him, the *rav* suggested that they donate the full amount to charity. And that's what they did. The entire sum was given to *tzeddakah*. Do you grasp the greatness of *gedolei Yisrael* when it came to money? Financial integrity was one of the cornerstones of their lives.

I once told a story about the Chofetz Chaim and connected it to a *pasuk* in our *parashah*. The *derashah* took place between *Shacharis* and *Mussaf* on Shabbos, *Parashas Mishpatim*. Following that talk, several of the listeners tried to prevent me from delivering the priestly blessing during *Mussaf*. They claimed that a person such as myself has no *ahavas Yisrael*, and so is not permitted to lift his hands and say, '*Who has commanded us to bless His nation, Israel, with love.*"

What was it that I said in that *derashah*?

I opened with the well-known story (whether it's true or not, I don't know, but this is what they say) that took place during the period of the Chofetz Chaim's travels. A certain thief in Warsaw stole his purse, containing the money he had earned from the sale of his *sefarim*. The Chofetz Chaim, realizing that the man was a Jew, ran after him. And as he ran, people heard him calling loudly to the thief, "I forgive you! The money is yours!" (The Chofetz Chaim knew that he would not be seeing either the purse or its contents again. In this way, he prevented the Jew from having perpetrated a serious theft.) "It's yours!" He shouted this in the street so that the thief would not be in possession of stolen money — and so that, when he later repented, he would not have to wander for years looking for him to repay him.

"Now, imagine to yourselves," I said in shul that day, "that the Chofetz Chaim had taken Ben-Gurion to court. The judges would doubtless recognize both of them. On one side, they see a litigant who is scrupulous about even the shadow of a shadow of theft, and who goes so far as to care about the halachic status of a pathetic thief from Warsaw. On the other side is Ben-Gurion, who is capable of uttering many untruths. Both of them stand up in judgment.

It is possible to decide the verdict with absolute confidence: If the Chofetz Chaim claims that Ben-Gurion owes him money, he is certainly speaking the truth. But the Torah says that this is not the way we render a judgment in our holy Torah. "Do not pervert the judgment of your destitute person in his grievance ... [If] a wicked man and a righteous one who stand before you in judgment. Do not say, "Because he is a *rasha*, I will turn the judgment away from him!"

There is no prior reasoning. Absolutely none! You must render a verdict according to halachah. We have the *Shulchan Aruch* that contains section upon section, investigations and examinations, witnesses and proofs. The *Shulchan Aruch* does not say that if one litigant is a *tzaddik* and the other is a *rasha*, the *tzaddik* wins. Nothing of the sort is written there.

But the group of listeners in the shul were furious at my alleging that Ben-Gurion was capable of telling many untruths and wanted to prevent me from offering the *Birkas Kohanim*!

Whatever happened, happened, but the concept is a true and wonderful one.

פרשת תרומה
PARASHAS TERUMAH

וְעָשׂוּ לִי מִקְדָּשׁ וְשָׁכַנְתִּי בְּתוֹכָם. כְּכֹל אֲשֶׁר אֲנִי מַרְאֶה אוֹתְךָ אֵת
תַּבְנִית הַמִּשְׁכָּן וְאֵת תַּבְנִית כָּל־כֵּלָיו וְכֵן תַּעֲשׂוּ.

"They shall make a Sanctuary for Me — so that I may dwell among them — like everything that I show you, the form of the Tabernacle and the form of all its vessels; and so shall you do" (Shemos 25:8-9).

THE SECRET OF THE BEGINNING OF PARASHAS TERUMAH

R' Yaakov Galinsky

There is a seemingly amazing *midrash* (*Yalkut Tehillim* 346), in which *HaKadosh Baruch Hu* comes, as it were, to complain to David Hamelech.

David Hamelech had pleaded with Hashem: *"One thing I ask of Hashem, that I shall seek: that I dwell in the House of Hashem all the days of my life ...*" Hashem said to David, "You started out by saying that you would ask for one thing — and suddenly, you added a long list: '*to behold the sweetness of Hashem and to contemplate in His Sanctuary ... He will hide me in His Shelter on the day of evil,*' and so forth."

Said David, "Master of the Universe, I learned from You. I am a good student. You said, '*What does Hashem, your God, ask of you but to fear Him,*' and so on. Then the Torah adds a few other things: '*To fear Hashem, your God, to walk in all His ways and to love Him and to serve Hashem, your God, with all your heart and with all your soul*'!"

An amazing *midrash*.

⌖ "One Thing" — "I Ask"

The commentaries wonder about David Hamelech's intent in using this terminology: "One thing I ask." Why did he express himself in this fashion? They suggest an answer that is sweeter than honey:

"One" refers to the *neshamah* — the soul. "I ask" ("*sha'alti*") implies that he has become a "*sho'el*" — a borrower.

A person's soul is referred to by four names: "*nefesh,*" "*ruach,*" "*neshamah,*" and "*yechidah.*" "*Achas sha'alti* — one thing I ask" refers to the "*yechidah*" aspect of the soul. That is, I am not a "*shomer chinam,*" an unpaid custodian, or a "*shomer sachar,*" a paid custodian. I am a "*sho'el,*" a borrower.

There are several categories of "*shomrim*" custodians, among them are: a "*shomer chinam*" who is not paid for the job, and who is responsible for loss if he was neglectful in his custodianship but freed from responsibility if the object under his care is lost or stolen. There is a "*shomer sachar,*" or paid custodian, who bears responsibility in the case of loss or theft but is not responsible for accidents beyond his control ("*oness*"). A borrower is responsible even in the case of such accidents, but not if an animal he borrowed dies in the normal course of its work. These laws are well known; you learned them in school.

And now, *morai v'rabbosai*, at that difficult hour when the Heavenly Court will ask a person, "Why did you sin? Why did you distress the members of your household? Why did you not go to shul? Why did you not study Torah?" a person will answer, "I did not commit a sin. I was a victim of circumstances beyond my control. Please, leave me alone and don't permit the destructive angels to punish me! I was an *oness*!"

The problem is, "*Achas sha'alti*" — one thing I ask." He is in the position of a borrower *vis-à-vis* his soul, and a borrower *is* responsible for circumstances beyond his control. "No excuses!" the Heavenly Court will declare. "Being an *oness* does not absolve you here." We live in this world as "borrowers" who are responsible even under such conditions.

What sort of protection do we have, then, to save us from being punished for our sins? What can we do to help ourselves? There is one escape hatch: "*If its owner is with him, he will not pay.*"

According to Jewish law, if the owner himself is involved in the business, then the borrower is acquitted as well. As the well-known *mishnah* states: "One who borrows [something] and also borrows its owner along with it, or else rents the owner['s services] along with it, is acquitted, as it says, '*If its owner is with him, he will not pay.*'" Therefore, the solution, as it were, is to join in partnership with the Creator. "*I shall dwell in their midst* — within each one's heart." When Hashem resides within him, a person may be acquitted even under such circumstances for, "*If its owner is with him, he will not pay.*"

The *Sefas Emes* mentions this with reference to the wicked Bilaam, who said (*Parashas Balak*), "*He perceived no iniquity in Yaakov, and saw no perversity in Israel.*" In other words, *HaKadosh Baruch Hu*, as it were, does not focus on the sins of the Jewish nation. Why not? Because, "*Hashem, his God, is with him!*" And, as we have said, "*If its owner is with him, he will not pay.*"

Now we can understand David Hamelech's request: "*One thing I ask of Hashem, that I shall seek: that I dwell in the House of Hashem all the days of my life.*" He made one very big request: "*that I dwell in the House of Hashem all the days of my life.*" In this way, he asks, as it were, to be Hashem's partner. Then he will receive protection against suffering: "*He will hide me in His shelter on the day of evil.*" Why? Because, "*If its owner is with him, he will not pay.*" He will escape all travail. "*He will hide me in His shelter on the day of evil.*"

(I have also heard a slightly different explanation. David Hamelech asked for one thing: "*that I dwell in the House of Hashem*"... "*if its owner is with him.*" However, incorporated within this major request are many additional details, for whoever has Hashem has everything.

David said to *HaKadosh Baruch Hu*: "I learned from You to make one large request that includes additional details; just as You demanded '*yiras Shamayim*' from us, which includes everything." Indeed, this was David Hamelech's wisdom: He knew enough to ask for the primary thing upon which many other good things are based, and through which we gain the world and everything in it.)

* * *

☞ All Are Kohanim

To be truly close to Hashem is our mission:
"Its owner with him."

I once heard a story from the rabbi of a shul in the United States. A strange thing happened to him. One Yom Kippur, a certain person attended the synagogue as he did every year on that day (and only on that day). Just before *Mussaf*, this Jew approached the rabbi and said, "Rabbi, take this check for $500. I want to be a Kohen."

The rabbi looked at him in astonishment. "What?!"

The man, whose entire consciousness was bound up in money and the monetary value of things, thought that perhaps $500 was too little to pay for such an honor. At once, he said, "Okay, I'll write a check for a thousand dollars. I'm very interested in becoming a Kohen — at least this Yom Kippur. Next year, we'll see."

Naturally, the rabbi refused. The man raised his offer to $2000. Unable to restrain himself, the rabbi burst out, "I can't imagine what you're thinking! Why do you insist on being a Kohen? If you were a regular shul-goer, maybe. But as things stand ...?"

The ignorant man replied, "I'll tell you the truth, Rabbi. My grandfather was a Kohen. My father was a Kohen. I want to be like them. I also want to be a Kohen!"

The rabbi smiled. "Well, in that case, it'll only cost you $500 ..."

We haven't come here today to tell jokes, but the opposite: to state that every person can be a Kohen, without paying a penny.

In *Parashas Yisro*, we are told, "*You shall be to Me a kingdom of ministers ('mamleches Kohanim') and a holy nation.*" The question is asked: How can everyone be a Kohen? Is it possible to acquire that status with money or through some other means?

The answer is: Yes.

"*You shall be to Me a kingdom of ministers and a holy nation. These are the words that you shall speak to the Children of Israel.*" This was the short speech that Moshe Rabbeinu was asked to deliver to *Bnei Yisrael* before the giving of the Torah. What was so important about these words, that they served as a precursor to *Matan Torah*? What message was hidden in Hashem's declaration that "*You shall be to Me a kingdom of ministers and a holy nation*"?

With reference to *korbanos* — ritual offerings — we tend to think that part of the *Korban Olah* is, as it were, given to the High Table in heaven, while another part is assigned to the Kohanim. There are other offerings in which the animal's owner also partakes of the meat.

This view is erroneous.

The Gemara says that Kohanim eat, as it were, at Hashem's High Table. In other words, the entire *Korban Olah* is given to the High Table, and then Hashem doles out a portion to the Kohanim seated around His Table. Personally, they have nothing of their own. Everything they have, they receive from *HaKadosh Baruch Hu*.

Rabbosai. As the time for *Matan Torah* approached, Hashem informed us that we, too, can be Kohanim! We can be sanctified as a "holy nation" and eat from the High Table. Observe the Torah as it should be observed, in all its detail, and you will all merit being a kingdom of ministers. In fact, *Chazal* tell us (in another place) that a certain verse starts out talking about the *Mizbe'ach*, the Altar, and ends with the *Shulchan*, the Table. This is to teach us that "as long as the *Beis HaMikdash* existed, the *Mizbe'ach* atoned for a person. But if there is no *Beis HaMikdash*, a person's own table atones for him." That is, my table at home can be a *mizbe'ach*, with my bread as a *korban* and my wine as the poured libation. Jews, being a "*mamleches Kohanim*" — a kingdom of ministers — can all eat at the High Table, sleep in Hashem's house, walk through His rooms, and stroll through His gardens. We are tourists in someone else's house. And all this occurs when we fulfill the precept of "*its owner with him*" and "*I shall dwell in their midst.*"

And if you are a guest in Hashem's hotel, you do not introduce forbidden things into your dwelling place. If someone tries to sell you things that do not comply with Hashem's will, tell him, "Do you think I'm the owner here? This house is not mine, except for tax purposes. This house belongs to Hashem, and I have no more authority than a guest. I will not bring something into Hashem's House that He does not want there!"

* * *

☞ *Hidden Treasure*

R' Elazar, in *Midrash Shir HaShirim* (*Shir HaShirim Rabbah* 1), says: "If you seek it like money, if you search for words of Torah as for hidden treasure, *HaKadosh Baruch Hu* will not deny your reward. This is comparable to a person who has lost a gem in his house. He lights several candles and torches until he finds it. If he does this much to find something that is part of the temporal world, how much more so with the words of Torah, which are linked to life in both this world and the next? Are we not obligated to seek them out like hidden treasure?"

The *midrash* continues: "R' Elazar said, 'No one has ever come to the *beis midrash* before me, nor has anyone ever left it after me. Once, I woke up early and found the trash collectors and straw gatherers outside. I said, 'If you will seek it like money and like hidden treasure, then you will understand fear of heaven. We are not even like trash collectors and those who gather straw.' " Do you hear?

In that *beis midrash* in the time of our great Sages, he was the first to open the doors and the last to close them at night! Then, suddenly, he saw that those who collect refuse and straw had risen even earlier than he. Distressed, he expressed a desire that we may equal their achievement.

Gems, concealed in the words of *Chazal*! Suppose a person seeks money and doesn't find it, and then goes into a grocery store to buy milk and cheese. "Where is your money?" the shopkeeper will ask. He answers, "I searched for some, but didn't find it. Believe me, I looked everywhere. Who could have done more?"

The grocer will tell him, "Sir, you may have conducted a wonderful search but here in this grocery, we don't buy things with good intentions."

When it comes to Torah, however, we are rewarded even for the search. As *Chazal* teach, "If a person intends to do a *mitzvah* and is prevented from doing so, it is considered as though he's done it." If only we sought Torah as diligently as businessmen seek money. If only we'd get up for *davening* the way shopkeepers rise early to tend to their stores. If we'd do that, the profit would be twofold: Apart from the Torah that we would acquire, we would also receive a reward for our intention and our search! Moreover, even if we end without accomplishing a thing — if we rose early to learn Torah but did not succeed, or woke early to go to shul but found the shul closed — we are rewarded as though we had done it. This is what the *midrash* means when it says, "If you search for words of Torah as for hidden treasure, *HaKadosh Baruch Hu* will not deny your reward." Your reward, for the search itself.

When making a *siyum* at the end of a tractate, we say, "We toil and receive a reward, but they toil and do not receive a reward. We want and they want ... We rise early and are rewarded, while they rise early and do not receive a reward." What is this trying to say? A shopkeeper gets up early to sell his wares, but the only payment he receives is for what he sells, not for the early rising. A Jew, on the other hand, "rises early and is rewarded." Even if, heaven forbid, nothing comes of his rising early, he is rewarded for it anyway.

A person can learn and learn and not understand a thing or reach a single halachic conclusion but that is not his concern. "If he is prevented from doing it, it is considered as if he did it." In fact, the *Chovos Halevavos* says that "the conclusion of a deed is in heaven's hands." You open a Gemara and struggle with it; the rest is not your concern. What you *are* obligated to do is to "intend to do a *mitzvah*" — to desire, to try, and to invest effort.

Let us consider for a moment: Why, actually, do we receive a reward for the search? Why, if a person intends to do a *mitzvah* but is prevented from carrying it out, is he rewarded anyway? If his heart is truly with Hashem — "*its owner with him*" — not only is he absolved if circumstances force him to transgress, but if prevented from doing a *mitzvah* he is still rewarded. Why? Precisely because "*its owner is with him.*" His heart is attuned to Hashem! He did his part, and the rest is in Hashem's hands. If he has done his part, no one demands any more of him.

R' Yehudah Hachassid, in *Sefer Hachassidim*, writes that one who invests effort in learning but finds himself unable to understand anything, will be taught the entire Gemara and will know as much as others — to his eternal happiness.

When a person searches with his heart fully attuned to heaven — when his heart is filled with genuine desire — then he brings HaKadosh Baruch Hu into himself and merits, "*I shall dwell in their midst*" and "*its owner with him.*" And then, "*He perceived no iniquity in Yaakov, and saw no perversity in Israel.*" Hashem does not regard our transgressions.

How fortunate is our lot!

WHAT AMMON AND MOAV SOUGHT IN THE BEIS HAMIKDASH

R' Yaakov Galinsky

*W*hen the gentiles converged on the *Beis HaMikdash* as it was being destroyed, all the nations hastened to search for silver and gold. Ammon and Moav, however, were interested neither in silver nor in gold. What did they want? They wanted the *Sefer Torah*.

"R' Shmuel bar Nachmani said in the name of R' Yonasan, 'When it says, "The enemy's hand was extended over all its delights," this refers to Ammon and Moav. When idol worshipers entered the *Heichal*, everyone turned to the silver and gold, while they turned to the *Sefer Torah*, saying, "This, which says, 'An Ammonite and a Moabite shall not enter the congregation of Hashem,' shall be burned with fire" (*Yevamos* 16b). Ammon and Moav said to themselves, "Let us enter the Holy of Holies and remove the *Sefer Torah*, which states, 'An Ammonite and a Moabite shall not enter the congregation of Hashem' and set it aflame." They could not bear this dictum and wanted to erase the words.'"

Ribono Shel Olam! You accursed gentiles, witnessing the sorry state to which the Jewish nation has fallen, seeing them exiled from Eretz Yisrael, what difference does it make to you what their Torah says? The Jewish people are scorned, they are at your mercy, and you, Ammon and Moav, still crave the possibility of joining the congregation of Hashem?

Apparently, they understood that it is better to be a persecuted Jew than a non-Jew. Better to live as a shattered Jew but to be counted as a member of Hashem's congregation than not to be numbered as one of the Chosen People at all.

See how exalted is the Nation of Israel.

When the nations of the world entered the Holy of Holies, the Gemara (*Yoma* 54b) tells us that they saw the *Keruvim* (Cherubim) embracing each other.

The *Ari Hakadosh* asks: In this *parashah*, it says that the *Keruvim* on the *Kappores* were facing each other. On the other hand, there is another verse that says, "*Their faces were toward the Bayis.*" The Gemara (*Bava Basra* 99a) cites this question and offers an answer.

This is no contradiction, the Gemara says. Both verses are correct. They reflect two different conditions in which the Jewish people may find themselves. When they are behaving in accordance with Hashem's will, the *Keruvim* face each other. However, when they are not fulfilling Hashem's will, the *Keruvim* separate and face the *Bayis*.

In that case, asks the Ari Hakadosh, how is it possible — at the height of the destruction, when Bnei Yisrael contravened Hashem's will and were punished with the burning of the *Beis Hamikdash* — that the *Keruvim* were embracing each other?!

The Ari offers an answer that can be delivered before the Throne of Glory on Rosh Hashanah:

It is true that the people of Israel sometimes act in accordance with Hashem's will and sometimes against it. That is true, with reference to themselves. With reference to the other nations, however, we are *always* in a state of those who perform Hashem's will!

The worst Jew in the world is better than the best non-Jew.

With this, we can begin to understand *Chazal's* words: "*HaKadosh Baruch Hu* said to Hoshea: 'Your children have sinned.' [Hoshea] should have replied, 'They are Your children: the sons of Avraham, Yitzchak, and Yaakov. Have mercy on them!' Not only did he not say this, but he said to Hashem, 'Master of the Universe, the whole world is Yours. Go switch them with another nation!' " (*Pesachim* 87a).

What, the commentators wonder, was Hoshea's intention in making such a statement: "Go switch them with another nation"? They explain that Hoshea was actually saying the following: "Indeed, Your children have sinned. If we look at Your children and see how they have behaved, we see that they have truly sinned. However, 'Go switch them with another nation'; in comparison with the gentiles, they are *tzaddikim!*"

The *midrash* says that, on Yom Kippur, *HaKadosh Baruch Hu* takes all the sins of the people of Israel and pours them onto Eisav's head, as it says, "*Titein avon al avonam* — Add iniquity to their iniquity" (*Tehillim* 69:28). Asks R' Yehonasan Eibeshitz, author of the *Tiferes Yehonasan*: If *HaKadosh Baruch Hu* wishes to atone for His children's sins, does He lack rubbish heaps on which to toss their sins? Must He throw them specifically onto Eisav's head? Is Eisav the best garbage can?

R' Yehonasan explains the meaning differently. When the heavenly prosecutors demonstrate all the many sins of the Jewish people, the defender — the angel Micha'el — retorts, "They are merely learning from Eisav. Eisav is to blame. While there is no denying that the people of Israel are a talented bunch and can sometimes be very adept students, the source of the blame still lies with Eisav."

The guilt is hurled onto Eisav, while *Bnei Yisrael* are spared, for the bottom line is: a Jew is good and upright.

"Who is like Your nation, Israel?"

פרשת תצוה ⟋
Parashas Tetzaveh

וְאַתָּה תְּצַוֶּה אֶת־בְּנֵי יִשְׂרָאֵל וְיִקְחוּ אֵלֶיךָ שֶׁמֶן זַיִת זָךְ כָּתִית
לַמָּאוֹר לְהַעֲלֹת נֵר תָּמִיד.

"Now you shall command the Children of Israel that they shall take for you pure, pressed olive oil for illumination, to kindle the lamp continually" (Shemos 27:20).

A Hole in the Wall

R' Sholom Schwadron

*I*f I didn't tell you from whom I heard the following, you would think I heard it from a *chassidishe* rebbe. After all, I come from a long line of *chassidim*. However, what will be said here today is written explicitly in the Gemara."

So begins R' Sholom Schwadron, a broad smile on his face.

" '*Pressed ... for illumination*' : Crush yourselves over *divrei Torah*."

If you wish to bask in the light of Torah — as in, "*The Jews had light and gladness and joy and honor*," with "light" referring to Torah

(*Megillah* 16b) — become crushed (invest all your time and effort) over words of Torah.

Let me tell you a story.

A Jew once asked the Kotzker Rebbe, "Why doesn't the Rebbe go out into the world to rescue souls? There is so much to be done! Why does the Rebbe remain secluded? True, *chassidim* come to his *beis midrash* and the Rebbe expounds deep Torah concepts to them. But why doesn't he go out into the world?"

The Kotzker Rebbe replied with a parable.

Three wealthy individuals were arrested and thrown into a cramped, dark prison cell that was actually nothing more than a hole in the ground. Who can describe the tortures that were the lot of government prisoners in those days?

Two of the men were clever and intelligent, while the third was a fool.

The guards passed some food into the hole in which the men languished. The foolish prisoner could not manage, in the darkness, to find the food or his spoon or even, sometimes, his own mouth! Everything seemed to fall from his fingers.

Pitying him, one of his fellow prisoners helped him. He would take the foolish one's hand and guide it to the food, and then help him transmit the food from hand to mouth. All day long, he helped his inept cellmate, guiding him at every turn: to stand up, to lie down to sleep, and so on.

The third man just stood aside. He did not help at all.

One day, the second one said to the third, "We are suffering together, here in this hole. You must surely have noticed the efforts I've been making to help this fool many times throughout the day, until he's managed to make some progress. Why haven't you aided my efforts at all? Why do you just stand aside?"

The third man replied, "I'll tell you why.

"We are in the dark. This hole is all darkness. And when darkness reigns and we can't see a thing, you and he toil almost to no purpose. You are investing tremendous effort into teaching him how to eat and how to move, yet it looks as though you'll never be done. He's already been here several weeks and you've worked hard with him, yet he's hardly learned a thing. I, on the other hand, have used the time to dig a hole in the wall with my fingers. When the hole is deep enough, some light will enter the hole. A bit of sunlight will find its way inside. A little bit of light dispels a great deal of darkness. And then, he'll be able to see and he will not need either you or me. He will be able to eat and drink on his own."

Do you understand?

"*The Jews had light and gladness and joy and honor.*" What was the first thing? The light of Torah. One must dig in order to let in the light. If there is Torah, there is light and then there is everything else: gladness and joy and honor. All because the light has penetrated a person!

How do we illuminate ourselves with this light? How do we obtain light from the Torah? Simply, "Crush yourselves over *divrei Torah.*" Toil over the labor of Torah. Engage in the words of Torah.

⌒ Two Hundred "I"s

There is another meaning hinted at in the words, "Crush yourselves"; crush the "I," the ego. Subdue your arrogance. The Torah does not tolerate a person who will not submit. Throw away your "I"! When you learn Torah, you must nullify your ego.

A certain Torah scholar, a man of exceptional understanding who had insight into people, once told me that he'd devised a little test. He counted the number of times that the person with whom he was speaking used the word "I." There wasn't a single person who didn't use the word "I" at least 30 times. And over the course of a full day, everyone used it at least 200 times: "I ate," "I told you," "I ... I ...I." Two hundred times a day! And we all know what is left of all this "I" at the end of the day: worms and maggots. "*Where are you going? A place of dust, worms, and maggots.*"

Someone told me that he had been born only five years earlier. He was referring not to a physical birth, but to the birth of a person; he became a *ba'al teshuvah*. Then he complained, "In the first year, year and a half, or two years, I experienced a great deal of *siyata d'Shemaya* (heavenly assistance) in the most awesome ways. At every turn, in all I did, my new life received help from Above. Help was poured down on me! But later, I started to lose it. The aid was not as forthcoming as it had once been. What happened? Why did this happen to me?"

Here is what I told him.

It says in *Koheles*: "... *nor does bread come to the wise, riches to the intelligent, nor favor to the learned ...*" (*Koheles* 9:11). The simple meaning of these words would indicate that the wise man does not acquire more bread than the foolish one and that many rich men are not very intelligent, for it is not wisdom that brings one's daily bread.

The Kotzker Rebbe asked, "All right, so bread is not acquired through wisdom. But why does the text mention only the wise men? Are they the only ones who do not have bread?"

And he answers his own question: "Yes, They, specifically, are the ones who lose out. They don't get the bread. Why? Because the people say to the 'wise one,' 'You are a great, wise man, so go and find bread for yourself! After all, you seem to know how to manage on your own. Go ahead!'"

The same thing applies to *ruchniyus* — the spiritual side of things.

At the start, you thought you had not yet arrived. You still felt lacking. As long as you thought that way, you received help from Above. Slowly, however, you began to think that you were already a *tzaddik*. "I"... "I"... So Heaven tells you, "If you're a *tzaddik*, you don't need any more help. You have arrived. Fine!" And the *siyata d'Shemaya* dries up.

☞ To Kindle a Lamp

"...pressed... for illumination, to kindle the lamp continually."

We are taught that a *mitzvah* is compared to a "*ner*," and the Torah to light. What is a "*ner*"? It is a receptacle for oil. The Torah is the "light" — that which burns within the receptacle. If the "*ner*," the receptacle for oil, has no light burning inside it, it is nothing. An unlit candle has no purpose. In the same way, if a person performs *mitzvos* but does not set aside time for Torah study or toil in Torah, his performance is not worth anything. That is why the first reference is to "light": "*The Jews had light.*" The light ignites the "*ner*" — "*to kindle the lamp continually*"!

May it be the will of our Father in heaven that we truly merit to kindle a lamp continually — a "*ner tamid*" — and that we merit a full repentance and a complete salvation, speedily in our days. Amen, Amen!

וְאַתָּה תְּצַוֶּה אֶת־בְּנֵי יִשְׂרָאֵל וְיִקְחוּ אֵלֶיךָ שֶׁמֶן זַיִת זָךְ כָּתִית לַמָּאוֹר לְהַעֲלֹת נֵר תָּמִיד. בְּאֹהֶל מוֹעֵד מִחוּץ לַפָּרֹכֶת אֲשֶׁר עַל־הָעֵדֻת יַעֲרֹךְ אֹתוֹ אַהֲרֹן וּבָנָיו מֵעֶרֶב עַד־בֹּקֶר לִפְנֵי ה'.

"Now you shall command the Children of Israel that they shall take for you pure, pressed olive oil for illumination, to kindle the lamp continually. In the Tent of Meeting, outside the Partition that is near the Testimonial-tablets, Aaron and his sons shall arrange it from evening until morning, before Hashem (Shemos 27:20-21).

"Do You Really Love Me?"

R' Sholom Schwadron

hat comes to mind when you hear the words, "*Hinei mah tov u'mah na'im, sheves achim gam yachad*"? ("Behold, how good and how pleasant is the dwelling of brothers, moreover, in unity.") R' Sholom asks the *bachurim* crowded into his room in Sha'arei Chesed.

Friends get together, at a *Simchas Beis Hasho'evah*, a wedding, or the like. They eat a little together, in a spirit of joy and companionship, and sometimes they sing together, "*Hinei mah tov u'mah na'im, sheves achim gam yachad!*"

But *chassidim* tell this story in the name of a certain great rebbe — I don't remember which one — as follows:

There were two villagers. In many villages throughout the world, the custom at the end of a hard day's work is to step into the local pub or tavern for a drink of whiskey.

Evening fell, and two villagers sat in their usual seats in the pub and sipped their drinks after clinking glasses, as was their custom. They drank a quarter of the glass, and then another, nursing those drinks for a full hour, until the whiskey started talking through their mouths. Suddenly, one villager turned to his friend and asked, "Do you love me?"

"Sure, I love you!" The second villager took another swig of his drink.

"Do you know my troubles?" asked the first.

"No."

"So how can you say that you love me? You don't have any idea about the things that are worrying me, what's going through my head, or why I can't fall asleep at night."

The rebbe was moved by the very true words spoken by that villager, and related them to his *chassidim*. He wanted them to understand how and when a person could truly be called an "*ohev Yisrael*" — a lover of Israel.

"*Sheves achim gam yachad*" — brothers dwelling together. At the very least, know what is troubling your fellow Jew. Sense the pain in his heart and understand what's on his mind. That is the minimum requirement for "*sheves achim gam yachad*," as that villager realized.

⮑ The "Yachad" of Moshe and Aharon

However, *morai v'rabbosai*, there exists a higher level of "*sheves achim gam yachad*" — of brothers dwelling together. It is common knowledge that twins, even when very young, often identify with each other's needs. If one cries, so does the other. Even as babies, they enjoy a "*gam yachad*" relationship, with each sensing the other's pain and crying along with him. But Moshe Rabbeinu's "*gam yachad*" was even more than this. It was literal! We can see this in our *parashah*, regarding the two brothers: Moshe Rabbeinu and Aharon HaKohen.

"*Now you shall command the Children of Israel that they shall take for you pure, pressed olive oil for illumination, to kindle the lamp continually.*" Why does the verse read, "*They shall take for you*"? Was the oil designated for Moshe? Wasn't it Aharon, his brother, who lit the Menorah?

The *Or Hachayim* asks this question, and the *Rosh Yeshivah* of the Mirrer Yeshivah stated that the *Shitah Mekubetzes* on *Kerisos* offers an answer as well.

In *Parashas Shemos*, Moshe Rabbeinu declines to go to Egypt at Hashem's behest, saying, "*Shelach na b'yad tishlach* — Please, Hashem, send through whomever You will send!*" (*Shemos* 4:13). The Torah then tells us, "*The wrath of Hashem burned against Moshe, and He said, 'Is there not Aharon, your brother, the Levite? I know that he will surely speak; moreover, behold, he is going out to meet you and when he sees you he will rejoice in his heart.*" At that moment, Moshe Rabbeinu was punished: He would not be the Kohen, but rather the Levite. Aharon, his brother, would receive the *Kehunah* (priesthood).

Rashi, on that verse, is the one who cites this opinion. "R' Yehoshua ben Karchah says, 'Every time the 'burning of God's anger' is mentioned in the Torah, a lasting mark is mentioned with regard to it. But this burning anger has no lasting mark mentioned with regard to it, and we do not find any punishment coming about through that burning anger. R' Yose said to him, 'A mark *is* mentioned with regard to this one, too: that which is implied by the next words of the verse, "*Is there not Aharon your brother, the Levite ...*" — who had been destined to be a Levite, not a Kohen. I had intended that the *Kehunah* would come forth from you, Moshe. Now that you have angered Me, it will not be so. Rather, he will be a Kohen and you will be the Levite, as it says (*Divrei Hayamim* 1 23:14), "*But as for Moshe, the man of God, his sons would be reckoned as the tribe of Levi.*' " In short, by saying, "*Send through whomever You will send*," Moshe was punished and lost the *Kehunah* to his brother, Aharon.

What was Moshe Rabbeinu's reaction to this personal loss? Let's take a look at three verses in *Tehillim* 133: "*Behold, how good and how pleasant is the dwelling of brothers, moreover, in unity. Like the precious oil upon the head running down upon the beard, the beard of Aharon, running down over his garments, so the dew of Hermon descends upon the mountains of Zion ...*' " (vs.1-3).

Who were literally "*gam yachad*" — unified? Moshe and Aharon.

"*Like the precious oil ... running down upon the beard, the beard of Aharon*": This is the oil that Moshe Rabbeinu used to anoint Aharon, and which ran down the beard. Why, it is asked, the use of the double "beard"? Did Aharon have two beards? Rather, the *midrash* tells us that the first refers to Moshe's beard, while "the beard of Aharon" refers to Aharon's beard. What is this meant to tell us?

Our Sages teach us that when Moshe anointed Aharon, and the oil ran from Aharon's head down to his beard like pearl drops, Moshe Rabbeinu grasped his own beard with a sense of actual physical pleasure, as though the oil was running down his own beard. "Moshe was afraid lest, heaven forbid, he may have misused the [holy] oil of anointment." So intensely did he take pleasure in Aharon's anointment to the *Kehunah* that he was afraid he might have misused the oil for his own personal pleasure.

This, *rabbosai*, is how Moshe felt about his punishment, as he anointed Aharon to the *Kehunah*, which had been taken away from him. He took such pleasure in his brother's happiness that he was afraid he had committed the transgression of misusing a holy object!

This is no philosophical meandering. It is the way it was. Awesome. Do we have an inkling into such an exalted level? Were we to live a thousand years, who knows if we could understand how one can achieve such purity of heart? That was what he was like, the man who received the Torah in heaven on our behalf.

⌒ The Dew of Hermon

Because Moshe was concerned lest he had committed a transgression, *HaKadosh Baruch Hu* told him not to worry. *"So the dew of Hermon descends upon the mountains of Zion."* Just as the falling dew on Mount Hermon does not constitute a misuse of a holy object, neither have you done so with the oil of anointment.

"So the dew of Hermon." What is the Hermon? It is a tall mountain that is frosted with ice all year round. Have you ever seen the Hermon? Snow and ice, cold and ice and snow. A reference, then, to dew falling onto any other spot in Eretz Yisrael would bear some meaning, but what sort of impression does dew make when it lands on the snows of Hermon?

Hashem said to Moshe Rabbeinu, "You are worried because you experienced physical pleasure. You have no body: You have purified your body to that extent." Moshe Rabbeinu purified himself until his body was able to ascend to heaven. It was not his soul that ascended, but his body! (The *pasuk* tells us that Moshe neither ate nor drank. Does the soul require food or water? This must, then, refer to a body so purified that it did not require the physical sustenance necessary in this world.) Moshe Rabbeinu did not blast off in a rocket in order to reach heaven and even if he had, he would never have arrived. The Gemara (*Chagigah* 13a) describes traveling the distance from earth to heaven, a process taking many thousands of consecutive years. How did he get there? Through a process of purifying himself and making himself holy, he reached a point where his body did not extract pleasure from this world: *"So the dew of Hermon descends upon the mountains of Zion."*

⌐ No Pleasure from This World

There was a great, holy *rav* in Jerusalem known as R' Nachum Shadiker. R' Nachum would fast from Shabbos to Shabbos, but on Shabbos, he would eat everything he was served. You must understand that had he even eaten only the way the other members of his household did on Shabbos, that would have been amazing in light of his prolonged fasting. The wonder was sevenfold because he sometimes ate even more than the others! He consumed everything that was served him, even if he was inadvertently served more than others had received. He ate it all in honor of the Shabbos.

Once, he spent Shabbos at his brother's home in the city of Rechovot — then a new, religious settlement. (The brother was also a great *tzaddik*.) Rechovot boasted a number of people who could be called "*leitzim*." Told that the emaciated visitor, on principle, ate everything that was put before him at the Shabbos meals, what did they do? They cooked five big kettles of soup and served all of it — 20 bowlsful — to the two brothers.

R' Nachum ate and ate. His brother, seated beside him, tried to do the same, and became violently ill. A doctor was summoned to his side, for he was in real danger. But R' Nachum? He finished his meal in honor of the Shabbos, and on Sunday resumed his fast. Just so you understand a little bit of the level of people such as this ...

Let us return to the business at hand.

Moshe asked whether he, heaven forbid, had misused the fragrant oil of anointment. Hashem reassured him: " '*Behold, how good and how pleasant is the dwelling of brothers, moreover, in unity.*' Just as Aharon, your brother, did not transgress, neither did you."

What are we to take from all of this? We can learn what the Torah is. We can see what sort of exalted world is inhabited by the Torah and by those who study it. Even if you were to fill every space in this *beis midrash* with volumes of original Torah thought, we would still not arrive at even the beginning of the Torah's sweetness. As it is written, "*The Torah of Hashem is perfect.*" After all the thousands of years of commentary, it is still whole and perfect. Nothing is missing.

Oh, how much we still have to learn and to understand about our holy Torah!

How They Became Intoxicated

R' Sholom Schwadron

*A*s bnei Torah, there's something I'd like to tell you.

Rabbosai, "My heart grew hot within me, in my contemplations a fire blazed." Was Purim created in order for us to make fools of ourselves? Is that why we drink? It is true that "a person is obligated to drink on Purim until he doesn't know the difference between 'Cursed is Haman' and 'Blessed is Mordechai.' " But how should a person get drunk? Should his intoxication create confusion and mockery? No!

R' Itzele Peterburger, a student of R' Yisrael of Salant, lay under a table on Purim — yes, literally under a table — and delivered a shmuess. A mussar discourse.

And one year, on Purim, R' Yisrael told his students that today, on Purim, a person is granted everything he asks for. Everyone who sticks out his hand is given. "What are you asking for, Naftali?" he asked his student, R' Naftali Amsterdam.

R' Naftali replied, "I'd like the head of R' Akiva Eiger, the depth of the Nesivos, the breadth of the Ketzos, and the heart of the Rebbe."

"No, no," R' Yisrael said. "The head is yours, the depth is yours, the breadth is yours, and the heart is yours. Work with those." Understand? Don't ask for the minds or hearts of great people. Use your own heart! These were the kinds of things that they heard on Purim.

The Rebbe Reb Zusha once said, "What use would it be to Hashem if I were like Avraham Avinu? So there would be another Avraham Avinu? No. Be Zusha!" Don't seek to be like Avraham Avinu. Be like Zusha. Be who you are meant to be.

"Then Haman said to King Achashverosh, 'There is one nation that is scattered abroad and dispersed among the peoples in all the provinces of your realm'" (Esther 3:8).

KERIAS SHEMA IN THE TRAIN STATION

R' Yaakov Galinsky

When Haman came to Achashverosh to incite him against the Jews, he said, "There is one nation that is scattered abroad and dispersed among the peoples." Asks the *midrash*: "Why the word '*echad*' ('one nation'), which seems unnecessary here? Every nation is 'one,' as opposed to 'two.' Why were the words 'one nation' emphasized?"

The *midrash* explains. Haman and Achashverosh strained to understand the secret of the Jewish people's continued existence. Here is a nation that lives scattered among 127 others and yet, they are one nation. Who or what unifies them? Why, if something happens to the Jews of India, do the Jews of another nation hasten to succor them?

When there was a blood libel in Damascus before World War I, Sir Moses Montefiore was summoned from England to help the Jews of Syria. The king of Syria at the time, meeting him, asked, "Sir, you are from England. What business do you have with a Jew who is in prison in Damascus? Explain this to me. You are English, not Syrian. How can this possibly affect you?" If a Syrian non-Jew had been sentenced to death, would a gentile from India have rushed over to save him? In short, we are a strange people, the Jews. Something unifies us.

Finally, Haman discovered the secret. It is the "*Echad*" — the "One" — that unifies all Jews. From Hodu to Kush, everyone said the same thing: "*Shema Yisrael, Hashem Elokeinu, Hashem Echad!*"

This "*Echad*" weaves us all together.

I have related several times what happened to me during the great war (World War II), when we fled from place to place. The war enveloped us on every side, and all of us sought a train to take us deeper into the heart of the country and out of the war zone. The trouble was, trains were not always available.

One day, I arrived at the train station in Bucharia. I did not have a ticket to continue the journey. Of course, I had no relative or acquaintance in the area to help me, so there was no chance of escape. The sun was sinking in the sky, and I knew that anyone found wandering around at night who was not a local resident would go directly to jail. And from there, to the World to Come.

About half an hour before sunset, I stood wondering what to do. Darkness was fast approaching, and (without a ticket) there was no train to carry me further on my way. Where to turn? If I hid under a bench in the train station, the watchmen would soon discover me.

Suddenly, I spotted an old man sitting at one end of the station, polishing shoes. *Perhaps he is a Jew*, I thought hopefully.

If I asked him, "Are you a Jew," and he was not, I'd be in deep trouble. *Ribono Shel Olam!* I stood helpless, knees shaking with fear. What to do? Then an idea popped into my mind. I approached the man, and in a voice choked with excitement laced with terror, I called out, "*Shema Yisrael, Hashem Elokeinu, Hashem Echad.*" (If he was a gentile, he would not understand what I'd said.)

The shoe-shiner raised his eyes and whispered at me, "*Baruch Shem kevod malchuso l'olam va'ed!*" in the old Bucharian dialect. A Bucharian Jew!

Rabbosai, I hid in that man's home for 11 days. He didn't understand my language, as I was from Poland, and he knew no Yiddish at all. He spoke Bucharian, of which I was ignorant. We communicated through sign language. And I was saved.

One night, with hot tears spurting from my eyes, I thought, *Had he been a gentile, heaven forbid, anything that I might have cried out to him in Polish would have been useless. "Get lost," he would have said, and sent me away not understanding a word. Ribono Shel Olam! What kind of bond did I have with that Bucharian Jew? He didn't speak my language, he didn't know my mother or father, he had never even seen a Jew from Poland before. But both of us, he and I, say the same, "Shema Yisrael." The tears streamed from my eyes, drop after scalding drop. What it is to be a Jew!*

There, in the wilds of Bucharia, I understood the wicked Haman when he said, "*There is one nation that is scattered abroad and dispersed among the peoples.*" On the one hand, the nation is scattered and dispersed throughout the world, among 127 nations. But they draw sustenance from the same air. That is the Torah.

⬅ Without Wings

It is imperative for us to know that the Torah is the connecting link between us all. It is also the oxygen of life for the Jewish people.

Without Torah, not only are we missing something, we have nothing. Without the oxygen of Torah, we suffocate.

In one place, the text says, "*I will increase your offspring like the stars in the heavens.*" Another verse compares the Jewish nation to dust: "*I will make your offspring like the dust of the earth and the sand that is on the shore of the sea.*" Our Sages ask: Are we like stars or like dust? A star rides high above, while dust lies down below.

The Gemara answers: "Fortunate is your lot, Israel. When you rise, you rise to the heavens" — just like stars — "and when you fall, you fall to the dust." Fortunate is your lot!

The commentaries ask an obvious question: We can understand Israel's good fortune in ascending to the level of stars. But where is the good fortune in descending to the dust of the earth? The Maharsha and others answer as follows: The good fortune of the Jewish nation comes about through what the Jew sees in all of this. He sees that, without the oxygen of Torah, he is unable to be even a simple gentile. Without Torah, he is worse than a gentile. He is down in the dust!

Rabbosai, is it not a shameful thing that Frankfurt contains a special prison for Israelis, so that they will not adversely affect the Germans? You are fortunate, Israel. See how you look without Torah. For if, heaven forbid, Jews can be like Germans, Dutchmen, Belgians, or the English, woe unto us. Therefore, *HaKadosh Baruch Hu* has given us a nature that either rises to the skies or sinks very low. This forces us to cling only to Torah.

Chazal compare *Knesses Yisrael* to a dove. Just as a dove has wings, people of Israel have their elders to lead them. There are many beasts and birds who would be something even without wings, but a dove without wings is nothing. Similarly, a Jew devoid of Torah is not a gentile. He is worse than a gentile.

"How fortunate is your lot, Israel!"

These days, we encounter *ba'alei teshuvah* everywhere. From where did this phenomenon arise? It came from "you fall to the dust." There are those who sank so close to the dust that they wondered, *How is it that we are worse than Belgians, worse than Russians? How did this happen to us? There must be something here.* I met one of these individuals in Toronto about a month ago.

I knew a certain jeweler in Toronto, from whom I would receive a nice donation whenever I came to his city to raise funds for our yeshivah. Two years ago, on another visit to Toronto, I walked over to his big jewelry store. To my surprise, there was no *mezuzah* on the doorway. What had happened? I stopped, retraced my steps, and went into a fabric store next door, also owned by a Jew.

"Tell me," I asked, "what happened to that fellow? Why is there no *mezuzah* on his door?"

"He's not here any longer. He sold the business," the shopkeeper told me.

"Who bought the store from him?"

"An Israeli." Do you hear that? Not a Jew — an Israeli.

"An Israeli without a *mezuzah*?!" I decided to go next door and try my luck. After all, the Jew wouldn't kill me if I asked for a donation for the yeshivah. I went in.

To my surprise, I found myself face to face with one of the biggest activists in the Histadrut. He recognized me, too. "Galinsky, what are you doing here?"

"I'm here on behalf of the homeland," I said.

"So what are you doing *here*?" (In other words, he was saying sarcastically, what is a patriot like you, so ardently supportive of the State of Israel, doing here in Toronto?)

"I got tired of getting a letter every month, summoning me to two months of army reserve duty," I joked.

In that relaxed atmosphere, I turned the conversation in a different direction. I asked him, "Here, in another country, maybe I'm allowed to ask you a difficult question. We once met in Ashkelon and had an argument: Should *bnei Torah* serve in the army or not? You are a reserve major in the army. How did you come to leave the country? After all, the State needs you! How much money did the State of Israel spend to train you for your position as an army major and now, you leave? What's the matter with you?" I gave him a lesson in Zionism ...

"Galinsky, stop it," he pleaded.

"I'll stop but the question that really pains me is this: The man who owned this store before you was a local Jewish resident, and there was a *mezuzah* on the door. And you've taken it down! I was sure the store had been sold to a non-Jew!"

Seeing that I had decided to rebuke him, he said quickly, "Rabbi Galinsky, how much did the former owner of this place give you for the yeshivah? I'll give you double. Just go away and stop talking."

I retorted, "I'll give back whatever you give me and go on talk-ing."

His wife, curious as to what was going on, joined our conversa-tion. He introduced me and said that we were both old-time Israelis. I continued to gently chide them: "Here in Toronto, there's no such concept as Israelis. There are Jews. Anyone who doesn't behave like a Jew, who knows what will become of him? If you don't have a shul to go to, who knows what will become of your children?" We parted on friendly terms.

Afterward, I went into the local yeshivah and requested from the *rabbanim* there, "Take care of that fellow."

Then, about a month ago, I met him in Toronto again. I discov-ered that he was going to shul every day. He whispered, "Rabbi Galinsky, you can even stay at my house. We keep kosher now."

What can I tell you? Give a Jew a little "mother's milk," and he comes to life. Poor fellows, what can you expect from them? Their mother was taken away from them. They were deprived of the nour-ishment they needed, the way Achaz did to the nation ...

⌒ *Achaz Knew the Secret*

The *midrash* asks, "Why was he called 'Achaz' (which means 'seized')? Because he seized the shuls and houses of study, saying, 'If there are no kids, there will be no goats; if there are no goats, there will be no flock; if there is no flock, there will be no shepherd; if there is no shepherd, there is no world.' This is what he said: 'If there are no young students, there are no scholars; if there are no scholars, there are no wise men; if there are no wise men, there is no Torah; if there is no Torah, there are no shuls and houses of study; if there are no shuls and houses of study, there is no *HaKadosh Baruch Hu* spreading His *Shechinah* over the world.' What did he do? He got up and locked the shuls and houses of study" (*Vayikra Rabbah* 11). He knew where the secret of the people of Israel is hidden.

The *midrash* then gives another parable. *Chazal's* parables must be read very carefully.

There was an elderly king who was childless. His heir, a young man, always thought to himself, *Well, the old king will soon be dead, and I will reign in his place.* And then, one day — mazal tov! A son was born to the king. Oh, no! All the former heir's plans bit the dust.

What shall I do? he asked himself. *If I kill the child, my head will be forfeited. I will be suspected, investigations will be instituted, and they will discover that I killed the heir to the throne.* A resolve formed in his heart, and he carried it out carefully. Whenever the nurse came to suckle the king's son, he would prevent her from entering, until the child died.

Achaz acted along the same principles. He knew that the Torah allows us to survive as an eternal nation, through every difficulty and every crisis, all exiles and all decrees. The Torah provides the nourishment we need for eternal life. It is our nurse. What did Achaz do? He closed the doors of the *batei midrash*. He did not permit the nurse to enter.

We can ask a question about the midrashic parable. Was the former heir a fool? He refrained from killing the child with his own hands, lest he himself be put to death as a result. In that case, wouldn't he be put to death now, when it was discovered that he had prevented the nurse from coming in to feed the starving child?

The answer is that he did not, heaven forbid, close the door in order to starve the child! No, he would earnestly claim. Naturally, he was concerned about the child's nourishment. He placed a tomato, a dirty cucumber, and other things on the table, and when the nurse arrived he told her, "Look, you are not needed. He doesn't need milk anymore. Leave him alone. He's big enough to get along on his own." The child, being hungry, ate the dirty cucumber and drank some bitter water. He had no other choice. Eventually, he died.

Achaz knew that as long as Israel remained bound to the eternity of Torah, they would not recognize a new king, or a new state, or a new head of state: nothing. They were under the reign of Torah.

How to solve this problem? To forbid them from learning would not work; they would rebel. Achaz decided, therefore, to prevent them as far as possible from studying the Torah, while at the same time placing all sorts of foolish substitutes on the table. Out of hunger, they would slowly, bit by bit, begin to try to nourish themselves from these other things, until the houses of study closed down.

A Jew without Torah tumbles all the way to the dust of the earth, sometimes descending lower than a non-Jew. With Torah, he reaches the heavens — very high indeed.

The Torah unites us and lengthens our lives, in every generation, time, and place. Whether in faraway Bucharia or in the wilds of Siberia, we are one eternal nation. "*O Guardian of the holy nation, protect the remnant of the holy nation; let not the holy nation be destroyed.*"

We all hope and pray that this oxygen will protect our health until the Redeemer comes. When *HaKadosh Baruch Hu* sees that we are trying, that we are doing all we can, He will do His part, and send us *Mashiach tzidkeinu*, speedily in our days. *Amen, amen!*

"And Esther's maidens came, as well as her chamberlains, and told her about it, and the queen was greatly distressed; she sent garments to clothe Mordechai, and to remove his sackcloth from upon him, but he would not accept them. Then Esther summoned Hasach ... and ordered him to go to Mordechai, to learn what this was about and why" (Esther 4:4-5).

A Frozen Rebbi Can't Answer

R' Sholom Schwadron

*M*ordechai learned of all that had been done; and Mordechai tore his clothes and donned sackcloth and ashes." How did Mordechai know? Did he hear it on the radio? "*Mordechai learned of all that had been done*" — from up above! However, were we to elaborate on the meaning of "Mordechai learned," we could be sitting here for two or three hours.

"*And Esther's maidens came ... and told her about it.*" How are we to understand this? Was Esther not aware of the decree against the Jewish people? "*Then Esther summoned Hasach ... and ordered him to go to Mordechai, to learn what this was about and why.*" According to the simple meaning of the verse, she did not understand why Mordechai had suddenly put on sackcloth and ashes and was crying loudly and bitterly in the city streets.

But *Chazal* comment otherwise, saying that Esther did know about the decree. She knew, because she had the power of prophecy. (Esther was one of the seven female prophets in Israel, as enumerated in the Gemara in *Megillah* 14a.) She was certainly aware; and yet, "*Mah zeh v'al mah zeh*" — "What was this about, and why?" She wanted to learn the reason for the harsh decree.

"*Mah zeh*": *Perhaps, she thought, the Jews had denied Hashem, of Whom they had said, "Zeh Keili v'anveihu*" ("*This is my God and I will glorify Him*").

"*V'al mah zeh*": Or perhaps the Jews had denied the two Tablets of the Covenant, about which we are told, "*Mizeh u'mizeh heim kesuvim*" ("*They are written on both sides*").

Mordechai sent word back to her. "*And Mordechai told him of all that had happened to him ("kol asher karahu") and about the sum of money that Haman had promised to pay into the royal treasuries for the annihilation of the Jews.*"

"Israel has not denied *HaKadosh Baruch Hu*," Mordechai told Esther, "nor has Israel denied the Tablets. Rather, the grandson of '*karahu*' has come upon us, as it says, '*Asher korchah baderech*' (Who happened upon you on the way' or, alternatively, 'who made you cold on the way')." She asks the reason for the terrible decree, and his answer is concealed in his message: "The grandson of '*karahu*' has come upon us."

"*Asher korchah*" — The one who took us and put us, so to speak, in the refrigerator. *Chazal* compare this event to a bathtub full of boiling-hot water, too hot for a person to enter. Finally, one godless person leaps in, even though he will be scorched in the process. They rush him to the hospital by ambulance and treat him. Everyone can see how badly he's been burned. Nevertheless, "though he was burned by the boiling water, he cooled it off for others." Now other people will also venture a foot into that tub, for even if he hasn't completely cooled the water, he has certainly cooled off their fear of it.

That is what Amalek did. The Children of Israel left Egypt with a high hand, and faith was strengthened everywhere as all the world witnessed wonders and miracles. The Finger of God, the parting of the Reed Sea, during which all the waters of the world parted as well ... Indescribable! And then, just when the heat of faith was at its peak, "*Amalek came.*" Though they were vanquished by Israel — "*Yehoshua weakened Amalek by the sword*" — they managed to cool things off. They demonstrated that waging war on the Jewish people was conceivable. And, in doing so, they erased from the minds and hearts of all the world many of the miracles and wonders they had witnessed. Therefore, "*Remember what Amalek did to you, on the way when you were leaving Egypt, that he happened upon you on your way.*"

Mordechai sent word to Esther, saying that the Jews had not acted against Hashem or His Torah. Rather, the people of Shushan had become cold — how cold! "The grandson of '*karahu*' came upon them."

What kind of cold are we talking about?

We find an example at the beginning of *Megillas Esther*.

The king threw a party and invited everyone. Two men were in charge of the feast. The first was the wicked Haman. His task was to supervise the representatives of the world's nations and to make sure that the banquet was as lavish as the king had ordered. And the second was Mordechai, to oversee the Jews. The king had the power to coerce, and he appointed Mordechai.

If Mordechai was in charge of the Jews, we may assume that the meat was kosher or rather, superkosher, *mehadrin min hamehadrin*, with every certification in the book! The same goes for the wine. Nonetheless, Mordechai Hatzaddik announced, "Don't go."

Despite his warning, however, 18,500 Jews did attend the banquet of Achashverosh. "Why should we be different?" they asked. "If we're invited to the party, we will go just like everyone else." And they went.

And at the party — well, you all know why Vashti was taken out and killed. I do not need to elaborate on that. The gentiles became drunk, as was their wont. They drank and became intoxicated, and behaved as they behaved. And not only that, but they took the holy vessels from the *Beis HaMikdash* and filled with wine the cups that had once been used for sprinkling blood in the *avodah* of the sacrificial offerings. And the Jews sat by and watched! That was why the decree was imposed. As the Gemara (*Megillah* 12a) tells us, the Jews were sentenced to death.

⬲ *"What Can I Do?"*

Let me tell you a story. It's a true story that I heard from a great person about a student of the Chofetz Chaim.

That student was the *rav* of a city. One day, he went to see the Chofetz Chaim, who asked him, "Well, what's the news in your city?"

The man understood that the Chofetz Chaim was not asking about the price of bread or milk or honey. He was referring to the city's spiritual state.

He sighed.

"What's happening with Shabbos?" the Chofetz Chaim pressed.

"*Oy, oy, oy* — the barbers don't close their shops on *erev Shabbos*, but only after nightfall. And there are other problems with Shabbos observance ..."

"Well, what have you done about it?"

"What can I do? The people don't listen. They don't want to listen. What can I do?"

"And what about family purity?"

"*Oy, oy, oy* — that's even worse. It's very bad."

"Well, what did you do about that?"

"What can I do? They refuse to listen!"

The Chofetz Chaim asked, "And what are you doing about the issue of education for the children?"

"That's in a very bad state. The children are sent to non-Jewish schools. And even in the Jewish schools, what are they learning? Not much. It's a terrible situation. But what can I do? They don't listen, and aren't interested in listening!"

"You couldn't do anything about Shabbos," the Chofetz Chaim said. "You couldn't do a thing about family purity. You couldn't act on behalf of Jewish education. But you could at least have fainted! Why didn't you faint?"

Jews sit by and watch as holy vessels are filled with wine! And where does this take place? In Achashverosh's profane palace, at a feast of degenerate drunkards. They are pouring wine into the holy vessels of the *Beis HaMikdash,* and no one is fainting. "Israel did not deny *HaKadosh Baruch Hu* and they did not deny His Torah. Rather, the grandson of '*karahu*' came upon them." That's why the decree was imposed! "Who made you cold on your way ..." The sin of coldness was the reason behind the terrible decree to decimate, murder, and destroy all the Jews.

My rebbi came up with a good comparison. When a person is sick, a doctor comes in and examines him. If the patient feels hot, the doctor will treat him. However, if the patient feels cool to his touch, the doctor says, "There is nothing to be done." If a person is cold, there is nothing to be done! This was the terrible message that Mordechai sent Esther. We have become cold. *Oy,* cold!

ᴥ A Frozen Rebbi Can't Answer

The following story is true. I was in America about 12 years ago, perhaps longer. A heavy snow fell, with about a meter and a half covering the ground. For a full week, I couldn't leave the house. There was no way to go into the street. Who could walk up to his knees in snow?

After a week, I went out. As I walked, I noticed a man in the distance. He looked like a rabbi. He was dressed like a rabbi, a little on the short side with spectacles on his nose.

I thought to myself, *I came to America, and I may have to speak in his shul. Who knows? He may be the rabbi of an Orthodox shul.* So I greeted him like an American. While he was still some distance away, I called out, "Hello, Rabbi, hello!"

He didn't answer.

What kind of person is this? I wondered. *I don't know you and you don't know me. But I greeted you. Why won't you answer me?*

Well, what could I do? Perhaps he was a proud person. Or maybe he hadn't really heard me so well. I came a few steps closer and nodded my head again. "Hello, Rabbi."

He didn't answer.

Now I became angry. *Why is he behaving this way? Is that any way for a person to act?*

I came even closer and then I realized why he wasn't answering. That "rabbi" had been fashioned by children. He was a snow-rabbi. A rabbi on ice ... a frozen rabbi, who couldn't answer.

Do you understand? He is the one "who came upon you and cooled you off on your way." When that person is a rabbi — but a frozen one — *oy, oy,* you can't expect anything from him.

Hashem will assuredly help us, if only we want it enough. And we will ascend in Torah and *yiras Shamayim* and good *middos,* and merit a full redemption, speedily in our days. *Amen, amen!*

"They were sitting and learning the laws of the mitzvah of Omer, for that day was the sixteenth of Nissan, and on that day the Omer had been offered when the Beis HaMikdash stood. Haman came over to them and asked, 'What are you busy with?' 'With the mitzvah of Omer,' they said. 'And what is the Omer: gold or silver?' They told him, 'It is neither gold nor silver, nor even wheat, but barley.' 'And how much is it worth?' he asked. 'Is it worth 10 talents of gold?' 'It is worth 10 ma'ah (coin of minimal value),' they answered. 'Then stand up!' he said. Your 10 small coins have triumphed over my 10,000 talents of silver!' " (Esther Rabbah, parashah yud).

LAUGHING AT THE WHOLE WORLD

R' Yaakov Galinsky

*C*hazal tell us that when Haman received Achashverosh's order to place Mordechai on the royal steed, he asked where Mordechai was to be found so that he could bring Mordechai to the bathhouse. He was told that, as the head of a yeshivah that numbered 400 students, Mordechai was delivering a *shiur* at that hour.

So Haman went to visit the yeshivah.

The most important prime minister in the world at the time walked into the yeshivah hall. He stood at the side of the *beis midrash* until the *shiur* was over. Then he approached some of the boys and asked, "What are you learning?"

"We're learning the *sugyah* of 'kemitzah,' " the students told him.

"And what is *kemitzah*?"[1]

---

1. [The first of four essential services of a *minchah* (meal) offering. The Kohen closes the middle three fingers of his right hand over his palm and scoops out the flour from the *minchah* to form the *kometz* that is burned on the Altar.]

"When the *Beis HaMikdash* will be rebuilt, and a *korban Minchah* or *Omer* will once again be offered, a *kemitzah* will be taken, and we are learning the laws." It was important to know how to fulfill these laws, as the work of *kemitzah* was a most difficult one that the Kohen would be required to carry out in the *Beis HaMikdash*.

Haman lifted his voice in fear. "Your *kemitzah* has defeated the 10,000 talents of silver that I gave!"

The commentaries ask why Haman became so agitated. Why did the fact that they were studying these particular laws disturb him so? Why did he cry out, "Your *kemitzah* has defeated my 10,000 talents of silver!"?

Rabbosai, listen well.

When informed that Mordechai was delivering a *shiur*, Haman thought to himself, *There is a decree out to destroy and annihilate all of the Jews. In that case, why is he giving a shiur? It must be a class in the laws of sanctifying God's Name. He's probably also telling his students about the World to Come that is ready and waiting for them. At most, perhaps he's teaching them about the prohibition against serving foreign gods, for which one must be willing to die rather than transgress it. There are many such things to learn.* For an edict had gone out to all 127 provinces, commanding that the Jews be destroyed. There would not remain even the memory of a Jew.

Then he walked into the *beis midrash* and asked, "Well, boys, what have you been learning?"

" '*Yibaneh Beis HaMikdash.*' " The *Beis HaMikdash* will be rebuilt!

Ribono Shel Olam! They have all been sentenced to death. The runners had already gone out with the decree to decimate every single Jew. And they are learning about the rebuilding of the *Beis HaMikdash*?!

And I, Rav Galinsky, ask you this: What were Mordechai's students really thinking when they studied the *sugyah* of *kemitzah*?

In their minds and hearts, they were thinking that the edict to "kill and annihilate" might be sent out to every address in the kingdom, but they weren't concerned. They had the Torah, which said that the *Beis HaMikdash* would be rebuilt, and when that happened the *Omer* offering would once again be brought. Therefore, their job was to learn — and learn well — all the laws of *kemitzah*.

Haman was astounded. Shaken and alarmed, he said, in effect, "If you have such a Torah that laughs at the whole world, to the degree that nothing else interests you ... There are decrees plastered up in every city declaring that the Jews are to be killed, yet young students are delving into the laws of *kemitzah* in preparation for a rebuilt *Beis HaMikdash* ... Against such a nation, I am lost."

Haman was not shattered when they came to hang him. He had long since realized the end was coming. He had witnessed the strength of the nation that had received the Torah, that was schooled in suffering but laughed at everything. "*Yibaneh Beis HaMikdash* ..."

Why do we laugh? Because our prophets have told us that the Redeemer will come and that He will rebuild the *Beis HaMikdash*! "*The One Who gave you Toras Emes* — a Torah of truth!" Write all the decrees you want. The Torah is truth.

The power of the Jewish people lies in our thinking not about the present, but about the future. It was witnessing this that disconcerted Haman. The *Rosh Yeshivah* and all of his students were able to look at the world as though it consisted of so many grasshoppers. It didn't matter to them — because they were the eternal people.

"For an edict which is written in the king's name and sealed with the king's signet ring may not be revoked" [Esther 8:8].

There's No Money, We're Killing Today

R' Reuven Karlenstein

e've been talking about money. We've mentioned Moshe's wealth, the treasures at the Reed Sea and in Egypt. Now, let's talk about Purim money.

In Haman's terrible edict, he wrote, "*And to plunder their posses-sions.*" This was also written explicitly in Mordechai's subsequent message: "*Plunder their possessions.*" The Jews were to plunder the gentiles' possessions. But there is a difference between the two.

Haman's edict said, "*to destroy, to slay, and to exterminate all the Jews, from young to old, children and women, in one day, on the thirteenth day of the twelfth month,*" followed by the words, "*and to plunder their possessions.*" Mordechai's edict, however, put the reference to plun-der before the date: "*to destroy, to slay, and to exterminate every armed force of any people or province that threaten them ... and to plunder their possessions, on one day ... namely, upon the thirteenth day of the twelfth month, that is, the month of Adar.*"

Both the Malbim and the Vilna Gaon deal with this question. The Gaon points to a deep secret that is hinted at here.

Haman knew that, were the plunder to take place on the same day as the killing of the Jews, the gentiles would not do the job properly. Each would think to himself, *What do I care if this Jew lives or dies? The important point is: I need money!* And he would not kill the Jews. Therefore, Haman divided the edict into two days: On the thirteenth day of Adar, there would be no plundering. That day was slated for killing only. Then, on the days to come, "*plunder their possessions.*"

Mordechai Hatzaddik, however, and his fellow Jews, were not interested in money. (Indeed, in the end, "*they did not extend their hands to the plunder.*" They did not touch the gentiles' money.) But Mordechai had a big problem, as the Alshich describes.

Achashverosh told Mordechai: "*You shall write regarding the Jews as you see fit.*" Should he not have said, "You shall write regarding the gentiles as you see fit"?

The Alshich explains. According to the laws of the kingdom, there was no legal basis for nullifying the king's earlier decree. As the *Megillah* explicitly states, "*For an edict which is written in the king's name and sealed with the king's signet ring may not be revoked.*" How, then? The solution was to interpret the law in such a way as to alter it. This was the only option Mordechai had at his disposal.

Well, Mordechai, as it were, was a good lawyer. He found a legal loophole. What did he do? He changed one point of the edict. Haman's decree had read, "*to destroy, to slay, and to exterminate all the Jews*" — period. Mordechai merely moved the period over, leaving out the end: "*To destroy, to slay, and to exterminate all*" — period. And who would do the killing? "*The Jews.*"

Here is a hint to an answer for our question as to what Achashverosh meant by "*You shall write regarding the Jews as you see fit*": That is, he granted permission for Mordechai to do as he saw fit with the words, "the Jews." Wonderful!

We learn from here that the entire miracle of Purim hinged on a single period: one dot.

Returning to the matter under consideration: Because an edict that had been signed and sealed by the king could not be revoked, there was also no way to erase the part of the decree that dealt with plunder. This aspect of the decree had to appear in the second announcement, even if the Jews were not interested in Amalekite money.

What did Mordechai do?

Here, too, he made a change. Instead of the reference to plunder coming *after* the part about destroying and killing, as in Haman's wording, Mordechai included it along with the destruction order — that is, it was to take place on the same day. And because the Jews were engaged in the *mitzvah* of wiping out Amalek, no one would have time to busy themselves with the matter of money.

And so it came about that the Jews scorned the money, the gold, and the silver. They engaged only in a *mitzvah*: "*They did not extend their hands to the plunder.*"

☞ *Throwing — and Catching — Tzeddakah Funds*

There were three elements in Haman's edict, dealing respectively with the spirit, the physical, and the monetary.

"*To destroy*" — the soul.

"*To kill*" — the body.

"*And plunder their possessions*" — the money.

Corresponding to these three things, three *mitzvos* were established on Purim. Countering the destruction of the spirit, *Chazal* instituted the *mitzvah* of *simchah*, of rejoicing, on Purim. For the killing of the physical self, we have a day of *mishteh*, of feasting with food and wine. And with respect to the money, we are told to give *matanos l'evyonim* — charity to the poor.

The Vilna Gaon draws a parallel between "*matanos l'evyonim*" and the act of plundering: Plunder involves vigorously snatching money, and we must give *tzeddakah* just as vigorously. Come to shul on Purim and see how Israel throws money at the poor! Plunder!

☞ *From the Holy of Holies to Shushan Habirah*

Where, everyone asks, did Haman obtain the wooden pole, 50 cubits tall, from which he intended to hang Mordechai? Have you ever thought about how high 50 *amah* — 50 cubits — really is? I remember once, before Sukkos, searching for a 6-meter piece of lumber and how hard it was to find one. Finally, we were directed to a special carpentry shop where the pole could be obtained. But, 50 *cubits*? Where did he find such a thing?

The answer is: from the *Mishkan*.

Some point out that *Chazal* identify the pole as a remnant of Noach's wooden ark, but they add that this does not pose a contradiction to the claim that it came from the *Mishkan*, for the *Mishkan* also contained wood from the ark. What is clear is that the *Pirkei d'Rebbe Eliezer* (*Perek* 49) states explicitly: "At that hour, what did Eliyahu, *zachur letov*, do? He appeared in the guise of Charvonah, one of the king's chamberlains, and said, 'There is a tree near Haman's house from the Holy of Holies, and it measures 50 cubits,

as it says, "*They made the hall of pillars 50 cubits in length*" ' (I Melachim 7:6). Immediately, the king ordered Haman to be hanged from
it, as it says, "The king said, '*Hang him on it!*'"

Anyone reading these words in *Pirkei d'Rebbe Eliezer* reacts with
astonishment: The Holy of Holies? The apex of holiness, the glory
of Hashem. On such a pole they hanged the corrupt and wicked
Haman?

The answer is that while the honor of heaven does filter through
the Holy of Holies (when a Jew *davens Shemoneh Esrei*, we are told,
"He should focus his heart toward the Holy of Holies"), it is also
served through the hanging of Haman. "*V'nahafoch hu*" — the great
turnaround in the fates of the Jews and their oppressors — was so
outstanding and so obvious, that it accrued to Hashem's glory, of
which the Holy of Holies is the focal point.

☞ Why Didn't He Kill Himself?

The Gerrer Rebbe, the *Imrei Emes*, once asked why Haman did
not kill himself when it became clear that he was destined to suffer the tremendous mortification of leading Mordechai astride his
horse through the streets of Shushan. How could Haman endure
such anguish, which must have been like a thousand deaths to him?
His suffering over Mordechai's ascendancy on the one hand, and
his own degradation on the other, were indescribable. Why, then,
did he not take his own life?

The *Imrei Emes* explains. Haman was prepared to endure anything, because he was patiently awaiting the great revenge that
was yet to come: "*To destroy, to slay, and to exterminate all the Jews.*"
Haman was conserving his strength to endure what he must, with
the goal of surviving to witness the total destruction of the Jewish
people. At that point, Haman did not yet realize that the seeds of
his own downfall had already been sown.

At first, things seemed to be going well. "*Haman told his wife, Zeresh, and all his friends everything that had happened to him.*" The Alshich reveals what he told her and the others. How did he explain it to them? With a painful smile, he said: "If you think that I've already spoken with the king about hanging Mordechai, and he became angry and therefore ordered me to dance before Mordechai in the streets, you are mistaken! You don't understand politics. I haven't even spoken to the king yet about hanging Mordechai. Here's what happened.

"A few different elements came together. The king couldn't fall asleep. That happens to a person sometimes, and it can certainly happen to a king. He became restless and asked that his Book of Chronicles be brought to him. For some reason, things worked out so that the book chanced to open up to that page. As you know, near morning I came to the palace on my own business. I wanted to speak with him privately, face to face. And because I was the first person to enter so early in the morning, before dawn, the king asked me, 'What should be done with a man whom the king wishes to honor?'

"I gave him the correct answer, and he saw fit to repay Mordechai in this fashion, with his highest minister honoring Mordechai. He granted me this 'honor' but, in essence, I'm only at the beginning of the road. Today or tomorrow, I will have that talk with the king about the main topic, according to plan, and all will be well."

But Zeresh and his advisers warned, "Beware! The situation is not so good. For, '*If Mordechai … is of Jewish descent, you … will undoubtedly fall before him.*'"

Haman reeled from their words. He became terrified. Who knew what would happen? He wanted to take his life then, but, "*They hurried to bring Haman.*" Amazing! Hashem did not give him an opportunity to escape. The king's servants quickly came to take him, and events unfolded to his downfall.

* * *

"To make known to the people of the world that what is written in the Torah is truth, for which mighty nation has a god to whom they are so close as Hashem, our God, is to us when we call Him?" This is the essence of the *Megillah* reading, the Rambam tells us. The nation of Israel was on a degraded level, and a decree of destruction was placed on the entire people. In one moment they repented, fasted, and prayed and instituted whatever corrective behaviors were necessary in order to improve, and everything turned around. To make known to the people of the world that what is written in the Torah is truth!

The Brisker Rav summarized this concept by saying that these are the thoughts expressed in *"Shoshanas Yaakov"*: *"You have been their eternal salvation, and their hope throughout generations."* Why? *"To make known that all who hope in You will not be shamed; nor ever be humiliated, those taking refuge in You."*

As the Rambam said, above: "To make known to the people of the world that what is written in the Torah is truth, for which mighty nation has a god to whom they are so close as Hashem, our God, is to us when we call Him?"

פרשת ויקהל

Parashas Vayakheil

שֵׁשֶׁת יָמִים תֵּעָשֶׂה מְלָאכָה וּבַיּוֹם הַשְּׁבִיעִי יִהְיֶה לָכֶם קֹדֶשׁ שַׁבַּת שַׁבָּתוֹן לַה׳ כָּל־הָעֹשֶׂה בוֹ מְלָאכָה יוּמָת.

"On six days, work may be done, but the seventh day shall be holy for you, a day of complete rest for Hashem; whoever does work on it shall be put to death" (Shemos 35:2).

Stoning

R' Shabsi Yudelevitz

The *parashah* begins with Shabbos observance and the punishment for its desecration. Listen to a story:

As is known, in the period before the world wars, the more prosperous members of a community exerted a strong influence on Jewish communal life. During that time, there lived in a certain city in Poland a wealthy Jew (we will not mention his name out of concern for his honor), who involved himself in the running of the community in a very forceful manner. His fellow residents treated him with great respect, their attitude a mixture of reverence and fear.

It happened that this wealthy Jew, in a moment of foolishness, began to publicly scorn Shabbos observance. As time went on, his spiritual state deteriorated to the point where he brazenly climbed aboard a coach harnessed to a pair of horses — on Shabbos. *Hashem yishmor*.

Of course, there was a turmoil in the town. The shuls were filled with talk, but no one could be found who dared confront the wealthy man in public. Most of the residents were afraid for their own skins, knowing that whoever angered that gentleman would pay a high price. He was known as a person who did not flinch at exacting a suitable revenge or pitilessly suing even the most respected members of the community.

His pious fellow Jews tried to think of a plan whereby they might deliver a public rebuke. As the time for Shabbos *Minchah* neared, word came that the rich man had decided to have his carriage harnessed and to travel through the city's streets, in a deliberate act of provocation. When he got tired of that, he announced to his son that he was leaving town, setting out immediately to visit one of his Christian friends in a nearby city. Suiting word to action, in the spirit of madness that gripped him, he left the city before Shabbos was over, his horses kicking heavy dust into his fellow townspeople's eyes. His pious neighbors wrung their hands in pain and despair.

On *Motza'ei Shabbos*, news began to circulate through the town. At first, the reports were unclear. Slowly, however, it became known that the rich gentleman had not succeeded in traveling even halfway to his intended destination. His carriage had overturned and the horses, startled and afraid, had trampled him to death with their flying hooves. As eyewitnesses related, so broken was his body that it was difficult to recognize him.

His family insisted on giving him a Jewish burial. Community activists helped organize a respectable funeral, and before the funeral procession set out, several prominent members stood up to deliver eulogies.

The first spoke of his integrity in business, the second praised his activism and the way he had served as a liason between the Jews and the Christians. The third speaker also made mention of the individual's good qualities. All three spoke of his tragic death in a road accident with rampaging horses.

Then the *rav* of the city, a gentle, elderly man, rose, as was the custom. Pale and shaken, he said, "My brothers, after hearing what the speakers before me have said, and the way they explained the departed man's death, I was reminded of a *pasuk* that we say every day: '*Some with chariots, and some with horses; but we, in the Name of Hashem, our God, call out.*'"

Raising his thin voice, he cried, "The first eulogizer explained the reason for his death: driving an unstable carriage that overturned at the side of the road. The second pinned the tragedy on the horses that trampled him to death. But we whose hearts are in tune with Hashem, our *Elokim*, know that Hashem brought this strange death upon him as a punishment for deliberately desecrating the Shabbos in public — in front of scores of city residents. '*But we, in the Name of Hashem, our God, call out!*'"

The *rav* was not finished. Bathed in perspiration, he hoarsely quoted the Gemara (*Sanhedrin* 37b) in tears: "Although the Sanhedrin abolished the law of the four deaths, they were not abolished. Someone who is sentenced to stoning will either fall off a roof or be trampled by an animal. Someone who is sentenced to burning will either end his life in a fire or be bitten by a snake. Here we see the fulfillment of the Gemara's words: death by stoning for *chilul Shabbos*, which comes about either through falling from a height or by being trampled by animals. *HaKadosh Baruch Hu* has brought about the death this man deserved!"

Several of the dead man's family members were roused to approach the *rav* angrily, but the rest of the crowd held them back. The man was duly buried, and the people went home.

The rich man's family members became known, after this tragic event, as upright Jews who donated money to the shuls and *batei midrash* of Poland, for the rectification and ascendancy of their father's soul. The big yeshivah that was erected through their support stood for decades, and by the beginning of World War II hundreds of God-fearing Torah scholars had emerged through its doors.

"*Some with chariots, and some with horses; but we, in the Name of Hashem, our God, call out!*"

Two Thousand Years

Y ou are about to hear a terrible story, a true story, which contains a hidden treasure, tangential but marvelous, about the holy Shabbos, the subject with which our *parashah* begins.

The *navi* Zechariah was stoned to death.

There were two prophets named Zechariah. The one in the Book of Zechariah was not stoned, but rather it was the *navi* Zechariah ben Yehoyada, the Kohen. As we are told in *Divrei Hayamim* II (24:20-22): "*A spirit of God came over Zechariah son of Yehoyada the Kohen. He stood above the people and said to them, 'Thus said God: Why are you transgressing the commandments of Hashem? You will not succeed, for you have forsaken Hashem, so He has forsaken you!' But they conspired against him and stoned him with rocks, by the command of the king, in the Courtyard of the Temple of Hashem ... As he was dying he said, 'May God see this and demand redress!'*"

Indeed, exactly one year later, to the day, the army of Aram fell on Jerusalem and wrought much death and destruction, as described there.

Long years passed, until Nevuzaradan entered the Courtyard and saw the blood of Zechariah the Prophet boiling and seething: the same blood that had been on that rock and seethed for about a hundred years, from the time of Zechariah's death to the destruction of the Temple.

Nevuzaradan asked, "What is this?" They were forced to tell him that this was the blood of Zechariah, a *navi* of Hashem, who had rebuked the people with a message from heaven, after which they got up and killed him. A terrible tragedy transpired there on that day, as Nevuzaradan, in an attempt to stop the boiling blood, slaughtered the elders of the Jewish nation: the Sanhedrin on the same spot. After that he killed young men and women and children, until even he recoiled from so much bloodshed and pleaded, as it were, for the blood to stop its endless seething. The blood subsided, and then started up again at double strength. Nevuzaradan repented and converted to Judaism (*Gittin* 57b).

Pay close attention. The Lithuanians knew of the "Novaradoker dybbuk." This was a case of "possession" of a Jewish *bachur* from Novaradok by a spirit (an errant soul that entered a living body). Chassidim also speak of an amazing dybbuk, and it is reasonable to suppose that both are referring to the same spirit, which started its journey in Novaradok, where it was brought to the home of the Vilna Gaon's student, R' Chaim Volozhiner, and afterward moved on to a different area and was taken to the Maggid of Kozhnitz.

According to eyewitness testimony by an illustrious Lithuanian figure (and as quoted in the *sefer* of *Hatzaddik* R' Shlomo), that young man used to walk along the streets of the city, meeting people and enumerating their sins. He would approach a Jew and tell him joyfully, *"Ich hub dir leeb."* In other words, "I love you! I love you!" In a spirit of friendship, he would then go on to list the sins that the fellow had done in the course of his life. The second man would shrivel with shame over this public announcement of his misdeeds in front of all the people on the street, and would immediately begin to entertain remorseful thoughts. Then the tone would change: "I hate you! I hate you!" And the *bachur* would lift his feet and flee.

Sometimes, he would escape even before the hateful portion. He would turn to the fellow as though pleading, *My dear brother, why are you going to such an extreme [in thinking remorseful thoughts]? What do you need to do that for?* In other words, why do you need to do *teshuvah*? However, seeing the other man persisting in this vein, he would part from him at a run. Apparently, the corrupt spirit was goading him on, for it is known that a person's desires and ambitions do not part from him after his soul separates from his body. The soul is parted from the body but not from its desires, which remain a part of the soul and cling to it. Perhaps only the suffering of punishment parts the soul from these drives.

The spirit revealed itself, saying that it had been the first one to hurl a stone at the prophet Zechariah.

For over a millenium he had been wandering about, without the option of entering *Gehinnom* to be purified of his sins. Thus, he had entered the body of this *bachur*, to find a brief interval of respite and calm.

Another amazing phenomenon was the fact that this spirit could not bear to be around Torah scholars. When he met a wicked person, he would hug and kiss him repeatedly. Let him come within four cubits of a righeous person, however, and he was unable to look him in the face. He would flee, muttering and cursing.

R' Yosef Shlomo Kahaneman, the Ponevezher *Rav*, once walked into the yeshivah dining room on Shabbos and saw that a number of tables were not covered with a tablecloth. The *rav* turned to a group of students and told them, "My dear *bachurim*! Listen. I have been told with regard to the Novaradoker dybbuk, that one Shabbos the *bachur* in whom he was residing was taken forcibly to the home of *Hagaon* R' Chaim Volozhiner. The *bachur* was beside himself, prowling here and there throughout the house as though seized by madness. He simply could not find a place to settle. Unable to bear the holiness of that house, he raced about in a frenzy. Finally, he found a small corner at one table, where the tablecloth had been folded back and the bare table stood revealed. At once, he leaped onto that place and kissed and embraced it (for only there was he able to settle). This is a true story." That was what he said.

Once, when the dybbuk was threatened with being taken to the Vilna Gaon if he did not remove himself, the spirit retorted, "I'm not afraid of him. The *Gra* doesn't deal with us (as stated in the *Gra's* introduction to '*Sipra D'tzniusa*)." So the Chofetz Chaim told his student, R' Shlomo Bloch. The dybbuk was then asked whether he knew the identities of the generation's 36 righteous men (the *lamed-vav tzaddikim* that are said to exist in every generation). He named many people unknown to them, and listed the *Gra* as well. However, he did not name the *Gra* among the first on the list. They asked him about this: Wasn't the Vilna Gaon foremost, or at least among the top three names, on the list?

Replied the dybbuk, "No — because he is *slightly* famous. Only a portion of his qualities are known."

☞ *On to the Maggid of Kozhnitz*

The *sefer* "*Shomer Emunim*" is the first source to mention the Maggid of Kozhnitz in relation to that spirit: "They once brought a certain person to the Rebbe of Kozhnitz in order to repair the soul that had entered (i.e., in the form of a dybbuk). They asked the Maggid who he had been in a previous *gilgul* and at what time. He answered that the soul had been experiencing pain and suffering for over 2,000 years because he was the first to throw a stone at the *navi* Zechariah. Ever since, he had wandered from place to place and known no peace. With Hashem's compassion, it was rectified through the holy figure mentioned here."

How did the dybbuk move between Novaradok and Kozhnitz? Or was it someone else, later possessed by the spirit that had been the first to hurl a stone at Zechariah? It is hard to know with certainty; however, what I am about to relate may shed some light.

"I asked R' Eliyahu Lopian," says R' Yaakov Eidelstein, *shlita*, "what became of that *bachur* who was walking around with a dyb-buk inside him." He replied that, to the best of his knowledge, word of the dybbuk had spread until many came to hear it speak, to attain the fear of punishment, and to learn of heaven's decrees for sins committed. In time, the matter reached the highest echelons of the government. Government officials were apprehensive that a magician was walking around among the Jews and the gentiles. Magic was legally forbidden in the country, and anyone caught practicing it ran the risk of a death sentence. Therefore, the *bachur's* situation fell into the category of "*pikuach nefesh*" — life-and-death danger. It was decided that he needed to be rescued, not only because of the spirit that had taken possession of him, but also because of the obligation to save a life. He was smuggled across the border to a place where the laws were different. That was how he left Novaradok, Vilna, and Volozhin. Eventually, he merited reaching a Jewish community that bundled him off to see the Maggid of Kozhnitz. There, the matter finally achieved rectification, as set down in the "*Shomer Emunim.*"

R' Moshe Holtzberg, *Rosh Yeshivas* Karlin Stolin, once revealed that details of the Maggid of Kozhnitz's encounter had reached him in an unbroken chain from the original source. He agreed to relate the facts to R' Yaakov Eidelstein, who describes it as follows.

At first, the Maggid attempted to exorcise the spirit from the *bachur's* body using special holy Names. When he whispered these names into his ear, the spirit laughed out loud and said, "You think to frighten me with such things? I knew all those names when I was still a child below the age of bar mitzvah. I come from the period of the Temple. I hurled the first stone at Zechariah Hanavi ..." The spirit broke down in tears. "Don't frighten me!"

The Maggid asked him, "How is it possible to rectify your soul?" (His goal was also to rectify this wandering soul, which had been suffering untold agonies for more than 2,000 years.)

"From the time I died," the spirit replied, "to this very day, there has been no Torah scholar who has tried to defend me. Were there someone to find some defense for me, my soul would be rescued and I would be able to rest." He stressed that it was necessary to defend him in all sincerity.

The Maggid thought, and found some merit in his favor, but told him that he would defend him only if the spirit would show him his essence. The spirit agreed, but stipulated that this must be done, "not here in the house or in the city, but in a field outside the city. I will show you if you will bring me to my rest."

The Maggid went out of the city and uttered aloud the defense he'd come up with according to halachah. Afterward he saw a pillar of fire, reaching from the ground to the sky. Whatever else he saw he did not say.

What was the defense? R' Moshe Holtzberg tells us: He found a halachic precept by which a mistaken understanding would have permitted him to hurl that stone. This misunderstanding of the law provided a certain defense. He thought the halachah was that a negative prophecy from Hashem may be changed as long as the prophet does not say it out loud. In his erroneous view, the *navi* Zechariah, having a negative prophecy as commanded by Hashem, should have refrained from speaking this prophecy in Hashem's Name, in order to try to save the people of Israel. Although "one who suppresses his prophecy is liable to death," he felt the *navi* should have sacrificed his life rather than say his prophecy. A *navi* is forbidden to do this, but this explains why he felt justified in stoning the *navi*.

כָּל־אִישׁ וְאִשָּׁה אֲשֶׁר נָדַב לִבָּם אֹתָם לְהָבִיא לְכָל־הַמְּלָאכָה אֲשֶׁר צִוָּה ה' לַעֲשׂוֹת בְּיַד־מֹשֶׁה הֵבִיאוּ בְנֵי־יִשְׂרָאֵל נְדָבָה לַה'.

"Every man and woman whose heart motivated them to bring for any of the work that Hashem had commanded to make, through Moshe — the Children of Israel brought a free-willed offering to Hashem" (Shemos 35:29).

SEVEN SOLUTIONS

R' Reuven Karlenstein

*T*his verse seems to use double language. There are words that seem redundant, and many have tried to explain the meaning behind this repetition. Let us now offer seven solutions to this question," begins R' Reuven Karlenstein. "*Rabbosai, herr zich ein.* Listen well."

1) R' Yehonasan Eibeshitz explains as follows:

The *erev-rav* also wished to bring their donation to the building of the *Mishkan*, but the *Bnei Yisrael* vigorously refused, saying, "Those who led us to sin with the Golden Calf shall not have a share in the *Mishkan*!"

The *erev-rav* stood there with their gold and silver, their pale-blue cloth and their purple, and all the other objects, and the Children of Israel opposed them: "No. You will not participate!" The question, as it were, hung in the air: How could they allow a loss to be incurred to the House of Hashem, by preventing the *erev-rav* from giving their donations? Should the *Mishkan* be the poorer because of their refusal?

So the Jews resolved: The *erev-rav* would not participate, yet the *Mishkan* would not lose by it. How? They counted up all the silver, copper, and so on that the *erev-rav* had brought — a hundred kilograms, a thousand kilograms, and so on — and then they told the *erev-rav*, "Leave it all at home. We, the *Bnei Yisrael*, will add this sum from our own pockets." The words in our verse, "*Every man and woman*," refer to the *erev-rav*, "*whose heart motivated them to bring for any of the work that Hashem had commanded to make*" — but it all came from the *Bnei Yisrael* themselves: "*the Children of Israel brought a free-willed offering to Hashem.*"

2) The *Chida* offers a different explanation, by way of a parable:

In shul after *Shacharis*, the *gabbaim* will often conduct a charitable fund-raising drive, saying, "*Ba'avur shenadav* ("Because he donated)..." One person calls out, "Five hundred dollars!" The *gabbai* continues, "Who will give more? R' So-and-So, how much will you give?" The *gabbai* points to each man in turn. One donates a $100, another contributes $50, still another $150, and so on, until the bidding is over and *Mussaf* begins.

After shul, the man who had offered $500 walks home, thinking, *I'm crazy. Why did I offer so much? What have I done to myself? The others barely offered $100, and I had to be the 'rich one'?"* He thinks it over some more. *Well, what can I do now? I said it;*

it's over. I will not take it back, heaven forbid! I'll pay up. But from now on, I'll think twice and act with restraint. I'll take better care of my money."

The *Chida* says, "When it came to donating for the *Mishkan*, there was no phenomenon of regret afterward. *Every man and woman whose heart motivated them to bring for any of the work:* From the initial offer to the actual bringing of the material, it was all a donation to Hashem, without any second thoughts."

3) The *Maharil* Diskin expounds on this verse:

The Gemara says that no one ever misused an *olah* offering of Hillel Hazaken, because he would consecrate it right before the slaughtering, when it was already in the Temple Courtyard, the *Azarah*. And this is precisely what the *Bnei Yisrael* did in this, their first donation to the House of Hashem. *"Every man and woman whose heart motivated them to bring for any of the work"*: When *"the Children of Israel brought," only* then did they consecrate what they had brought as *"a free-willed offering to Hashem,"* so that it would not be improperly used.

4) *Rabbosai*. When a Jew prepares himself and engages in a *mitzvah* — for example, going to buy his *arba'ah minim*, to bake matzos, to build a *sukkah*, and so forth — his reason tells him, "Reb Yid, take your children along with you! Let them participate in the mitzvah!" Take them to buy the *arba'ah minim*. Show them all the laws of baking *matzos*. Show them at home, afterward, how to gather it into a basket in order to obligate one in the *mitzvah* of *hafrashas challah*, and show them how to do this with a blessing. Show them how to fulfill the *mitzvah* of covering the blood on *erev Yom Kippur* after the slaughtering for *kapparos*. The same goes for the other *mitzvos*. Share it with the children!

In the great *mitzvah* of donating for the building of the *Mishkan*, the *Bnei Yisrael* did not come alone. *"The Children of Israel brought"* — together with their *kinderlach*, their "children" — *"a free-willed offering to Hashem."*

5) The "*Kehillas Yitzchak*" explains by means of a true story:

The Maharsha had a yeshivah that was suffering from terrible overcrowding. They needed a new building, but there was no money. What to do? "Make money from the building itself." How? By conducting a "cornerstone-laying" ceremony and selling the honor to the highest bidder. That's what they decided to do.

A certain Jew living in that city wanted the honor of laying that cornerstone. However, he wished to remain modestly anonymous. He refused to let his name be announced as the contributor. Going to the *gabbai*, he requested, "I'd like to make a deal with you. At the bidding, you announce, 'Five hundred dollars — going once!' Then you go on to raise the bidding, according to the crowd: Six hundred, seven hundred, and so on. Don't you worry, even if someone calls out, 'A thousand!', you go ahead and announce, 'A thousand one hundred.' And so on — 2000, 2500, 3000, 3500 ... Of course, no one is to know who is really raising the bid. Do your job faithfully and raise the price at my expense — as high as necessary."

"But what happens when the bidding is over?" questioned the *gabbai*. "You'll have bought the right to lay the cornerstone, and everyone will discover who the donor is."

"No. Announce that the donor wishes to honor the *Rosh Yeshivah* (the Maharsha) with the laying of the cornerstone. That will settle the matter in the best possible way."

And that's the way it was. In a ringing voice the *gabbai* began to announce the bidding, and every time the price went up, he raised it again. Finally, the crowd gave in. "He got it, he got it." But who was the happy winner? Silence reigned in the big room. And then the *gabbai* called out again, "The donor wishes to honor the *Rosh Yeshivah* ..."

When the ceremony was over, the Maharsha summoned the *gabbai* to learn the name of the person who had presented him with this honor and had donated such a large sum toward the new yeshivah building. Apologetically, the *gabbai* explained that his lips were sealed.

"All right, don't tell me his name," the Maharsha said. "But tell him that, if he agrees, I'd be happy to meet him." The *gabbai* delivered the *Rosh Yeshivah's* message.

Only hours later, the man knocked on the door of the holy Maharsha's room. Seeing him, the Maharsha exclaimed in surprise, "You're the donor? Since when are you such a wealthy man? Where is all the money we never knew about?"

"The *Rosh Yeshivah* is right," the man replied. "I am not a rich man. But because I am childless, I wished to earn the merit of the Torah learned by yeshivah students."

"Is that so?" the Maharsha cried. "Then I will add my blessing! By this time next year, you will have a son, and he will study Torah in our new yeshivah building."

A year later, a male child was born to the man and his wife. Years later, when the boy had grown into a youth, his father wished to register him in the yeshivah. For various reasons, the yeshivah administrators declined to accept him. The father smiled painfully and told them, "I will take care of this matter." He went in to see the Maharsha, and the *bachur* was immediately accepted, no questions asked. (There is a *pasuk* that says, "Behold! The heritage of Hashem is children; a reward is the fruit of the womb." *Chazal* explain that when the Children of Israel returned from the foot of *Har Sinai*, they all conceived sons.)

"*Every man and woman whose heart motivated them to bring ...*" What was their reward for this? They brought an offering — *Bnei Yisrael* — to Hashem. In other words, they merited bringing children into the world, and those children were like a donation to Hashem's legions, as it were. And because it came about in the merit of this donation, it was considered part of the gift to Hashem. (See the "*Kehillas Yitzchak.*")

6) The Alshich expounds: The people of the generation of the desert thought to themselves, *If only I had the ability, I would donate to the Mishkan, the Menorah, the Shulchan, the Aron — everything. I would even sell the clothes on my back. What's a kilo of gold? I want to bring 200 kilo to complete the whole job! But what can I do, I don't have it. Everything that I have I've already given to the House of Hashem — the maximum.*

When he thought this sincerely, Hashem considered it as if he'd donated everything. This, the Alshich says, is hinted at in the verse, *"Every man and woman whose heart motivated them to bring ..."* What did their hearts long to bring? Everything! It was as if the Children of Israel brought all *"the work that Hashem had commanded to make, through Moshe."*

How does it come about that a good intention is thus joined to deed? *"A free-willed offering to Hashem."* It is because it is a gift to Hashem. A gift given to flesh and blood is measured only by what is actually given, but Hashem wants our intention and our heart as well — and that is precisely what they gave!

A person says, "I can't do it. I just can't do it!" He should be aware that his desire and intention earn him *siyata d'Shemaya* — heavenly assistance — to succeed beyond his actual powers. And he is credited with the accomplishment, even though it was beyond him, because he wanted to do it, he longed to do it, and acted to the very best of his ability.

In general, *Chazal* teach us, a good intention is considered tantamount to the act itself. The Torah says that Moshe Rabbeinu "erected the *Mishkan*." Moshe did not have the physical strength to put up the *Mishkan* on his own. Rather, he *wished* to erect it. When he picked up just one wooden pole with this desire in his heart, "it was erected by itself," and heaven credited him with the entire deed. Because he wanted to do it and was prepared to do it, it was as though he actually did it.

7) The seventh explanation is an original approach:

"A Tabernacle for His presence has the King to Whom peace belongs made of the wood of Lebanon: Its pillars He made of silver; His resting place was gold; its suspended curtain was purple wool, its midst was decked with implements bespeaking love ..." (Shir HaShirim 3:9). Gold, silver, copper, and more were brought in to bedeck the exterior of the House of Hashem. But what did they bring to the interior of the Tabernacle?

They brought their hearts — filled with love.

The Jewish people burned with a fierce desire to sacrifice themselves for their beloved Creator. But what could they do? Hashem would not accept them as sacrifices. So the *Bnei Yisrael* took this powerful longing to give themselves to the *Mishkan*, and poured it with all their hearts into their donations of silver and gold ...

They brought silver, gold, and wool to adorn the *Mishkan* on the outside: "*His resting place was gold; its suspended curtain was purple wool.*" But inside? "*It was ... decked with love!*"

Thus, when the Torah speaks of every man and woman bringing their offerings for all the work of the Tabernacle, their donation became doubly holy because they brought it "decked with love." The outside was gold, and the inside was lined with love for Hashem.

May Hashem grant us merit!

פרשת פקודי ❧
PARASHAS PEKUDEI

אֵלֶּה פְקוּדֵי הַמִּשְׁכָּן מִשְׁכַּן הָעֵדֻת אֲשֶׁר פֻּקַּד עַל־פִּי מֹשֶׁה עֲבֹדַת הַלְוִיִּם בְּיַד אִיתָמָר בֶּן־אַהֲרֹן הַכֹּהֵן.

"These are the reckonings of the Tabernacle, the Tabernacle of Testimony, which were reckoned at Moshe's bidding. The labor of the Levites was under the authority of Issamar, son of Aharon the Kohen" (Shemos 38:21).

WHY MOSHE SUBMITTED A REPORT

R' Reuven Karlenstein

W*hich were reckoned"*: The word "*pokeid*" is used in this verse, a word that carries a connotation of loss. Rashi says that Moshe Rabbeinu made a reckoning as to how much gold, silver, copper, and so on was used in the making of the *Mishkan*. He submitted, as it were, an official financial report.

Hashem called Moshe His most faithful servant. Why, then, is he called upon to submit a reckoning about income and expenses? *Chazal* explain that Moshe paid heed to the words of the cynics and heretics of his generation, who taunted him for becoming wealthy from the work on the *Mishkan*. In response, he said, "All right, we'll finish the job and I'll submit a report."

The *Midrash Tanchuma* states:

"Who caused him to sit down and make a reckoning for the *Mishkan*? Why did he make a reckoning? *HaKadosh Baruch Hu* believed in him, saying (*Bamidbar* 12:7): '*Of all My House, he is the most faithful.*' So why did Moshe make a reckoning? Because he heard the cynics of his generation who said, 'A person is in charge of the work on the *Mishkan*, of the talents of gold and silver, with no oversight and no accountability. Do you expect him *not* to grow rich?' Hearing this, he told them, 'When the work on the *Mishkan* is completed, I will submit a reckoning to you.' And when the job was done, he said, 'These are the reckonings of the Tabernacle ...' "

It goes without saying that the men who spoke so slightingly of Moshe were those of little significance in the generation, or how would they ever have dreamed of voicing such thoughts?

As we know, all cynics dip into the bucket of truth. Their most frequently repeated outrageousness is built around a small kernel of truth, on which they have erected a veritable tower of questions, explanations, thoughts, and opinions. It was doubtless in such a way that they dared to speak out against the Man of God, Moshe Rabbeinu.

Still, we must ask: Why and how did it occur to them to suspect Moshe of taking money from the work of the *Mishkan*?

⌒ A Simple, Heretical Calculation

I've found a "*Be'er Yosef*" that offers an explanation. As we know, the Israelites were a wealthy nation, with all the treasures of Egypt and the *Yam Suf.* "There was no one in all of Israel who did not have 90 donkeys laden with the silver and gold of Egypt" (*Bechoros* 5b). But Moshe Rabbeinu had none — neither the wealth of Egypt nor of the Sea. He had been occupied with removing Yosef's bones from Egypt. Poor fellow — while everyone else was filling their chests with treasure, he was occupied with Yosef's bones! The same thing happened when the Jews collected the vast treasure at the parting of the Reed Sea: "Come and see how beloved *mitzvos* were to Moshe Rabbeinu: All of Israel was busy with the booty of the Sea, while he was occupied with a *mitzvah*, as it says, 'The wise of heart will take *mitzvos*' (*Sotah* 13a).

How did Moshe actually become wealthy? Rashi, in *Parashas Ki Sisa*, reveals what is brought down in the *Midrash Tanchuma*: "Hashem's blessing brings riches. This was Moshe's blessing. *HaKadosh Baruch Hu* told him, 'Carve for yourself two Tablets,' and showed him a block of sapphire in his tent. And Moshe carved from it, and Hashem said, '*Carve for yourself* — the remainder is yours.' From here, we learn that one who engages in Torah receives his livelihood from the Torah and becomes prosperous and successful."

Now, let us make a simple calculation. When did the carving take place? On the seventeenth day of Tammuz. For on that day, the two Tablets were broken, and on the following day Moshe carved two new Tablets, ascended the mountain for another 40 days, and returned on Yom Kippur.

On the day after his descent — one day after Yom Kippur — Moshe Rabbeinu announced that he would be collecting donations for the construction of a Tabernacle, and each morning the people streamed in with their offerings. Suddenly, within a day or two of the start of the drive, the people saw that Moshe's tent was filled with gold and silver. "What's going on here?" they asked themselves. Moshe, who had been destitute, was suddenly wealthy. There was no stock market in the desert, nor any sort of business. In that case, what had happened? Had he brought money down with him from up Above? After all, he had descended with the Torah, not gold! So the cynics reflected.

Of course, they had no inkling of "Carve for yourself" — the fact that Moshe had carved the Tablets and become a rich man before he went up the mountain. In short, they speculated that, since he had instituted the mammoth drive for the *Mishkan* immediately upon descending the mountain, and since Moshe Rabbeinu himself was in charge of what was collected, a simple calculation could be made, along the lines of "one and one are two."

"We're not saying that he shouldn't get rich. He's worked hard on building this *Mishkan*. But it is reasonable to assume that the money in his tent is the money that came from the donations." And they began to spread this "logical" rumor.

In that case, why are they considered heretics? Why are they called "cynics of the generation"? They might be deemed mistaken, perhaps, or rumormongers, but why cynical and wicked?

The answer is: Even if you have the best questions and the most reasonable answers, to speak thus about a *tzaddik* is simply heresy!

Rabbosai, there is a powerful lesson for us here. If a person builds a precise case, using block upon block of proofs and logical deductions, and then uses the case to speak badly of a *tzaddik*, he is an *apikoros*, a heretic! We can point to this illustration: a group who had a good question and a good answer that seemed to them eminently logical to the point that Moshe Rabbeinu agreed to submit a financial report. But they will forever retain the pejorative label of "*leitzanei hador*," cynics of the generation.

"In his 'first world,' he is like a king. Everyone is concerned for his welfare and longs to see him, and all hug and kiss him because he's just a year old. In the 'second world' he is like a pig, rooting in the rubbish and playing with excrement. The 'third world' is comparable to a kid (a young goat), prancing about before his mother, playing before his father and mother, dancing to and fro and frolicking here and there, and all are happy with him" (Tanchuma, Parashas Pekudei, siman gimmel).

HOW MANY IDENTITY CARDS DO WE HAVE?

R' Yaakov Galinsky

When I was still in Poland, they used to tell a story. In Poland, the gentiles worked hard for pennies every day. They drew water and chopped wood. There were many gentiles who worked in Jewish homes, until they came to be fluent in the Yiddish tongue.

One evening, at the end of a hard day's work, one of these gentiles passed a shul and noticed someone he recognized: a poor Jew, standing near the shul collecting alms. In the Jew's hand was a large number of coins. The gentile came closer, looked into the poor man's hand, and asked, "How much money have you got there?"

"Three *zloty* (the equivalent of about 3 shekels (or 75 cents)," the Jew answered.

"How did you come to have so much?"

The poor man replied, "The Jews all pass by here between *Minchah* and *Ma'ariv*. About 300 people go into the shul, and because Jews are a compassionate people, all I have to do is shout, 'Jews, give a donation!' and each of them throws me a coin. In that way, I've managed to collect 300 pennies."

The gentile was impressed. *Am I crazy*, he asked himself, *to work a full day for just 10 shekels? Tomorrow, I'm going to stand near the Jewish synagogue and ask for handouts.*

The next day, accordingly, he slept all through the day and roused himself near evening to hurry over to the large area in front of the shul. In Yiddish, he began to call, "Compassionate Jews, give a poor man a donation!" Seeing him, the Jews began giving him their pennies. He collected a great deal.

Still, he wasn't happy. Why? Because, on the other side of the plaza sat another Jew who, for some reason, had received much larger sums than he. Where the gentile had been given penny and half-penny coins, the other man had received as much as 10 cents at a time.

When *Ma'ariv* was over and the congregation had gone home, the gentile asked his fellow alms-collector, "Can you tell me your secret? Why did they give you so much more than me?"

"I am a *ger tzedek* (a righteous convert)," the man replied. "Jews have a special sympathy for a *ger tzedek* — and they give more."

On the following day, the gentile returned to the shul and called out — again in Yiddish, of course — "Compassionate Jews, take pity on a poor *ger tzedek.*" The Jews gave him with a lavish hand. Still, he noticed another Jew sitting on a side chair and receiving as much as 20-cent or even half-*lira* coins.

After *Ma'ariv*, he went over to that Jew and whispered, "Why do they give you more?"

The poor man answered, "I am the grandson of the Ba'al Shem Tov. Being a descendant of *tzaddikim*, they give me more."

The next day, the gentile came early and began to shout, "*Rabbosai*, give a donation to a *ger tzedek*, the grandson of the Ba'al Shem Tov."

That day, he did not receive a penny.

He called and called until his voice was hoarse, but the Jews just passed him by with a smile. He did not understand the contradiction in his own claim: One can either be a righteous convert or the grandson of the Ba'al Shem Tov — but not both!

That was the fatal flaw in the gentile's plan. But we sometimes experience the same problem. We live a contradictory life, and therefore our children's upbringing does not always go smoothly. A person has to decide what he is: a *tzaddik* or not a *tzaddik*, scrupulous over *mitzvos* or negligent. The trouble is that he is still unclear about his own identity, and when a parent is weak in this area, it is hard for him to educate his children properly.

⁀ Who Are You?

In *Kerias Shema*, we say, *"Teach them thoroughly to your children and speak of them while you sit in your home."* Asks the Chasam Sofer: "It should have said, *"Teach them thoroughly to your children, and they shall speak of them."* After all, we are speaking here of the children: Teach them, and they will speak of these things at home and outside.

The Chasam Sofer explains, "Teach them to your children" — if you wish your children to learn, if you wish to thoroughly fulfill the edict of "teach them to your children," then *you* must learn. In other words, you must serve as a role model and an example for your children. *"And speak of them while you sit in your home, while you walk on your way, when you retire, and when you arise."* When children see their father, after a hard day's work, run to shul to learn instead of staying at home to relax and rest, then the child will know that it is a good and worthwhile thing to break one's inclination: the way their father subdues his desire to rest when he is tired, in order to set aside times for Torah study.

However, if the father fulfills the verse, *"Tell His words to Yaakov and His laws to Israel,"* but does not carry them out, what can he expect from his children?

Shlomo Hamelech said, *"A poor man's wisdom is despised"* (*Koheles* 9:16). A question may be asked: The Torah scholars of Israel were poor men, but was their wisdom despised? Does anyone look at a wise man's bank account to see whether he takes risks and is poor or not? If a rabbi is not wearing an expensive suit, is his wisdom despised?

Chazal reveal the meaning behind this verse. "A poor man's wisdom is despised": This is referring to an entirely different sort of "poor man." It is talking about a scholar who preaches, "Do not take a bribe," when he, himself, takes bribes quietly on the sly; "Do not lend money with interest," and he provides interest-added loans, and so on. That sort of wisdom is indeed despised! "Was the wisdom of the destitute Rabbi Akiva despised? Rather, what is a 'poor man'? Someone who is despised for what he says, such as an elder who preaches, 'Do not pervert justice,' when he perverts justice; 'Do not show favor in judgment,' when he shows favor in judgment'; 'Do not take a bribe,' when he takes bribes; 'Do not inflict pain on a widow and orphan,' when he inflicts pain on them. This man is called 'poor' and his wisdom is despised. The contradiction in his life is his poverty!"

What, you may ask, causes people to live contradictory lives?

The *Chovos Halevavos* tells of a king who met with a certain wise man. "Tell me please," the king asked, "who are you?"

The wise man replied, "I am a king over the one whom you serve."

The king stared at him in astonishment. "I am the king. He is babbling nonsense!"

Furiously, the king demanded an explanation of the man's words. The wise man willingly explained:

"I am a king over my *yetzer hara* — my nature — while you are a slave to your nature and your inclinations. Therefore, I am a king over the one you serve. Who, then, is the true king: you or I?"

Let us take a look at a wonderful *midrash*.

Shlomo Hamelech repeated the word "*hevel*, futility, seven times at the start of *Megillas Koheles*: "*Haveil havalim, amar Koheles, haveil havalim, hakol havel!*" "Futility of futilities!" said *Koheles*, "Futility of futilities! All is futile!" These expressions correspond to the seven "worlds" that a person sees in his lifetime. In other words, he switches ID cards seven times over the course of his life:

"Until he is a year old, everyone loves him and kisses him on the head." Every calls him by endearments during the period when he bears that "identity card." At 2 and 3 he is more like a pig, eating and dirtying himself the way that animal does. He is given, then, a pig's ID card, and is no longer considered quite as adorable.

At 10, he is like a young goat, "prancing about before his father and mother." Now he no longer resembles a pig, but a kid.

At 20, before his marriage, he is like a horse, lifting his head and stepping proudly along.

Then he marries, takes a wife, and becomes like a donkey: "The fifth world resembles a donkey, who is saddled with a wife and son and daughters and goes to and fro and supports his family and is burdened by his children." And so it goes, until the age of 40.

In the "sixth world," he bears a new identity card: as a dog, "who moves insolently here and there, taking from this one and giving to that one without embarrassment."

Growing still older, he begins to resemble a monkey (see the *midrash*). The *Tanchuma* adds additional details. Then *Chazal* conclude, "All this applies to the wicked." These seven eras in a person's life are descriptive of a *rasha* — a wicked person. Of *tzaddikim*, however, it says, "*And the king, David, was old.*" Although he was old, he was a king.

This is very hard to understand. Is the 3-year-old who dirties himself and others called a *rasha* — wicked? Is a prancing 10-year-old wicked? What do *Chazal* mean when they say that this description refers to the lives of the wicked? At most, we might call them by the labels that the *midrash* gives them: a pig, a kid, a donkey, a monkey, and so on. But *resha'im*? Wicked? Why do they deserve this kind of designation?

Elsewhere, *Chazal* discuss the definition of a *rasha* and a *tzaddik*. "*Resha'im* are under the dominion of their hearts, whereas with *tzaddikim*, their hearts are under their dominion." In other words, one who conquers his inclinations is called a *tzaddik*; the opposite is a *rasha*. Now we begin to understand.

The "seven worlds" that are described as making up a person's life — dog, pig, donkey, etc. — are not essential. They are the nature of things when a person lives as the whim moves him. But is there anyone who is unaware that there are those who have reached the "third world" that resembles a dog, for example, but are *not* insolent as dogs and do not behave in the way that the *midrash* describes? When they must "take from one and give to another," they do so with modesty and consideration. And does a 10-year-old have to behave like a young goat? And why is a 20-year-old suddenly like a horse? This only holds true when his nature holds the reins. "*I created a yetzer hara; I created the Torah as its antidote.*" If a person involves himself in Torah study, he receives the strength to resemble a human being — not an animal. This is wisdom: not to be like a donkey, a horse, or a dog; to acquire a different sort of identity card.

To acquire an identity card to last all his life, instead of a different one for each new era, an identity that changes along with his age and situation as his nature dictates. Rather, this is the ID card of a king: "But of *tzaddikim* it says, '*And the king, David, was old.*' Although he was old, he was a king."

If he announces one day, "I am a righteous convert!' and the next, "I am a grandson of the Ba'al Shem Tov!" everyone just laughs at him. Decide who you are! One day you attend *shiur*, the next two days you skip it; one day you *daven* with a *minyan*, and the next day you sleep late. Like a young goat, or a horse, or a monkey, letting himself be tugged whichever way his friends pull him, sometimes getting up on the right side and sometimes on the left.

May Hashem help us all!

⌐ *"The Angel Walked With Him"*

The following are portions of a *Midrash Tanchuma*, translated from its original language.

"... *HaKadosh Baruch Hu* tells the angel appointed over the souls, 'Bring me a certain soul that is in *Gan Eden*, whose name is So-and-So and which appears thus and thus,' for all the souls that are destined to be created have all been created, from the day the world was formed until the day the world will end, and all are called by human names, as it says (*Koheles* 6:10): 'What was has already been given a name.' "

At once, the angel goes and brings that soul before Hashem, and the soul immediately bows before the King of kings, *HaKadosh Baruch Hu.*

Hashem says to the soul, "Enter into a certain drop belonging to So-and-So." The soul opens its mouth and says, "Master of the Universe, I am satisfied with the world in which I have lived from the day I was created. Why is it Your will that I enter into that putrid drop, when I am holy and pure and formed from Your Glory?" *HaKadosh Baruch Hu* replies at once to the soul, "The world into which I am introducing you is a more beautiful world than the one in which you have been living. In the hour you were formed, you were made specifically for that drop." Immediately, Hashem introduces it there against its will, and afterward the angel returns and puts the soul into the mother's womb and summons two angels to guard it so that it will not leave there, and will not miscarry. And a light is placed above its head, as it says, (*Iyov* 29:2-3) "*If only I could be as in the earlier months, as in the days when God would watch over me; when His lamp would shine over my head, etc.,*" and [the soul] is able to see from one end of the world to the other.

The angel takes it out and brings it to *Gan Eden*, and shows it the *tzaddikim* sitting in honor with their crowns on their heads. The angel says to that soul, "Do you know who these people are?" "No, sir," says the soul. The angel then tells it, "These whom you see were formed at the start just like you, in the womb of their mothers, and they emerged into the world and kept the Torah and *mitzvos*. That is why they merited to come upon this great good that you see. Know this: You are destined to leave the world, and if you are meritorious and keep Hashem's Torah, you, too, will merit to sit among these people. If not, be aware that you will have earned another place." In the evening, [the angel] takes [the soul] to *Gehinnom* and shows it the wicked ones, whom the destructive angels are beating with sticks of flame, and who are wailing aloud without incurring mercy. And the angel says to the soul, "Do you know who these are?" And the soul says, "No, sir." The angel says, "These people being burned were created like you and went out into the world and did not keep the Torah and Hashem's laws. Therefore, they have come to this shame that you see. Know this: You are destined to leave the world. Be a *tzaddik* and do not be a *rasha*, and earn life in the World to Come."

HaKadosh Baruch Hu warns it about everything, and the angel takes it around from the morning to the evening and shows it the place where it will die and the place where it will be buried, and then takes it over the whole world and shows it the righteous and the wicked and shows it everything, and in the evening he restores it to its mother's womb. And Hashem provides a bolt and doors, as it says (*Iyov* 38:8), "*As He dammed in the sea with bolted doors,*" and (*Yeshayahu* 51:16), "*And I have placed My words in your mouth — and with the shade of My hand have I covered you.*" And Hashem tells it, "Until here you may come and do not go further."

The embryo remains inside its mother for nine months. For the first three months, the unborn child lives inside its mother on the lowest level; during the three middle months it resides on the middle level; and during the final months it lives on the highest level. And when the time comes to emerge into the light of the world, it turns over and descends in a moment from the top to the middle and from the middle to the last. And everything that its mother ate and drank, it eats and drinks and does not excrete anything, which is why it says (*Iyov* 5:9), "*Who performs great deeds that are beyond comprehension, [and] wonders beyond number.*" Finally, it is time to emerge into the air of the world.

At once, that same angel comes to him and says, "My son, know that you were created against your will and now know that you are being born against your will, and against your will you will die, and against your will you are destined to render an accounting before the King of kings, *HaKadosh Baruch Hu.*" And he does not wish to leave from there, until [the angel] strikes him and extinguishes the lamp that has been lit over his head, and takes him out into the air of the world against his will.

The baby, upon leaving, immediately forgets everything that he saw and everything that he knows. Why does a baby cry on leaving [the womb]? [It cries] over all that it has lost: a world of peace and rest, and the world that it has departed. At that moment, the seven worlds pass over him. The first world resembles a king, whose welfare interests everyone and whom all yearn to see. The seventh world resembles a monkey, whose visage is different from that of all other creatures, who asks about everything and eats and drinks like a youth and plays like a baby, so that even his children and the members of his household laugh at him and curse him. When his time finally comes, that same angel appears to him and asks, "Do you recognize me?"

"Yes," he says. "Why have you come to me today, of all other days?"

The angel says, "In order to take you out of the world, for the time has come for you to die."

At once, he begins to cry, and raises his voice from one end of the world to the other, and no creature recognizes or hears his voice except for the rooster alone, and he says to the angel, "You've already taken me out of two worlds and put me into this world!" And the angel says, "I told you that you were created against your will and born against your will, and against your will you live and against your will you will render an accounting before *HaKadosh Baruch Hu*. These are the four camps that Hashem revealed to Eliyahu."

ספר ויקרא

SEFER VAYIKRA

פרשת ויקרא

PARASHAS VAYIKRA

דַּבֵּר אֶל־בְּנֵי יִשְׂרָאֵל וְאָמַרְתָּ אֲלֵהֶם אָדָם כִּי־יַקְרִיב מִכֶּם קָרְבָּן
לַה׳ מִן־הַבְּהֵמָה מִן־הַבָּקָר וּמִן־הַצֹּאן תַּקְרִיבוּ אֶת־קָרְבַּנְכֶם.

*"Speak to the Children of Israel and say to them: When a man
among you brings an offering to Hashem: from animals —
from the cattle or from the flock shall you bring your offering"
(Vayikra 1:2).*

*"The speaker spoke truly, saying, 'If not for those who go
mad, the world would remain desolate,' for there is no madness in the world comparable to the madness of man" (Rambam, in his introduction to Seder Zeraim).*

"IF NOT FOR THE MADMEN"

R' Sholom Schwadron

Who is he who sacrifices himself as a *korban* to Hashem?
Let us learn.

"Speak to the Children of Israel and say to them: When
a man among you brings an offering to Hashem: from animals — from

the cattle or from the flock shall you bring your offering." The midrash says, " 'When a man among you brings an offering to Hashem' — hada hu dichsiv (that's what it means when it says) — I have found one man in a thousand, and in all of this I have not found a woman."

Here is a general principle: When the midrash says, "hada dichsiv," as it does here, stating "hada hu dichsiv, I have found one man in a thousand," it means that both verses can be explained from each other. (That is, 'When a man among you brings an offering" and "one man in a thousand" are mutually explainable.)

The midrash also tells us, "When a man among you brings an offering to Hashem — hada hu dichsiv, 'Haben yakir li Efrayim' ('my treasured son, Efrayim)." What is "yakir"? The word connotes something precious.

The midrash links the above verses together, saying that the "one man in a thousand that I've found" is a precious person — "haben yakir li" — of whom it also says, "When a man among you brings an offering to Hashem"! As we shall see below.

⬭ More Precious than a Kohen Gadol

There are 10 things in the world that are called "precious," and they are as follows: The Torah, prophecy, wisdom, understanding, foolishness, folly, wealth, tzaddikim, the deaths of the pious, chesed, and Israel (Vayikra Rabbah, perek beis.). Let us study the first and last of these.

"The Torah is called precious, as it says, 'More precious than pearls is she.' Israel is called precious, as it says, 'Haben yakir li Efrayim.' "

Chazal say (Sotah 4b): " 'More precious than pearls is she' — she is more precious than the Kohen Gadol who enters the innermost sanctum, to tell you that even a gentile who engages in Torah is like the Kohen Gadol entering the innermost sanctum."

Where did Chazal learn this parallel? How do they know that "more precious than pearls" means more precious than the Kohen Gadol entering the innermost sanctum? Surely they learned this with their heaven-sent insight; yet how are we to understand it? How are we to derive this understanding from the Torah itself?

My rebbi taught me the following. Let us say that a merchant walks into a store where diamonds are sold. Generally, the diamonds' owner will tell the buyer, "This diamond is worth $1000; the diamond next to it is more valuable and costs $1500; the third is worth $2000," and so on. However, if there were a piece of pretty colored glass worth perhaps 300 *shekels*, and the buyer were to point to it and say, "And that diamond is more precious than this piece of glass, for the glass costs only 300 shekels while the diamond is worth a $1000," the buyer would laugh at him. "What does one have to do with the other? We are speaking of diamonds and comparing their relative worth. But a piece of glass that only resembles a diamond …?"

If we say that the Torah is more precious than diamonds, that is a mockery. What does Torah have to do with diamonds? Diamonds are merely stones! There is no comparison between them.

Therefore, *Chazal* reflect that the verse is surely not referring to ordinary diamonds in the marketplace, or to ordinary pearls, but rather, a pearl of real value: the *Kohen Gadol* entering the innermost sanctum. *That* kind of precious pearl! The Torah is more precious than that.

When did the *Kohen Gadol* enter the Holy of Holies? On Yom Kippur. On the greatest day of the year, he stepped into the holiest of all places: a thing far more precious than pearls! This demonstrates just how far we must strive to achieve when we learn Torah: "like the *Kohen Gadol* entering the innermost sanctum."

It was an awesome time. "The *Kohen Gadol* would make a *Yom Tov* when he safely left the Holy of Holies!" Were a person to learn Torah with this thought in mind — and I include myself as well — how devotedly we would cling to Torah, and how deeply we would love it.

At one time, I served as *Mashgiach* in Yeshivas Tiferes Tzvi. One morning, as I walked among the rows of students, I noticed one of them with his head fallen forward onto his chest. He would wake up and then, a few seconds later, drop off again. This happened time after time. I became anxious. Approaching the *bachur*, I leaned over and whispered, "What's the matter? Why are you so tired?"

"I didn't sleep at all last night. I never closed my eyes. That's why I'm so tired."

I was even more surprised. "Why didn't you sleep all night?"

"Well, yesterday the *rav* spoke about how Torah is 'more precious than pearls.' So I stayed up to learn all night." I had told them this thought from my own rebbi, about how precious Torah is, more than the *Kohen Gadol* entering the innermost sanctum. *Gevaldig!* In short, the Torah is precious.

⤚ *Precious Israel*

The last item on the list that the *midrash* provides is "Israel": "The people of Israel are called precious, as it says, '*Is Efrayim my favorite son or a delightful child, that whenever I speak of him I remember him more and more? Therefore, my inner self yearns for him; I will surely take pity on him — the word of Hashem.*'"

The *midrash* explains how one precious person is formed out of a thousand: "In the way of the world, a thousand children enter the study of *Chumash*." When a child is brought to *cheder*, the first thing he is taught is *Chumash*; therefore, "a thousand children enter the study of *Chumash*." And of that thousand, a hundred will go on to *Mishnah*.

From these hundred who go on to study *mishnayos*, 10 will continue on to Gemara.

Of the 10 who go on to learn Gemara, one remains to teach Torah to others — "*Hada hu dichsiv*, I've found one person in a thousand." The one in a thousand is the most precious of goals. It is for his sake that all the rest of the thousand are sustained, for without the thousand, the one would not emerge. Every single Jew is a partner in this exalted mission, for they are part of the thousand who enter *cheder* to learn *Chumash*.

What have we learned to this point? That all of Israel are called "precious," because of the Torah that is called "precious." And that one person in a thousand (who goes out to teach) is the most precious goal of all: a fragrant offering to Hashem.

It is this person who is held up as an example at the start of our *parashah*: "*Speak to the Children of Israel and say to them: When a man among you brings an offering to Hashem ...*" Who is the man among you who will bring an offering to Hashem? The one man in a thousand who gives himself as an offering to Hashem.

You might think that I was repeating a "*vort*" from some great rebbe, but no. These are the words of *Chazal*, in the *midrash*! One who offers himself: he is the one who is called an "*adam*," a person. And how precious he is!

The verse continues, "*from animals — from the cattle or from the flock.*" That is, that precious offering, the "*man among you*," is exalted above all other created beings, for Hashem did not create anything without a purpose. Animals — cattle and sheep — were created for the man who will give himself as an offering to Hashem.

☞ "If Not for the Madmen"

Now we have arrived at the Rambam that is quoted at the beginning of this section. The Rambam writes, "If not for the madmen, the world would remain desolate." If I didn't know that this was said by the Rambam, I'd have thought the comment was made by a *tzaddik* from a previous generation. But the Rambam said it! "If not for the madmen." By the way, I once heard Yankel Rogeshkover remark that the Rambam actually used the reflexive word, "*mishtagim*" — literally, those who are not only mad, but who make themselves mad.

In his introduction to *Seder Zera'im*, the Rambam discusses the verse, "*The sum of the matter, when all has been considered: Fear God and keep His commandments, for that is man's whole duty.*" *Chazal* comment, "That is man's whole duty: the whole world was created only for this *mitzvah*." The Rambam explains as follows (I will not quote his exact language, only the general concept):

A person travels through a mysterious land. He is accompanied by suffering and the hardships of the road: frigid winters and searing summers. Sometimes he goes to warmer climates and sometimes to snowy ones. He wanders for 30 years, for 40: in America, in Africa, in mountains of darkness, and other places. He digs beneath the earth to unearth coal. He works and he labors. For what? For the gold that he will receive when his work is done.

In other words, that is the goal. For the person who labors 40 years in order to receive thousands of dollars, that is the primary goal: to put money in his wallet.

But is this the true purpose?

No. How do we know that? Because that same person continues working. Even with money in his wallet, he does not rest.

After years of work, he takes the money that he's amassed over the course of 45 years, ends his traveling, and returns home. And there, in his hometown, he hires a contractor to build him a house. He gives the money to the contractor.

This, then, is clearly the goal and the purpose: to give the contractor money to build him a house. The Rambam describes the way the house is built: stone upon stone, one row of bricks on top of another. Wall by wall, the building goes up. Remember, I'm not speaking of a fantasy novel, but of the Rambam! The contractor builds, stone by stone and row by row, until the house is standing: a fine-looking and sturdy structure, able to endure for at least 300 years. The house's new owner is aware that he has only a limited number of years of life left on this earth, for which a house of wood or even straw would have sufficed.

Perhaps the new homeowner believes that all his decades of hard work were aimed toward this goal: to build himself a strong, beautiful house. In truth, however, this is simply madness: to work so hard for so many years, only to build, in his final days, a house that can stand for hundreds of years. In a spirit of foolishness, he believes that this was the whole purpose. "Is there any folly or madness like this? So, too, are all the pleasures of this world. They are completely false and foolish, but they are the reason for the settlement of the world" (in the Rambam's words).

What is the truth? This, says the Rambam, is not the purpose. Then what is?

Why does the world function well? Because there is one man in the world whom Hashem favors. "*A man among you brings an offering to Hashem.*" The purpose is to ensure that this man lives a pleasant and comfortable life. As Shlomo Hamelech said, "*The sum of the matter, when all has been considered: Fear God and keep His commandments, for that is man's whole duty.*" That lovely and sturdy house that the long-laboring man has built will serve a personal function for that one man who finds favor in Hashem's eyes. When this God-fearing individual is walking in the field one day, feeling cold, and he comes upon that house, he will be able to enter it and be warmed. When the weather is hot and his head is heavy, the shade of the house will cool him. It was for this that the home-owner indulged in a fit of madness, but not only he. Thousands of people: quarry workers, cement men, bricklayers, carpenters, engineers, and so on — thousands of people participated in this building. And for what purpose? So that those who are called "precious" in the world — "*my treasured son, Efrayim*" — will be served in some way.

"*For that is man's whole duty.*" The entire world was created for this.

The world is built and managed by "madmen." And the goal of it all is, "*When a man among you brings an offering to Hashem.*" Let us merit great good, and be among those who are perfect in His service!

"Is it not true that there is no ordinary person who smells the (harsh) smell of burning feathers without becoming nause-ated by it? Why did the Torah say, 'he shall cause it to go up in smoke'? In order that the Mizbe'ach should be full and beautified with the offering of a poor man" (Rashi on Vayikra 1:17).

The Mikveh that Freed the Miser

R' Shabsi Yudelevitz

*B*ecause we have gathered here today on a *tzeddakah*-related matter, you are going to hear something that I have never told before," began R' Shabsi.

We have gathered here on the matter of heating the *mikvehs* in the outlying settlements. Others have spoken here before me. Among those seated here are some wealthy individuals who can give enough money to supply the *mikvehs* with heat for several years. But even the poor men in this audience can give enough for a month or two, and their merit will be enormous: reaching to the heart of heaven. See the *midrash* on this week's *parashah*: how important the poor man's offer-ing is considered, to the point where the wings of doves were burned in order to beautify his *korban*. As *Chazal* tell us: "Is it not true that there is no ordinary person who smells the (harsh) smell of burning feathers without becoming nauseated by it? Why did the Torah say that, *'he shall cause it to go up in smoke?'* In order that the Mizbe'ach should be full and beautified with the offering of a poor man."

The *midrash* cites an awesome story about King Aggripas and a poor man who would bring birds to be offered in the *Beis HaMik-dash* every day. You can read that *midrash* for yourselves. What we can learn from these stories is that even someone who is poor and cannot afford to bring an offering worth a thousand *lirot*, but only turtledoves and young doves that he bought for 20 *lirot*, can offer them to provide a "*rei'ach nicho'ach* — a pleasing fragrance" — for Hashem! My brothers and friends, we are all like one person with one heart. Let us rouse our hearts for the repair and heating of the *mikvehs* in these distant areas. And then the merit of the "*Taharas Hamishpachah b'Yisrael*" organization will be ours as well: for contentment and joy and salvation, as a group and as individuals.

Listen to a story about *tzeddakah, morai v'rabbosai.*

The chief rabbi of Jerusalem in the previous generation was a respected *gaon* by the name of R' Shmuel Salant. He ran the city with great wisdom for decades.

During a certain period, a new *mikveh* came under construction. This was a very urgent project in Jerusalem of that time. The work was begun, but was halted due to a lack of funds. The city's residents, as we all know, were destitute, and the pennies that they donated were not sufficient to complete the *mikveh*.

One day, R' Shmuel Salant suddenly put on his coat, picked up his cane, and announced to his household that he was going out to see Wittenberg, a well-known and wealthy man, to try and persuade him to contribute to the building of the *mikveh*.

His family and other community members were astonished. Wittenberg, though very rich, was known as a downright miser. They had no doubt that the *rav* was wasting his time and energy. *Rabbosai*, do you know what stinginess is? It is a very harsh disease. Just as, for example, an ordinary person would be incapable of cutting off his own finger, so does the miser feel about parting with money from his pocket. He is simply incapable. It is really hard for him. He is very unfortunate: a victim of a serious ailment.

Neither his family nor the community activists said a word to R' Shmuel Salant. In silence, they watched him set off on his mission.

R' Shmuel approached the rich man's house, into which he was welcomed with honor.

The chief rabbi sat down in an armchair and made his plea for a donation for the new *mikveh*. You must understand that a person who is suffering from the disease of stinginess finds it hard to overcome his nature, even if he is well aware of the urgency of the matter and even if the chief rabbi of Jerusalem in person is seated before him, outlining the holiness of the *mitzvah*.

When the *rav* finished speaking, total silence reigned. Wittenberg did not move a muscle. He sat in silence.

Suddenly, Wittenberg opened his mouth and asked, "Honored *rav*, I am curious. There is no one wiser than you in our holy city, and the *rav* does not generally act in such a foolish way — coming to me for money for the *mikveh* — when both the *rav* and all the rest of the community know that I never give anything even to the most important personages. Surely, the *rav* knows that I will not give a penny to the *mikveh*, either. In that case, why did the *rav* bother coming to my house?"

R' Shmuel Salant picked up his cane, looked at the man, and said, "I will explain. One day, you will die. You will be buried like all other Jews, and worms with eat your flesh and your body will rot and decompose. You will stand in judgment in heaven like every Jew: 'Before Whom you are destined to render an accounting!' One of the questions that you will be asked will be, 'Why did you not assist in the building of the *mikveh*, thereby weakening purity among the people of Israel?' You will no doubt be quick to defend yourself, answering, 'I did not donate money because they never came to ask me. People had already stopped knocking on my door. (In other words, they'd given up on me.)' Therefore, I have come to your home today" — R' Shmuel raised his voice in fear and trembling — "I have come to ask you for money, in order to remove that possibility. Even that answer will not be available to you when you stand in judgment before the heavenly court!"

Wittenberg began to tremble violently from head to foot. He said to the chief rabbi, "Please, let the *rav* take the keys to my safe and take out anything he wants. But please, don't make me watch while you do it!" So powerful was his innate stinginess, that even when he had made up his mind to give, he could not watch it happening.

The *rav* did as he had been told.

I have heard that, from that moment, a change began to take place in the man. A crack had been made in his miserliness. That first act of giving helped him free himself of his stingy nature. This incident was the "eye of the needle" that, at the end of the process, had widened until it was like a vast hall. From that day, Wittenberg changed, and became a major philanthropist. Here in Jerusalem there is a neighborhood known as "Batei Wittenberg," where the city's pious poor can find free housing. Near the end of his life, this man had the privilege of amassing a great deal of merit for the World to Come, and served as an example to many of truly heartfelt generosity.

The difficulty in raising money for the *mikveh* had been worthwhile, if only to free a miser from his stinginess — as well as from a harsh judgment in the next world. The merit of his *mitzvos* will stand him in good stead. And today, your merit in the *mitzvah* of *tzeddakah* — to heat the *mikvehs* — will protect us from every trouble and anguish and ailment. Be strong and be blessed!

"There is a story of a woman who brought a handful of meal, and the Kohen ridiculed her, saying, 'See what they are sacrificing! What is there to eat in this; what is there to sacrifice?' A vision came to the Kohen in a dream, saying, 'Do not ridicule her, for it is as though she is sacrificing her life.' We can learn a 'kal v'chomer' (comparison) from this: If someone who does not sacrifice a live being is considered as if he has sacrificed his life, how much more so is a person who has actually sacrificed a live creature considered as though he's sacrificed his life!" (Vayikra Rabbah, parashah 3).

THE RICH MAN'S LAST NIGHT

*H*ere is an amazing story from a wise Torah figure: We were walking carefully among the tombstones in the big Vilna cemetery, when our eyes suddenly glimpsed a fascinating text on one stone. "Here lies [the man's name], son of [the man's father], who left the world on [date of death] and was buried on [date of burial] ... '*She spreads out her palm to the poor, and extends her hands to the destitute.*'" Here, the text ended.

A line from "*Eishes Chayil*" on the tombstone of a Vilna man, instead of a woman? Amazing! Had such a thing ever been heard of before?

Our curiosity was piqued. We wanted to learn the story behind that stone. We decided to look into the sources. In the archives of the old *Chevrah Kaddisha*, we discovered an explanation. We found the man's name and the story behind him. A wonderful tale ...

The man lived in greater Vilna. He was a charitable and giving individual. His wealth was a byword in all the neighboring towns, and his generosity matched his wealth. He gave abundantly to needy Jews. "*Praiseworthy is he who contemplates the need; on the day of evil Hashem will deliver him.*"

For many years, this man poured out his fortune on the destitute and the needy, and all were awed at his great joy in giving *tzeddakah*. He simply loved scattering largesse on the poor. He relished the process of transferring his money to their empty pockets. He literally pursued charity!

Then came a difficult period, when this *tzaddik* slowly began to lose his fortune. His business stagnated. One loss led to another, until the man had no more cash. He still retained his opulent home filled with gold and silver ornaments and utensils, but there was no more money for the poor.

All of Vilna speculated as to why such a generous man had deserved such a harsh fate. Here was yet another example of the inexplicable: the "*hester panim*" of our time ...

The talk reached the ears of the community leaders, judges, and rabbis. These great men of Torah and piety decided to sit in court and plumb the depths of this matter: Why did he receive such a harsh punishment?

Several wise men met together and investigated the man's lifestyle, until they discovered his sin:

The man had not heeded the words of *Chazal*, who have instructed, "*The profligate shall not give more than one-fifth.*" In his zeal to give *tzeddakah*, he had given out far more than a fifth of his possessions.

What was there for this charitable man to do, now that he had no ready cash available to give to the poor? He began to satisfy his desire in a new way: by distributing a portion of his vessels and ornaments from his home. He handed over objects from his own house.

Seeing what he was doing, the *Beis Din* devised a strategy whereby they might rescue him from destroying his entire home. "You are under house arrest," they told him. "You are not permitted to leave your home!" The *dayanim* hoped in this way to prevent the poor from encountering the man in the streets of the city, forcing them to seek alms at other hands.

But the area's poor, who knew their benefactor well, did not despair of finding ways to seek donations from him. They began to knock on the windows of his home. They collected near his home late at night to wail over their deprivations until he was roused from sleep, and was touched.

Every night, he tossed to them everything that came to his hand: dishes and silver candelabra, watches and other valuable objects that still remained in his house. Gradually, the house emptied out. There was no more gold or silver, yet the man happily continued to give, energetically pursuing *tzeddakah* despite the halachic strictures.

Until, *rabbosai*, the last night came.

The last night. At midnight, two poor men rapped on his window in tears. Overcome with compassion, the former rich man went inside to search for some object of value that he might hurl their way. He searched and searched, but found nothing. All of his things were snugly residing in other homes.

The poor men did not give up. "Pity us and our hungry families!" Once again, the householder searched through the cracks and crevices of his cupboards until he found a spoon of pure gold, which he had received from his father-in-law on his wedding day ... But he had only one spoon, and there were two poor men crying at his window! What to do?

The man scratched his head, thought a moment, and came up with a simple idea. He broke the spoon in half. One of the poor men received the handle, and the other, the bowl of the spoon.

The poor men rushed off to sell the gold in exchange for cash to relieve their families' plight.

In the morning, the householder was dead. He had returned his soul to his Creator. It had been his last night on earth.

It was decided to etch this story, with which his life had ended, on the man's tombstone: "*She spreads out her palm to the poor, and extends her hands to the destitute.*" The man had given his "palm" — in Hebrew "*kaf,*" which also means "spoon" — to one poor man, and his "hand" — "*yad,*" meaning "handle" — to the other.

(This is a true story as told by a reliable source, who heard it from R' Yosef Dov Soleveitchik, who saw the tale inscribed in the archives of the *Chevrah Kaddisha* of Vilna.)

A PORTION OF THE DERASHAH, TOLD INCIDENTALLY

*T*he entire Oral Torah is hinted at in the Written Torah. It is known that the Vilna Gaon, in his old age, learned only *Chumash*. Why is that? It was because he knew the entire Torah, whether it be the Written Torah, the Oral Torah, the *Talmud Bavli,* the *Talmud Yerushalmi,* the *Sifri,* the *Sifra,* the *Mechilta,* the *Tanna DeVei Eliyahu,* or what have you. He knew every word. And in his old age he studied deeply to understand how the entire Oral Torah is hinted at in the *Chumash* — the Written Torah.

Which brings us to an amazing story ...

R' Chaim of Volozhin had a younger brother, R' Zalmale, an awesome *gaon*. R' Chaim had great respect for his brother. Once, when R' Zalmale was still a *bachur*, as the two spoke of deep Torah matters, R' Chaim was deriving such pleasure from his brother that he promised, "For your wedding, I will hire a band."

R' Chaim kept his promise and hired musicians and instruments. The wedding was attended by a huge crowd because their father, R' Yitzchak, was an important and honored person and it is reasonable to assume that the entire city was invited. The celebration lasted many hours. When all the guests had finally departed and gone home, R' Zalmale asked R' Chaim, "*Nu?* Didn't you say you would hire a band?" He hadn't even heard the music, so immersed was he in his great and holy thoughts. That was R' Zalmale.

A leading Torah figure was once asked, "What is the uniqueness of the Vilna Gaon? They say he knew *Shas* the way we know *Ashrei*. Well, R' Zalmale also knows *Shas* the way we know *Ashrei* — completely by heart."

"True," came the answer. "Both of them know *Shas* the way we know *Ashrei*. But the Vilna Gaon also knows *Shas* the way we would say *Ashrei* from the end to the beginning — backward. "*Selah, yehallelucha, od, beisecha, yoshvei, Ashrei,*" and so on."

פרשת צו ~

PARASHAS TZAV

"Master of the Universe, it is known to You that, during the time that the Beis HaMikdash stood, when a person sinned and brought an offering, only the fat and blood were [placed on the Altar], and that would suffice to atone for him. Now, I have sat in fasting and my fat and blood have become diminished. May it be Your will that my fat and blood, which have become diminished, will be considered as though offered before You on the Mizbe'ach, and let me be forgiven!" (Berachos 17a).

WEEPING COPIOUS TEARS

Rav Benzion Yadler Regarding The Patriarch of the Porush Family

id you know R' Naftali Tzvi Porush?" the elderly *maggid* asked those seated around him at the table in the Katamon neighborhood of Jerusalem.

"No," they replied.

"I never saw him, either, as he passed away during the lifetime of his holy friend, R' Nachum of Shadik. But I heard about him from a firsthand source."

There have always been Jews who have sacrificed their fat and blood through fasting, learning Torah in a state of abstinence. One of these Jews was R' Naftali Tzvi Porush, who spent the last years of his life in Jerusalem.

Hagaon R' Yitzchak Blazer — better known as R' Itzele Peterburger and a student of R' Yisrael Salanter — also spent the final years of his life in Jerusalem. He told me that he had known R' Naftali Tzvi when they still lived in Europe. It is known that R' Naftali Tzvi Porush led an outstandingly ascetic lifestyle: All year long he did not engage in mundane talk, being committed to a *ta'anis dibbur* (a fast of speech) from Rosh Hashanah to Rosh Hashanah. He wrote down what he had to say, and even then only the barest minimum that was necessary.

He did not eat more than a few "*kezeisim*" of bread soaked in water, and even this morsel he did not chew, but swallowed whole, in order not to take pleasure from this world. He was careful to wear only white flaxen clothing to avoid the risk of *shaatnez*. This he wore in the winter as well, never donning a woolen garment. He never slept more than a few hours in 24, and those few hours were not spent in a bed. (Because of all of this, he was labeled a "*porush*" — an ascetic — and from thence derived his family name, Porush, which has endured in Jerusalem to this day.)

And still, he did not feel satisfied in his service, and always feared that he had not fulfilled his obligation. Therefore, on the occasion of R' Yitzchak Blazer's passing through his town, he had his vow against speaking nullified in order to go see him. This is what he said:

"You are a student of *Hagaon* R' Yisrael Salanter. You must surely have *ruach hakodesh* (a Divine spirit). Therefore, I ask you to guide me in my service of Hashem and tell me of my sins, in order that I can repent!"

"As he said these words, he was weeping copiously," related R' Itzele Blazer. "But I had nothing to tell him."

R' Blazer continued his story.

Time passed, and when I traveled to Kovno, R' Naftali Tzvi went there, too. He asked me to come with him to see R' Yisrael Salanter, who lived in that city. I agreed.

I described R' Naftali Tzvi's greatness to R' Yisrael, telling him that R' Naftali's soul endured tremendous suffering and yet he wished to impose on himself even further self-abnegation with additional asceticism, as repentance for sins.

The moment he entered, R' Naftali Tzvi said, "I am certain that Rebbi has *ruach hakodesh*. Please guide me in my service of Hashem."

R' Yisrael, in his wisdom, replied as follows.

"I think, based on the wisdom of our Sages — may their memory be a blessing— that the greatest sin of all is ingratitude, as our Sages have remarked in several places. The greatest good that *HaKadosh Baruch Hu* gives a person is his physical health, for it is through the health of his limbs and body that he retains the possibility of serving Hashem. Therefore, anyone who does not care for his bodily health is considered ungrateful."

This is what I heard from R' Itzele.

The rebbetzin, R' Itzele's wife, once related that, as a child in the city of Vilkomir, she merited serving the "*porush*" several times in the home of her father, who was the *rav* of Vilkomir. This was during the period when the ascetic had exiled himself to Vilkomir for five years of asceticism in secret, in preparation for his move to Eretz Yisrael. He learned Torah in a hut at the edge of the city, sleeping little and fasting from Shabbos to Shabbos. He always broke his fast at the *rav's* home, where the rebbetzin sometimes gave him the *challos* for *Kiddush*. For two and a half years he endured this way, until his weakened body succumbed to serious illness. Doctors were summoned. They categorized his illness as grave. Community activists quickly brought in a specialist from Peterburg, to whom they paid a large sum — 300 silver *rubles* — to work diligently until R' Naftali Tzvi was cured.

When he had recovered from his illness, he was invited to see the *rav* of Vilkomir, who use every word of beseeching to convince him to change his habits and reduce his self-imposed suffering, in light of the condition he had brought upon himself and the expense incurred by the townspeople. He found R' Naftali Tzvi's mind very hard to change. The *rav* tried again and again, until at last he managed to convince him to at least break his fast on Tuesdays.

R' Naftali Tzvi secluded himself once again, and for another year and a half, he toiled in Torah and service to Hashem day and night without rest. Then, once again, he fell gravely ill. At this point, the *Beis Din* decreed that he must change his habits. He agreed to be satisfied with fasting every day but stopping at nightfall to eat a meager meal of bread, salt, and a little water. In this way, he completed the originally resolved five-year period. Joyfully he returned home to actualize his dream of moving to Jerusalem.

Together with his wife and two of their children, he set out on a ship from Odessa. The journey took three months. Three days before the ship reached safe harbor in Kostanzin, the ship was split in half, with him and his older son on one half while his wife and younger son were on the other. They floated on the water and miraculously managed to reach the harbor. In all his travails he saw the Hand of Hashem; after all, Eretz Yisrael is acquired through suffering.

From Kostanzin they traveled to Yaffo. From there they were forced to make their way to Jerusalem by camel. From the camel's back dangled two baskets, one on either side. In one of these baskets rode the slender father and his son, while the mother and other son rode in the second basket. At long last, R' Naftali Tzvi arrived in Jerusalem, to involve himself in Torah and *mitzvos* in holiness and purity. He lived in an apartment in the courtyard of *Churvas R' Yehudah Hachassid.*

A corner of this area was partitioned off with the use of a curtain, and into this "four cubits of halachah" not even the members of his household entered. This was where he pored over his Talmud and *poskim* night and day, without pause. His abode was near that of the holy *gaon* R' Nachum of Shadik, and the two conducted a nightly "*tikkun chatzos*" at the Western Wall. There, in a set corner at the end of the square, they lamented the destruction of the *Beis HaMikdash.*

R' Naftali Tzvi left this world in the cholera epidemic of 5626 (1866), and was greatly honored in his death. Those who accompanied him to his final resting place sat on the ground and wept bitterly. In the great eulogy delivered by R' Nachum of Shadik, he cried heartrendingly, "When the rest of us finished the five books of Moses on Simchas Torah, he finished the *Talmud Bavli, Yerushalmi, Sifri, Sifra, Midrash Mechilta,* and all four parts of the *Shulchan Aruch,* which he knew by heart."

One week later, R' Naftali Tzvi's holy dear friend, R' Nachum of Shadik, likewise passed on.

וְהָאֵשׁ עַל־הַמִּזְבֵּחַ תּוּקַד־בּוֹ לֹא תִכְבֶּה וּבִעֵר עָלֶיהָ הַכֹּהֵן עֵצִים בַּבֹּקֶר בַּבֹּקֶר וְעָרַךְ עָלֶיהָ הָעֹלָה וְהִקְטִיר עָלֶיהָ חֶלְבֵי הַשְּׁלָמִים. אֵשׁ תָּמִיד תּוּקַד עַל־הַמִּזְבֵּחַ לֹא תִכְבֶּה.

"The fire on the Mizbe'ach shall be kept burning on it, it shall not be extinguished; and the Kohen shall kindle wood upon it every morning; he shall prepare the burnt-offering upon it and shall cause the fats of the peace-offerings to go up in smoke upon it. A permanent fire shall remain aflame on the Mizbe'ach; it shall not be extinguished" (Vayikra 6:5-6).

"It Shall Not Be Extinguished"

R' Benzion Yadler

A simple Jew entered the house of one of the *mussar* greats, complaining that *mitzvah* observance was very difficult for him. The demands of his varied business enterprises made it impossible for him to be Torah observant, may Hashem have mercy. What to do? He had come to consult with the Sage and to pour out his heart. "It's too hard for me. I can't do it," he sighed.

The wise man sent him to a nearby farming village. "There you will find an answer to your question," he said.

The man went. The moment he entered the village, he met a villager standing on top of a wagon filled with lumber and arranging the wood in piles. The Jew stopped to watch.

The villager turned to the visitor and said, "There beside the wagon, on the ground, are a few planks of wood. If you please, sir, do me a favor and hand them to me."

"They're heavy," the Jew answered apologetically. "I come from the city, and I'm not used to carrying such heavy loads. I'm sorry, but I can't help you."

The villager looked at him from the heights of the wagon and retorted with a bit of well-known farmers' wisdom: "If you don't want to, you don't want to. I have no right to force you. But please don't say, 'I can't.' Say, 'I don't want to,' because if you wanted to, you'd find a way to do it. Nothing stands in the way of the will!"

Later, at the end of the day, the businessman returned to his own city. The Sage said, "Remember those words. They will serve you as a guidepost and an answer to your question. The will is the powerful foundation for keeping the Torah and *mitzvos*. There is no excuse such as, 'I can't observe the Torah because of my business concerns.' Can't you? The truth is: you don't want to!"

R' Yosef Yoizel of Novaradok used to say, in Yiddish, "*Nit kenen is nit du. Nit vellen iz du.*" ("'I can't' doesn't exist. 'I don't want' exists.")

How does one achieve the will to "want"? The desire comes with the study of *mussar*. The study of *mussar*!

Listen. When I once asked the holy *Maharil* Diskin for advice about strengthening myself in Torah and *avodah*, he said, "Strengthen yourself with the study of *mussar* with great dedication and humility, and it will help you."

His student, R' Zerach Braverman, told me that he was once summoned to the *Maharil* Diskin. His rebbe showed him that he always kept the *sefer* "*Sha'arei Teshuvah*" in his *tallis* bag.

R' Tzvi Michel Shapira used to say jokingly, "If a person wants to be God fearing with ease, let him not study *mussar*. Then he will be in his own eyes God fearing and pious, without any difficulty at all.

In my *derashah* last Shabbos, I linked the study of *mussar* to the words, *"The fire on the Mizbe'ach shall be kept burning on it, it shall not be extinguished; and the Kohen shall kindle wood upon it every morning; he shall prepare the burnt-offering upon it and shall cause the fats of the peace-offerings to go up in smoke upon it. A permanent fire shall remain aflame on the Mizbe'ach; it shall not be extinguished."* The holy Torah is hinting that, if we truly desire to have the flame of love for Torah and fear of heaven burning constantly within us, it is not enough to avoid pouring water on the flames or extinguishing them with our hands. Rather, we must keep adding wood to the fire at all times, so that the fire will not go out of its own accord.

They say that R' Yisrael Salanter reviewed the *sefer* "Mesillas Yesharim" for eight consecutive years, until its concepts were etched into his heart so that he might properly focus his energies, weigh his words, and walk in the footsteps of the righteous.

⌇ Hundreds of Times

Our *mussar* Sages have provided us with an important principle: to invest no less energy in the study of *mussar* than in the study of halachah and *pilpul*. *"v'yagata u'matzasa"*: Only through toil and effort are achievements made. I was once present, years ago, at a penetrating *mussar* talk delivered by a renounced *rav*. In his talk, he repeated a statement of *Chazal* hundreds of times: "HaKadosh Baruch Hu is willing to overlook the sin of *avodah zarah* (worship of foreign gods), but He is not willing to overlook the sin of *bitul Torah* (wasting time that might be used for Torah study)." Again and again he repeated these words over the course of half an hour, and so powerful was the impression they made that it pierced my heart like a needle. For days afterward, these words of *Chazal* reverberated in my ears. They gave me no rest until I went to see the *Maharil* Diskin and asked him: "Please tell me, Rebbi, what sort of things can be classified as idle talk, and what are the acceptable parameters of the sin of *bitul Torah*?"

The *gaon* asked me: "Which time are you talking about: the hours you spend in yeshivah, or the time you spend outside it?" I replied, "I'm asking in a general way." Immediately, he stood up, went over to the bookcase, and took down a *Mishnayos, Seder Nezikin*, and opened to *Maseches Avos (perek gimmel)*: "One who walks on the road while reviewing [a Torah lesson], but interrupts his review and exclaims, 'How beautiful is this tree! How beautiful is this plowed field!' — it is considered for him by Scripture as if he bears guilt for his soul." The commentary of the Rav (R' Ovadiah MiBartenura) writes: "Despite the fact that through his interest in the tree he is blessing Hashem Who created the world, nevertheless, he is considered guilty for his soul, because he interrupted his learning." The *Maharil* Diskin concluded, "We can derive a *kal v'chomer* from here: If a person who is walking along the road during a time that was not designated for learning, and who distracts himself even for a *mitzvah*-related matter, is considered guilty, how much more so would a person in yeshivah, where all his time is designated for Torah study during those hours, be considered guilty if he interrupts his learning."

At that same meeting, I spoke with the *Maharil* Diskin about the study of *mussar*. He provided me with guidance, saying that the study of *mussar* is essential. In his opinion, it is best to study *mussar* in the *beis midrash*, quietly and discreetly. Ever since, I have not deviated from his advice in the matter of *mussar* study, with regard to both the form that study should take as well as its great importance.

פסח ⸄
PESACH

"Behold! I send you Eliyahu Hanavi, before the great and awesome day of Hashem. He shall restore the heart of fathers to children and the heart of children to their fathers, lest I come and strike the land with destruction" (Haftarah, Shabbos Hagadol, Malachi 3:23-24).

"BEHOLD! I SEND YOU ELIYAHU."

R' Sholom Schwadron

I heard two stories from my father-in-law, *shlita*, said R' Sholom Schwadron, about the revelation of Eliyahu to the Chofetz Chaim, *zt"l*.

When he was still living in Lithuania, those close to the Ponevezher Rav knew that he had witnessed a revelation of Eliyahu to the Chofetz Chaim. He refrained from relating details of the story, putting off those who asked with the words, "I'll tell you some other time."

Near the end of his life, in the Ponevezher Yeshivah, when a group of young yeshivah men stood around him and he spoke to them about the greatness of the Chofetz Chaim, he moved from topic to topic until he suddenly came to "the revelation of Eliyahu." This is what he said:

"I was standing in line to go in to see the Chofetz Chaim. I stood near the door, and when my turn came I suddenly saw a person open the door of the Chofetz Chaim's room and walk inside. The man stayed there for about half an hour. The others waiting in line complained, asking why I didn't go in. I told them that the stranger had been in the room a long time and had not yet emerged.

"When he came out, I went in to the Chofetz Chaim.

"As I approached, the Chofetz Chaim asked, 'Did you see that man?'

" 'Yes,' I answered.

"The Chofetz Chaim then said, 'Fortunate is he who greets him with "Shalom" and whom he greets with "Shalom" in return.' "

The Ponevezher Rav did not reveal whether or not he had greeted the man.

Here is an additional story about a revelation of Eliyahu.

In the Chofetz Chaim's youth, he would sometimes visit the small towns of Poland in order to gather groups of young *bachurim*, establish a yeshivah for them, and teach them Torah. When the yeshivah was on its feet, he would avoid taking credit for it, referring its success to the *rav* of the town who had worked so hard for the students. R' Zelig Privalski was a student in one of these *yeshivos*. Here is what he had to say:

Once, as we sat and learned with the Chofetz Chaim, a man with a slightly strange appearance entered the *beis midrash*. The Chofetz Chaim went over to him and the two stood near the *bimah*, conversing for a long time.

Seeing the Chofetz Chaim spend such a long time talking to the stranger, some of the *bachurim* surmised that the stranger was a *talmid chacham* and decided to shake his hand in greeting. Others remained in their seats, waiting patiently. And still others made fun of the man's outward appearance and clothing.

When the two had parted and the man left, the Chofetz Chaim praised those who had greeted the stranger, and condemned those who had mocked him. Of this latter group, he said, "You will certainly not succeed in your learning." We understood from his words that those who had greeted the man had merited the blessing of, "Fortunate is he who greets him …"

וַיּוֹלֶךְ ה׳ אֶת־הַיָּם בְּרוּחַ קָדִים עַזָּה כָּל־הַלַּיְלָה וַיָּשֶׂם אֶת־הַיָּם לֶחָרָבָה וַיִּבָּקְעוּ הַמָּיִם. וַיָּבֹאוּ בְנֵי־יִשְׂרָאֵל בְּתוֹךְ הַיָּם בַּיַּבָּשָׁה וְהַמַּיִם לָהֶם חוֹמָה מִימִינָם וּמִשְּׂמֹאלָם.

"Hashem moved the sea with a strong east wind all night, and He turned the sea to damp land and the water split. The Children of Israel came within the sea on dry land; and the water was a wall for them, on their right and on their left" (Shemos 14:21-22).

A PICTURE OF THE WORLD

R' Sholom Schwadron

I have an appreciation for art, and I sometimes think that the whole world has gone crazy in its art, in its music, in its clothing: in everything. In the old days, I would see beautiful paintings and take pleasure from the handiwork of the old masters. But today? Strange pictures. And the songs? I travel from Jerusalem to Tel Aviv, and all I hear is boom, boom, boom. Today's "art" is a strange thing, as is its music.

The songs and paintings of our day come to mind when the *Ksav Sofer* says, with reference to the splitting of the Reed Sea: To what can this be compared? To an artist who paints the king's horse, as we will see below.

"*On that day, Hashem saved Israel from the hand of Egypt, and Israel saw the Egyptians dead on the seashore. Israel saw the great hand that Hashem inflicted upon Egypt; and the people revered Hashem, and they had faith in Hashem and in Moshe, His servant.*" They saw the great hand! And so, they felt reverence for heaven and, after that, "*they had faith in Hashem.*"

Was it only now that they believed in Hashem? In the previous portions, before the parting of the *Yam Suf*, it says, "*The nation had faith.*" Before all the miracles and wonders occurred, Moshe Rabbeinu protested to Hashem, "But they won't believe me!" Hashem replied, "Israel are believers and the children of believers" (*Shabbos* 97a). In that case, what happened now? What is the meaning of, "*they had faith in Hashem*"? Was this the only time they believed?!

It is also difficult to understand, "*the people revered Hashem, and they had faith in Hashem.*" How could they have reverence if they lacked faith? An unbeliever does not revere! Should the text not have said, "*They had faith in Hashem,*" and then, "*the people revered Hashem*"?

These questions were asked by my rebbi, who answered them with a marvelous principle which everyone is obligated to review:

Just as *HaKadosh Baruch Hu* is limitless and timeless, so can faith in Hashem be limitless and timeless. The more I believe, the more I am able to believe.

Indeed, they had faith even before "*the people revered Hashem,*" for it *is* possible to revere without having faith, but even greater faith is possible. After "*the people revered Hashem,*" they rose far higher, to a very sweet level of faith. And what was that? It was faith with their own senses, when the senses themselves believe in Hashem — an exalted level indeed. "*Israel saw the great hand that Hashem inflicted upon Egypt ... and they had faith in Hashem!*"

We live in the world for 70 years or, if we are exceptionally strong, 80 years. Let us at least know that it is possible for us to continually rise in *emunah*, in faith, and that there is *emunah* that exists before "*the people revered*" as well as *emunah* afterward — more and more and more.

⌁ Within the Sea on Dry Land

The following question is asked in the name of the *"Noam Elimelech"* (Reb Elimelech of Lizhensk). At first, the Torah says, *"The Children of Israel came within the sea on dry land"* (*Shemos* 14:22), after which (ibid., v.29) it says, *"The Children of Israel went on dry land in the midst of the sea."* His explanation:

The *Bnei Yisrael* walked in the midst of the sea, which had turned into dry land. "A maidservant on the Sea saw what Yechezkel ben Buzi Hakohen did not [merit to] see." In that great hour, they witnessed the wonders of Creation and were granted prophetic insight: to the point where *emunah* became etched into their hearts and they knew in the most immediate way that Hashem is the Creator of heaven and earth. Their wonder encompassed not only the water that had split, but also the dry land itself.

I ask you: How do I walk around on dry land? How? Isn't *that* an amazing thing? It is only because I have always lived on the dry land that rests on great waters — *"Who spreads out the earth upon the waters"* — and have long become accustomed to the fact that the world hangs in space like a giant ball, that I am not overcome by the wonders of nature each and every moment. But the nation of Israel, who experienced all the miracles, achieved a marvelous level: *"Hodu l'Hashem ki l'olam chasdo* — Praise Hashem, for His lovingkindness is everlasting."* Hashem's *chesed* is not only on the sea, but on dry land as well.

As we have already mentioned (in *Parashas Beshalach*), the Ksav Sofer wove a parable about an artist who painted a portrait of the king's horse. He painted it on a large canvas, in painstaking detail, so that the painting resembled a live horse in every respect. Then the artist stood the canvas up on the street, certain that everyone who passed would be moved by the greatness of his art.

To his surprise, the passersby did not seem to be moved at all. He thought and thought, until he understood the simple reason for this. *I painted the horse so well that people think it's a real horse! And in that case, what is there to get excited about?*

What did that artist do? He took a pencil and drew a line to bisect the horse into two parts. Once this was done, everyone marveled at the portrait and realized how very talented the artist really was. So the Ksav Sofer says in the "*Noam Elimelech*," "There is no artist like our God." The world is an amazing painting, a banner lifted aloft, but it is only when Hashem cuts the painting in half, when He splits the Sea in two, that the world understands the miracle that is the entire world. And all acknowledge and praise Him.

"*How abundant are Your works, Hashem; You have made all of them with wisdom! The earth is filled with Your possessions.*" The marvels are not only in distant places, but even as close as a person's heart. What manifold and varied emotions exist inside the human psyche: anger, joy, hatred, love, and so on. An endless array!

My rebbi used to say that people travel to America to see the Statue of Liberty, to France for the Eiffel Tower, to London or Honolulu to see new and breathtaking sights. What a waste of their money! Explore, rather, the terrain of the human heart! The whole world can be found there. The heart contains so many paradoxes, so many traits and emotions. "There is no knowing the hearts of kings!" A person grows accustomed to these things, which is why they no longer move him. If, however, he were suddenly to see the world split in half, he would become filled with wonder at everything, even the dry land itself. "*On dry land in the midst of the sea.*" That is what occurred at *Kerias Yam Suf*, the splitting of the Reed Sea.

⌒ The Murderer at the Table

Since we have mentioned the verse, "*How abundant are Your works, Hashem; You have made all of them with wisdom! The earth is filled with Your possessions,*" I will tell you what my rebbi used to say to explain the words, "*The earth is filled with Your possessions.*"

My rebbi compared this to a show.

There was once a gangster in America by the name of Al Capone, a degraded person who enjoyed dealing out death and suffering. Now, suppose a show was planned in which all the viewers of the world could see the Chofetz Chaim sitting in a room together with — *l'havdil elef havdalos* — that murderer.

We might expect that the moment the Chofetz Chaim entered that room, he would pull an iron bar from his pocket and give the killer what he deserves. But, no! We see Al Capone seated calmly opposite the Chofetz Chaim. He asks the Chofetz Chaim a question; the Chofetz Chaim thinks for a moment, then gives an answer … Then the Chofetz Chaim quotes the Rambam, while the other man cites the Ravad …

People would have paid a fortune to see the spectacle: Al Capone and the Chofetz Chaim.

"And Hashem formed the man of dust from the ground, and He blew into his nostrils the soul of life." What is the soul of life? It is a piece of the Divine, carved out from beneath the Throne of Glory. Such is the soul and human intelligence. And what was this soul blown into? *"Dust from the ground."* Does this refer to the dirt in our backyards, in which we grow tomatoes? No. It refers to the dust from which Fascism grows, and Communism, and every kind of degraded phenomenon in the world! Hashem took these two extremes and put them together. For a show that lasts an hour? No. For 60 or 70 years, *"and man became a living being."* Gevaldig! *"How abundant are Your works, Hashem!"*

(When we see people who have corrupted themselves, we are liable to fall prey to despair. But man is told: "Do not despair. You can take this body and make a soul out of it. Or, if not an actual soul, at least a subjugation of the body to the soul — a good partner. Like the subjugation of a murderer to the Chofetz Chaim. And then, how nice everything would be!)

Upon leaving shul on Friday night, a man goes home and pours himself a cup of sweet, red wine. He makes *Kiddush*: *"Thus, the heaven and the earth were finished, and all their array."* He offers testimony to the renewal of the world, and forms a "partnership" with Hashem in the Creation. He drinks the wine; the body drinks the wine. And then body and soul, together, consume the fish, meat, and other delicacies. Who eats? The body and soul together — partners. Isn't that so? The Chofetz Chaim makes *Kiddush* and Al Capone drinks the wine. The Chofetz Chaim says "*Hamotzi*" and Al Capone eats the challah and fish.

We marvel at this extraordinary Creation each morning, as we cry out loud, "*How abundant are Your works, Hashem!*" The dust of the earth is filled with "Your possessions" — that is, the possessions that belong to heaven: the soul that fills the body.

Miracles and wonders!

GEMS ON THE HAGGADAH

THE TEACHER STARTED IT!

R' Shabsi Yudelevitz

*T*he Torah spoke about four sons: One wise, one wicked, one simple, and one who does not know how to ask."

This is how things look in our day: One son goes to yeshivah and another does not, while a third ... don't ask. The four of them sit around the table, as their father struggles to find the common denominator among them all.

What does the wise son say? Today's "wise son" learns the same Torah as that long-ago one, and he asks the same venerable questions: "*What are the testimonies, the statutes, and the social ordinances which Hashem our God has commanded you?*"

"*As for you, instruct him regarding the laws of Pesach: After the Pesach offering, no desert is to be eaten!*" There is no problem with this son. The father knows how to get along with this one.

Then comes the wicked son's turn. Telling this son the laws of Pesach, as he did the wise son, is out of the question. He will not understand them. What, then? "*Therefore, you should blunt his teeth, and say to him: 'It is because of this [service] that Hashem acted for me when I came forth out of Egypt. For me — but not for him! Had he been there, he would not have been redeemed.*"

"Blunt his teeth" does not mean to strike him in the mouth. For if you were to strike him, he would simply strike back ... twice as hard.

They tell a story about the principal of a well-known Tel Aviv school who walked into a classroom and saw a student hitting the teacher!

"What's going on here?" the principal demanded.

"He started!" retorted the student, pointing accusingly at the teacher. "The teacher began the fight; I only gave him back twice as much as he gave me."

To "blunt his teeth" means to weaken the power of his teeth. Teach him a lesson and get rid of him, fast.

☞ Ruining the Merchandise

Why don't we enter into debate with the wicked son? Why not engage in a question-and-answer session with him? The Dubno Maggid offers a parable to explain:

A Jew was walking down the street a few days before Pesach, when he saw rugs from India on sale at a good price. He decided to buy one.

When he walked into his house with the rug over his shoulder, his wife asked, "What is that?" He explained that he'd received a bonus that day and had bought the rug.

"Don't you know that we don't have money to buy matzah, wine, and potatoes for Pesach? Why did you buy a rug?!" she protested bitterly. "What is to become of us? Why did you buy it?" In distress, the wife decreed, "You've got to return that rug to the seller!"

"But he won't want to take it back."

"I have an idea," she said. "Pull a thread from the rug, take it back to the store, and complain that the rug you bought was defective. It sheds threads."

That's what he did. The next day, he marched into the store and shouted, "This is a defective rug that sheds threads! Why did you sell me such shoddy merchandise?"

The shopkeeper hurried over to a drawer, took out the money he had received from the customer the day before, took back the rug, and returned the money. The customer went home in high spirits.

A few minutes later, a car pulled up in front of the rug store. A prosperous gentleman stepped out, holding a rug. Walking into the store, he complained that his wife had found a stain on the rug. "You sold me something that isn't new. I'm not interested in this! I want my money back!"

The shopkeeper refused. Arguments ensued. It was only after half an hour of raised voices that the rug seller finally agreed to exchange the stained rug for another one (but not to return the man's money).

A man who'd observed both interchanges waited for the customer to leave, then asked, "Tell me, please — why, when the first customer came in here half an hour ago, did you return his money at once, while the second had to argue for so long before you agreed to exchange his rug?"

The shopkeeper smiled. "You don't understand business. I'm an old hand at this. I know what my customers are like and I see them clearly. Let me explain.

"The minute I laid eyes on the first customer, I realized that I was dealing with a poor beggar who somehow, inadvertently, had bought a rug. As always, once the deal was done, he regretted the purchase and decided to come back here with various complaints. What would have been the point of arguing with him? If I'd exchanged his rug for another, he would have been back two days later with another excuse to return it: either more pulled threads, or a ripped piece at the side. He simply doesn't want to keep the rug. He will do everything in his power to get his money back, and in the end he'll destroy my whole shop ... While the second customer was a wealthy man who was really interested in the rug. If not this one, he'll buy another. With him, there was a purpose in fighting it out and driving a hard bargain."

It's the same way here, says the Dubno Maggid. With a *rasha*, a wicked person, there is no point arguing. He is simply not interested in buying your merchandise. The *rasha* comes only to complain. Were you to enter into debate with him, he would only destroy, only pull out all the threads and wreck the shop. Therefore, we refrain from holding conversation with him. "Get out of here!" we tell him. "*Blunt his teeth*": Weaken the danger that he represents and send him on his way. "We're not talking to you!"

"ONE WHO IS WISE, ONE WHO IS WICKED ..."

⌒ Wise or Righteous?

I once heard the following question from an elder of Jerusalem: Why do we say, "One wise, one wicked"? Why not say, "One who is a *tzaddik* and one who is a *rasha*"?

He answered that there is a rebuke hidden here aimed at those who wish to make innovations in each generation.

If the father is a *tzaddik*, then the son will also be a *tzaddik*. If the father is God fearing, then most probably the son will not be a *rasha* but will continue in his father's way. But if the father is a "*chacham*" — if he is "wise" (that is, too smart for his own good) — he will begin to use his cleverness with respect to Torah. "It won't matter if I behave a little differently, if I step out of the guidelines ..." Says the author of the Haggadah, "It's not a good idea to be too smart for your own good. If you are clever, then your son will be even cleverer: While you bend the rules to make things a bit more lenient for yourself, your son will become totally lenient. He will become a *rasha*."

And the grandson? He will be detached from any concept of spirituality. He will be confused, not knowing how to behave, for he will say to himself, "My grandfather is clever and my father is wicked. I don't know what's happening to us. Who am I?" And because he will be utterly confused, he will be a "*tam*" — the simple son. And when that "*tam*" has a son of his own, this great-grandson of a "wise man" who has never in his life seen a Seder, neither in his father's home nor in his grandfather's, what will be left of him? He will know nothing: "*She'eino yode'a lishol*" — one who does not even know how or what to ask.

"One Who Is Wise ..."

⌇ Rasha Before Tam

R' Naftali of Ropshitz once asked: Why does the *rasha* come before the *tam*? On the surface, the simple son would appear to be better than a wicked one, and thus should precede him.

The answer is that the *rasha* still has a chance, if he repents, whereas the *tam*, in general, is already lost.

⌇ "Tam": Positive or Negative?

There is another question to be asked. We have seen the word "*tam*" used in a positive sense: "*Yaakov was an 'ish tam,' a dweller in tents.*" This sounds as though being a "*tam*" is a praiseworthy thing. And yet, in the Haggadah, "*tam*" is not listed first, as an asset. The solution is simple:

When one stands beside a *rasha*, he is not allowed to be "*tam*." One cannot be simple minded when confronting wickedness. Yaakov Avinu was a "*tam*," in the *beis midrash*. "*Tam, a dweller in tents.*" But when he went out to meet wicked people, he demonstrated his shrewdness, for one is obligated to behave craftily with the crafty. When dealing with the wicked, it is necessary to be alert and even devious.

"At first our forefathers were idol worshipers, but now the Omnipresent has brought us near to His service."

"ALEINU!"

The custom, when meeting the parents of a prospective son- or daughter-in-law, is to tell the *mechutanim* of your family's *yichus*. "I am a grandson of such and such a *rav*, the famous *tzaddik* from such and such a city ..." In the Haggadah, we find that the opposite is true.

Have you ever heard one *mechutan* tell another, "At first our forefathers were idol worshipers"? Is that any way to begin the Haggadah? Would it not have been more fitting to say, "At first, our forefathers were the holy men, Avraham, Yitzchak, and Yaakov"?

Before we resolve this question, let us first see who said those words: "*At first our forefathers were idol worshipers.*" Who said it, and why? It was Yehoshua who spoke these words at the end of his life (*Yehoshua* 24:2).

As they entered Eretz Yisrael, Yehoshua established the prayer of "*Aleinu*," an awesome prayer that reaches up to the very heart of heaven.

When Yehoshua brought his people into the Land and they witnessed miracles and wonders that had never before been seen, they all saw the glory of Hashem. Jericho was conquered by the shofars.

Yehoshua stood up and proclaimed, "Aleinu l'shabe'ach la'adon hakol …, It is our duty to praise the Master of all, to ascribe greatness to the Molder of primeval creation, for He has not made us like the nations of the lands …"

After the conquest of Jericho, Yehoshua imposed a ban on taking booty. Achan broke the ban, taking the booty, and members of the nation fell. The *Bnei Yisrael* were in great pain.

Yehoshua rolled on the dust of the ground and asked Hashem, "What has happened to cause these sudden tragedies? We are going out to war, and falling." Hashem said, "The booty has been taken." Yehoshua instituted a lottery, which pointed to Achan. At first, Achan refused to confess his crime. Yehoshua said, "*Give honor to the God of Israel!*" Achan confessed.

"*Then Yehoshua said to Achan, 'My son, please give honor to Hashem, God of Israel, and confess to Him. Tell me, please, what you have done; do not withhold from me.' Achan answered Yehoshua and said, 'Indeed I have sinned against Hashem, God of Israel; thus and thus have I done. I saw among the spoils a lovely Babylonian garment …'*" (*Yehoshua* 7:19-21).

Achan stood, surrounded by his family, just moments before he was to be stoned to death. He recited his final *viduy* (confession). What did he say? "*Al kein nekaveh*" — Therefore we put our hope in You, Hashem, our God …" (The first Hebrew initials of "*al kein nekaveh*" spell out Achan's name.) Before his death, he recognized how one may stumble into sin, and the price that is exacted for such a stumbling … Then he prayed to Hashem: Let this punishment that I am about to receive instill fear into others and deter them from sin, so that the glory of heaven will be increased. "*To remove detestable idolatry from the earth*" (The vessels that he stole were used for idol worship). "And the false gods will be utterly cut off! Then all humanity will call upon Your Name, to turn all the earth's wicked toward You." See how sinners end up! They lead "the good life," but see how their lives of sin end, by leading them into the grave! "*All the world's inhabitants will recognize and know that to You every knee should bend.*" When, *Chazal* ask, should we bend the knee?

On the day of death. *"To You ... every tongue should swear."* When? On the day of birth, "When he is sworn: Be righteous and do not be wicked." *"Every tongue should swear!"*

These two paragraphs, *"Aleinu"* and *"V'al Kein,"* are recited three times a day. The first is a description of the Creator's greatness by those who carry out His will. Yehoshua composed these words — a paean to Hashem's glory — when he stood triumphant before the fallen walls of Jericho, when the sun stood still in Givon and the moon in the Valley of Ayalon, when Hashem hurled large stones down on the enemy at Beit Horon. These miracles were a testimony to heaven's honor, both above and below. *"It is our duty to praise the Master of all ... He stretches out heaven and establishes earth's foundation!"*

And then, the flip side of the coin: Achan's open confession of failure to withstand the temptation of sin, and the punishment of death.

In other words, it is incumbent upon us, each and every day, to stand up and recognize the Creator's greatness, and to acknowledge, as well, the punishment that we incur for transgressing His will.

Before Yehoshua's death, he delivered a powerful speech, in which he reminded the Children of Israel of their heritage. When was this?

After the Land had been conquered with open miracles, Yehoshua gathered together all the people and told them, *"Thus said Hashem, the God of Israel: 'Your forefathers — Terach, the father of Avraham and the father of Nachor — ... served the gods of others."*

Do not think that Avraham Avinu was born in Meah Shearim. Avraham was born among the gentile nations. *"At first, our fathers were idol worshipers!"* Avraham grew up in a home filled with idols.

"But I took your forefather Avraham from beyond the River and led him throughout all the land of Canaan." Avraham forged a path that ran contrary to the entire world; they stood on one side, and he on the other. He had to fight his family, his parents, and his surroundings: a difficult battle of body and soul. It wasn't easy.

After that, Yehoshua told the people, you went down to Egypt: "*I sent Moshe and Aharon, and I plagued Egypt ... I brought your fore-fathers out of Egypt and you arrived at the sea. The Egyptians pursued your forefathers with chariot and horsemen to the Sea of Reeds ... Then you dwelled in the Wilderness for many years ... Then you crossed the Jordan and came to Jericho ... not by your sword and not by your bow. I gave you a land for which you did not labor and cities that you did not build, yet you occupied them; vineyards and olive groves that you did not plant, yet you are eating from them*" (Yehoshua 24:5-13). So announced Yehoshua before the assembled nation. I have con-quered the land for you, and you are dwelling in Eretz Yisrael, a land filled with everything good. Make your calculation and come to a final decision:

If you wish to observe Hashem's commandments and walk in the path of Torah — wonderful. If not, I am taking my wife and children and proclaiming: "*But as for me and my house, we will serve Hashem!*" Should the need arise, then just as Avraham was willing to fight the gentiles, I will fight the Jews! I am not willing to live together with those who prefer to lead the life of a secular state. Therefore, know this: "*If it is evil in your eyes to serve Hashem, choose today whom you will serve: the gods your forefathers served across the River, or the gods of the Amorite in whose land you dwell. But as for me and my house, we will serve Hashem!*" (ibid., v.15).

Avraham's forebears were idol worshipers. Hashem removed him from their midst and took him across the River. If, heaven forbid (says Yehoshua), you are interested in continuing their practices, I will part ways with you and will depart together with my household. All the hard work I've done in the conquest of this country and the establishment of our homeland — all the long years of warfare to bequeath her to the Children of Israel — are worth nothing in my eyes if you will serve foreign gods! So cried Yehoshua to the people of Israel before his death.

The *Bnei Yisrael* promised not to defile themselves with idol worship. "*It would be sacrilegious for us to forsake Hashem, to serve gods of others.*" Yehoshua made a covenant with them and then went to his rest. "*Yehoshua, son of Nun, the servant of Hashem, died at the age of one hundred and ten years. They buried him in the border of his heritage in Timnas-Serach, which is in Mount Efrayim ...*" (ibid. vs. 29-30).

⁀ Running from the Marror

I'd like to highlight one small sentence from Yehoshua's speech: "*But I took your forefather Avraham from beyond the River and led him throughout all the land of Canaan ... and I gave him Yitzchak. To Yitzchak I gave Yaakov and Eisav. To Eisav I gave Mount Seir to inherit, and Yaakov and his sons went down to Egypt.*"

Rabbosai, he uttered one sentence that speaks volumes: "*To Eisav I gave Mount Seir to inherit, and Yaakov and his sons went down to Egypt.*" Eisav, apparently, had it all: power, officers, a huge state in *Har Seir*. And what did Yaakov have? He and his sons went down to Egypt, poor men.

Why were they, specifically, the ones to go down to Egypt? Because Eisav fled his debt. The Children of Israel went down to Egypt to repay the debt of their grandfather, Avraham Avinu, to whom Hashem said, "*Your children will be strangers in a land that is not their own.*" Eisav, however, put aside the IOU, handing it over to Yaakov and making his escape to *Har Seir* (as explained in *Pirkei D'Rebbe Eliezer*). Afraid of the *marror* — the bitter herb — Eisav fled.

Why did Eisav run away?

He was like the gentile who was (mistakenly) invited to be a guest in a Jewish home on Seder night. How pathetic, how unfortunate — a gentile on Seder night ...

[We have read a similar story earlier, but it is worth repeating for the message is powerful.]

They brought him home. The chairs were prepared with pillows as the gentile waited impatiently for the meal. At long last, they opened the wine bottles. After *Kiddush* he gulped down a glass of wine. Then came "*U'rchatz*" and "*Karpas*," when he was given a small portion of vegetable. Ravenous by now, he thought he'd go out of his mind. Still, he remained silent. *Soon enough, they'll bring in the second course,* he thought hopefully.

"*Maggid!*" They droned on and on, until he felt as though he were about to explode. An hour later, when he was about to get up and leave, they washed their hands and gave him round matzos that nearly broke his teeth. He had never eaten anything like them before. He was furious. Girding himself with patience — salvation surely could not be far off — he waited. Then came the *marror*, the bitter herbs. Seeing his host happily taking a large portion of *marror*, the gentile did the same. When they all took a bite, so did he — and began to gasp. *What are they trying to do to me?* He got up and, cursing, left the house in a rage, to walk the streets hungry till morning.

The next day, he told his Jewish neighbor what he'd been through on the previous night. "Wine, potato, and terrible bitter herbs!"

The Jew responded, "Oh, you fool. You were nearly at the end. Had you waited just a few more minutes, after the *marror* would have come '*Shulchan Orech*' with all sorts of delicacies to eat. Did you have to flee just when the *marror* came? With a bit more patience, you would have had every good thing!"

Eisav fled. There are people who find themselves in a difficult situation. Their lot is bitter — and they get up and run. They are the fools who run when the *marror* comes.

Eisav saw an IOU for a debt to be paid, so he ran away. Hashem said, If your desire is to flee, then take *Har Seir*: "To Eisav I gave Mount Seir to inherit." But Yaakov and his sons were unafraid of the *marror*. They went down to Egypt to experience the travail, the fiercy furnace: "*And Yaakov and his sons went down to Egypt.*"

"The sorcerers said to Pharaoh: 'It is a finger of God!'"
(Shemos 8:15).

A FINGER AND A HAND

*I*t is a finger of God!" In another place, it says, "*And Israel saw the great hand.*" What is the difference between a hand and a finger? What is the significance of the two termino-logies?

Suppose a person were walking down the street and he saw someone wagging a finger from a window on the third floor, in the universal symbol for "Beware!" It would not enter his mind to think that there was only a finger up there. Obviously, the finger is connected to a hand, and the hand belongs to the body of the person issuing the warning from his vantage point up above.

Similarly, heaven shows a person a finger. A finger does not strike hard. It is just a warning: Listen, you're not doing so well. The plagues of blood, frogs, lice — all of these were warnings: "*A finger of God.*"

A waiting period follows. If the person heeds the warning (that behind the finger lies something much worse), then all is fine. But if he clings to his position, then the hand is taken out. And a hand, as everybody knows, is used for hitting!

Pharaoh was shown blood, frogs, lice, and so on. "*The sorcerers said to Pharaoh: 'It is a finger of God!'*" This was the warning finger, the least of punishments. However, "*Pharaoh's heart was hardened.*" That was when he was shown the great Hand, as witnessed by all of Israel: "*Israel saw the great hand that Hashem did to Egypt, and the people revered Hashem.*"

Not long ago [this lecture was given in 1992] we in Eretz Yisrael were shown a finger. We received a warning (the Gulf War). Thirty-nine missiles landed, corresponding to the 39 prohibited labors of Shabbos, which Jews have been transgressing as they desecrate the Shabbos. It was only a warning. There were still no deaths. A single missile killed numerous soldiers in an American military base, but here in Eretz Yisrael there was no loss of life.

Let us do *teshuvah*, and Hashem will have compassion on us and hasten our redemption.

פרשת שמיני ⇜
Parashas Shemini

"Tzaddikim are in the habit of accepting Hashem's treatment of them as justice. Avraham accepted his decree as a just one, as it says, 'I am dust and ashes.' Yaakov justified his decree, as it says, 'I have been diminished by all the kindnesses and all the truth' … Moshe told Aharon, 'Aharon, my brother, your sons died only for the sake of His holy Name' … Because Aharon knew his sons to be beloved of Hashem, he remained silent and was rewarded for his silence. From here, they said, 'Anyone who accepts [his decree] and is silent, it bodes well for him'" (Yalkut, Parashas Shemini).

Napoleon Gets a Beating

R' Yaakov Galinsky

When we look at the story of R' Akiva and Rachel, the first thing we see is how much a woman can accomplish through her devotion, her self-sacrifice, and her tenacity.

Rachel saw abilities in R' Akiva that indicated the potential for greatness, and that was why she dedicated herself to his success. But what a steep price in self-sacrifice she paid! Isolated from her family, Rachel remained alone (and doubly alone after R' Akiva went off to learn for 24 years). She gave up all her father's wealth — he was one of the three richest men in Jerusalem — and she and R' Akiva, who married in the winter, lived in a cow stall and slept on straw. That was their furniture: straw (as brought down in *Nedarim* 50a).

Avos D'Rabbi Nassan adds further interesting details about the complaints that R' Akiva's neighbors made, and what he replied to them. See what it says there.

Chazal tell us that there was a furor in heaven: such self-sacrifice on the part of a woman — R' Akiva's wife! Finally, they sent down Eliyahu Hanavi. When we learn this Gemara and hear that Eliyahu Hanavi was sent, we tend to expect that he will doubtless build them a nice cottage right away.

The Gemara goes on to say that Eliyahu knocked on the door and said, "Hello. Please do me a kindness. My wife has given birth and I have no straw to place beneath her head." R' Akiva and his wife shared the poor man's distress and gave him straw. Afterwards, R' Akiva said to his wife, "Do you see? I thought I headed the list of unfortunate people in this city, but there are others in even worse shape than we are: like that man, who doesn't even have straw in his house."

The commentaries ask a powerful question. If heaven took the trouble to send Eliyahu Hanavi down to our world (a great distance with four "stations" along the way, as the Gemara tells us: "Micha'el in one, Gavriel in two, Eliyahu in four" [*Berachos* 4b]), then why didn't he give them a dwelling place? Why, as we might have expected, didn't Eliyahu build R' Akiva a pleasant garden apartment in the Geulah section of Jerusalem?

The answer is as follows: Had that happened, they would have had a place to live, but a R' Akiva would not have emerged from there! They would have had a cottage, but we would have not had a R' Akiva.

A person suffers, and he complains. But he has no idea how much good can sprout from that suffering ... just as R' Akiva flourished only through penury.

Let me tell you a story. Napoleon conquered large portions of Europe. Then he decided to take on Russia.

When the second campaign was launched, winter had already begun. As everyone knows, Russian winters are brutal. Napoleon besieged one city, but was not successful in bringing it to its knees. After a week of siege, and then a second, the city did not succumb. Heavy snow fell, causing more trouble for him.

One morning, one of his generals came to him and said, "Your majesty, we cannot go on this way. We must either advance or leave the field. Our soldiers, camped out in open fields, are beginning to rebel."

Napoleon said, "I have already considered the situation, and here is what I have decided. You and I will take off our army uniforms and disguise ourselves as simple peasants. We will slip into the enemy's city and see what sort of conditions prevail there. If we see that they are organized and that they still have food, we will leave this place. If not, we will know that they will soon fall into our hands, and this knowledge will encourage our soldiers."

The two, dressed as simple peasant farmers, set out on the side roads that led into the city, and eventually entered a restaurant in the center of town. As they took their seats, they heard the city's soldiers chatting with one another: "What will become of us? The kitchen is bare. It's a week since I've eaten bread. We'll all die of hunger!"

The second retorted, "A week? I haven't tasted fresh bread in two weeks!"

Hearing this, Napoleon was encouraged.

Suddenly, one of the soldiers sitting in the restaurant told his commanding officer, "That man sitting in the corner of the room is Napoleon!"

"What are you talking about? Are you crazy?" The officer was astonished.

"I was once in a certain city when Napoleon held a military parade, and I saw him. That's him ..." Overhearing him, Napoleon and his general were frightened.

Speaking more loudly now, the soldier continued to build his case. "You don't have to believe me, but why not go over to him and ask to see his papers?" What a predicament for Napoleon!

At that moment, the general roused himself and began to berate Napoleon, seated across the table from him, at the top of his voice: "Well, bring me some beer already! Why haven't you brought it yet? I gave you money. Did you decide to keep it for yourself?"

The other diners began to laugh raucously. "What a Napoleon he's imagining! Apparently, hunger has addled his wits."

Napoleon stood up to fetch the beer and fell down. The general came over to him and slapped him. "I don't want to see your face around me!" With the general still beating Napoleon, the two made their exit from the restaurant and ran for their lives.

On their return to their base, the general approached the emperor and said, "Your majesty, please forgive me. I struck you, humiliated and degraded you."

"What? Have you any need to beg my forgiveness? You saved my life! Had you not revered me so greatly, I would already be hanging on the gallows. Thank you very much for the humiliation you dealt out to me, and for the blow you struck me. Thank you!"

What do we learn from this story? At times, we receive a few slaps on the face from *HaKadosh Baruch Hu*. We complain. But, my dear ones, you have no idea how that suffering may have saved you. By being exposed to mortification and scorn, you know not how much you have profited!

"He rebukes the one whom He loves." Fortunate is he whose father loves and rebukes him. If people would sense that they have a Father above, they would not complain quite so loudly about their miserable lot in life. Rather they would "subjugate their hearts to their Father in heaven." They would understand that we are all in His hands. Everything is in His hands: health, children. It is all His; we only serve as a *"shamash"* to safeguard Hashem's property, no more. He does as He sees fit. Hashem wants us to place our hearts in His service. This is worth millions, as we saw in the *midrash* at the start

of this *derashah*: "*Tzaddikim* are in the habit of accepting Hashem's treatment of them as justice."

May Hashem rescue us quickly!

אַךְ אֶת־זֶה לֹא תֹאכְלוּ מִמַּעֲלֵי הַגֵּרָה וּמִמַּפְרִסֵי הַפַּרְסָה אֶת־
הַגָּמָל כִּי־מַעֲלֵה גֵרָה הוּא וּפַרְסָה אֵינֶנּוּ מַפְרִיס טָמֵא הוּא לָכֶם.
וְאֶת־הַשָּׁפָן כִּי־מַעֲלֵה גֵרָה הוּא וּפַרְסָה לֹא יַפְרִיס טָמֵא הוּא לָכֶם.
וְאֶת־הָאַרְנֶבֶת כִּי־מַעֲלַת גֵּרָה הִוא וּפַרְסָה לֹא הִפְרִיסָה.

"But this is what you shall not eat from among those that bring up their cud, or that have split hooves: the camel, for it brings up its cud, but its hoof is not split — it is unclean to you; and the hyrax, for it brings up its cud, but its hoof is not split — it is unclean to you; and the hare, for it brings up its cud, but its hoof is not split ..." (Vayikra 11:4-6).

TOMORROW, TOMORROW, TOMORROW

R' Shabsi Yudelevitz

*L*et me tell you a brief story. The passenger seated next to me on a plane was a zoologist. Do you know what a zoologist is? An expert with knowledge of animals, for zoos. This was a Jewish millionaire professor who knew about most of the animals that exist on this planet.

During the long flight, as he sat beside me, he told me about all the ambitions he'd had in his life, and about his present job at the university, teaching Zoology. "I've already seen three of my students become big professors themselves," he said proudly. In short, he chatted amicably with me, like an old friend. He was very interesting.

At one point, the plane staff served a non-kosher meal. "*And Hashem opened the donkey's mouth*" ...

In distress, I said to him, "How can you eat that kind of food?

Aren't you a Jew?"

He became annoyed with me for interfering with his meal. "Listen, what Moses said does not obligate me, because he died 4,000 years ago!"

"God said it," I told him. "And God is alive and well."

"Rabbi, don't get mad," he requested. "If you can prove that God said which meat one is permitted to eat and which not, if you can prove that, I will submit to your view and repent."

"All right. But remember what you said. If I prove it to you, you will stop eating that food."

"Listen, Rabbi, it would be a waste of your time and energy. A few years ago, I debated a certain rabbi for four hours, and he didn't beat me."

"I don't need four hours. Four minutes will be enough. In four minutes, you will be lying on the ground, as it were, and admitting that I'm right."

He looked at me, eyes round as saucers. "Uh — four minutes?"

"Yes. No more than that is necessary."

"How?"

"Wait patiently, and I'll show you ... Professor, do you know the signs of *kashrus* in an animal?"

"What?"

"Let me explain. The signs of *kashrus* that are described in the Torah are split hooves and bringing up its cud. These are the two signs of a kosher animal, as written explicitly in the Torah, and as any Jewish youngster knows.

"Now, let me ask you, Professor. What is the law if you have an animal with only one of those signs? An animal that either has split hooves or brings up its cud?"

"Half kosher and half non-kosher," he replied.

"What are you talking about? There's no such thing as half-and-half. It's either kosher, or it's not."

"All right. It's non-kosher," he said.

"You're right," I agreed. "An animal with only one of the signs is non-kosher and forbidden to eat!"

I looked at him. "Now, listen well. Moshe Rabbeinu wrote in the Torah that there are four animals — the camel, the hyrax, the hare, and the pig — that have just one sign … and only those four. Just them. All other animals either have both signs or neither one. Tell me, did Moshe Rabbeinu study zoology in your school? Was he a professor in the study of animals? No.

"Perhaps Moshe Rabbeinu went out hunting and got to know the animals in the forest? No. He also never worked in a zoo in his life. He grew up in an Egyptian palace, not the jungles of Africa. In that case, how did he know that there are no other animals of this type? And who knows better than you, Professor, that from the giving of the Torah to this day — a period of 4000 years, during which nearly the entire planet has been explored — no other animal has been found in all the world's forests and jungles that has just one sign. A fifth one has never been found to be added to the list of those four. How could Moshe Rabbeinu possibly have known this?"

I continued, borrowing the words of the Gemara: "(*Chullin* 60b), 'Was Moshe Rabbeinu a zookeper, or a hunter? From where did he know this? Rather, it is to tell you that the Torah is from heaven!' So says the Gemara. In other words, Hashem, Who created and knows what He created, was the one to tell Moshe all these things, which Moshe then transmitted to us."

When I was finished with my lecture, I noticed that several of our fellow passengers, in front of and behind us, had stopped eating and gathered round. Seeing that five minutes had passed, I apologized for the extra minute.

I looked at him, and he was white as chalk.

"Rabbi, you've convinced me," he said, and added, "I will finish eating, and then I will repent."

"Go away. You're lost," I snapped.

He'd been convinced. He knew the truth. And yet … "I'll finish eating first." He couldn't stop in the middle of his meal, poor thing. How terrible. He was convinced, but he wanted to finish eating. That's what a person is like.

R' Sholom Schwadron once quoted *Shir HaShirim* (5:2), "I was sleeping but my heart was awake. A sound — my beloved is knocking. Open for me ... for my head is filled with dew, my locks with the rains of the night." *HaKadosh Baruch Hu* is knocking at our door, rousing us to *teshuvah*. He is knocking! And what do we say to *HaKadosh Baruch Hu*? (The text continues) "*I have removed my chemise; how shall I put it on? I have washed my feet; how shall I soil them?*" I've already bathed and put on my pajamas. It's hard for me to wake up ... I can't do it today ... I'll do *teshuvah* tomorrow (when I finish eating my airline meal). Next week, I'll set aside times for Torah study. Tomorrow, I'll work on improving my *middos*. And so life goes by ...

Tomorrow, tomorrow, tomorrow. "*I have removed my chemise; how shall I put it on? I have washed my feet; how shall I soil them?*" All of life goes by like a fleeting dream, with the hope of "tomorrow."

What is "tomorrow"? Today! There is no tomorrow!

Sometimes, when we wake up after a great deal of knocking, it's already very late. For the difficult and awesome day comes, of which it says, "*But my beloved had vanished, had gone.*" He's gone. Yesterday, I came, and you slept. Now it's too late! "*I sought him but found him not; I called him, but he did not answer me.*" Ah, the longing starts, but all a person has is longing: "*I adjure you, daughters of Jerusalem — if you find my beloved, what will you tell him? That I am lovesick.*"

Rabbosai, just a little while ago, there were missiles. Missiles! Have you forgotten? I can see on your faces that it happened a hundred years ago ... But it was only a few years ago that we were wearing gas masks. It was then that "*kol dodi dofek*" — that my beloved knocked on the door, when our hearts felt constricted with longing. *Ai, ai,* "*Bring us back to You, and we will return!*" we pleaded. And now, we've nearly forgotten. Ah ... "*My beloved had vanished, had gone. My soul went out when he spoke. I sought him, but found him not; I called him, but he did not answer me.*"

And now, *HaKadosh Baruch Hu* wants at least our longing. "*If you find my beloved, what will you tell him? That I am lovesick.*" I am sick with love for Hashem.

How fortunate you are, *baruch Hashem*, that you have merited on this night to gather together. We can all say to Hashem: We miss you. We long for you, *Ribono Shel Olam*! We can open our eyes. We can see the truth, the Divine light, and we can desire to be close to Him and to fulfill His commandments with care.

Our longing will ascend to the Throne of Glory on this holy day, in the merit of the *"Or Hachayim hakadosh,"* and we will merit a *geulah sheleimah*, speedily in our days, *amen*!

"He saw a drunkard lying in the marketplace, and a measure of water spilling on him, and boys and youths striking him with stones and ropes and throwing mud in his face and into his mouth …

The chassid said to himself, 'I will go to my father and bring him here, and I will show him this drunkard and the humiliation they are heaping on him. Perhaps he will prevent his mouth from drinking in the tavern and getting drunk. And that's what he did. He brought him there and showed him [the drunkard].

What did the old father do? He moved up close to the drunkard and asked him for the name of the tavern in which he'd had the wine that had made him so drunk …" (Midrash Tanchuma).*

A GAN EDEN FOR DRUNKARDS

R' Yaakov Galinsky

R' Sholom Schwadron once talked about a time when they were digging sewer holes in Sha'arei Chesed (where he lived). The stench was awful; it was impossible to pass nearby. In the morning, when he walked to shul wearing his *tallis* and *tefillin*, he would run like a young boy in order not to linger near that bad smell. There was no fresh air to breathe in the entire area.

One morning, as he returned home from shul and was approaching the place, he prepared to start running. Suddenly, to his surprise, he saw that the workers were sitting and eating their breakfast next to the sewer. One of them was feasting right inside the hole! The men chatted peacefully with one another ...

The sight made a strong impact on him, and R' Sholom concocted a number of powerful *derashos* to the merit of those sewer workers.

We too, with this story, can understand the meaning of the *mishnah in Maseches Avos*:

"*Akavia ben Mahalalel says: Look at three things and you will not fall into the hands of sin*" (*Avos* 3:41). *Akavia ben Mahalalel* declared that if a person looks and makes the following calculation, he will not fall into the hands of sin: "*Know where you come from, and where you are going, and before Whom you are destined to render an accounting.*"

Asks R' Eliyahu Lopian: I don't understand the beginning of this *mishnah*. "*And you will not fall into the hands of sin.*" Does sin have hands?

The explanation is simple. Listen, and understand.

As we know, "No one commits a sin unless a spirit of madness enters into him" (*Sotah* 3a). It happens that a person is attacked by folly and does what he does, may Hashem have mercy. They tell him, "At least be ashamed of yourself! You did an *aveirah*. You fell into madness; be embarrassed! He is like a person who has a nervous attack in the middle of the street and, feeling terribly embarrassed, covers his face and hides at the side of the street. (And when the *yetzer* comes around a second time, tell him, "Enough! Leave me alone. You embarrassed me enough with that madness. Enough!") *Chazal* tell us: "*A person who commits a sin and is ashamed of it is forgiven for all his sins.*" Hashem is merciful and knows that the Torah was not given to angels. We walk through this world of lies, deceit, and falsity — well, what can we do? A person sometimes goes mad for a few minutes.

The evil inclinlation is afraid of this sense of shame, for it is advantageous to man. So it hurries to prepare "medicine" for this "ailment." It attempts to win over the sinner's intellect. The *yetzer* tells him, "Was this really an attack of madness? Never! What you did was not even a sin! This was something you had every right to do, even in the middle of Main Street. You have nothing to be ashamed of. And if anyone tells your otherwise, then *he's* the one who should be ashamed of himself. Not you!"

This is the danger. As we all know, mad people claim that everyone else is crazy. The drunkard does not say that his head is feeling dizzy, but rather that the floor is spinning around. Here, too, the sin confuses him to the point that he doesn't even know he's had a lapse into madness.

Rabbosai, as long as a person realizes that his actions are reprehensible, his chances are good. However, we see people who have become used to wallowing in the sewers, sitting there at their ease as though in a luxury hotel. Things that once disgusted and sickened them are practically the norm for them by now. And how did they reach this point? Through the principle of, "*A person sins, and repeats his sin.*"

"R' Huna said: If a person transgresses and then repeats it, it becomes [as though] permissible to him ..." (*Yoma* 86b). The more one repeats a transgression, the further his thoughts sail from the shores of truth. "I'm doing a big *mitzvah*! What sin are you talking about, anyway?" Do you understand? He's convinced that he'll actually receive a portion of *Gan Eden* for the "*mitzvos*" he's doing.

(R' Yaakov Galinsky's voice grows quiet.) Here is the dangerous point. From sin itself, it is possible to run away, as it says, "*Flee from sin.*" The great fear is that "*One sin drags another in its wake.*" We are afraid of sin's hands, grasping him and not letting him budge. He is held in the iron fingers of sin! And the sin offers him a new kind of *Gan Eden*. These are the "hands of sin."

We plead with *HaKadosh Baruch Hu* daily, in *Birkas HaMazon*, to bless us, "*as our forefathers, Avraham, Yitzchak, and Yaakov, were blessed — bakol, mikol, kol (with everything, of everything, everything).*" In other words, as explained in *Bava Basra* 17a, Hashem gave Avraham, Yitzchak, and Yaakov a taste of the World to Come while they were still in this world. Let us also reach that level, through Torah and *mitzvos*: to taste *Gan Eden* in our world. And who is a "*ben Olam Haba*" — one who merits the World to Come? He who, in this world, is already in the next!

What does the *yetzer hara* do? Obviously, it is incapable of offering the *Gan Eden* of Avraham, Yitzchak, and Yaakov. So it says, "Wait a second, don't rush away. I'll give you a different sort of Paradise. I have a substitute!" And, as R' Sholom relates, they have their *Gan Eden* in the sewers.

These are the "hands of sin."

☞ The Drunkard and the Sewer

The *Midrash Tanchuma*, in our *parashah*, declares, "The drunkard, while still under the influence of his wine, sits joyfully as though he is sitting in *Gan Eden*." The *midrash* cites a true story to illustrate this point; a story of our holy *Chazal*.

A certain student, who was a *chassid*, had been blessed with a father who drank a great deal of wine. Whenever the father fell down in the marketplace in his drunkenness, boys would hurl stones and sticks at him and cry, "See the drunkard!"

Regarding this spectacle, his son "was mortified to death." Seeing his father lying in the muddy street, he would say to himself, "*Ribono Shel Olam*, I am receiving so much shame from my father. It would be better not to see, not to be in the world!"

Each day, he would go over to his father's home and respectfully argue, "Father, why go out into the street or to a tavern? If you want to drink, I'll bring the best wines to you, right here at home. Father, I will bring you the best wines being sold in this country. Just don't go out drinking in the tavern, for you are a source of shame both to me and to yourself. Your rolling around in the streets is harming my marriage prospects and will harm the entire family. Please, do me this favor," he pleaded … once, twice, three times … scores of times, until his father finally promised to do his drinking at home.

Twice a day, morning and evening, the son came to visit his father to prepare him all sorts of good things to eat along with fine wine and whiskey.

One day, rain was pouring down. The *chassid* went out to the marketplace on his way to *daven* in shul. As he passed through in the marketplace, he saw a drunkard lying in a puddle of water, while boys were hitting him with rocks and sticks and throwing mud in his face and into his mouth. Each time he would spit it out, they would laugh. Said the *chassid* to himself, *Here is an excellent chance. At this moment, my father happens not to be drunk. I will go get my father and bring him here, and I'll show him this drunkard and the humiliation to which he is being subjected by these boys and youths. Perhaps he will refrain from drinking at home and becoming drunk.* And so he did. He brought his father, certain that the terrible sight would persuade his father to stop drinking.

What did his old father do? He went over to the drunkard and bent over him.

The son, in his innocence, thought that the father was bending over the man in order to explain that his behavior was neither nice nor beneficial. Alas, no. He went close to the drunkard and asked for the name of the tavern in which he'd drunk the wine that had made him so drunk! "What good wine you must have imbibed," he said, "if you're lying here and don't even feel them putting mud in your mouth. Wonderful! Give me an exact address where I can find such wine …"

The son was shaken. "Father, is this why I brought you out here? I wanted you to see the mockery they're making of him, for that is what they do to *you* when you're drunk. Perhaps you will stop drinking wine even at home?"

The father recognized his son's pain, but said apologetically, "My son, I promise you, I have no other pleasure or *Gan Eden* than this." Hearing these words, the *chassid* went away, disconsolate.

This is the drunkard's Paradise …

When he first started drinking, no doubt he did feel embarrassed. Had anyone shown him the spectacle of drunkards rolling in the mud then, he would have abandoned the practice. But he continued drinking. *It's not so terrible to have something to drink,* he told himself — until the drinking became his *Gan Eden.* Even when he is wallowing in the mud and children are beating him, he is in *Gan Eden.* "He said to him, 'My son, I promise you, I have no other pleasure or *Gan Eden* than this!'"

What argument can one use with a person who has reached this state? He is firmly in the grip of sin. He is living in a drunkard's Paradise.

⌒ Gan Eden for Policemen

Recently, I happened to have a conversation with someone who is living in a "Policemen's Paradise."

On Thursday, I received a call from the Israeli police. A police officer introduced himself, then asked, "Rabbi Galinsky?"

"Yes?"

"We have a complaint here against you."

"What is the complaint?" I asked. "What could anyone possibly complain about me, except for the fact that I am still in the world? What do you have against me?"

"We have nothing against you. It's simply this: A woman has lodged a complaint. She and her husband handed their son over to a mission, and you harrass them on the phone all day."

I told him, "I'm not aware of this story. If only I knew who that woman was, perhaps I could influence her!"

"I'm not interested in excuses or stories," the officer said. "If you wish to put an end to this matter, come and testify that you do not know them, and that's that."

This was in the beginning of *Chodesh Elul* and I had no time to spare, but we made an appointment. The next day, at 4:30 p.m., I arrived at the police station in Ramat Gan. Shabbos was due to begin at 6:30. I went in and asked for the officer who'd spoken to me on the phone.

They told me that he was not there. Only the accused had bothered showing up; the accusers were not present. Have you ever heard of such a thing? I waited another quarter-hour, then went over to the desk and asked, "What's going on here? I was told to come at 4:30. The officer said he'd be here, but he isn't. What happened? Maybe you didn't pay him his salary and that's why he didn't come in …"

They asked me to wait. "Wait a minute," they said. But the "minute" didn't end, and Shabbos was coming.

They told me that a different investigator would "deal with" me.

"All right," I said. "But please tell him that today is *erev Shabbos*, and I don't have a lot of time."

The investigator came out of his office and apologized: "I'll just finish up with a different client, then I'll be ready for you."

At long last, I went in.

"What do you want?" he asked.

"What do *I* want? You people want something from *me!*"

He had no idea what I was talking about. I explained the story and why I'd been asked to come down, and that the officer who'd called me was not around.

"Fine. Take a pen, write your story on a piece of paper, and we'll be done." He dictated: "I, Yaakov Galinsky, ID number so-and-so, hereby assert that I do not know the _____-family who have lodged a complaint against me, and I have nothing against them."

"Just a minute," I protested. "I do have something against them. I just don't know them."

"This is the language we use here at the police station! That's the way you have to write it," he insisted.

"In Bnei Brak, where I live, it is known that there is is a 'Nusach Sefard' and a 'Nusach Ashkenaz.' However, I've never heard of a 'nusach Police' …"

"I want you to write!" He was starting to get angry.

"I can't write lies. You are interested in having me sign on the words, 'I have nothing against them.' However, don't I have something against them? How does a Jewish woman hand her children over to a mission? Of course I have something against her!"

"All right, I won't insist. Write whatever you want, and let's end this." (He was in a hurry to go home, as was I.)

Before I got up, he asked, "Tell me, please, if I may, what do you do in your private life?"

"If I have the time, I sit and learn."

"What is it with all you Bnei Brakers — 60 years old, 50 years old, 40, 30 — you sit and learn. What is this? What's going on there? Learning?!"

"Sir," I said, "listen. If, for example, you wanted to argue with me about chocolate — which is the best-tasting chocolate — I would not spend a lot of time discussing it with you. I'd simply go into a store with a Bnei Brak *hechsher*, buy you a bar of chocolate, and give it to you. You'd make a *berachah* and have a taste. Afterward, we could argue, right? That's what David Hamelech said when he warned us not to argue with anyone. Rather, *Taste, and see that Hashem is good.* Therefore, here's what I suggest. Next week, in Ashkelon, a seminar for *ba'alei teshuvah* will be held. You can participate. No one is forced to do anything. You'll just listen to a few lectures — have a little taste. Afterward, we'll talk. Take your wife along. It costs $290. I'll pay; you know that we religious people have dollars under our mattresses. I'll pay the price out of my own pocket and won't ask you for a penny."

"How do you know, Rabbi Galinsky, that I happen to have a vacation coming up next week?" he asked with a smile.

"I guess, when it came to that detail, I must have *ruach hakodesh*," I told him.

I returned to Bnei Brak, went over to R' Shechter, and said, "Listen, here's what happened. I was in the police station, and a certain officer seemed like a refined sort of person. He mentioned, among other things, that his grandfather was an ultra-Orthodox man from Hungary. Please sign him up for the seminar. If he wants to pay for it himself, fine. If not, I'll pay, and it will be a merit for me."

Listen to what happened next. On *erev Yom Kippur* morning, I received a phone call. "Rabbi Galinsky?" It was that police officer. "Congratulate me. I started putting on *tefillin* today."

Do you understand? All I did was give him a taste of a different sort of *Gan Eden*.

People are immersed in all sorts of "Paradises." They'll laugh at you, eat breakfast in the sewers, and mock those who pass by and hold their noses: "You are in *Gehinnom*, and I am here in *Gan Eden*!" But when one has had the privilege of tasting the *Gan Eden* of Avraham, Yitzchak, and Yaakov, he wakes up.

Let us merit happiness and blessing in this world and the next. And let us end by quoting R' Chanania ben Akashya: *"HaKadosh Baruch Hu wished to confer merit upon Israel … Make the Torah great and glorious!"* (*Yeshayahu* 42:21).

פרשת תזריע
PARASHAS TAZRIA

בִּי אֲנִי ה׳ אֱלֹקֵיכֶם וְהִתְקַדִּשְׁתֶּם וִהְיִיתֶם קְדֹשִׁים בִּי קָדוֹשׁ אָנִי וְלֹא
תְטַמְּאוּ אֶת־נַפְשֹׁתֵיכֶם בְּכָל־הַשֶּׁרֶץ הָרֹמֵשׂ עַל־הָאָרֶץ.

*"For I am Hashem, your God — you are to sanctify yourselves
and you shall become holy, for I am holy; and you shall not
contaminate yourselves through any teeming thing that creeps
on the earth" (Vayikra 11:44).*

R' AKIVA EIGER IN THE ROOM OF THE DEAD

R' Sholom Schwadron

I once heard the following *derashah* from the Hommeler *Rav*,
in Meah Shearim. Incidentally, I'd like to emphasize that I
am grateful to Hashem that I merited hearing him. He was
one of the few individuals who ingrained me with *yiras Shamayim*.
When I was a forlorn orphan boy I very much enjoyed listening to
his *derashos*, and they revitalized my soul.

Here is what he once said, in the manner of *darshanim* throughout the ages:

"*You are to sanctify yourselves and you shall become holy, for I am holy.*" *Chazal* say, "*V'hiskadishtem*" — "*You are to sanctify yourselves*" — refers to the first waters, while "*and you shall become holy*" refers to *mayim acharonim* [*Berachos* 53b].

"*V'hiskadishtem*" — the prior waters. A person takes bread or challah and sits down to eat. He recites the blessing, "*... Who sanctified us with His commandments and commanded us about netilas yadayim, the washing of hands.*" What is the meaning of *netilas yadayim*? The simple meaning is known. Shlomo Hamelech established the obligation to wash our hands prior to eating bread.

However, *netilas yadayim* is alluded to in the Torah. The Hummeler *Rav* said as follows: As we know, when one accompanies the dead or leaves a cemetery, one washes his hands. Why? The holy books explain that it is possible, when a person dies, that a neighbor or acquaintance or even a family member was the cause of his death, heaven forbid. The person may have been afflicted with suffering and travail that broke his heart and curtailed his life, or perhaps he was hungry for bread and his fellow townspeople did not notice or help him. Other people may have caused him to die, heaven forbid. Therefore, we wash our hands after a funeral, as if to say, "Our hands did not spill this blood, and our eyes did not see it."

The Gemara, in *Sotah* 38b, asks: Would we imagine that the elders of the *Beis Din* were those who killed this person? And yet, they are required to wash their hands over the *eglah arufah*, and to say, "Our hands did not spill this blood." The Gemara explains that if there is no suspicion of actual bloodspilling, the hands are washed and one says, "Our eyes did not see." We did not see him suffering and leave him without support or sustenance.

Similarly, when we return from a funeral, we wash our hands, as if to say: "My hands are clean in this man's departure from the world." The same applies to the washing of hands over food! the *maggid* thundered. We wash our hands before eating food: a bit of bread and herring for breakfast, for example. How did you acquire this food? You paid for it with money. How did you come by that money? Did you cheat someone, transgressing the prohibition against deceiving one's fellow man? Did you demand money from someone that he did not actually owe you, thus taking money unjustly? If so, your hands spilled this blood. The bread is stained with blood: the blood of your fellow man, of your friend, your neighbor, the blood of the Jew whom you robbed. *Oy vey!* cried the Hummeler *Rav.* Therefore, when washing our hands before a meal, we recite the blessing, *"Who sanctified us with His commandments and commanded us on the washing of the hands."* Eat the meal with hands that are pure. Pour clean water over your hands and purify them: Our hands did not spill blood for this food.

☙ *From Prior Waters to Mayim Acharonim*

The Rebbe of Lublin — R' Meir Shapiro — had something else to say about the ideas hinted at in these words.

"V'hiskadishtem" — these are first waters: This refers to the stringent laws of family purity. *"You shall warn the Children of Israel from their contamination"* ... *"That soul shall be cut off from its people."* These are the *"mayim rishonim"* — the "first waters."

R' Meir Shapiro adds that *"v'hiskadishtem"* does not refer only to water. Water is the bare minimum. The Torah wants more and more. It wants us to become holy! And don't think that this is a difficult thing to do, for you will have help from Above. All you have to do is want it! I have many stories that touch on this point. If a person truly desires to be holy, he will witness an outpouring of assistance from his own intellect and from heaven. Full barrels of knowledge, full barrels of purity and holiness. These are the "first waters."

"And you will be holy" — this refers to the *mayim acharonim:* the nine *kabin* (measures) of water that is poured over a body when it returns its holy soul to its Creator. If a mother and father safeguard the first waters, they will merit these final waters. But if, heaven forbid, they did not observe the Torah's laws as they should, the nine *kabin* will have no effect, for the destructive angels are not afraid of this water.

There is a story told of R' Akiva Eiger, who went into the purification room where a dead body lay awaiting burial. As they stood beside the corpse, R' Akiva Eiger suddenly asked his companion, "Do you want to see something?" The man replied in the affirmative.

R' Akiva Eiger took his handkerchief and passed it before the other man's eyes. The man was struck with terror and nearly fainted. What did he see? He glimpsed scores of destructive angels hovering over the dead man as it lay in the purification room. *Rabbosai*, this concept is very simple. The way we live is the way we die!

R' Meir Shapiro continues. *"For I am holy"* — this is sweet oil. A person who has merited making himself holy, becoming a perfect *"tzelem Elokim"* (image of God), is permitted to anoint his body with oil — to adorn the *tzelem Elokim*. Hillel Hazaken, when on his way to anoint his own holy form, explained as much to his students:

"When Hillel Hazaken parted from his students and started to walk away from them, his students asked him, 'Rebbi, where are you going?'

" 'To do a *mitzvah*,' he told them.

" 'And which *mitzvah* is that?' they asked.

" 'To wash in the bathhouse,' he told them.

" 'Is that a *mitzvah*?' they asked.

"He told them, 'If they erect statues of kings in theaters and circuses, and pay a salary to the man who dusts and washes them, and accord him honor for doing this job, am not I, who was created in His image, as it says, *'For in the image of God He made man,'* even more so?" (*Vayikra Rabbah, perek* 34).

Baruch Hashem, we have talked about good things. May *HaKadosh Baruch Hu* grant us the merit of ascending in Torah and *yiras shamayim* and good *middos*, and may we merit the *geulah sheleimah* speedily in our days, *amen! Chazak u'varuch* — be strong and be blessed!

> *"Naaman, the commander of the army of the king of Aram,
> was an eminent man before his master and well honored, for
> through him Hashem had granted victory to Aram. The man
> was a great warrior — a leper ... 'Go and bathe seven times
> in the Jordan'"* (II Melachim 5:1,10).

THREE QUESTIONS AND ONE ANSWER

R' Sholom Schwadron

☞ The First Question

My rebbi asked an awesome question on this passage, and then
followed it up with further questions.

Naaman, the commander of the army of Aram, was a *metzora* — a
leper. He consulted doctors and tried all sorts of remedies, but nothing healed him. A Jewish girl who had been captured in war lived
in Naaman's household, and she whispered to Naaman's wife that it
would be worth his while to go up to Eretz Yisrael, where there lived
a man of God, Elisha, who had the power to cure his leprosy.

Having no other options — a leper is considered as though dead
— and with the knowledge that no medicine had been able to help
him so far, Naaman decided to follow the captive girl's advice.

The king of Aram sent a letter to the king of Israel, stating that
his military commander was coming to see him and begging him to
at any cost do what he could to improve Naaman's medical condition. The king read the letter, and tore his clothes. *"Am I God, to
make people die or live, that he has sent me to cure a man of leprosy?"*
(He was concerned about the consequences, should he fail to effect
a cure.) The prophet Elisha heard about the king's distress and sent
word to him, saying, *"I will cure him. Let him come and know that there
is a prophet in Israel."*

Naaman was given an appointment. He came in an opulent carriage, with fine horses and footmen in elaborate ceremony. Elisha was not impressed. He did not invite him into his house, or even go out to meet him in the courtyard. All he did was send someone to the door to tell the commander of Aram's military forces, "Go bathe in the Jordan seven times, and you will be completely healed."

As you know, the lives of world leaders are wrapped up in pride and honor, especially honor, and competition to see who has more of it. They tell of a certain king in history who ruled over the entire civilized world. He said: "Every person has his desire and his ambition. If he is a simple soldier, his desire is to become an officer. If he is an officer, his goal is to move up to being a general. If he is already a general, his ambition is to be assistant to the king; and if he is already a king, his desire is to rule over another land, and still another, until he rules over the entire world. And if he already rules over the entire world, what is his desire then? His desire is toward overweening pride."

It says in *Tanach* that the prideful Naaman became angry. *"Behold, I said [to myself] that he would surely come out to me, and stand and call in the Name of Hashem, his God, and wave his hand over the [diseased] area — and the leper would be healed!"* Instead, Elisha is sending messengers to meet me at the door, and advising me to go bathe in the Jordan River, as though there were not enough rivers in my own country! *"Then he turned and went in a fury."* He refused to do as Elisha suggested.

His attendants coaxed him to change his mind. What harm can befall you if you believe in him and do as he tells you? "Had the prophet told you to do a difficult thing, would you not have done it?" All he did was tell you to bathe in the Jordan and you will be healed!

Naaman listened to their advice, and immersed himself in the Jordan. His flesh returned to the condition of a young boy's skin — perfectly clean. At that moment, something stirred powerfully in his heart. Having witnessed such an incredible miracle, the commander in chief of Aram's army returned to the home of the Elisha, *navi* of Hashem, and begged permission to shower him with gifts. Elisha, however, refused to accept them. Not a single one.

Amazed, Naaman resolved to convert to Judaism. Because it was impossible for him to become a *ger tzedek*, but only a *ger toshav*, that is what he became.

And what, asked my rebbi, of the men who accompanied him? Why did they not convert? After all, they had been bigger believers than Naaman was. Where did they all disappear to? Why did they not convert as well? A good question.

Then my rebbi went on to ask another one.

⌒ The Second Question

Parashas Korach deals with a great controversy. Korach was no ordinary man, but he became ensnared in the coils of a quarrel and fell into the depths (may Hashem safeguard us). "When a person disagrees with his rebbi, it is as if he is disagreeing with the *Shechinah*." The controversy generated terrible punishments and tragedies. Korach's people were swallowed up, burned, and decimated by a plague. Afterward we are told, *"The entire assembly of the Children of Israel complained on the morrow against Moshe and Aharon, saying, 'You have killed the people of Hashem!'"* Whereupon Hashem instructed them to take twelve sticks and place them before Hashem in the Holy of Holies. *"It shall be that the man whom I shall choose — his staff will blossom."* In this way, the controversy would finally subside.

"Moshe laid the staffs before Hashem in the Tent of Testimony. On the next day, Moshe came to the Tent of Testimony and behold! the staff of Aharon of the house of Levi had blossomed; it brought forth a blossom, sprouted a bud, and almonds ripened. Moshe brought out all the staffs from before Hashem to all the Children of Israel; they saw and they took, each man his staff." At last, the controversy was over.

My rebbi asked: If the blossom of Aharon's staff could cause the controversy to subside, Hashem could have instructed them to take the staffs at the start of the episode, saying, "The staff that will blossom belongs to he whom I have chosen." In this way, the fire of controversy might have been quenched at the onset. Why, as it were, was there a need for earthquake, fire, and plague? What was the purpose of all of these calamities?

⌁ The Third Question

Tanach describes an incident involving Eliyahu Hanavi, who had an argument: With whom? With Achav, king of Israel. *Ai, ai,* what a wicked man that was! And he was married to a woman even more wicked than he. "There was none such as Achav, who was incited by Izevel, his wife."

He had a Jewish friend who served as a minister of the state — the state of *Gehinnom*. His name was Chiel.

Chiel decided to settle down: Where? In Jericho.

Yehoshua had cursed anyone who would rebuild Jericho: "*Cursed before Hashem be the man who rises up and rebuilds this city, Jericho; with his oldest [child] he will lay its foundation and with his youngest he will set up its gates.*" And this man wanted specifically to build Jericho. "On principle," they call it.

He had seven sons, and he lost them all. When he laid the foundation for his home in Jericho, his firstborn died. He sat *shivah*. He continued to build, row after row of stones, and his second son died. Firm in his "principle," he mustered his strength and continued building, and the third son died ... until, at the completion of the house, as the doors were put in, the seventh died. He sat *shivah*. They came to comfort him.

Because he was a government minister, the king himself came to pay a "*shivah* call" as did Eliyahu *Hanavi*. The two met. Achav, king of Israel, asked Eliyahu a question: " 'The curse of the student has come to pass.' That is, Yehoshua, who was Moshe Rabbeinu's student, imposed a curse that came true. This much cannot be denied, for I have seen it come to fruition: '*With his oldest [child] he will lay its foundation and with his youngest he will set up its gates.*'

"But," said Achav, "the teacher's curse has not been realized. The Torah says, '*Beware, lest ... you turn astray and serve gods of others and bow to them. Then the wrath of Hashem will blaze against you. He will restrain the heaven so there will be no rain.*' Yet I, Achav, walk to the chapel of my foreign gods, and I have to use an umbrella! The teacher's curse has not come to pass."

Eliyahu Hanavi replied, "You dare ask such a question? As Hashem lives, you will have no rain!" With this vow, Eliyahu sentenced Israel to three years of drought!

But what purpose, we may ask, did this vow serve? Eliyahu was also a "student." In that case, Achav could ask the same question: "The curse of the student, Yehoshua, came to pass, but that of Moshe was not realized."

There are several possible explanations. Here is one of them:

Eliyahu was saying to Achav, "When are you asking these kinds of 'clever' questions? When you're seated at the table with 400 prophets of the Ba'al, 450 prophets of Asheirah, and the wicked Izevel — all of you eating and guzzling to your heart's content. When you stuff yourself and are full, you ask questions. But when famine comes, and you are eating potato peels plucked from the rubbish, then you will no longer be asking questions."

Indeed, that was how it was.

☞ Let's Make a Symposium

For three years, there was famine in Israel. When the three years were up, Eliyahu once again met King Achav.

"You are the enemy of the Jewish people!" Achav called out to him.

Said Eliyahu, "*It is not I who is the enemy of Israel, rather you and your father's house [are], by forsaking the commandments of Hashem; and you have trapped Israel in idol worship!*"

Do you know what Eliyahu proposed next? "Let's make a symposium!" Do you know what a symposium is? A conference. Let's gather together all of Israel. You build an altar to your foreign gods, and I will set up an altar to Hashem. Whichever altar receives fire from heaven will belong to the true God, and you will see with your own eyes that Hashem is God!

Achav agreed. His "*tzaddikim*" collected a band of false prophets. Facing them on *Har Carmel* were the people of Israel. Two bulls were brought. These two bulls were alike in every feature and quality and born from the same mother, so that no one could say that Eliyahu had bought, as it were, a special bull.

The prophets of the Baal tried until noon. They danced, yelled, and tore their flesh with swords — all in vain.

Chazal tell us something terrible. They built a hollow altar and put Chiel inside — the man who had already lost all seven of his sons. They put him in with kerosene and matches. He was to light the kerosene under the altar to let up a flame. That was the plan. What did Hashem do? He sent a snake to bite Chiel, and that was that ... The false prophets were beside themselves. "Baal, answer us!" they cried until midday, but there was no one to answer.

(How did Chiel come to such foolishness? All of his children had already died and yet, he remained stuck fast in his evil ways! My rebbi once told me that the greatest of all desires is, "He who knows his Master and plans to rebel against Him." If he succumbed to that desire, he is to be pitied.)

Then Eliyahu Hanavi built an altar, and ordered large quantities of water to be poured over it. He prayed to Hashem and was anwered. A fire descended from heaven and consumed the bull, the wood, and the stones — and licked up the water as well. And the people cried, "*Hashem hu ha'Elokim!* Hashem — He is the God!"

They executed all the prophets of the foreign gods: 850 false prophets in all.

Achav, greatly shaken by this spectacle, repented for 22 years. For 22 years, he did *teshuvah*.

My rebbi asked: When Achav asked his question about the curse of the student coming to fruition but not that of the teacher, Eliyahu could have suggested the "symposium" right there and then. He could have shown the entire nation the bull and the fire, and they would all have repented. Why inflict three years of famine on them first?

We are going to answer all three of these questions at once. To review: The first question deals with Naaman, who converted, while the men who had come with him remained gentiles. The second question was about Moshe Rabbeinu. Why didn't he introduce the staffs at the start of the controversy? And the third is about Eliyahu Hanavi. Why didn't he stage his "symposium" earlier?

My rebbi offered a single answer for all three of these questions! It is a very fundamental one. Please pay attention, and you will understand.

☞ Showing Miracles to an Animal

By way of introduction: The Torah tells us, "*And Hashem Elokim formed the man of dust of the ground ...*" We added (in our discussion of *Parashas Tzav*), that it is with reference to this creation that the verse exclaims, "*How abundant are Your works, Hashem; You have made all of them with wisdom! The earth is filled with Your possessions.*" The earth is filled with the possessions of heaven. Hashem attached a holy, exalted, spiritual soul to the dust of the ground. There is no single limb or sinew, no portion of the body from its head to its toe, that is not a joining of body and soul together. Awesome! And it is from the power of this marvel that free will arises. Man is the only creation in the world that possesses the ability to choose freely. There is no other! (There are those who say that an angel has choice, but in its intense awareness and awe of the Exalted, it does not stray into sin.)

When a person chooses good and allows his soul to triumph over the physical, he is called a *tzaddik*. Incidentally, it must be pointed out that *tzaddikim* work very hard in order to achieve this. For a person to rise above nature requires effort. It's not something you can buy in a store. (This is why we can ask a *tzaddik* to pray on our behalf, and his blessings come true, because a *tzaddik* lives his entire life on a plane that is above nature. And so, measure for measure, he has the ability to cure illnesses that cannot be cured in the natural way.)

However, a person who drowns in the sea of *ta'avah*, of desire (as *Rabbeinu* Yonah describes it) — and it doesn't matter how he drowns, quite quickly or very, very slowly, may Hashem have mercy! — is allowing his body to rule over his spiritual force. In that case, he is capable of causing great damage. What damage! What destruction! More than all the beasts and all the animals, more than all the poisonous snakes. We have seen evil men — Hitler, Stalin, and others, may their names be blotted out — who were far worse than wild animals. They allowed the physical to rule over their souls! And so, "*He is likened to the silenced animals*" (*Tehillim* 49:13).

Now, think about this. Take an animal, put a *tallis* on it, and place it in the *beis midrash*. Give that animal a *siddur* and tell it, "Please, animal, *daven*!" You can show it signs and miracles, but would there be any point?

Here is the answer to all three questions. If we show miracles to a person who is drowning in a sea of desire, it is like showing them to an animal. He will open his eyes, gaze in amazement, and after a moment return to his desires, to his dirt, and to all the sins in the world.

The clever Korach drowned in the sea of desire for controversy, and became like an animal. And not only he succumbed, but his entire congregation. Had Hashem said, at the start, "*Let every man take his staff*," nothing would have come of it. They would have cried out, "Aaaah …" They would have reacted with excitement to the miracle — and that's all. Then they would have gone home, and the next morning the controversy would have renewed itself.

However, *rabbosai*, after Korach and his people were swallowed up and burned and afflicted with plague, the physical self was broken. The material stuff, or *chomer*, of which the body is made up has the same letters as "*chamor*," or donkey. These days we don't see donkeys in the street, but in my childhood I saw them. The donkey is the laziest of creatures. When it refuses to walk, what does its driver do? He pokes it with a stick, whereupon the donkey jumps up and begins to walk. Only after the body was broken did the time come to bring on the miracles! Only then did *HaKadosh Baruch Hu* order the staffs to be brought, saying that the staff that flowered would belong to the man of Hashem's choice. At that point, there was a purpose to the miracle.

Had Eliyahu reacted to Achav's question by saying, "Bring two bulls" and so forth, they would have seen the miracle of the descending fire, and what would they have said? They would have exclaimed, made gestures … and that's all.

Let me tell you something that I heard from a man who was an officer in the army. Many years ago, there were two Yemenite youths who tried to attack Lord Moyne. (They were Eliyahu Beit Tzuri and Eliyahu Chakim.) The youths wanted to kill the lord (who was appointed by the Egyptian ambassador), but they were caught and sentenced to hanging. After they were put to death, they were buried in Egypt, and it was only some 30 years later that the Egyptians returned the bodies in caskets. And the bodies were completely whole. Even the rope around their necks was recognizable. Amazing! (The Gemara says that those who are put to death by *Beis Din*, and those who are put to death by the nations of the world, there is no man who can stand in their place.)

Recently, I was visited by an officer who participated in the burial of those two young men. There were a few other people in my house at the time, and I urged them to listen to the story, as told by someone who had been there. He told them what other witnesses had already testified to, for he, too, was an eyewitness: that the bodies were whole. Then he added that, among those who'd been standing by when the coffins were opened were several doctors, who stood open mouthed as the bodies were taken out of the coffins, looking as though they had been put to death the day before. How did those doctors react? "Egypt's soil is dry."

Syria has the same kind of soil, onlookers commented. Why, when an ordinary corpse is brought over from Syria, is it impossible to differentiate as much as a single bone?!

"All right," they admitted. But what came after that admission? They went home, to think about money and eat steaks. You can't show an animal a miracle.

Only after the Jews had suffered a famine for three long years, when the body of *Klal Yisrael* and of Achav had been broken … Only after Achav sent Ovadiah out to find some grass for the five horses that had not yet died of hunger … Only then was he ready to do *teshuvah*.

During the Six-Day War, Ben-Gurion exclaimed, "Miracles and wonders! Miracles and wonders!" That's how he spoke on the radio, do you remember? But what happened the next day? Everything was different. "We, in our strength …" May Hashem have mercy.

"*Hashem created a person straight, and they make all sorts of calculations.*" If a person truly desires to walk the straight path — if he possesses a faithful desire, strong and true and honest — then Hashem helps him be straight! He showers down *siyata d'Shemaya*! "*He who comes to be purified is helped.*"

פרשת מצורע
PARASHAS METZORA

There was once a man who would sit and expound, and he said, "There is no single hair for which HaKadosh Baruch Hu did not create a wellspring all its own, so that one will not benefit from that of its neighbor." Said his wife: "And you are planning to go out [of the Land of Israel] in order to make your living? Remain here, and Your creator will provide for you. He listened to her and he remained, and his Creator provided for him" (Vayikra Rabbah 7:3).

A GOOD LAWYER

R' Yaakov Galinsky

There was a certain Kohen who would inspect discolorations on the flesh to see if they were *tzara'as* (a physical manifestation of a spiritual punishment), as the Torah says, "*If a person will have on the skin of his flesh a s'eis, or a sapachas ... he shall be brought to Aharon the Kohen, or to one of his sons the Kohanim. The Kohen shall look at the affliction on the skin of his flesh ...*" (Vayikra 13:2-3).

He was having a hard time making ends meet, and finally decided to leave home for an extended period abroad, in order to make a living. He told his wife, "I am to be leaving home soon, with your consent, but people are accustomed to coming to me to show me their discolorations. It's hard for me to leave the country without appointing a substitute in my place. How can I leave people without someone to answer them? So I will teach another Kohen how the discolorations look, and he can fill my place."

The first lesson dealt with the case where hairs are seen within the sore: "*And it has changed hair to white*, etc." He introduced the subject with a fundamental principle: "If you see a hair whose source of moisture has dried up, you will know that he is afflicted. Each and every individual hair was created with its own 'spring' from which to drink. If the spring dries up, so does the hair." If, heaven forbid, a dried-up hair is found on a person's head or anywhere else on his body, that is a sign that he has been afflicted. A wellspring of life has dried up in his body, for each individual hair has its own wellspring from which it draws its sustenance. If the hair has dried up, this is a sign that the moisture source has dried up as well — an indication that he is afflicted.

The wife listened to what he was teaching and understood a deeper significance. "How many hairs does a person have on his body?" she interjected.

"The answer is, tens of thousands. And each hair has its own source of moisture. No hair drinks from its neighbor's 'spring.' Each and every one of those tens of thousands of hairs has its own source of livelihood!"

Tens of thousands of springs! And Hashem can't give *you* the sustenance you need? If Hashem created a separate spring for each individual hair to drink from, won't you — a person with so many hairs, who is responsible for supporting your children — be supported by Hashem?" With that, she withdrew her consent for him to leave the country in search of a livelihood.

He listened to her, stayed in Eretz Yisrael, and fresh sources of income came to him.

Rabbosai, this man was strengthened in his *emunah* in the merit of his wife, and had time left over to engage in Torah study and thus become even further strengthened in *emunah*.

⌒ *"I Don't Lack for Money"*

I remember a story that may be useful for providing strength and encouragement.

A certain wealthy man came to the Chofetz Chaim and said, "*Baruch Hashem*, I don't lack for money. And, *baruch Hashem*, I am not old. Then again, I am not young, and I have six children. I've decided to include a yeshivah as my seventh child. In other words, I've come here to draw up a will, in which I will write that my considerable property is to be divided into seven portions. However, there is a condition attached: When my life is up, I would like the Chofetz Chaim to learn *mishnayos* for the elevation of my soul."

The Chofetz Chaim lifted his eyes and said, "*Reb Yid*, I have two questions for you, for your words are puzzling to me.

"Let us say, for example, that you have 700 *rubles* and six children. You would like each child to take 100 *rubles* and the yeshivah to take 100 *rubles* as well. A very nice wish. But what I don't understand is why you are waiting until after your death. Give the yeshivah the 100 *rubles* right now! Why take a chance on your children hiring a good lawyer after your passing, to prove that they are the sole heirs, to the yeshivah's detriment?

"My second question is this: Is it I who needs to learn *mishnayos* for the elevation of your soul? *You* learn! You are still alive. *Reb Yid*, learn yourself!"

A person wants to secure himself through others. Let him, instead, secure himself 100 percent through his own efforts. He is dealing with eternal life. Why take chances?

Rabbosai, as the Chofetz Chaim once said, there is nothing there. In *Shamayim*, it is impossible to obtain even a torn, stained page of

Gemara from some *genizah*. You may search for a page to learn from, but there is none. If you search for just an old *siddur* so that you can look inside and say a few words, there is none. The only *sefarim* we'll find there are those that we bring with us! "You are still alive. Learn *mishnayos* while you are still here!" the Chofetz Chaim adjured.

☞ Don't Be a Fool

They say that R' Yisrael Salanter once told a student:

There are four parts to the *Shulchan Aruch* — and there is a fifth part as well. What is that? "Don't Be a Fool." *Rabbosai*, the greatest foolishness is to lose one's own life.

Sometimes a person awakens to the fact that he musn't lose his life or waste its substance. Afterward, however, he falls asleep again, and returns to routine. Let me tell you something. I was once driven by car to deliver a *derashah* in a *moshavah* near Rechovot. As the car entered the settlement and moved quickly along the winding road, we passed a group of horses munching grass at the roadside. One of the horses became startled by the passing car. In its panic, it reared up on its hind legs. Amazing! Have you ever seen a horse do that? One might think that it wasn't a horse at all, for it was standing on two legs. But when the car moved on, the horse resumed its usual, four-legged stance. It went back to being a horse. The wonder was gone.

That is how a person is, when he decides to use his life properly, but then so quickly forgets and returns to routine. In the Gulf War, we saw miracles. Our prayers were as they should be, our *teshuvah* was wonderful. Together, we roused ourselves to use the time we've been allotted in our lives to designate more time for Torah study and the like. But the moment the car passed by ...

☞ Mussar for R' Sholom Schwadron

"You have plenty of time. You have the rest of your life ahead of you," the evil inclination tells a *yeshivah bachur* or a grown man.

In this way, a person remains with his "life ahead of him," until it's already behind him — finished.

The Vilna Gaon once said that a person should think three things: As if he has only one day left to live, and he has one page of Gemara in front of him, and he is the last Jew in the world. In this way, he will succeed. For if Eliyahu Hanavi were to come along and say, "Sir, I'd like to inform you that this is your last day on earth," would you run to the bank to withdraw cash or run to the *Beis Midrash*?

Hitler (may his name be blotted out) wanted there to be just one Jew left in the world — in memory of the Jewish nation. Think of what that last Jew would be thinking about on the last day of his life. "The world rests on my shoulders! Judaism depends on me! The continued existence of Torah depends on me!" Every minute would be used to its very fullest. *Chazal* tell us, "Therefore, man was born unique, to teach you that sustaining a single soul in Israel is tantamount to sustaining an entire world." Be proud! Did you know that you are responsible for the entire world? You are unique.

R' Sholom Schwadron relates that R' Eliyahu Lopian told him one night, "Bring me a *shtender*." When he brought the *shtender*, R' Elya stood beside it as though preparing to deliver a *mussar* talk to R' Sholom. Then R' Lopian called to him, "R' Sholom! R' Sholom! If only I had your black beard ... If only I had it! If I had a black beard like you, I would know what to do with my life." The talk was over ... a *mussar* talk from rebbi to student. A loving lecture for the student's benefit.

A person is never satisfied with the amount of money he has. He wants more and more. And when he realizes that money will not accompany him to his grave, he suddenly has a genuine desire to give it to *tzeddakah* but only after his death, when it will be up to his children to make sure that the yeshivah receives some crumbs. "You are alive!" the Chofetz Chaim says. "You are capable of helping yourself. Don't be a fool!"

Let us increase our Torah study and charity. Let us and our children seize life!

וּסְפַרְתֶּם לָכֶם מִמָּחֳרַת הַשַּׁבָּת מִיּוֹם הֲבִיאֲכֶם אֶת־עֹמֶר הַתְּנוּפָה שֶׁבַע שַׁבָּתוֹת תְּמִימֹת תִּהְיֶינָה.

"You shall count for yourselves — from the morrow of the rest day, from the day when you bring the Omer Hatenufah (the Omer of the waving) — seven weeks, they shall be complete." (Vayikra 23:15).

A MODERN-DAY DONKEY

R' Sholom Schwadron

Y ou shall count for yourselves." How and what are we to count?

One day of the *Omer*, two days of the *Omer* ... until we reach 49 days — seven weeks, or seven times seven.

The intention of the *Sefirah* is to arrive at *Kabbalas HaTorah*: *"Until the morrow of the seventh week you shall count, 50 days; and you shall offer a new meal-offering to Hashem"* — on the festival of Shavuos.

I once heard R' Eliyahu Lopian discuss why we call *Shavuos* by that name. After all, the essence of the holiday is the receiving of the Torah. Wouldn't it be more fitting to call the day by some other name, such as "*Chag Kabbalas HaTorah*" or "*Chag HaAtzeres*"?

In R' Elya's view, this name is meant to teach us that receiving the Torah is impossible without prior preparation. If you wish to receive the Torah, get ready. Count seven full weeks until the "*Chag HaShavuos*," the Festival of Weeks, and the giving of the Torah.

☞ For Yourselves

"*You shall count for yourselves.*" What does the word "yourselves" convey? The simple meaning is that each and every person must count.

However, in the pathway of *derush*, there are all sorts of counters of days and weeks.

One person may count to himself, *In another 49 days, I will have to appear in court.* And another may count, *In another 49 days, I will win the lottery!* The difference between the two is vast. Both of them are counting, but a single look at their faces demonstrates the difference, as great as the difference between heaven and earth.

Therefore, the Torah tells us, "*You shall count for yourselves.*" Count the days of the *Omer* — for yourselves. The *Sefirah* should be something that belongs to you, that is close to your heart (and, as the Gemara states in the laws of *Yom Tov*: "For yourselves, for all your needs.") Count the days for yourselves! Sense that the goal is to achieve the greatest happiness.

☞ The Omer Hatenufah

"*From the day when you bring the Omer Hatenufah.*"

"*Omer Hatenufah*": The simple meaning of this term is the "raised" offering. A deeper way of looking at it would be that the *Omer* raises the person who brings it. It elevates him.

The *Omer*, brought on Pesach, is made from barley. From the day that it is brought as an offering, we count 50 days, and then, "*You shall offer a new meal-offering to Hashem.*" This new offering, the two loaves, are made of wheat.

Why is the *Omer* offering of barley, and then two loaves of wheat?

According to the *Zohar HaKadosh*, we are, in effect, saying to *HaKadosh Baruch Hu*: "Master of the Universe, we know that until we have received the Torah we are considered like animals. Therefore, we bring you an offering of animal food: barley."

Animal food is degrading, true! For if we have even the slightest similarity to an animal, we should feel a certain amount of degradation.

The problem is that a person eats animal food, and commits sins, heaven forbid — an animal act — or drowns himself in the lust for money, but he does not feel degraded.

David Hamelech says: "*Man is glorious but [if he] understands not, he is likened to the silenced animals*" (*Tehillim* 49:13). Man has a most glorious thing inside him: an exalted soul, carved from beneath the Throne of Glory. But if he does not understand this, and does not use his soul properly, "*he is likened to the silenced animals.*" (There are those who are only "likened" to animals; there are others who actually are "silenced.")

How terrible. This morning, a man passed by my house with his son, both of them yawning. Why? Neither of them had slept the night before. What did they do all night? They ate snacks, played loud taped music, and pranced around like year-old calves. In the morning, they went to bed. *Nu*, is this not like an animal?! *Rachmana litzlan*.

☞ Adam HaRishon's Tears

Adam *HaRishon* was cursed because he ate from the *Eitz Hada'as* — the Tree of Knowledge of Good and Evil. Why did he eat from the tree? Because he wanted to know! Not the kind of knowledge our scientists talk about, but much more. Nevertheless, he was cursed, because Hashem had ordered him not to eat.

What was the curse? "*Thorns and thistles shall it sprout for you ... By the sweat of your brow shall you eat bread ...*" Before he can eat bread, he will have to undergo ten labors: plowing, planting, harvesting, threshing, grinding, and so on. By the time he reaches the point where he can eat of the bread, he is ready to expire. A curse.

You may be thinking to yourselves that the Torah was just talking about those days, and that only farming entails this sort of labor. Agriculture is not so difficult today. These days, fields are plowed with a huge, tanklike machine, the harvesting is done with the help of another specialized machine, and there are all sorts of other labor-saving devices. There is a machine to collect sheaves of wheat ... soon there'll be a machine to eat the bread! So we can relax and enjoy ourselves. We can rejoice in our labor ...

But, *rabbosai*, Adam HaRishon was intelligent. How intelligent he was! He was the work of Hashem's own Hands! And when Adam heard Hashem tell him, "*Thorns and thistles shall it sprout for you*," tears streamed from his eyes. He said, "I and my donkey will eat from one trough" (*Pesachim* 118a). Adam HaRishon wept. Do you hear?

Why did he cry? Would he and his donkey really eat out of one trough? His donkey will eat in his stall, amidst dirt and rocks, while man will sit at a table covered with a pristine white cloth, forks, silver spoons. Why did he cry and say that he and his donkey would eat from a single trough? And, specifically, were he alive today, what would there be to cry about?

The answer is — a modern-day donkey. A donkey with spoons and forks and gigantic machines.

For if a person is forced to deal with the earth all day long, with straw and thorns and thistles, and only thus is he enabled to receive his portion of daily bread, then his is a donkey's life. It doesn't matter if he eats with a golden fork afterward, or if his work is done with the help of a huge combine. Adam wept because, "I and my donkey will eat from one trough." Everything pertaining to this world is ephemeral: here one minute and gone the next. If we are forced to work "by the sweat of your brow," we are forced to expend so much time on this-worldly matters simply in order to have bread to eat. Therefore, "I and my donkey will eat from one trough."

Thus, "*you shall count for yourselves.*" Know that when you count the *Omer* you are counting "for yourselves." From the day you bring the *Omer Hatenufah*, you are elevated. First you bring the barley offering: animal food. Then, day by day, as we counted, we moved away from the gates of pollution and entered the gates of purity, until we arrived at *Matan Torah*. "*I will lift you on the wings of eagles — and I will bring you to Me.*" For when there is Torah, we are exalted. We are removed from the other nations, let alone from the animal world. "*I will bring you to Me!*"

May Hashem save us and redeem us for the glory of His Name. Be strong and blessed.

[More on *Sefiras Ha'Omer* in *Parashas Bamidbar, iy"H*.]

פרשת אחרי מות
PARASHAS ACHAREI MOS

וְנָשָׂא הַשָּׂעִיר עָלָיו אֶת־כָּל־עֲוֹנֹתָם.

"The he-goat will bear upon itself all their iniquities" (Vayikra 16:22).

"HaKadosh Baruch Hu takes all of Israel's sins and gives them to the wicked Eisav, as it says, 'The he-goat will bear upon itself,' and there is no he-goat [sa-ir] except for Eisav, as it says, 'Behold, my brother Eisav is an 'ish sa-ir.' "

WHAT WERE WEDDINGS LIKE BACK THEN?

R' Yaakov Galinsky

There is a marvelous *midrash* in our *parashah* (*Yalkut* 5577), as quoted above. The *midrash* continues, "Eisav said, 'How much power I have, now that you have placed all of Yaakov's iniquities on me.' At that time, *HaKadosh Baruch Hu* took their iniquities and placed them on his clothing, which became red, as it says, 'Why are your clothes red?'" On Yom Kippur, Hashem takes the sins of the Jewish nation and, as it were, pours them over Eisav's head. He already has so much iniquity, let him have a little more.

The *Tiferes Yehonasan* (R' Yehonasan Eibeshitz) asks: If *HaKadosh Baruch Hu* wants to atone for Israel's sins, does He lack for garbage cans into which to cast them? Is Eisav's head a trash can? He explains that the meaning is other than the obvious one. What is it?

The many sins of Israel are brought to the Heavenly Court in prosecution against them. The defender — the angel Micha'el — says, "*Ribono Shel Olam*, Eisav is to blame in all these transgressions! They are only students. True, the people of Israel are talented and they are good students, but they are only students." In this way, he speaks in our defense. Hashem listens to his claim and takes our iniquities, as it were, and throws them onto the wicked Eisav.

We are not to blame. The "street" influences us. But let us at least know from where our sins are derived.

The Gemara (*Zevachim* 113a) cites an opinion that the *Mabul* (the Great Flood) did not take place in Eretz Yisrael. *Tosafos* asks, and the *Zohar HaKadosh* elaborates on a similar question: In that case, why was there any need for an ark? Hashem could just have put Noach and his family in Eretz Yisrael.

The answer, according to the *Zohar*, is as follows. While the *Mabul* did not actually take place in Eretz Yisrael, its harmful influence caused extensive damage to Eretz Yisrael as well, and anyone who lived there died.

Our homes are open to the public domain and are influenced by the street. Ironically, were we not influenced by the people of the street, who are busy day and night with trivial and worthless pursuits, they would be inestimably influenced by *us*! For when one sees the picture correctly, the influence of a *ben Torah* is indescribable!

A small person is naturally influenced. Many individuals have become observant after spending a Shabbos among God-fearing folk. Why? Because they had the picture wrong. They thought that life is lived among the garbage, and that pleasant conditions are to be found only where they are. Therefore, they reasoned, if they, who live "properly," have problems, those observant Jews doubtless are drowning in them ... Thirty years ago, I attended a wedding in a certain hall. In the adjoining hall, another wedding was taking place between two semisecular people. Once the meal was over, they didn't have much to do, so the celebration ended at 10 p.m. Whether or not they said *Birkas HaMazon*, I don't know. (I believe they set up a small *mechitzah* for the *chasan* and recited the *Sheva Berachos*.) I heard a man and wife decide, "Let's see what's going on in the hall next door." I told myself, *I'll follow them and hear their reactions.* Moving closer, I heard the woman tell her husband, "Look at those poor things, sitting separately. But how they're dancing! They're so happy! See how their legs are flying. They are really dancing!"

Why am I telling you this? So that you will know that *they* are the "poor things" who are influenced by us in all sorts of ways, both directly and indirectly.

☞ A Sword in the Beis Midrash

The Gemara relates that, when Sancheriv besieged Jerusalem, King Chizkiyahu stuck a sword in the *beis midrash* and announced that anyone who did not engage in Torah study would be pierced with that sword. The king knew that as long as there is Torah in Israel, there is no danger. Danger gains the upper hand only when, heaven forbid, the voices of Torah are silenced.

A very valid question is asked about this. Why did he thrust a sword into the entrance of the *beis midrash*? Is that where the sword was necessary? Let him put the sword in the middle of a busy thoroughfare, where Jews stroll in idleness. Why in a *beis midrash*?

The answer is: He knew that, should there be slackening of the learning in the houses of study, all parts of the nation would be influenced. On the contrary, only in the *beis midrash* would the sword be useful. Outside, on the street, not even a cannon would suffice.

You, *bnei yeshivah*, must know that if there is weakness anywhere out there, it is because of our weakness here inside! Were the learning in the *beis midrash* stronger, our behavior toward one another more devoted, our fear of heaven more powerful, they out there would also be better people. This is our reality. For the Jewish people are responsible for one another. Like electrical circuits, we are connected to each other. The responsibility rests only on us: to uproot the thorns, to clean up our act, and to be whole and perfect in our private lives.

⌐ Why a New Suit?

We have spoken about people being influenced at a distance. Now, let us talk about *chilul Hashem* (the desecration of Hashem's Name) with respect to those close to us. I will speak openly.

In our own circles, a terrible situation has arisen: debts that are not paid to *gemachs* (free-loan societies), the grocery store, and so on. When checks bounce, there is a great *chilul Hashem* in seeing how a person who appears God fearing on the outside is lax about stealing. The same applies to our dealings with neighbors, especially in communal apartment buildings where we may come to transgress the prohibition against stealing a neighbor's sleep, or even stealing outright. If someone returns home late at night and makes noise, people will think, *Those yeshivah men don't care about their neighbors.* And so, apart from the transgression itself, there is also *chilul Hashem*.

You may say, "There are people far worse than we are," or "We're not to blame, the street is to blame." True! As the *midrash* says, our sins are poured onto Eisav's head. But it's still no excuse.

One of the things that lead people not to repay debts is as follows: Until a generation ago, a person knew that what he had, he had, and what he didn't have, he didn't have! Today? "I must have it!" Who says you must? Who decided that? If Hashem has given you money, fine. But to accumulate debts and not repay them, and thus cause trouble for others, who taught you that? Where have we picked up such behaviors? Which work of *mussar*, which *midrash*, tells us to live by what we don't have? Is this the way previous generations behaved? We've learned it from the street!

A person says, "Believe me, for my part I'd be glad to walk around wearing a sack. I only bought a nice suit for others. But what happens? I wear my new suit, and no one even says, 'Thank you!'!" A person lives for others. Is this the way to make a *kiddush Hashem* (a sanctification of God's Name)? When I spoke recently, I quoted a story from the book, "*The King's Son and the Nazir*." In that talk, I dwelled mainly on the parable itself. Today, I will focus on the parable's meaning.

The story tells of a person who was a servant of Shlomo Hamelech. When he was freed, Shlomo told him, "Because you have served me honestly, I will give you a gift. I will teach you the language of the birds and the beasts. You will be able to understand what the animals are saying, what birds talk about and the words of the wild beast. However, I give you this gift with one condition attached: If anyone finds out that you understand the language of animals and birds, on that day, you will die."

The servant promised not to reveal the secret to anyone. The king began to teach him.

Upon returning to his home, the man overheard his donkey and ox conversing. The ox was complaining to the donkey, saying that he had no more strength left for the daily grind of hard work. He never had time off from the job. What to do? The donkey replied, "They say that donkeys are stupid. Apparently, you are a donkey."

"What do you mean?" the ox asked in surprise.

"I'll give you a simple piece of advice," returned the donkey. "Do as I do. I pretend to be sick. When they give me food, I don't eat.

When they offer me water, I don't drink. Then they decide to give me a day off to rest."

Hearing this, the animals' master began to laugh. "What's so funny?" asked a member of his family.

"Uh …" He found some sort of excuse and evaded the question.

The next day, when the ox was given food, it refused to eat. They gave it water, but it wouldn't drink. So they made the donkey do the ox's work as well as its own! The donkey began to regret that it had ever given the ox the benefit of its advice. It returned from the field worn and weary.

"Well, how did it go?" the donkey asked the ox.

"I really want to thank you for your idea," the ox replied.

"Listen," the donkey said. "I heard that if you don't work tomorrow, they're going to slaughter you. Who needs a sick ox?"

Shaken, the ox resolved to work as usual the next day.

Once again, the master laughed. His brother noticed, and asked, "What's so funny? This same time yesterday, you laughed as well!"

Once again, the man took refuge in excuses and evasions. But his brother said, "That stuff won't work with me. I'm not going to let you off the hook. Tell me!"

"I can't tell you," pleaded the householder. "If I do, I'll have to die."

"I don't care. You have to tell me!"

Seeing that he had no choice, the man promised to tell him the next day. He began to write his will.

His dog, sensing his master's dejection over the prospect of losing his life on the following day, tagged along after him with hanging head. He felt sorry for his master, who was about to die. As he passed near the chickens, they set up a noisy squawking.

"Aren't you ashamed of yourselves?" scolded the dog. "Our master is about to die, and you're making so much noise?"

One of the roosters replied, "If our master is crazy, are we to blame? I have 10 wives, and just let one of them say a word. But he, our master, can't deal with just one person putting a little pressure on him? Let him die!"

Hearing this, the master thought, *Perhaps he's right. Who says I have to tell him?* He entered the house, picked up a stick, and waited until his brother came in, demanding the story. When he came, the man cried, "One, two, three!" and hit his brother three times with the stick. "Who says I have to die for you?!"

Rabbosai, this is the principle that we must learn.

A man lays down a principle: "I have to have this." Or a woman insists to her husband, "We simply must have Italian marble counters." Or any other empty "needs"! And they lay down their lives for these decisions. It's no shame to live with what one has! I remember, about 50 years ago, when a certain wealthy individual made a wedding for his daughter in Tel Aviv. Afterward, guests described the event enthusiastically. "Do you know, they served expensive meat at that wedding to hundreds of guests." But other people, lacking the same means, managed to get married without costly meats. In Jerusalem, they would throw a wedding with just one cake. How? They began to ask each of the guests, "Have you had a slice?" And each guest avoided answering, feeling uncomfortable about taking the first slice. So they drank a *"l'chayim"* and danced up a storm, while continuing to ask the guests, "Have you had a piece of cake yet?" In short, they never cut the cake. It remained intact until the next day, and the couple was married anyway!

Today, we have some stupendous halls. On whose tab? Where have we learned to act this way? In which school was our generation educated? Which *Shulchan Aruch* states that one must live in this fashion? We ought to engage in a bit of soul-searching.

I've gone on long enough on this painful topic. We must learn a little *mussar*. And Hashem will help us, so that we will really be able to overcome all the obstacles and understand what is truly *Gan Eden* in this world. Knowing where that *Gan Eden* is hidden; that is the important thing. And let us merit all that is good, *amen!*

"On the first of Nissan, Aharon's sons died. Why are their deaths mentioned on Yom Kippur? To teach that, just as Yom Kippur atones, so does the death of tzaddikim atone. Why was the parashah of Miriam placed in juxtaposition to the parashah of Parah Adumah? To teach that, just as the ashes of the parah purify, so does the death of tzaddikim purify" (Yalkut Shimoni, II Shmuel, remez 155).

HASHEM'S EULOGY

Stories and selections from the hesped (eulogy) R' Yaakov Galinsky, shlita, delivered for the Steipler Gaon, zt"l

R*abbosai! Rabbosai!* Let us imagine for a moment that we have been asked to deliver a eulogy for Moshe Rabbeinu, *a"h."* So began R' Elchonon Wasserman's eulogy for the Chofetz Chaim.

"Who would be prepared to undertake the responsibility of standing up and eulogizing Moshe, the man of God? Who would have the strength to cry and to eulogize? However, there is no need, for the Torah, as it were, has already done the work for us. In just a few words, the holy Torah delivered a great eulogy on that crowning example of humanity, Moshe Rabbeinu: '*So Moshe, servant of Hashem, died there.*' Everything is included in these words. There is nothing more to add! '*So Moshe, servant of Hashem, died there.*' Anything that might be added would only detract.

"Why, we might ask, is 'Hashem's servant' such a desirable title?

"It is because of the well-known halachah: 'Whatever a servant acquires is acquired by his master' (*Pesachim* 88b). A servant has nothing; it all belongs to his master."

R' Elchonon went on to relate a story from the *midrash*.

A wealthy businessman set out for a distant country together with his devoted servant, leaving his only son at home. Then, one day, the man began to feel unwell, and his heart was filled with foreboding.

What shall I do? My son has no idea that my days are numbered, he thought in distress. *And when I close my eyes, heaven forbid, my servant, who knows about all my assets, will hurry to seize them. Once he has taken all the hidden treasures he will go on his way, leaving my only son with no knowledge that his father has died.* So he thought in anguish, as his eyes flowed with tears of parting from this world.

He thought it over, and made a decision.

From his sickbed in that foreign land, he summoned his servant and said, "My dear servant, I have a feeling that my days are numbered and that I will soon return my soul to its Creator. I am very grateful to you for serving me so faithfully all these years. Therefore, I would like to repay you. I have decided to write a will leaving all my property to you. All of my assets: silver, gold, land, and movable objects. However, I would like to give a gift to my only son as well. Therefore, I am putting an addendum on the will, saying that he has the right to search among all my belongings and to take one thing for himself as a memento. Let him choose what he will — one thing." The master went on to write the document, which he then handed to his servant. A few days later, he closed his eyes forever.

The servant was overjoyed. He hurried home to inform the "only son" of his father's passing. He described the last, difficult days: the father's parting words for his only son, the tears, the prayers, the final *viduy*, and, most important, about the document in his pocket.

The son mourned, shedding bitter tears over the sudden loss of his beloved father. When the seven days of mourning were over, he went to Rabban Gamliel to ask in astonishment, "Did my father's wits disappear in his last days, when he wrote such a will for an only son who loved him so much?!"

Rabban Gamliel said, "You don't understand just how clever a father you had. Filled with apprehension over his servant, he behaved with great wisdom. He gave you one thing, but he didn't say what it was. Take the servant! *'Whatever a servant acquires is acquired by his master.'* It's all yours! Once you have acquired the slave, you will have everything."

"*So Moshe, servant of Hashem, died there*"! The angels wept, and the *serafim* and the *ofanim* and the holy Torah. Indescribable! And what was it they called Moshe? A servant. The hand of a servant is like the hand of his master, and whatever the servant acquires belongs to his master. On his own, he has nothing.

Morai v'rabbosai, anyone who knew the Steipler Gaon from his youth to his old age saw a servant of Hashem. He didn't understand why he was accorded so much honor. Several times, when I entered his room, he would ask me, "R' Yaakov, can you explain to me why the children follow me about in the street? Am I 'abnormal'?" Which children was he referring to? When he went to shul on Shabbos, the local children were the only ones who dared to venture near, while the adults stood back and gazed at him from a distance. These, he didn't see (as his vision was impaired). "Why are the children following me?" he would ask. "Who am I? What am I? I'm just doing my duty. Does anyone owe me anything?" (In other words, I am just a servant, carrying out his duty.)

☙ One Dark Night

Let me tell you a wonderful episode that I witnessed about 50 years ago. In those good days, I was learning in the *yeshivah ketanah* in Novaradok.

The custom in yeshivah was that, when a young student sensed a cooling off in his spirituality — these days, they call it a "crisis," but back then they referred to it by saying that he'd cooled off a bit in his *yiras Shamayim* — the *mashgiach* would advise him to travel to the big Novaradok Yeshivah in the city of Bialystok, in order to strengthen himself. That's what happened to me. At a certain stage, my desire to learn diligently became weakened, and the *maggid shiur* told me, in a friendly, encouraging spirit, "Here's a train ticket and a warm letter of recommendation. Go learn for a few weeks in the Novaradok Yeshivah in Bialystok. There, they will warm your heart and ignite your soul."

Anyone who knew Novaradok in its glory knows that it was a factory for *yiras Shamayim*, service of Hashem, and character development. A stranger would not understand. Anyone who has never tasted Novaradok from close up would not understand the kind of *yiras Shamayim* factory I'm talking about. Fortunate is he who has merited it.

I took the long, exhausting trip to Bialystok, and finally arrived with the letter in my hand.

It was a cold winter afternoon. I was received pleasantly by the *Rosh Yeshivah*. He read the letter and made all the necessary arrangements for me. Then he told me, "Yaakov! Rabbeinu Yonah says, 'If a person does not arouse himself, what use is all the *mussar* and rebuke?' In that case, what purpose will be served by my giving you words of *mussar* and inspiration, when you are capable of learning *mussar* on your own?

"You know what? Go to a certain shul on the next street: 'Beis Rochel' is the shul's name. The shul will be empty. Take along a *Chovos Halevavos* and a candle and go there. You will have time and space for learning *mussar* at your leisure. Afterward, we'll talk."

Listen to what happened.

I set out. I arrived. I opened the door of the big shul. It was empty and dark when I got there at a late hour of the night.

The moment I opened the shul's door, before I lit the candle — literally, as I held the match in my hand — I noticed a small candle flickering in the women's section, a pinpoint of light in the darkness. Suddenly, I also heard a voice chanting melodiously. Someone had arrived before me and was sitting in the women's section. The sweet voice glided quietly down from the heights of the women's balcony. It mourned; it repeated; it yearned. I moved closer, climbing on tiptoe and listening closely. This is what I heard:

"Shmuel said to R' Yehudah (*Eruvin* 54a), 'Sharp one, grab and eat, grab and drink, because this world from which we must eventually depart is like a wedding celebration [inasmuch as it begins and ends within a short period of time] ...'" He quoted the words of *Chazal* just as they appear, without additions. "Shmuel said to R' Yehudah, 'Grab and eat, grab and drink, because this world … is like a wedding celebration …!'"

I stood transfixed. I had never heard this kind of thing. The voice grew stronger and stronger, reaching a crescendo of passion: "Grab and eat! Grab and drink!" And so on, repeated dozens and dozens of times.

The *mussar* chant pounded at my head and bounced against the *Aron Kodesh* with joy, with fervor, with grief: "Because this world is like a wedding celebration …" R' Shmuel was telling his son the following: "Know that this world is like a wedding hall, where all sorts of food and drink and many kinds of delicacies are arranged. Anyone who wants to can reach out a hand and take some. Anyone who does not reach out a hand will have nothing. When the wedding is over, the guests leave one by one and the light is extinguished. Darkness reigns. There is nothing there. Whatever you have taken is yours; what you have not taken, you don't have. Therefore, 'Grab and eat, grab and drink!' Seize the moment!"

[In tears] Do you know who it was that sat there with his candle and repeated these words of *Chazal*?

It was a *bachur* by the name of Yaakov Yisrael, from the town of Hornosteipel.

Looking at the *sefer* '*Kehillos Yaakov*,' seeing all the wonders, studying the incredible righteousness and brilliance, we find that they are all founded on this one *mussar* lesson, repeated over and over: "Grab and eat! Grab and drink!" To weep and to whip the soul into a passion with these words that Shmuel Hagadol spoke to his son, who wished to make life good for him and so warned him that this world is like a wedding celebration. He who takes will have. As much as he takes will be what he will eat for all eternity.

In his youth and after, that *bachur* from Hornosteipel was a tree that grew into astounding greatness.

⪜ "L'chayim!"

I must tell you something marvelous. A certain Jew told me this story, and R' Chaim Kanievski confirmed it. One day, after *davening* "*vasikin*" in the Steipler's home, the man opened the door and saw father and son (R' Chaim, he should live long and be well) drinking a "*l'chayim.*" Respectfully he withdrew, and only returned when they were done.

Later, he asked R' Chaim what had occurred on that occasion.

R' Chaim replied, "My father had struggled for three days over the meaning of a *mishnah* in *Maseches Challah.* That morning, when I walked in, my father told me, 'Let's drink a *l'chayim*. This morning Hashem illuminated my eyes. I understand the *mishnah* in *Maseches Challah.*' "

This *gaon* and *tzaddik* was not satisfied with little. He burned with the ambition to conquer yet another *mishnah* in *Maseches Challah.* "Grab and eat, grab and drink …"

⪜ A Quarter of an Hour

A certain man in Jerusalem, a *maggid shiur* in a yeshivah, had a student with exceptionally weak skills who was unsuccessful in his learning. Over the course of six years, the student had made only minimal progress in the study of *mishnayos* and a little *Shulchan Aruch.* Finally, the *maggid shiur* decided to travel to Bnei Brak to see the Steipler. He wrote down his question (as the Steipler was hard of hearing): The Gemara states that a person who learns for five years and sees no success in his learning has no chance of succeeding. What should I do with this weak student of mine who is getting nowhere? In the *maggid shiur*'s personal opinion, the student had no real future in yeshivah.

The Steipler read the note and asked to see the *bachur.* When the student entered, he asked him, "Do you know how to learn a *mishnah* or a paragraph in the *Shulchan Aruch?*"

"Yes," the *bachur* replied.

"Did you know how to learn *mishnayos* before you came to the yeshivah?"

"No," the *bachur* said.

"Before you entered the yeshivah, did you understand a paragraph in the *Shulchan Aruch?*"

"No."

The student left the room.

The Steipler turned to the *maggid shiur* and said, "My dear friend, why do you say that he has seen no success in his learning? What kind of *maggid shiur* are you? He knows a little *Shulchan Aruch!* He understands a *mishnah!*"

That was the Steipler's greatness. For all his own genius in Talmud and halachah, he attached inestimable importance to yet another paragraph of the *Shulchan Aruch,* still another *mishnah* that the yeshivah student had acquired.

A certain *bachur* of Sepharadic descent told me that he once came to see the Steipler and wrote, "Rebbi, I have no desire to learn."

"I thought he'd get angry at me and maybe even scold me," the *bachur* said.

"Instead, the Steipler said, 'Please, sit down.' I sat, and he said to me, 'You have no desire? Learn for a quarter of an hour (for you cannot imagine the value of a quarter-hour of study). Afterward, get up and stroll around for a bit. Return and learn another 15 minutes, and so on. In that way, you will slowly acquire a desire to learn.' "

⌐ The Unfortunate Fox

R' Yochanan completed *Sefer Iyov* and said, "A person is destined to die, an animal is destined for slaughter; everything is destined for death. The Gemara (*Berachos* 17a) asks the following question: How are we to understand the fact that, in R' Yochanan's *beis midrash,* they conducted a *siyum* on *Navi?* Let me explain.

R' Yochanan lived a hard life, a life that might be labeled a "*Sefer Iyov*." Ten of his children died during his lifetime. He buried 10 children. And as he buried the 10th, he kept a tiny bone with which to comfort other mourners grieving for their children. "See this bone? It is the bone of the 10th child that I buried," he would tell other mourners, in consolation. Such greatness is hard to fathom.

However, when Reish Lakish, his Torah-learning partner, left this world, R' Yochanan's strength abandoned him. He could not go on. Over and over, he cried in anguish, "Where is the son of Lakish?" Finally, out of his mind with suffering, the Sages pleaded for mercy on his behalf and he departed this world. (Why did they not pray that he be healed? There was no purpose in this, for he would only have grieved once again over the loss of Reish Lakish. He had no one with whom to learn ...) *Rabbosai*, can we fathom the levels of such angels? A man who, upon the death of his 10th child, was clear headed enough to keep a bone with which to comfort other mourners but who, when Reish Lakish died, went out of his mind.

And when that same R' Yochanan experienced a "*Sefer Iyov*" in the most personal way, what conclusion did he reach? He said, "*Rabbosai*, a person is destined to die, and an animal is destined to be slaughtered, and everything is destined for death. Fortunate is he who toils in Torah and grows great in Torah and creates *nachas ruach* for his Creator!" This is the sum total of life. What else is left to a person? Only the work of a lifetime of Torah.

Koheles states, "*A person emerges naked from his mother's womb, and naked will he return.*" When a baby is born, as R' Meir points out, its fists are clenched as though to seize the entire world. When he leaves this world, his hands are open, as though to say, "Look, I haven't taken anything with me!" "*Naked will he return.*"

Chazal cite a *midrash* on this verse: a parable about a fox that loved grapes, and went off in search of a vineyard. Finding one, it walked around in dizzying circles but was unable to find an opening through which to enter. Walking further, the fox finally discovered a small aperture, too small for it to squeeze through. The fox fasted for three days, growing weak and thin, until it was able to enter and eat its fill of grapes. But when it tried to leave the vineyard by squeezing back through the hole, the fox found that it could not, for it had grown fat again. What did the fox do? It fasted for another three days until, weak and feeble, it left the vineyard.

On its departure, the fox turned to the vineyard and exclaimed, "Vineyard! Vineyard! How pleasant is your fruit, and how sweet your grapes. But what use are they to me? Hungry I went in, and hungry I went out." As it says, *"Naked I emerged from my mother's womb, and naked will I return."*

What are we to learn from this parable, beyond what we already understood from the verse, *"Naked I emerged"*?

Let us imagine that the fox had come and asked us, "I would like to eat grapes. Here is a vineyard, but its opening is too narrow. What shall I do?" What would we have answered?

We would have said, "Fox! Fox! Suffer a little and fast three days. Then, when you succeed in slipping inside, do not eat anything. Only taste a bit, to give yourself strength, and then pick clusters of grapes and toss them outside the fence. Do not eat and grow fat. Just pluck the grapes and throw them over the fence, and they will be waiting for you to feast on when you get there."

That is the parable. And the lesson to be derived from it? My dear brothers! Why does a person come naked and leave naked, if it is within his power to toss bundles of "grapes" into the Next World? So that we will have them there, on the other side of the fence! As we began by saying: "Grab and eat, grab and drink …"

"Prepare yourself in the anteroom, so that you may enter the hall."

☞ We Are Shoemakers, Too

The Maharil explains why a son stands beside his father's death-bed and says, *"May His great Name grow exalted and sanctified."*

Here is the question. We believe in the survival of the soul. "*Chanoch went with Elokim and was no more, for Elokim had taken him.*" The soul remains; Hashem merely moves it from the anteroom to the hall. In that case, why all the tears? Why the weeping and the pain when a Jew departs this world?

The answer is that when a Jew leaves this world, whoever he is, there is a lessening of heaven's honor.

Therefore, the son stands up and declares: "What is missing, *HaKadosh Baruch Hu*, in my father's departure, I will make up to you: '*Yisgadal v'yiskadash Shemei rabba! May His great Name grow exalted and sanctified!*"

So said R' Elchonon Wasserman. He continued:

"There were towns in which the various craftsmen would unite to *daven* and learn in their own respective shuls: shoemakers, wagon drivers, tailors, and others. There was the "Blacksmiths' Shul," the "Wagoneers' Shul," and so on. How did those poverty-stricken folk have the money to build private shuls, when they hardly earned a living? They would gather together and announce that everyone should reduce his food budget by one penny, and then another, and toss the coins into the communal pot. Over time, a great deal of money was collected, until a *beis midrash* was built for the shoemakers. In other words, even shoemakers have the possibility of building if the community unites and strengthens itself.

"The Chofetz Chaim has passed away and left a void in the world. Each person, as an individual, may not have the power to fill that void, to get up and say, '*Yisgadal v'yiskadash Shemei rabba.*' We are poor shoemakers of little ability. But even shoemakers and wagon drivers, working together as a community, have the power to fill the lack. We can build a beautiful shul. Because a *tzibbur* — a community — is a '*gaon*'. A *tzibbur* is a '*tzaddik*'."

We have the power to join together, to imitate the ways of the Steipler Gaon and his ilk. Every person can gather a few crumbs. For example?

In the Bialystok Yeshivah, they said that no one ever drank from a cup. They drank directly from the faucet. Why? Because there were *bachurim* who had brought personal cups from home, as was the custom in yeshivahs in those days. Lest someone inadvertently drink from a cup that was not his, they all refrained from using cups at all, and drank from the faucet instead.

As we have said, we can learn from his ways what is important and what is not significant at all: what to "grab" and how to grab *mitzvos*.

On a visit to Eretz Yisrael, R' Avraham Yaffen, *zt"l*, son-in-law of the Alter of Novaradok, suggested to me that we visit the Steipler Gaon.

We entered the room late one night, and saw the Steipler eating his meal. On the table were slices of black bread and a cup of clear water. In a dish was a piece of herring. As we entered, he greeted us with an apology for his simple dining: "After all, we are all Novara-dokers." With that, he threw a cloak over the whole subject, as it were, and moved the conversation into other channels.

The *Rosh Yeshivah*, R' Avraham, whispered to me, "*Der zelber Steipler* (the same Steipler): in Novaradok, in Bialystok, and in Bnei Brak." He remained the person he had been throughout. (As Rashi wrote on the words, "*And Yosef was in Egypt.*" Yosef remained firm in his righteousness, whether he was in his father's home, or under Potiphar's roof in the polluted land of Egypt, or ruling over Egypt. He was Yosef. He didn't budge.) Just as food and drink did not interest him in yeshivah, just as he subsisted then on a bit of bread and water, so now, too, his only concern was to seize another *mitzvah*, to seize more Torah. "Grab and eat! Grab and drink!" Another page of Gemara ... another *perek* of Mishnayos ...

In the latter part of his life he served as a shining example of "His learning was never interrupted"; even "*bein gavra l'gavra*" — between one *aliyah* to the Torah and the next — he would mur-mur *mishnayos*. Time was precious in his eyes. As he walked down the street he would constantly recite *mishnayos* from memory. Who hasn't seen that? As we waited for the *chasan* to emerge from the *chuppah* at his grandson's wedding, we saw his mouth moving with *Tehillim* and *mishnayos*. More than once, when I went to see him, he would say humbly in greeting, "What can an old man do with his last days but say *mishnayos?*"

To young *bachurim* coming to seek his blessing, he would repeatedly advise, "The main thing is not to waste time. Then you will succeed."

Let us salvage time, so that it does not escape us. Let us seize everything that we can.

פרשת קדושים ⇐

Parashas Kedoshim

Self-Love — L'Mehadrin!

R' Benzion Yadler

I remember, decades ago, when a secret society was established in Yerushalayim for the purpose of helping one's fellow man. The idea was that each member of the society would help his friend.

I went to see the Brisker Rav, the gaon hakadosh R' Yehoshua Leib Diskin, to tell him about this society and to ask his opinion of it. At first he said, "What difference does it make?" In other words, he tried to put me off. However, I persisted, telling him that, in my view, such a society was good and worthwhile as it was founded on the principle of "V'ahavta l'rei'acha kamocha" ("You shall love your fellow man as yourself").

The gaon hakadosh told me that this society did not fall into that category at all. Rather, it belonged in the category of self-love: You watch my back and I'll watch yours. I'll help you so that you'll help me. Today he's concerned for his friend; tomorrow his friend will take care of him. This is contradictory to the mitzvah in the Torah, which says that one must love every Jew, even if he is not a member of the same society, and even if that someone has done him a bad turn, as it says, "Do not take revenge and do not bear a grudge." In fact, you are actually obligated to do that person a good turn!

The Rav concluded: "Heaven forbid that you should join such a society, for it runs counter to the Torah."

"You shall be for Me a kingdom of priests and a holy nation."
Why? Because I, Hashem, am holy, so you must be holy, as I
have sanctified you … HaKadosh Baruch Hu said to them,
"If you have merit, you are called a 'congregation of holy
ones.' If you do not have merit, you are called a 'bad congre-
gation,' as it says, 'Until when, for this bad congregation?' "
(Midrash Tanchuma, Parashas Kedoshim).

Trussed for the Fire

R' Sholom Schwadron

*L*et me tell you a terrible, true story. R' Eliyahu Lopian
related the following to me:
"The *rav* of the city of Aliska, a great *tzaddik*, told me that in
his youth he once looked through the community archives of the town
of Lisa — where R' Yaakov, author of the *Nesivos Hamishpat* served
as rabbi — and he saw a terrible story written there. The incident
involved the daughter of the *Nesivos*. This daughter was a widow.

"This widow was about to marry off her daughter, the granddaughter of the *Nesivos*. The two women boarded a wagon to make
the trip to a nearby city to purchase clothing and wedding necessi-
ties for the bride.

"The gentile wagon driver, knowing the purpose of the trip and
knowing, too, that there was money in their pockets, changed direction. Instead of traveling out of the city, he went directly to his own
home on its outskirts. There he quickly summoned his friends, who
together robbed the women of all the money in their purse.

"The gentile gang was afraid that the two would give them away
to the police. They quickly tied up the women with ropes, lit a fire in
the oven, and went out to bring additional wood to strengthen the
flames into which they intended to throw their victims, killing them
and burning their bodies until there was nothing left but ash. In this
way, they hoped to avoid leaving behind any trace of their crime.

"Mother and daughter lay on the ground bound with ropes. While the robbers waited for the fire to grow, they sat around the table and began to discuss how to divide up the money. The wagon driver demanded a double share, as he had initiated the entire scheme. His colleagues objected, saying that the loot ought to be divided equally. The argument grew more heated. Suddenly, the door burst open. In the doorway stood a German officer who had been passing outside and heard the raised voices. The gang got up and ran for their lives.

"Seeing the way they fled, the officer realized that this was no ordinary argument but something more serious. He entered the room and looked around, and was stunned to see two women on the ground tied up with ropes and weeping. With a few questions as to why they had been tied up and what had happened, he learned the entire story.

"Picking up a knife, he cut them loose, returned their money — which still lay on the table — and set them free.

"That night, the *Nesivos* came to his daughter in a dream and said, 'Know this: When I was told of the trouble you two were in, I rose up to a high place and pleaded for mercy for you. I was not answered. And why wasn't I answered? Because you had transgressed the prohibition of *yichud* — being alone with the gentile.

" 'I went up to an even higher place and begged for the lives of my daughter and granddaughter. I asked that the merit of the Torah I disseminated in the *Nesivos Hamishpat* stand to their credit, and my plea was answered. You were saved. From now on, be careful about this serious prohibition!'

"The daughter told the story to the heads of the Lissa community, who wrote it down in their archives as a permanent remembrance."

So concluded R' Eliyahu Lopian.

"It is a mitzvah for every person to love every single individual in Israel as himself, as it says, 'V'ahavta l'rei'acha kamocha.' Therefore, one must recount another's praises and protect his money in the same way that he protects his own money and wants honor for himself. He who seeks to gain honor through the degradation of another person has no share in the World to Come" (Rambam, Hilchos De'os, perek vav).

A Very Large Fork and Spoon

R' Yaakov Galinsky

By way of introduction, let me tell you a story.

I once went to see the Ponevezher Rav, who turned to me and said, "R' Yaakov, let me ask you a question. A person dreams that he goes into a great forest and is attacked by lions, bears, tigers — an entire zoo. How can this Jew be helped?"

I looked at the Ponevezher Rav, trying to understand his point. The Rav continued:

"I'll tell you. You can do only one thing: wake him up, and the dream will vanish."

I still didn't know what the Rav was trying to tell me. He quickly explained.

"The same holds true with your *derashos*, R' Yaakov. There is no need to give the people *mussar*. Just wake them up, and when they wake, they will begin to improve on their own. (Everyone knows his own weaknesses and how to shake himself free of them.) What is needed is to awaken the listeners from their sleep!"

Rabbosai. Even without the Ponevezher Rav's words I do not think, heaven forbid, that I own the privilege of giving others *mussar*. But, as R' Chaim Brisker said, "When I speak in front of an audience, I am speaking to myself, and the audience is listening. And if you were to tell me, 'In that case, stand in a corner by the wall and talk to yourself!' — were I to do that, they would say that I wasn't normal. Therefore, I speak to others."

* * *

I have had various occasions to speak on the topic of "*V'ahavta l'rei'acha kamocha*," and I have mentioned this well-known story. Even if you've already heard it, it is worth hearing again.

R' Shimshon Wertheimer served as chief rabbi of Vienna about 300 years ago. He was drawn into debate with priests over the words, "*Attah bechartanu mikol ha'amim* — You have chosen us from among all the other nations." This refers to the status of Israel vis-à-vis the gentiles. The priests complained about the Jews' special sense of being chosen, as it says, "*I will separate you from the nations and you will be a nation for Me.*" They argued with him endlessly, until at last the king said, "Honored rabbi, let us put an end to these arguments. You have one chance to prove that you are correct: with a practical demonstration. If truth is on your side, you will provide clear proof that there exists a difference between a gentile and a Jew."

"All right, Your majesty. I will show you, in a tangible way, the difference between a gentile and a Jew. Just prepare a lavish feast, for the gentiles separately and for the Jews separately. At this feast, things will become clear."

Invitations to the banquet were sent out. On the following Tuesday, they announced, the king would be serving a lavish meal. From the hour of 6 to 8 p.m., the gentiles would feast at the king's table; from 8 to 10 p.m. the Jews would dine (under the supervision of Rabbi Wertheimer). The rabbi explained the need for two separate feasts by saying that the Jews' food was not that of the gentiles. "With Hashem's help, at that meal you will be able to see the difference between the nations."

The gentile guests — important citizens in the capital city — arrived to find the tables before them laden with all sorts of delicacies. However, one thing was missing: forks and spoons. A servant was sent to find out the reason for this apparent oversight. After a few moments, he returned and announced in the king's name: "Do not touch the food without a fork and spoon." So the guests waited. Long minutes passed. Finally, waiters entered the room bearing forks measuring four feet or longer! The spoons were equally long. "You must eat only with these forks!" the guests were told.

The gentiles began to wonder: *How can we reach the food? Has the king gone mad?* (If you think about it, you will realize that, with a fork of that length, it was not feasible to grasp the fork's handle and move the food from the tines into the mouth.)

They tried various methods: perhaps this way, or perhaps that. The first 10 minutes passed in unsuccessful trials. For their part, they would long since have begun eating like animals, with their hands, but this they had been forbidden to do. Waiters circulated among the guests to warn repeatedly in the king's name, "You must not touch the food without a fork or spoon." After two hours, the food remained as it had been. The signal was given that the meal was at an end.

We're not moving, the gentiles grumbled to themselves. *We'll wait and see what the Jews do. If they are given normal-size forks and spoons, we'll lodge a complaint.*

The Jews went to a second banquet hall, where kosher food had been prepared for them. They washed their hands. And they faced the same situation: no forks or spoons. They sat and waited. From the side, the gentile spectators saw four-foot-long forks and spoons carried in to the Jewish guests. They waited expectantly to see what would happen.

The Jews smiled. They thought the situation over. And then, every Jew picked up food with his fork and fed the man sitting on the opposite side of the table. A quarter of an hour later, the food was gone!

"Your majesty," said Rabbi Wertheimer. "Do you see the difference between a gentile and a Jew? Why did the idea to feed each other occur only to the Jewish guests?"

The truth, *rabbosai,* is that if I help my friend to eat, he will also help me, and both of us will benefit. This notion did not occur to the gentiles (who concluded: neither you nor I will have any food).

Jews, steeped in the teaching of "*V'ahavta l'rei'acha kamocha*," were capable of thinking in this direction, but the gentiles were not. The gentiles' situation was comparable to that of a miser who had never given charity, and was drowning in the sea at Tel Aviv. The lifeguard raced toward him, shouting, "Give me your hand!"

"But I never give!" the miser shouted back, and sank deeper into the sea to become prey to the fish. The gentile does not truly recognize the concept of "another."

We were living by the precept of "*V'ahavta l'rei'acha kamocha*" back at the giving of the Torah. In the Pesach Haggadah, we say, "Had you brought us close to *Har Sinai* but not given us the Torah — that would have been enough!" Why? Because at *Har Sinai*, we became as one. Even then, *rabbosai*, they didn't say, "I will do and I will listen," but rather, "We will do and we will listen." Each man thought of his neighbor. If I have something good, I want to pass it on to my neighbor as well: the foundation of everything.

⌐ Lighting the Dark

When I was a child, they told me a story.

In those days, electricity was not yet a household staple. People would light a kerosene lamp in their homes. And in the winters, as you know, Jews would get up at 3 or 4 o'clock in the morning to learn and to recite *Tehillim*.

One *erev Shabbos*, a Jew prepared his kerosene lamp so that it would burn through the night and until 9 o'clock the next morning; for in Russia it could be 9 a.m. before daylight penetrated a house.

He woke at dawn and found that the lamp had gone out. Perhaps he had neglected to put in enough oil. In short, there was no light. What to do? He had a gentile neighbor, but asking a gentile to light a lamp for him on Shabbos was forbidden. Then he had an idea. He knocked on the neighbor's door and called, "Get up, quick! I've brought you some vodka from the city. You've never tasted such vodka in your life. Get up!"

The gentile jumped out of bed and raced over to drink the vodka. As he came into the house, he asked, "What's the matter with you? It's so dark in here, I could fall and break my head and both legs!" At once, he went over to the lamp and lit it. The Jew was overjoyed, for when a gentile lights a lamp for his own needs, the Jew is permitted to benefit from it as well. He handed his neighbor a glass, and the gentile drank his fill.

"Do you want another one?"

"Why not?" The gentile drank more and more, until his head began to spin and he decided that it was time for him to return to his bed. He got up, went over to the lamp, extinguished it, and left.

As long as the gentile was interested in drinking, he left the lamp burning. After his needs had been met, however, he did not spare a thought for the Jew who might want light. He simply put the lamp out and went home. This is the difference between the people of Israel and the nations of the world.

If a person lives only for himself, he doesn't care if others suffer. He does not recognize anything outside himself. This is very bad.

But the Torah cries out: "*V'ahavta l'rei'acha kamocha!*" You must be concerned about the next person! This is the purpose of life: for a person to think, *How can I do a chesed?*

"*Olam chesed yibaneh* — The world is built through kindness."

Hashem created man's nature in such a way that, the more he gives, the happier he is. This is how man fulfills the purpose of Creation. The purpose of Creation is to do *chesed*!

☞ R' Dessler Speaks

"The wicked Turnus Rufus asked R' Akiva: 'If your God loves the poor, why does He not provide them with a living?' " (*Bava Basra* 10a). "If you people think that Hashem loves poor folk, why don't they receive food directly from Him?"

Why do they receive it in an indirect way, with the rich man receiving money and the poor man required to knock on his door? The rich man may or may not decide to open the door to him, according to his temperament at that moment, and it is only wishful thinking to hope that he will provide all of the poor man's needs at one time. And if you say that Hashem is angry at the poor, and that's why He leaves them hungry, in that case, how do the wealthy dare give them bread? This can be compared to a king who becomes angry with his servant and has him thrown into jail, allotting him only a bit of bread and water. Were someone else to go in and provide the prisoner with cooked meat and fish, the king would grow angry with *him*. "If I put him in jail, that means that he is deserving of punishment. Don't try to help me!"

R' Akiva counters: "To what is this really comparable? To a king who becomes angry with his son, and has him thrown into jail. The law is the law, even with regard to a son. But if someone were to come along and serve the boy food on the side, the king would not be angry, for it benefits his own child. We are called Hashem's children, as it says, *'You are children to Hashem, your Elokim.'* "

Moreover, why did Hashem arrange matters in such a way that the poor man must go to the wealthy one? In order to save the rich man from the judgment of *Gehinnom*. Since there are wealthy people who have *Gehinnom* waiting for them, when a poor man comes along and knocks on his door for help, by taking charity the poor man takes away his *Gehinnom*. So say *Chazal*.

R' Dessler asks the following question. We can accept the first explanation, that we are the children of Hashem. But the second — "in order to rescue the wealthy from *Gehinnom*" — seems strange. Must a poor man suffer in order to save the rich man from suffering? He could simply say to Hashem, "*Ribono Shel Olam*, let the rich man sit in *Gehinnom* as long as he pleases — on his own account. Not at my expense! Do I want to be poor and suffer mortifications and humiliations as well?"

This, says R' Dessler, shows how far the power of benefiting another person extends. One person does a favor for the next, even at the expense of his own mortification. This is the purpose of the Creation.

☞ "Let the Donkey Testify in the Heavenly Court!"

As an additional proof, he cites a Gemara that makes the same claim.

If a person sees a donkey collapsing beneath its burden, there is a *mitzvah* for him to unload that burden from the donkey's back. Similarly, if he is walking down the street and sees a Jew carrying a load of merchandise which he lacks the strength to load onto his donkey, the halachah is that unburdening the animal takes precedence over loading it, for in unloading there is the additional benefit of sparing the beast some suffering, as it is in distress from the heavy burden on its back.

Then the Gemara adds something new. If you see both of those donkeys in the distance, one with its heavy burden needing to be unloaded and the other about to have a load placed on his back, and you suddenly realize that the owner of the second donkey, waiting to be loaded, is an old enemy of yours, then the order is reversed. Instead of giving precedence to unloading the first donkey, you must run to help your enemy load his donkey. Why? In order to vanquish the evil inclination. By assisting one's enemy, the Torah tells us in effect: In your heart, you'd be glad to let your enemy stand there till tomorrow morning. Therefore, do the opposite of your desire.

"But why should the laden donkey suffer?" asks R' Dessler. "Does it have a *yetzer hara*? That donkey could come before the Heavenly Court and complain, '*Ribono Shel Olam*, I was standing there with a heavy burden, and a Jew came over, but instead of helping me, he went over to another donkey. Why? Because that donkey's owner was his enemy and he wished to conquer his evil inclination. Am *I* to blame for that?!'"

This shows us that even a donkey — should it fall within its power to help rectify a human soul by conquering the evil inclination — is obligated to suffer to that end. For the purpose of Creation is only *chesed*!

A kosher fish has two signs: fins and scales. A kosher animal has split hooves and chews its cud. Such "signs" have an overriding importance, to the point where lost objects are returned to the accompaniment of signs. In that case, what is the "sign" of a Jew, to tell us that he is the son of Avraham, Yitzchak, and Yaakov?

The signs are three traits — "bashfulness, compassion, and lovingkindness" — for the Jewish nation is distinguished by *chesed* and devotion to others.

☞ In Return for Charity

Let's mention one more point, and with this we will conclude.

R' Chiya told his daughters: "When a poor man knocks on the door, quickly give him what he asks for, so that when the hour of your need comes, you will also be given quickly."

Surprised, the daughters of the wealthy R' Chiya asked, "Father, have you come to curse us that we will be poor one day?"

"Heaven forbid," he told them. "But this is what the Torah teaches us in the verse dealing with *tzeddakah* (*Devarim* 15:10): '*You shall surely give him, and let your heart not feel bad when you give him, for in return for this matter, Hashem, your God, will bless you in all your deeds and in your every undertaking.*'" The world, *Chazal* explain, operates in a cyclical manner. A person never knows what will happen to him tomorrow. Therefore, he should be prepared and train his body to face any situation. How does one accomplish this?

First, he must know that he is not alone; his fellow Jew will be with him in any adversity. The Jewish people are a single entity with many limbs, with each limb fulfilling its own mission within the body.

☞ Responsible for One Another

When a Jew learns that all of *Klal Yisrael* is one, he will understand that he is just a small wheel in a large machine. Just as he helps his friend physically, he will help him spiritually as well. He will certainly take care not to damage any member of *Klal Yisrael*. *Chazal* explain this with a parable:

There is a ship carrying a great many passengers, each with his own comfortable cabin. Suddenly, one passenger picks up a gun and begins shooting bullets into the wall of his cabin. Immediately, the other passengers begin screaming at him, "What are you doing?!"

He stares at them uncomprehendingly. "This is a democracy, isn't it? In my own space, I can do whatever I want!"

Whereupon the others shouted back, "You fool! Are we not all traveling on a single ship? Are you the only passenger here? While it is true that you have a private cabin, you are not alone. Every action that you take has the ability to sink the entire ship!"

The same applies to *mitzvos* and *aveiros*.

Let us involve ourselves greatly in *"V'ahavta l'rei'acha kamocha,"* helping our fellow man do *mitzvos* and perform good deeds. Whether he is a family member, a spouse, a child, a sibling or anyone else, how great a merit this will be for us.

Let every man strengthen his neighbor!

"Lo sonu ish es amiso (Each of you shall not aggrieve his fellow)" (Vayikra 25:17).

The word "es" indicates the inclusion of a certain category, as is known to those who study the Talmud. Asked the Chofetz Chaim: In that case, what is the inclusion in this verse? And he answered: "Each of you shall not aggrieve his fellow" — this includes even himself.

No Excuses/ What Did We Learn in Novaradok?

R' Yaakov Galinsky

*M*orai v'rabbosai, the *Talmud Yerushalmi* (*Gittin*, end of the sixth *perek*) quotes R' Yishmael son of R' Yose, who bewails the gap between the generations, specifically, between the generation in which his father lived and his own. The difference is as great, he says, as that between the Holy of Holies and the most mundane of the mundane. How are we to understand R' Yishmael's pain?

As we all know, the generations tend to deteriorate. The quality of the people of the world diminishes with the passage of the centuries. This is, and has always been, the nature of the world. Those who are distant from the time of Creation and the giving of the Torah are less outstanding in both wisdom and piety.

However, there is also an unnatural condition, in which this deterioration speeds up painfully. Today, for instance — over the past three decades or so — we have seen a deterioration encompassing several generations. That was why R' Yishmael son of R Yose grieved and said that the deterioration since his own father's generation, such a short time before, had been sharp and precipitous, like the drop from the Holy of Holies down to the most mundane.

If we speak about the Novaradok *yeshivos* before the Holocaust — where my friends and I were only a short generation ago — we are looking at an indescribable deterioration.

What did we learn in Novaradok?

One central principle was that a person must not deceive himself. The Chofetz Chaim once asked a question on the injunction, "*Lo sonu ish es amiso* — Each of you shall not aggrieve his fellow." The word "*es*" as those who study Gemara know, is meant to teach us that some unexpected category is to be included in this injunction. What is meant to be included here? The Chofetz Chaim answers: "*Each of you shall not aggrieve his fellow* — including yourself.*"

Yes, *rabbosai*. We have come to pay a visit to the "*olam hasheker*" — the world of falsity. When one comes here, everything must be checked to see if it is genuine. When Shaul, in great distress, asked the woman to raise Shmuel Hanavi's spirit (*Chagigah* 4b; cited at length in *Midrash Tanchuma, Parashas Emor*), Shmuel — known as "*Ish HaElokim*," or the "Man of God" — said that when he was in this world, he sensed that he was in a false place.

☞ *What Shmuel Taught Us*

What else did we learn in Novaradok?

Man is "so small, yet so great," our Torah giants teach. He must be aware of both sides: the greatness that resides within him, as well as the pettiness.

In Novaradok they taught us the argument that is quoted in the Gemara (*Yoma* 87b) regarding the *Ne'ilah* prayer. Rav says that this is a new *tefillah*, while Shmuel disagrees, saying that we do not have the power to create new *tefillos*; all we can say during *Ne'ilah* is one thing: "What are we, what is our life?" So says Shmuel.

Who was Shmuel? By his own testimony (*Berachos* 58), the pathways of Heaven were as clear to him as the streets of his own city. A holy *gaon* — indescribable!

By the way, let's ask a question. I can understand how Shmuel discovered heaven's pathways; he learned them from the Torah. But the streets of his own city? I, Yaakov Galinsky, have been living in Bnei Brak for about 50 years, and I hardly know any of its streets. I am familiar with a few streets where various shuls are located and so on. How did the holy Shmuel know the streets of his city the way he knew the pathways of heaven?

I was once in Mexico to raise funds for my institutions. When I stood up to deliver a *derashah*, I asked this question, and offered the following answer. "Because Shmuel was a *Rosh Yeshivah*, he was forced to know the city streets and addresses for the purposes of fundraising and strengthening the yeshivah." Of course, I said this because I, too, was visiting for the purpose of raising money for my yeshivah.

Present at that talk was the well-known Rabbi Dr. Moshe Rothschild of Bnei Brak, who had apparently also come to raise funds for a new hospital in Bnei Brak. When he heard the question, he pounded on the table and said, "R' Yaakov, Shmuel was a doctor, as it says in the Gemara. In that case, he had to be familiar with all the city streets in order to save lives."

In any case, a man of such spiritual power, a *Rosh Yeshivah* and doctor, at the end of those 40 days of mercy and forgiveness — days that are exalted above all the days of the year — where had he arrived? At the point of saying, "What am I and what is my life?" I am nothing. I am zero.

Shmuel taught us that, at the end of those 40 days, at the great hour of *Ne'ilah*, we should say, "What am I and what is my life?" I am zero. And then, we will be great.

☞ A Generation of Excuses

We learned other things in Novaradok. We learned not to make excuses.

If you were to ask a certain individual, for example, why he is not scrupulous in his halachah observance, or why he does not behave more appropriately with his family members, he will reply with a host of excuses. Everyone tries to justify himself, to fool himself into thinking that he's "O.K." Were you to ask someone, "Do you learn enough? Do you *daven* enough?" He would doubtless answer, "*Baruch Hashem*, there are people who are a lot worse than me." Or, putting it another way: "What do you want from me? Am I so bad? There are people who do real *aveiros*. Compared to them, I'm a *tzaddik*!"

A lifetime of excuses.

HaKadosh Baruch Hu, as it were, took man as his partner: "*Hashem took the man and placed him in Gan Eden, to work it and to guard it.*"

"*To work it*" — this refers to Torah study.

"*To guard it*" — this refers to *mitzvos*.

Man was meant to learn Torah with Hashem in *Gan Eden*. Hashem told him, "*Of every tree of the garden you may freely eat; but of the Tree of Knowledge of Good and Bad, you must not eat thereof.*" But Man did eat from that tree.

Hashem entered into discussion with him, asking, "*Have you eaten of the tree from which I commanded you not to eat?*" And Adam, to make a long story short, replied, "*The woman whom You gave to be with me — she gave me of the tree, and I ate.*"

Afterward, the woman was questioned, too. "*And Hashem said to the woman, 'What is this that you have done!'*" To which Chavah replied, "*The serpent deceived me, and I ate.*" Both of them had excuses.

Adam, in accordance with his exalted level, was punished and sent out of *Gan Eden*: "*So Hashem banished him from the Garden of Eden, to work the soil from which he was taken.*"

Chazal tell us, *rabbosai*, that had Adam admitted his sin instead of offering excuses — "I have done wrong! I have sinned!" — he would have remained in *Gan Eden*!

The proof? After Adam and Chavah were expelled from *Gan Eden*, and Kayin killed Hevel, Adam asked him, "How were you punished?" Kayin replied, "I did *teshuvah* and my judgment was lessened." Whereupon Adam exclaimed, "Is that the power of *teshuvah*? If only I had known …!" At once, Adam Harishon stood up and said, "*Mizmor shir l'yom haShabbos, tov l'hodos laHashem* — A psalm, a song for the Sabbath day. It is good to thank Hashem." The word "*l'hodos*," however, may mean more than just to thank. It can also mean to admit, as in "*Modeh v'ozev, yerucham* — If a person admits to his sin and abandons it, he will be treated with compassion." *Tov l'hodos laHashem!*

From here, we learn that there is no *Gan Eden* with excuses.

Shlomo Hamelech said, "*If you seek it like money and like hidden treasure, then you will understand the fear of Hashem.*" When it comes to money, there are no excuses. Imagine a person walking into the grocery store, filling his cart with merchandise, and when the shopkeeper asks for money, the person earnestly explains, "Believe me, I've been looking for work all day but haven't found a job." How would that shopkeeper respond? "In this place, we pay with money — not excuses."

"*If you seek it like money*": If you want *Gan Eden*, don't look for excuses. Seek to fulfill your obligations, for there is no *Gan Eden* with excuses.

☞ A Mussar Talk from the Polish President

Listen to another nice thing that I learned in the Novaradok Yeshivah in Bialystok.

I attended that yeshivah on the eve of World War II. Food shortages were rampant, to the point where we had no bread to eat.

Without bread, it is impossible to learn. The *Rosh Yeshivah* came to me and said, "The Jewish bakeries have promised bread for the students. However, these are dangerous times, when the sight of a yeshivah student walking to the bakery could be risky. Therefore, I thought that you, Yaakov Galinsky, might be able to avoid being seen by the soldiers, to slip into the bakery and get the bread, for you are short and slim. If you wear short pants and a cap, you will look like a young boy. You can walk at the side of the main road near the town square, turn right and left, and reach the bakery. Ask them to fill your sack, which you will take along with you. Bring back as much as you can carry."

I set out. Without going into elaborate detail about events of those days and of that fateful day in particular, I walked along with downcast eyes. As I neared the town square, I sensed that something was happening. The street was quiet. I asked a gentile who was walking along beside me whether some sort of event was about to take place. He replied, "If you wait, in about five minutes you'll hear the president." I believe it was the president of Poland himself who addressed the crowd in the town square.

As it was dangerous to continue walking, I waited. The president began his speech. He spoke about the debate in the Polish Parliament concerning whether to submit to Hitler's demands to cede the port of Danzig to Germany or go to war instead.

"My dear citizens, everyone knows that a heated debate has been taking place in Parliament. Danzig is surrounded on three sides by German territory. Anyone who wishes to travel to the other side of Germany (by way of Poland) requires a visa or, alternatively, must take a long detour. Hitler is demanding that we give him just Danzig. If we do so, he says that he will refrain from war." Parliament was divided as to whether or not to accede to Hitler's demand.

"Were I certain," said the president, "that he would be satisfied with Danzig, I would give it to him. We have another port city to use in its place. However, Hitler does not want Danzig! He is interested in Warsaw. He just wants Danzig as an easy, effortless shortcut.

In that case, we will end up by fighting a war over Warsaw. So it is worth our while to begin now. Why hand over Danzig for no purpose? Let us fight over Danzig, so that our way will be made easier in the future. I hereby announce a total rejection of Germany's demands, and the onset of hostilities."

With that announcement came the start of the war. The bakery owners who had attended the speech did not return to work. Panic set in; everyone began to think about saving his own skin. There was not a single Jewish bakery open. I returned to yeshivah empty-handed.

As I approached the yeshivah door, I was asked, "Where is the bread we've been waiting for?" I told them that there was no bread, because the president of Poland had delivered a *mussar* talk.

"Oh, Yaakov and his jokes," the *bachurim* said.

I told them what had occurred, and then explained what I'd meant by a "*mussar* talk." The president had touched on a topic that is close to our own hearts: the war against the evil inclination.

The *yetzer hara* comes to a *bachur* and tells him, "During the last half-hour of third *seder*, don't learn. I don't need more than that, just that half-hour." A smart person will understand that the *yetzer* does not want third *seder*; it is interested in your not learning at all. That's what the Polish president said. Everyone has a red line that he will not cross. The *bachur* will fight with all his might for morning *seder*. In that case, why engage in war only after the *yetzer hara* has already become a tall mountain? Let him start fighting over that last half-hour of night *seder*.

One person's red line might be Shabbos observance. The *yetzer hara* will come to him with a request to disregard seemingly "light" *mitzvos*. Says the president of Poland, as it were: If you disregard light *mitzvos* now, you will end up battling over Shabbos observance. Why wait? Fight over those small transgressions now, so that you will win the war before it becomes too powerful for you."

R' Galinsky concludes:

My father learned in Yeshivas Radin, and he told me that each year, at the start of *Chodesh Elul*, the Chofetz Chaim would deliver the same talk. Listen to what he said.

As everyone knows, *esrogim* did not grow in Poland. They were imported from Italy and other places. As the result the minimum price for an *esrog* was $500. (I lived in the city of Rav Mishkovsky, father of the *Rosh Yeshivah* of Kfar Chassdim, and if memory serves me correctly, I believe that, of the entire shul, only the *rav* had an *esrog*.)

The Chofetz Chaim asked the *bachurim*, "How many *mitzvos* do we fulfill with an *esrog*? One positive commandment: '*You shall take for yourselves on the first day a pri eitz hadar.*'"

When it comes to Torah study, on the other hand, continued the Chofetz Chaim, every word is a positive commandment. In a single minute, it is possible to learn 200 words — the equivalent of 200 *esrogim*. Multiply 200 by $500. In five minutes, you've earned five times 200 *mitzvos*, or 1,000 positive commandments, and so on.

In that case, how can a person have five free minutes without using them to learn or waste five minutes in the midst of his learning?!

פרשת אמור
PARASHAS EMOR

"R' Chiya wept. R' Yochanan asked, 'Why are you crying?' He said to him, 'Because you will have nothing left for your old age.' He said to him, 'Is it a light thing in your eyes what I have done? I have sold something that was created in six days and acquired something that was given in 40 days.' When R' Yochanan died, his generation said of him (Shir HaShirim 8:7), 'Were any man to offer all the treasure of his home to entice you away from your love, they would scorn him to extreme'" (Midrash Rabbah, Emor).

CONCEPTS

R' Yaakov Galinsky

C oncepts, *rabbosai!* You don't pick up concepts in the street. If a person is in the street, he breathes the street's air; how, then, will he acquire the Torah's concepts? Let us see.

I'd like to share with you a concept of *Chazal*, just to serve as an example.

The Gemara tells us that Abaye was orphaned of both father and mother from birth. His father died even before he was born; his mother died at his birth. She had time only to give him the name Nachmani.

There were two *Amoraim* who were friends: Rabbah and Rav Chisda. Rav Chisda was a very wealthy man, while Rabbah was terribly poor. Rabbah was so destitute that he didn't have even barley bread to eat. Why, asks the Gemara, did Rabbah not accept a few pennies from Rav Chisda with which to buy bread and milk? The Gemara's answer: "*He who hates gifts will live.*"

Now, in Rabbah's neighborhood there lived a boy who had been orphaned from birth: Nachmani. Someone was obligated to take him in and to raise him. Who took him in? The destitute Rabbah.

In a rich man's home, every child must have his own bed and closet and nightstand, delicacies at every meal, and so on. In such a home, it's hard to manage with even one child. Where should he sleep? What should they buy him? What kind of meat should they feed him? In the homes of the poor, on the other hand, they somehow learn to manage. The little food they have can be stretched to feed one more. One more child can be taken in.

In short, the holy Rabbah took in Abaye. Where did the name "Abaye" derive from? It contains the initials, "Asher ben Yerucham, *yasom*" (Asher, son of Yerucham, an orphan).

We can readily perceive how sad poor Abaye's life must have been. He had no mother to escort him to *cheder*, no father to learn with him. It is reasonable to suppose that there were days when he brought no food in his schoolbag, for there was no food at home. When the other children brought sandwiches to school, Abaye would not ask them to share their food with him, for his adoptive father did not take gifts even from his dearest friends (i.e., Rav Chisda). We may assume that those around him regarded Abaye as a poor, unfortunate orphan. They shook their heads in distress as they saw him walk along the side of the road.

Now, listen well. The Gemara (*Nedarim* 41a) states the following: "Abaye says, 'There is no poor man except in understanding.'" That is, true poverty exists only in a paucity of wisdom. If one lacks food to eat, that is not real poverty; rather, it is poverty in understanding that pierces the heart of heaven! (I once heard another explanation for the words, "There is no poor man except in understanding": A person who feels that he is lacking something is not poor, but rather lacking in understanding.)

The Gemara continues: "In Eretz Yisrael they say, 'If you have acquired wisdom, what do you lack?'"

These are the concepts of Abaye, orphaned of father and mother and raised in the home of destitute people. This wise Jewish leader proclaims: The truly poor, unfortunate person is he who lacks wisdom. However, if one has acquired wisdom, why should he care whether or not he has enough to eat? If he has acquired wisdom, what is he lacking? *Rabbosai*, we have lost sight of the true concepts.

In our *parashah*, the *midrash* on the verse, "*You shall take on the first day*" cites, among other things, the story of R' Yochanan.

R' Yochanan was walking on the road from Teveryah to Tzippori, leaning on R' Chiya. As they passed a field, R' Yochanan pointed at it and said that this field had once belonged to him but he had sold it in order to study Torah. They continued on their way, and presently came to a vineyard. R' Yochanan told his student that this vineyard, too, had belonged to him, but he had sold it for the sake of the Torah. As they neared Tzippori, R' Yochanan pointed at an olive grove which had belonged to him, and which he had sold in order to be able to learn Torah. R' Chiya began to cry.

"Why are you crying?" asked R' Yochanan.

"Because you have not left anything over for your old age," R' Chiya replied. One who has sold all his property in his 30's and 40's may not have a penny left for his old age, to buy medication near the end of his life. And if R' Chiya was crying, he knew what he was crying about! (One commentary gives his opinion that R' Chiya was not aware that the sale had been made for the purpose of Torah study.)

R' Yochanan reacted to his student's tears in the following way. "Is what I have done light in your eyes? I have sold something that was created in six days and acquired something that was given in 40 days."

When R' Yochanan left this world (having passed through his old age peacefully, even without the properties), the people of his generation said of him, "If a person were to give away all the fortune of his house in exchange for the love that R' Yochanan had for the Torah, he would be extremely scorned!"

Those people understood the concept of trade! They were true businessmen who understood that *"her merchandise is better than any other merchandise."*

We lack genuine love for the Torah. We have steeped ourselves in non-Jewish concepts. Yes, *rabbosai*, we are not to blame: the gentiles have taught us. As the *midrash* in our *parashah* hints, what does *HaKadosh Baruch Hu* do with the sins of Israel on Yom Kippur? He pours them over Eisav's head, as if to say, "*You* are to blame for everything they do. You are the teacher of sins. You are the source." (As we see in the episode of Shimon and Levi, when Yaakov Avinu accused them of using "stolen weapons" ("*klei chamas*" — that is, the weapons of Eisav). We have learned concepts from the gentiles and we must throw them aside and not lose our direction. The Gemara says that the Jewish people resemble a dove. Just as a dove, by its nature, will not fly out of sight of its dovecote — the moment it realizes that it is about to lose its way, it returns home — so, too, are the people of Israel.

Rabbosai, we must be very careful not to lose the direction which our fathers taught us. *"They left Me, the source of living waters, to dig broken pits."* They are offering us counterfeit goods! Instead of pure water to drink, they are giving us the drops and crumbs of foreign nations.

⌇ Gold Rings and Rubbish

There is a well-known story, *"The Prince and the Nazir."*

The prince was deeply involved in the ways of the world, and the *nazir* spun him a parable:

There was once a rooster who knew that after Shabbos there was a lot of food to be found in the rubbish. That was a big day for him, and he was very happy as he approached the garbage cans.

The can that he went to happened to contain, along with the leftover food that the woman of the house had thrown away, her gold ring, which had fallen off her hand as she cleared away the garbage. The rooster rooted around in the rubbish with his feet and mouth until he found a heel of bread. Wonderful stuff — bread amid the trash! He continued rooting further, pushing aside bags and other inedible stuff, until he saw a cholent potato. Excellent! Suddenly, his bill hit the ring. Angrily, he tossed the ring aside and continued his rooting.

"Don't be like that rooster in the rubbish," the *nazir* cautioned the prince. "Think a bit about what you are tossing aside in your life: about which golden rings you may be pushing away, and what you are taking for yourself out of life." He rejects the pleasures of the soul, which are of inestimable worth, and crows with glee over the joys of the rubbish heap.

⌇ Three Candies

The Chofetz Chaim related the story of a certain child who was suddenly orphaned of his wealthy father. His father had been a diamond merchant who worked at home, and he died while in the act of polishing a diamond.

The boy was left with his widowed mother. The brokenhearted woman did not leave her home to buy what was necessary, to the point that the pair began to be hungry. What did the poor child do? He opened a drawer, took out a diamond, and raced off to a food store.

On his arrival, he asked the owner for three candies.

"That'll be 20 cents, please," said the seller.

The boy took out the diamond. "I don't have 20 cents, but I have a diamond."

The shop owner looked at the diamond with gleaming eyes. He thought a moment, then said, "My boy, I won't give you candies for it. If I do that, when you grow up and understand, you will send me an invitation to court. You will sue me, saying, 'Because I was young and foolish, you took a diamond for me in exchange for three candies!' And then what good will any of it be to me? I will sit in prison, behind bars. Therefore, I will not give you the candies. You are small and do not understand!"

The Chofetz Chaim concluded, "If a person knew the worth of 'Amen, yehei Shemei rabba,' if he knew the value of one instance when he refrained from hurting someone's feelings, he would seize those rings instead of the trash that is left in the can after Shabbos. The problem is that he wants to trade a diamond for three candies or a gold ring for a potato."

Rabbosai, how great is the joy of a person who has merited collecting many *mitzvos*! Shlomo Hamelech said, "*She joyfully awaits the last day.*" *Chazal* explain that when a person directs his life toward its proper goal, in his last moments on earth he is shown the reward waiting for him, and he laughs with joy as his soul ascends upward.

But there is a *yetzer hara*, friends. As the Chofetz Chaim relates in his famous story:

There was a great general who had won numerous military victories. As he approached old age, he prepared to retire from his duties. The king said that he wished to repay him for his many years of devoted service.

The royal advisers asked, "Is is possible to pay a man who has done so much for country, nation, and king?"

"True," answered the king. "But I will do the little that I can." So saying, the king granted his general the authority to enter the royal treasury for a quarter of an hour's time, and to take anything he wanted.

Hearing this, the treasury minister hurried to the king in agitation. "Your majesty, do you know what can be taken in a quarter-hour? It is possible to empty the treasure-house of its main valuables. Why did you give the general permission to do such a thing?"

So the king met with his advisers for a second round of consultation. How to extricate himself from this predicament without retracting his initial decision, which had already been publicized before many witnesses?

It was resolved: The general loved ice cream and music. They would do their best to distract him with these things during those crucial 15 minutes.

That's what they did. They erected a big ice-cream stand at the entrance to the treasury, featuring a variety of ice creams in all colors and flavors, and announced, "Free ice cream! Step right up and get your free ice cream today!" At the same time, a band played music.

The moment the general saw the ice cream, he began to grab some. Some five minutes passed as he enjoyed his ice cream, and then he began to walk toward the treasure-house door. A few steps before the entrance, a special violinist whose music he adored began to play. In this way, additional minutes were lost. Finally, the general went in and began to seize valuables. He was only able to emerge with treasure worth a few thousand by the time the quarter-hour was up.

"What have you done?" his family berated him. And he berated himself: *What have I done?* But it was too late. The king's advisers rubbed their hands with glee over the episode's successful conclusion.

Our world is filled with music and ice cream, with sights and sounds, with drums beating at full strength. Merely glancing their way distracts us from the treasures.

As we noted elsewhere, have you ever seen an experienced street peddler selling rugs? He puts on a magnificent show, demonstrating the rug's beauty, extolling its fine points and the excellent price using a gamut of gestures and distractions. Afterward, the gullible customer will tear his hair and cry, "Why did you trick me?" But by then the rug peddler is long gone, a grin on his lips as he rubs his hands together and continues to prey on other innocents.

ᔉ Going Bankrupt

Rabbeinu Yonah, in his *Shaarei Teshuvah*, explains how a person establishes the remorse that is the first step in doing *teshuvah*. He says that among the things a person should think about is, *How did I come to exchange an eternal world for an ephemeral one? In other words, what kind of bankrupt businessman am I? Is this any way to do business? Instead of involving myself with mitzvos, whose reward is inestimable, I spent my time rooting around in the rubbish.*

Chazal say: "There is no reward in this world for *mitzvos.*" Why not? The Chofetz Chaim explains that there are simply no coins with which to pay for a *mitzvah.* If a person were to walk into a bank in Bnei Brak with a check for a million dollars in his hand, he would be told, "We don't have that kind of cash here. Go to our central branch." That's how it is with *mitzvos.* In this world, there is no way to acquire the kind of payment that is beyond any value: unequaled pleasure. Payment for *mitzvos* can take place only in the Next World. Let us truly understand what a *mitzvah* is.

With Hashem's help, we will accrue a great many golden rings.

וּלְקַחְתֶּם לָכֶם בַּיּוֹם הָרִאשׁוֹן פְּרִי עֵץ הָדָר כַּפֹּת תְּמָרִים וַעֲנַף עֵץ־
עָבֹת וְעַרְבֵי־נָחַל וּשְׂמַחְתֶּם לִפְנֵי ה׳ אֱלֹקֵיכֶם שִׁבְעַת יָמִים. וְחַגֹּתֶם
אֹתוֹ חַג לַה׳ שִׁבְעַת יָמִים בַּשָּׁנָה חֻקַּת עוֹלָם לְדֹרֹתֵיכֶם בַּחֹדֶשׁ
הַשְּׁבִיעִי תָּחֹגּוּ אֹתוֹ. בַּסֻּכֹּת תֵּשְׁבוּ שִׁבְעַת יָמִים כָּל־הָאֶזְרָח
בְּיִשְׂרָאֵל יֵשְׁבוּ בַּסֻּכֹּת.

"You shall take for yourselves on the first day the fruit of a citron tree, the branches of date palms, twigs of a plaited tree, and brook willows; and you shall rejoice before Hashem, your God, for a seven-day period ...You shall dwell in booths for a seven-day period; every native in Israel shall dwell in booths" (Vayikra 23:40-42).

"You shall not take revenge and you shall not bear a grudge against the members of your people" (Vayikra 19:18).

AFRAID TO BUY AN APARTMENT

R' Reuven Karlenstein

*T*he Alshich Hakadosh asks why the holiday of Succos is called by that name. After all, the festival encompasses a number of different *mitzvos*: *nisuch hamayim*, the pouring of the water, *arba'ah minim*, the four species, and more. Why, then, was the holiday not called "The Festival of the Water-Pouring" or "The Festival of the Four Species"?

It would be worth our while to take a look at the style of the text, for his language is penetrating and powerful. However, here is the gist of his idea. *Rabbosai*, listen.

Everything that a man achieves in terms of piety and righteousness in this world depends on one thing alone: the degree to which he lives in this world as a temporary resident. The more he views money and property as transient and unimportant — and the more he views the Next World as the primary focus — the higher he ascends. For this reason, the Torah emphasizes the *mitzvah* of *succah*, for the essence of this *mitzvah* is leaving our permanent home and going into a temporary one. The Torah, as it were, is proclaiming that the festival of Succos is there to remind us of this world's temporary nature.

The Chasam Sofer writes that the seven days of Succos correspond to the 70 years of a person's lifetime. Both periods of time must be viewed as temporary.

☙ "You Shall Not Take Revenge …"

Our early commentaries have shown us ways and reasons for a person to easily fulfill the obligation of not taking revenge or bearing a grudge.

☙ One Perspective

A person lives with faith and trust, knowing that the Creator's Hand guides everything. No one can hurt a person, or cause him harm, or take something away from him, unless Hashem wills it to be so. When a person suffers at the hand of another, he must remember that "*Hashem told him to curse me*" (in the words of David Hamelech). True, the afflicter doubtless has his personal calculations, and he will be punished for his actions. But the pain we suffer through those actions was decreed by Heaven. In that case, why take revenge? "*You shall not take revenge and you shall not bear a grudge*"!

There lived in Bnei Brak, on Rav Shach's block, a man known as "Tailor Green." In his youth, this tailor was close to the "Sandlar." The tailor told me some stories about him. Listen to one of them.

R' Yaakov Ribikow, the "Sandlar," was once injured in a traffic accident. After his discharge from the hospital, he was summoned to court to give testimony about the incident.

At the start of the proceedings, the judge asked him, "Your name is So-and-So?"

"Yes."

"You were walking down _____ Street in Tel Aviv on the date of _____?"

"Yes."

"A car knocked you down? You were in an accident?"

"Yes."

The judge then presented the driver, and asked, "Was this the man who was driving the car and caused your accident?"

"No. It was not him."

"Then who was it?"

"*HaKadosh Baruch Hu.* He wanted that accident to happen. He decreed that it happen to me."

The judge was at a loss. He was silent for a moment, then pounded on his table and cried, "Order in the court!" — after which he began again.

"Were you walking down the street; were you hurt; was it on that date?" and so on. When he came again to the question, "Is this man standing before you the one who caused your injury?" the Sandlar replied, "No."

"Then who?"

"My accident came from *HaKadosh Baruch Hu.*"

The judge became angry. "One more answer like that, and you will be ejected from this court with a fine — for contempt of court!"

The Sandlar looked at him and said, "I am not laughing at this court, heaven forbid. I am speaking seriously. I am being careful to speak the truth, which is that this man was not the perpetrator (for Hashem is the Master of all powers in this world)."

The judge glanced around the room, collecting himself. He began to understand that this man before him was indeed speaking in all seriousness ... (The driver had done something wrong and would be punished for his wrongdoing. But he was, after all, only a "stick" in the hands of the hitter. Were you to be asked, "Who struck you?" you would not answer, "The stick," but rather, "The man who wielded the stick.")

"You shall not take revenge and you shall not bear a grudge," the Torah commands. The man who harmed you did wrong, and will be punished for what he did. That is Hashem's business. But what affected you happened with heaven's full knowledge and its precise decree.

Second Perspective

The entire nation of Israel is one creation. As we know, "With 70 souls (lit., soul) did your fathers descend to Egypt." Seventy souls, yet they were called "one soul."

By the way, I heard a fantastic *vort* in the name of the Satmar Rav. He explained the *berachah*: "... Who creates numerous living things with their deficiencies; for all that You have created with which to maintain the life of every being." The nations of the world are called "souls," as is stated regarding Eisav, "the souls of his household." But the Jewish people are referred to as "one soul," as is stated "All the souls (lit., soul) of the House of Yaakov who came to Egypt." Hashem created "many souls," i.e., the multitude of nations — millions — and also all that they are lacking, "their deficiencies." And for what purpose did He create all this? "To maintain the life (lit., soul) of every being." These are the Jewish people, who are called "one soul."

To summarize: Since the Jewish people are one, how is it possible to take revenge? Can one hand take revenge on a second hand?

Let us explain in a different manner, as an allegory:

Someone came to a dentist and asked him to pull out two of his top teeth and two on the bottom.

"It seems that you are in pain," said the dentist. "Let me take an X-ray and see what the problem is."

"No, I don't need an X-ray. Nothing hurts me."

"So why do you want the teeth extracted?"

"If you really want to know, I'll tell you. Yesterday I was eating a hard piece of bread and as I was chewing I bit my tongue. It started bleeding; quite a bit of blood oozed. I became angry at my teeth that had harmed me: such chutzpah! So I decided to have them extracted! They are truly *mazikim*."

The dentist told the man that he was quite mixed up. "Both the teeth and the tongue," he explained, "are 'you.' Who do you think bit you? You did it to yourself."

So it is with revenge. How can you take *nekamah* from another Jew? We are all one.

There is no reason to exact revenge, for this whole world is nothing but "child's play."

Sometimes we see two children fighting with all their might, pulling each other's hair, hitting, crying, screaming, and battling with desperate fervor. Going over to ascertain the cause of the war, we find a small toy which each of the contestants claims as his own. "Oh, what are you two hurting each other for?" you laugh. Any adult would react in this way.

Rabbosai, up in heaven they are laughing at us: at the way people take revenge and bear a grudge, waging wars and creating quarrels over the "playthings" of this world. Over what trivialities people will shed blood! Over what nonsense …

If a person knows what is eternal and what is transient, he will not seek revenge. Why take revenge, when it is all a silly game? Child's play.

"*You shall dwell in booths for a seven-day period; every native in Israel shall dwell in booths.*" The Gemara, in *Succah* and *Kiddushin*, draws various halachic teachings from this verse. R' Yehonasan Eibeshitz adds, by way of *drush*, "*You shall dwell in booths for a seven-day period*": You will all sit in a *succah* for seven days, and only seven days. However, "*every native in Israel*" — that is, someone who is a true citizen, meaning a *tzaddik*, who is called a "citizen," like Avraham Avinu who was known as "Eitan *Ha'ezrachi*" (Eitan the citizen) — "*shall dwell in booths*" all his life. In other words, he will live in a temporary world all of his life, for he knows that this world is transient and unimportant.

I heard a story from the son of R' Baruch Toledano. *Gevald!* Who remembers R' Baruch, a holy flame of fire? I merited seeing him when, near the end of his life, he left Morocco and came to live in Bnei Brak.

When he came to this country, he bought an apartment in order to fulfill the commandment of settling in Eretz Yisrael. He was not a man of means, but because he wished to merit this *mitzvah*, he gathered sums from here and there, small loans and so on, until he had enough to pay for an apartment. After the purchase, he had the flat painted and repaired. When the work was completed, his family came to him and said happily, "Ah, *baruch Hashem*, we can move into the apartment now." He rejoiced along with them, but said, "I will rent out this place and use the money to rent a flat somewhere else. I will live in a rental flat."

Astonished, his grandchildren asked, "But why? Isn't it better to live in your own house?"

"I will not live in my own house! It's always been that way. I didn't live in my own place in Morocco, either. I was afraid to. I am afraid!"

His grandchildren did not understand what he was afraid of. The income-tax people? The government? His holy mouth went on to explain his meaning:

"I am afraid that I may begin to feel that this is my permanent residence, that I am established in this world ..." In a rental apartment, the landlord may come at any time and request that he vacate the apartment. It is easier to feel that one is a temporary dweller. In his own place, however, he was afraid that he might deceive himself with the illusion that this was his purpose, that this was his eternal life.

Rabbosai, "every native — every citizen — in Israel shall dwell in *succos*!" The *tzaddik* always lives in a *succah*. He endures the searing sun, the pouring rain, the cold. There is no air-conditioning and no heating. He is in a temporary dwelling. He has no gold and no silver: all is temporary. The important thing is the *mitzvos*, and conquering his *yetzer*, and absorbing himself in Torah study. *These* are the world!

I see that you'd like to hear another story. Here are two.

R' Michel Yehudah Lefkowitz once told me the following:

Each year, the Steipler Gaon would come to him to buy an *esrog*. R' Michel had *esrog* trees in his yard, grown from an *esrog* that he'd been given by the Chazon Ish himself. Before the Steipler selected an *esrog*, his face would be tense and closed. Afterward, however, all at once his face became unrecognizable, as though he'd discovered an amazing treasure. Anyone who has never seen this sight cannot understand, said R' Lefkowitz.

In short, each year after choosing his *esrog*, joy would suffuse the Steipler's face. He would put his hand in his pocket and take out money. He would give more than the *esrog's* worth, for R' Michel was not an *esrog* merchant who knew the exact price for each *esrog*.

"I had no set prices; what the customer decided to give, he gave. I knew that one did not argue with the Steipler over money matters, so I kept quiet. He handed me the money and, filled with great happiness, showered me with thanks and blessings.

"One year, however, I saw him take out a sum of money that was worth double or triple the value of the *esrog*. This time, I couldn't keep silent. I gathered my courage and said, 'The money that the *Rosh Yeshivah* is giving me is not connected to this *esrog* at all. He must have given me the money for no reason, for this amount has nothing at all to do with the true value of the *esrog*.'

"He heard me out with deep seriousness. Then, seizing my two hands he said, 'Let us think about what you are giving me and what I am giving you. You are giving me an *esrog* — a *mitzvah*!! What is a *mitzvah*? A *mitzvah* is everything! And what am I giving you? Money. What is money? Nothing. Nothing! In that case, what is the argument? You are giving me everything, and I am giving you nothing.'

"It is hard to describe the *yiras Shamayim* that entered my heart when he said these words, with such simplicity and such natural enthusiasm. The world is a temporary place for people like that, and money is nothing. Zero."

☞ From Dust to Dust

In my childhood, I heard a story that apparently never happened. But, *rabbosai*, the lesson it teaches is a powerful one.

There were once two brothers whose father left them a huge lot worth a great deal of money — perhaps a million and a half dollars — in north Tel Aviv. It was impossible to divide the lot fifty-fifty; it would have to go to either one brother or the other.

A *din Torah* was convened. Arguments ensued; the quarrel escalated and became a public matter, until the case finally reached the court. Finding a solution seemed hopeless. Weeks and years passed, with the feud alive and well between the two brothers — and not only the brothers, but their children and their children's children. No one wanted to look at his own relative because of that lot! May Hashem have mercy. (In order to make a profit from the lot, they lost out in every way: They lost family, their health was affected, they lost peace and tranquillity ... not to speak of their *middos*.) What's there to say? A lot worth a million and a half dollars!

Well, years passed and the two brothers began to age, with no solution in sight. There was someone who acted as a go-between for them, and from time to time he would exclaim, "What's the use of an empty lot from which neither of you has any benefit?"

One day, they heard about a *mekubal* (kabbalist) who was said to be able to see right into heaven. All he would do is take a look at someone's face, and he could say whether heaven had a claim against the person. The two "*tzaddikim*" decided to go to this *mekubal* and hear what he had to say. "We'll ask him whom the lot belongs to!" They agreed to abide by his ruling.

Before long, they set out. They entered the *mekubal's* room and asked their question, laying out both sides' arguments and the troubles that had attended the case for so long.

The man was supposed to answer with *ruach hakodesh* (that is, what Heaven had to say about that lot and to whom it belonged). He thought a few moments, and then said as follows: "Listen, I can't answer a question like this in my house. I have to go to the lot itself, in Tel Aviv." They listened to him with reverence, and took him out to their car.

They traveled to the lot. He leaned on them, walking slowly, until he was standing in a corner of the lot. Looking around, he asked, "So this is the lot that you've been busy with?"

"Yes," they answered.

He looked around again, lost in thought. Suddenly, he lay down — flat on the ground. He put his ear to the ground. The brothers began to tremble with awe. They had never seen anything like this in their lives. Then the *mekubal* began to carry on a conversation with the ground.

"… What?'

"… Yes …"

"… What?" As though listening to something and responding, back and forth. The brothers nearly fainted.

When he was finished, he felt very weak and asked them to help him to his feet. After all, he was not a young man. When they had helped him up, he said, "All right," as though the matter had become clear to him. They seated him on a chair and he began to speak.

"I asked the ground to tell me, once and for all, 'To whom do you belong: to Berel or to Getzel?'

"Listen well to what the ground said.

"It said as follows: 'I do not belong either to Berel or to Getzel. Both Berel and Getzel belong to me. They are mine.'

"*Ribono Shel Olam!* '*A person comes from dust and will return to dust.*' What are you fighting about? Why the lengthy quarrel?"

When a person is aware that this world is a temporary place, he understands where to invest his energies: to "keep his eye and his focus on his work, all the days of his life" (in the words of the *Mesillas Yesharim*). He knows what to seize and what to work on.

☙ A Pinprick

There is a mystifying *midrash*: "Iyov complained about the *Middas Ha'Din* (the attribute of justice). *HaKadosh Baruch Hu* showed him a *succah* with two halachically acceptable walls and a third wall just a *tefach* high." The *Aruch LaNer* explains. He says that all the questions that trouble a person during his lifetime — questions such as why the righteous suffer or the wicked flourish — arise when he believes that this is the primary world. However, once he understands that the primary place is over there, in the World to Come, everything falls into place. If a good person suffers in this world, it is in order to benefit him later, in the Next World. And that world is eternal. This is an awesome concept, *rabbosai*! So why trouble ourselves with such painful questions?

The *Mashgiach* of Slabodka explained with a parable.

Suppose a person was to be told, "You are guaranteed a long, happy life. You will lack for nothing, neither health nor wealth nor satisfaction. However, there is one condition: At the start of your life, you must receive one pinprick."

"I'm not interested," he says. "That will hurt!"

Anyone with a particle of sense would gaze at him pityingly. What is a pinprick, when compared to a lifetime of happiness?

Said the *Mashgiach*: And all this does not even compare to a person's life in this world and his eternal life in the next. All his suffering is less than a pinprick in comparison with eternal life! "*HaKadosh Baruch Hu* showed him a *succah*." Look! This world is temporary! It is a transient world, a passing world, a world that vanishes like a fleeting dream. The Next World is the lavish hall. So don't complain about the *Middas Ha'Din*.

☞ Do It Today

I'd like to tell you a true story. This is no parable, but something that occurred the first time I traveled to America.

We traveled on a commercial airliner that is no longer operating. The owners wanted to squeeze use out of every inch of space. In short, the plane was very crowded. The air was stuffy, and with our hand luggage at our feet there was simply no room to move. One

Jewish passenger, realizing that he was facing a 12-hour flight under these conditions, decided that he couldn't bear it. What did he do? He knew that there is a second story (first class), where conditions are very different. The passenger made up his mind: "I've got to move up there, no matter what!"

The passenger climbed upstairs, intending to pay for a first-class seat. He was stopped by a guard, who said, "You can't go in there."

"Why not? I see that there are empty seats!"

"Don't you understand? You can't go in there. Do you know how much those seats cost? The price you paid down below is less than half the amount you'd pay up here!"

"If that's the problem, I'll pay! Let me in."

"No, no. No entry."

"I'll pay the full amount!"

"No, no."

The man continued to argue. Seeing that it was impossible to get rid of the pest, the guard came closer and said forcefully, "Mister, in order to get in here, you have to pay in the airline office. There's no paying here, only down below. Right now, no entry!"

Down below, in this world. This is where we pay. *"Today is for doing them and tomorrow is for receiving the reward for them."* We must prepare ourselves in the anteroom in order to be able to enter the hall. Know that we are in this world on a temporary basis. *"Better is one hour of mitzvos and good deeds in this world"* — a *mitzvah* done with "heart," with wholeness; a *mitzvah* done with joy. And *"Talmud Torah k'neged kulam"* — Torah study is equal to all of them together.

Prepare yourself in the anteroom. That is the festival of Succos.

פרשת בהר-בחקתי
PARASHAS BEHAR-BECHUKOSAI

"The reason it says "halichah" (walking), is to teach that one must engage in Torah even on his travels … It says, 'While you walk on the way' — in his love for [Torah], he will review it constantly" (Ohr HaChaim).

A Storm Wind on Motza'ei Shabbos

R' Sholom Schwadron

*I*f you are reminded of something that has to do with communal life, that is a clear sign from heaven that they want you to speak about it," my rebbi, R' Eliyahu Lopian, told me. I have just remembered a story about the Ohr HaChaim Hakadosh. An amazing story.

The Ohr HaChaim was a prosperous man. Because he did not wish to take pleasure from other people's money, he worked at a trade: as a goldsmith. He made money and became a wealthy man.

How did he behave in his prosperity? His practice was to have an ox slaughtered every Thursday and to distribute the meat of the entire ox to the city's Torah scholars.

One week, as Shabbos neared in the Ohr HaChaim's city, an animal was slaughtered in the central slaughterhouse and was found to be a *tereifah*. Another animal was slaughtered, and then more and more — 13 in all — and every one was declared a *tereifah*. Only the Ohr HaChaim's ox was kosher. Of course, this was a golden opportunity to do some very good business; he could sell his meat at a high price. But he did not deviate from his usual custom. He did not sell the meat, but rather distributed it to Torah scholars as he did each week.

There was a certain rich man in town who wanted to eat meat that Shabbos. He went to the Ohr HaChaim's house and asked to buy some meat in honor of the Shabbos.

"What can I do?" the Ohr HaChaim said. "I've already distributed nearly all the meat. I only reserved one portion for a certain *talmid chacham* [he named the man] to whom I haven't had a chance to give it yet. I have nothing to sell you."

The rich man began to protest. "You call *him* a *talmid chacham*? Who is he, anyway?" and so on, heaping scorn on the Torah scholar.

On *Motza'ei Shabbos*, it was revealed to the Ohr HaChaim that, because he had stood by and listened to a Torah scholar being scorned and had not rebuked the speaker, a harsh decree had been imposed on him. (As *Chazal* have taught us, Hashem is exacting as a fine hair with *tzaddikim*.)

Heaven then revealed that there was a chance for him to atone for what he had done, if he went into exile for a full year.

Hearing this, the Ohr HaChaim immediately put on clothing suitable for exile, and left home.

Naturally, the Ohr HaChaim Hakadosh, even in exile, was able to learn from memory and did not stop thinking his Torah thoughts. His departure took place at the start of the week of *Parashas Bechukosai*.

As you know, *morai v'rabbosai*, in *Parashas Bechukosai* the Ohr HaChaim wrote 42 explanations of the verse, "*Im bechukosai teleichu* — If you shall walk in My ways." He developed those explanations during his time in exile (as he personally and literally fulfilled the *teleichu* — you shall walk — while toiling in Torah).

He left home on *Motza'ei Shabbos* and walked the roads until the following Friday. On that day, he passed near a forest that was situated close by a town. Through the trees he heard a Jew chopping down trees for firewood, and with every tree he cut he cried, "*Lichvod Shabbos kodesh!* — In honor of the holy Shabbos!" The Ohr HaChaim understood from this that the town had a community of pious Jews, including the wood-cutter himself, with his enthusiastic cries of "*Lichvod Shabbos kodesh!*"

He approached the man. "*Sholom aleichem!* Would it be possible for me to stay with you for Shabbos?"

"Certainly!"

The two went home together. The Ohr HaChaim prepared for Shabbos and went to shul with his host to say *Shir HaShirim, Kabbalas Shabbos,* and *Ma'ariv.*

Afterward, an announcement was made to the effect that the *rav* of the city would deliver a *derashah* after the meal. When the two men returned home, they had their Shabbos *seudah.* The Ohr HaChaim was served fish, meat, and other delicacies: true *hachnasas orchim* (hospitality to guests).

When they were done, the host asked his guest (not knowing who he was), "I need to go hear the *rav* speak. What shall I do with you?"

"I will go along with you."

The city's *rav* was a good and wise man. The moment he began to speak, the Ohr HaChaim realized that he was a *talmid chacham,* and rejoiced over the opportunity to listen to him. Of course, no one in the audience recognized the guest or knew who he was. He sat among the rest of the audience like everyone else.

During the course of the talk, the *rav* revealed awesome secrets. Suddenly, he added, "Today, in *Shamayim,* I heard 14 explanations on the first verse in "*Bechukosai*" that were originated by *Harav Hatzaddik* R' Chaim ben Attar." And he went on to expound on the 14 explanations that he'd heard from heaven.

When he'd concluded, the Ohr HaChaim stood up and and said respectfully, "Yes, that is what Chaim ben Attar said."

The men in the audience were appalled at the way he said, "Chaim ben Attar," without preceding the name with a respectful "*Rav*" or other title. Heaven itself had declared Chaim ben Attar a *tzaddik*, and here was this fellow treating him with such irreverence! They were furious.

The *rav* of the city told the others, "Let's forgive him this time. Perhaps he wasn't paying attention to what I said."

The next morning, after *davening*, another announcement was made: "The *rav* will deliver a talk after the Shabbos *seudah!*"

The Ohr HaChaim walked to the *derashah* together with his host. In the course of the talk, the *rav* said, "Today, on Shabbos, I heard in *Shamayim* another 14 explanations from *Harav Hatzaddik* R' Chaim ben Attar."

Once again, the Ohr HaChaim stood up and said, "Yes, yes, Chaim ben Attar said that."

Now the crowd was really angry. But the *rav* prevented them from acting. "No, no, don't do anything to him. Even now, we can judge him favorably, and forgive him."

At *Seudah Shelishis*, the *rav* gave a third talk. "Today," he said, *Shamayim* revealed to me the last 14 explanations said by *Harav Hatzaddik* R' Chaim Attar." Whereupon the Ohr HaChaim stood up and agreed, "Yes, Chaim ben Attar said that."

This time, the *rav* did not prevent the *gabbaim* from responding. They got up and began to berate the visitor for his insolence. Then they decided to punish him further.

There was a rule in that town that, if someone transgressed, he would be placed in a central corner of the shul, and a large sign proclaiming his despicable actions would be hung over his clothes. The sinner would be watched, making escape impossible, and everyone who passed by would spit near him or even on him. It was decided to punish the visitor in this way; a punishment that, of course, was used only rarely in that community.

Apprehensive lest he disappear from town before Sunday, they consulted with the *rav*, who permitted them to place him under house arrest. They put him inside and closed the door.

On *Motza'ei Shabbos*, after *Ma'ariv* and *Havdalah*, a terrible storm wind began to roar through the city. The wind uprooted all the trees and began detaching roofs and walls from houses. The whole city was in a state of collapse. The *rav*, who was a *tzaddik*, asked for Divine guidance as to the cause of this sudden storm. He was told: "Every *Motza'ei* Shabbos, *Harav Hatzaddik* R' Chaim ben Attar recites a certain Name [of Hashem] with specific intentions in order that the world might continue to exist. But since he is locked in a house and did not make *Havdalah* and have those intentions in mind while saying that holy Name, the world is in a state of destruction."

The *rav* thought for a brief moment, and understood that the reference was to the strange episode that had taken place in their town that Shabbos, that it was R' Chaim ben Attar who had been placed under house arrest.

He had the door unlocked at once, and fell before the Ohr HaChaim, begging his forgiveness and atonement. The Ohr HaChaim made *Havdalah*, and the storm subsided.

Afterward, it was revealed to him that the humiliation he had suffered had atoned for his misdeed, and that his week of wandering had fulfilled the decree of exile. He could now return to his home in all happiness!

וְכָל־מַעְשַׂר בָּקָר וָצֹאן כֹּל אֲשֶׁר־יַעֲבֹר תַּחַת הַשָּׁבֶט הָעֲשִׂירִי יִהְיֶה־קֹּדֶשׁ לַה'.

"Any tithe of cattle or of the flock, any that passes under the staff, the tenth one shall be holy to Hashem" (Vayikra 27:32).

"Im bechukosai teleichu — If you will go in My decrees: One might be able to think that this refers to the fulfillment of the commandments. When it says, 'And observe My commandments …,' see that fulfillment of the commandments has been stated. What, then, do I maintain is meant by 'If you will go in My decrees'? That you should be laboring in the Torah." (Rashi)

"ON THE WRONG SIDE OF THE BED …"

R' Sholom Schwadron

When R' Akiva was still unlearned and uneducated, he once passed a spring and saw a stone in which a hole had been etched by the water.

What is this? R' Akiva said to himself. *How can water make a hole in a stone?*

"Akiva," he was told, "don't you know that water streaming onto a rock can pulverize it?" So teach *Chazal*.

Why did R' Akiva ask this question? Didn't he already know that water has the power to do this? And what is the meaning behind the answer he was given? Listen to something wonderful.

R' Akiva pondered the question and wished to understand how water can create a hole in a stone. After all, the first drop to fall onto the stone does not make a hole. Apparently, it makes no impression at all. In that case, if the first drop does nothing, then the second drop is just like the first and leaves no impression. And if the second leaves no mark, then the third drop is just like the first ... and the hundredth would be like the first, and the thousandth. How, then, do we come to see a hole in the end?

He was told, "This forces us to say that the first drop also left its mark on the stone. We don't see the impression that it made, but it did something! The impression may be microscopic, but it is there nevertheless." Let me tell you something interesting.

When a shul was built here in Sha'arei Chesed, the *gabbai* requested of the architect that the floor of the women's section be built with no supporting pillars beneath, so that people would be able to sit and *daven* under the *Ezras Nashim*. The architect agreed.

In those days, constructing such a large area without supporting pillars was just not done. Therefore, when the job was completed, the *gabbai* was worried. He asked the architect, "Who will guarantee that the roof won't collapse over time — in 30 years, perhaps?"

"Relax," the architect said. "I have a little machine here" — he took it out and showed it to him — "that I place against the floor of the *Ezras Nashim*. If, over the next hundred years, the floor that we have poured will drop even a little bit, this machine will register it now. Do you understand? You can see the mark registered on the machine now. It may be a minuscule amount, but you can see some change!"

The same applies to the water and the stone. We must say that the first drop leaves a mark. What kind of mark? The lightest of impressions. Our senses are certainly not capable of discerning it, but it's a reality. That is the power of billions. Each drop after the first — the second, third, hundredth, thousandth, ten-thousandth, millionth — leaves its minuscule mark, very gradually forming a tiny hole. These things move very slowly.

A person learns Torah and thinks at the *shiur's* end: "The Torah made no impression on me. I learned, but I remained exactly the same." No. You are not the same! Anyone who thinks about this, who understands it, knows that this is the true reality.

I have students with whom I learned perhaps 50 years ago. Ten years later, I didn't recognize them. They had changed or improved out of all recognition. On the other hand, there were some students who, once they left the *shiur*, remained the way they had been when they left. Why? Because they didn't learn Torah, or else they had stopped learning with regularity. Anyone who learns — whether he wants to or not, whether he understands what he learned to its depths or not — will inevitably rise. "*I created an evil inclination; I created the Torah as the antidote to it.*"

This is the pronouncement that we hear at the start of *Parashas Bechukosai*: "*If you will go in My decrees* — you should be laboring in the Torah." We must toil in Torah, for this is the gift we were given, to earn us merit in both this world and the next.

Now listen.

Iyov asked a deep question.

The Gemara, in *Bava Basra* 16a, states, "Iyov wished to exempt the entire world from Hashem's judgment." What did he say? "*Ribono shel Olam*, You created an ox with cloven hooves; You created a donkey with uncloven hooves; You created the righteous and the wicked; You created *Gan Eden* for the righteous and *Gehinnom* for the wicked. Who can stay Your Hand?"

What was he saying? What was his meaning?

Iyov was a *tzaddik* as well as a great philosopher. He looked at our world from every angle, and saw that most people die as they were born. For example, if a person is born with a hot temper, from birth to death he walks the same path. He is born a young hothead and dies an elderly hothead. Anyone with a perceptive eye can recognize by the gestures of the baby's hands and feet in his crib that he is bad tempered. The child grows up and goes to kindergarten. The teacher gives him a toy. He clutches the toy, and anyone who dares come near will earn a swift kick. "It's mine!" Then he grows up a little more and goes to grade school. Just let someone take his pen — *oy vey!* He becomes a teenager and then a grown man. You greet him in the morning, and he's liable to respond with a scowl or worse.

Why? Why does he act that way?

"He got up on the wrong side of the bed," observers murmur to themselves. In other words, they don't know why. That's just the way it is. He got up on the wrong side. The way he was born is the way he lives his life and the way he departs it: angry, angry, angry to the very end. He is still angry on his deathbed — furious with the Angel of Death.

Or take a miser, for example. This is a bad, hard trait. There are people that I knew when we were all children. One of them, back in Talmud Torah, bought and sold cigarettes. He would purchase a pack of cigarettes and sell them one by one, earning a profit on each cigarette that he sold. In this way, he used all his abilities to amass money, and strengthened his native miserliness more and more. He was a money-lover from birth.

R' Eliyahu Lopian once told me that there lived a renowned miser in Lomza. The man's son was the same way, r"l. When the father passed away, they laid him on the ground and the son sat beside him.

Suddenly, the son stood up, bent over, and began to grope around beneath his father's body. "What in the world are you looking for there?" he was asked. And listen to his terrible answer: "When we moved my father from his bed to the ground, a button popped off my coat. I'm looking for the button."

"Is this any time to care about a button?" they asked in amazement.

In the most natural possible way, the son replied, "Do you think a button isn't worth something? It's worth a penny!"

He was searching for a button — the stingy fellow! As he lived, so he died.

A person who is born with a haughty nature is accompanied by that nature all through his life. And jealousy — oy, there are people who are jealous. Of what and whom? Of nothing. They are that way from birth to death. They get sick with jealousy, they are consumed with bitterness: *Why does he have and I don't? May his name be blotted out!* he thinks in his envy, cursing others in the foolishness of his heart. Why should you care what another person has?

What will you profit by your envy, except to rot your bones?

A person sees a doctor because he isn't feeling well.

"Have you become enraged lately?" the doctor asks.

"Yes! I was furious!"

"Then perhaps you should stop," the doctor suggests.

No. He can't calm down. *Why does my neighbor have more than I do? Why?* He can't stop. He's burning up inside!

In that case, says Iyov, if a person cannot change his nature, he is like an animal, like an ox, for example. Can an ox change, one fine day, into a donkey? No! Can a donkey change into an ox? No. "You created an ox with cloven hooves" — a sign of purity. "You created a donkey with uncloven hooves" — a sign of impurity. In the same way, "You created the righteous and the wicked." You created people who are good natured or bad natured. They cannot change. This is what Iyov asked his friends.

Why, then, they replied, did Hashem command a person to be God fearing, if he can't change his nature? The Gemara continues: "*HaKadosh Baruch Hu* said: I created the evil inclination, but I created the Torah as an antidote to it." If a person studies the Torah, he will change his nature.

R' Simchah Zissel (a student of R' Yisrael Salanter) explained that repentance is proper and enduring only with Torah. Without Torah, Iyov is correct, for without Torah one cannot change his nature. Indeed, most of the world's population who do not study Torah find themselves unable to alter their basic natures. A person may study geography or history, zoology or psychology — any subject he wants — and he will remain the same person. The way he was born is the way he will die.

This, incidentally, was Lot's error. Lot left Avraham Avinu's yeshivah because he said, "It's impossible. I can't do it." He was mistaken, for had he continued to learn in his uncle Avraham's yeshivah, he would have succeeded. "*I created the evil inclination and I created the Torah as an antidote for it.*" Even if the change would not have occurred overnight, it would certainly have happened gradually, as we have described above.

What Else Did We Learn from R' Akiva?

R' Yaakov Galinsky

The Gemara, in *Bava Kamma* 41b, says that R' Shimon Ha'amsoni expounded on every "*es*" that appears in the Torah, in the following way: He said that wherever the word "*es*" appears — as in "*Vayekadesh es ha'am*," "*Lo sisa es shem Hashem Elokecha*," "*Kabed es avicha*," and so on — R' Nechemiah Ha'amsoni said that every "*es*" indicates something additional that is hidden.

The Gemara says, however, "When he reached the verse, "*Es Hashem Elokecha tira*" ("*You shall fear Hashem, your God*"), he stopped his commentary, for he did not know how to explain the "*es*" implicit in fear of Heaven. As he put it, "Just as I received a reward for expounding, I will receive a reward for desisting." Then along came R' Akiva, and explained that "*Es Hashem Elokecha*" hints at the inclusion of *talmidei chachamim*. (See the Maharsha.)

Why was R' Akiva, specifically, the one who offered this insight?

The answer is that R' Akiva was the symbol of *kavod haTorah* — honor for the Torah. As we learn in *Sotah* (49a), "Since R' Akiva died, *kavod haTorah* has been nullified in the world."

Listen to a parable that R' Akiva told:

A fox once saw fish darting from place to place in the water, intent on escaping. "What are you so afraid of?" he asked them.

"We are afraid of the fishermen who are hunting us," they replied.

"I have an idea," said the fox. "Why should you all be crowded together in a 'ghetto' in the water, and then have to live in fear of fishermen? I have a big villa, complete with parking lot, anything your little hearts desire. Come live with me!"

One of the fish responded to his proposal as follows: "They say that you're the most clever of the animals, but you're talking like a fool. If we are in fear for our lives here, in our natural medium, in the water that we need to breathe, how much more so in a place where we are assured of death!"

And so, the fish outsmarted the fox.

R' Akiva told this parable to Pupus ben Yehudah, when Rome decreed that any Jew caught teaching Torah in public would be severely punished. R' Akiva continued to deliver widespread *shiurim*, as though the government had said nothing at all. Meeting him, Pupus ben Yehudah asked, "What's the matter with you? Aren't you afraid?" Whereupon R' Akiva responded with this parable, which is cited in *Berachos* 61b. The Torah is not a nice storybook. The Torah is life. It is our lifeblood, and the air we breathe. We cannot live without it.

In his own lifetime R' Akiva demonstrated, through personal example, how very much the Torah is life. He showed us the power of Torah and how far one can go with it — right up to the very heavens!

Now, go out into the street. Walk over to any Torah scholar who happens to be passing by, and ask him, "Who caused you to become such a fine *talmid chacham*?"

"My father," he might answer. Or, "My mother," "My grandmother's tears," and so on. No one will answer, "I achieved all this by myself!" Yet R' Akiva achieved everything with just the power of the Torah.

Then R' Akiva said, " '*Es Hashem Elokecha tira* — You shall fear Hashem, your God': The '*es*' indicates inclusion of Torah scholars." In other words, do you wish to see a demonstration of the power of Torah? Take a look at me!

No one pressured me to learn. No one urged or persuaded me. No one registered me for "*cheder*" at the age of 3, and from there to the upper grades in yeshivah. The *Midrash Hagadol* describes all the suffering that R' Akiva underwent. *Maseches Avos D'Rabbi Nassan, perek* 5, describes how R' Akiva went to *cheder* together with his own son, and sat in the same class. "He and his son went and sat before the *melamed*. He said, 'Rebbe, teach me Torah.' R' Akiva grasped the top of the slate and his son wrote down the *alef-beis* for him and taught him till *tav*." Imagine how the third-graders reacted when they greeted a new classmate who was over 40 years old. His wife encouraged him, telling him that it was all worthwhile! All the anguish and the mortification were worthwhile! Take a look at the *Midrash Hagadol* — wonder of wonders.

R' Akiva, at every stage of his life, could say, "This is the power of the Torah, to achieve tremendous things in a person's soul." From an ignorant boor to a man of God — to the point where Moshe Rabbeinu asked that the Torah be given through R' Akiva. Witness the essence of a true *talmid chacham*!

☞ R' Shimshon of Ostropoli's Secret

I can't explain, but in order for you to understand what the Torah can make of a person, let me tell you a profound *vort* from a great *mekubal* — R' Shimshon of Ostropoli (who was murdered *al kiddush Hashem*, in the sanctification of Hashem's Name in the pogroms of *Tach v'Tat*).

As we know, the *Aseres Harugei Malchus* — the 10 Torah giants who were killed in holiness and purity — were taken to serve as an atonement for the sale of Yosef. "*And you shall carry the sin of your fathers.*"

How many of Yaakov Avinu's sons took part in the sale of Yosef? Nine. Yosef is obviously not in the count, as is Binyamin, who wasn't there. Reuven, too, had gone to his father. In that case, why were 10 killed and not nine?

Another question: Why was R' Akiva one of the 10 who were killed? After all, he was the son of converts. His parents were not descended from Yaakov Avinu.

R' Shimshon of Ostropoli asked both of these questions. And he revealed that both the questions and the answers are hinted at in the verse in *Parashas Bechukosai*.

"*Any tithe of cattle or of the flock*": This hints at the question, Why did R' Akiva, who was a shepherd of cattle and sheep, die? The other nine who were killed are referred to in, "*any that passes under the staff.*" The word used for "staff" is "*shevet*" — as in, "*under their fathers, heads of their shevet* (tribe). But "*the tenth one*" was added — why? So that he "*shall be holy to Hashem.*" Because the nine brothers included the

Name of Heaven in the sale, as *Chazal* tell us, *HaKadosh Baruch Hu* took R' Akiva as an atonement. I do not wish to elaborate here, but the essential point is that Hashem chose R' Akiva, demonstrating again how great and awesome he was: this R' Akiva who, until the age of 40, was ignorant and had never learned a thing. He would say, "If you show me a *talmid chacham*, I'll bite him like a donkey!" And he, through his diligence, came to know Torah. He learned it from the persistent drops of water that fell onto that stone and penetrated it.

You can grow wise, grow pure, restore your soul — achieve everything! You can become a true *talmid chacham*! Fortunate is he who toils in Torah.

> *"Im bechukosai teleichu* — If you will go in My decrees"*:
> One might think that this refers to the fulfillment of the commandments. When it says, "And observe My commandments
> ..." see that fulfillment of the commandments has been stated.
> What, then, do I maintain is meant by "If you will go in My decrees"? That you should be laboring in the Torah" (Rashi).

THE SHTENDER, THE SHTENDER!

R' Sholom Schwadron

Can you imagine such a thing: to observe the *mitzvos* at home but not outside? Walking into your house and putting on *tzitzis*, but leaving them in the closet when it's time to go out to work? Wouldn't anyone who thought that way be misguided?

However, there are apparently people who have to be told this. Rashi explains that there was some thought that the Torah came forward to speak to certain individuals, telling them, "*Im bechukosai teleichu* — If you will go in My decrees." In other words, *mitzvah* observance applies not only to the time you spend at home, but also when you go out.

Then Rashi goes on to explain that "Go in My decrees" refers to toiling in Torah. There should be no time that one is *not* toiling in Torah!

A few days ago, I heard a story from a *talmid chacham* who heard it from the hero of the story himself.

As a young *bachur*, he studied in the *beis midrash* of R' Elchonon Wasserman. (This predated the opening of the yeshivah at Baranovich.) His students learned with him in a large shul in a certain town.

A group of men from the town conducted their own *shiurim* in that same shul. About 10 men sat on the eastern side of the big room, while R' Elchonon taught his *shiur* on the lower level, on the western side.

One morning, in the middle of the *shiur* — literally, as R' Elchonon was speaking to us — one of the men from the town approached him with a request. "We are making a *siyum* on a tractate and would like to ask your honor to say a few words."

"Very well. I'll come," R' Elchonon replied.

He stopped in the middle of the *shiur*, ascended to the other side of the shul, and began to deliver a *derashah* to the men seated there.

We students thought that he would speak for just a few minutes, but he began to warm to his theme. Five minutes went by, and then 10. "Let's step outside for a little fresh air," some of the *bachurim* whispered. One or two left, until everyone was gone.

The *bachur* who told this story was the youngest of the group, and he stayed. "I was afraid to leave because the *Rosh Yeshivah* might return to his place at any moment. *At least one of us should be here,* I thought to myself. So I didn't go out."

R' Elchonon finished his talk and returned to the western side of the *beis midrash*. He stood by his *shtender* and resumed his *shiur* where he had interrupted it earlier. He spoke to empty tables and benches.

I felt uncomfortable. He was talking only to me. There was no one else there. I got up and hesitantly asked the *Rosh Yeshivah*, "Shall I call them in?"

R' Elchonon looked at me apologetically, and explained that he hadn't even noticed that no one was there. "All right, yes, yes, go call them," he said happily.

This is an illustration of "toiling in the Torah." He didn't notice!

Well, now that we've begun with a story let's go on to another. What you are about to hear is a true story.

The Ponevezher Rav was R' Elchonon's *chavrusa* (study partner) for three years in the *kollel* of Radin. They learned with total diligence, to the point where he once said that he was prepared to render an accounting before the Heavenly Court on those three years in complete tranquillity, for he could not be faulted for any "*bitul Torah.*" Incidentally, he added, even when he had to step out to the washroom he asked R' Elchonon's leave. "My *chavrusa* needs to know where I'm going. It's not right to just walk away."

In short, it was during this period of diligence that someone came in with a telegram while R' Elchonon was immersed in a *sugya* about *shechitah* (ritual slaughter). He took the telegram, read it, and it said that a son had been born to him in his distant home. He recited the blessing and then immediately went on: "Therefore, according to what we've just said, it's clear that there is no *shechitah* except in the end ..." That is, he resumed the subject he had been in the middle of before he read the telegram!

When they had finished learning, he went over to the Chofetz Chaim and asked for a "mazal tov." "A son was born to me," R' Elchonon said. Then he went on to ask, "What does Rebbi say? Should I go home for the *bris?*"

The Chofetz Chaim responded with a question of his own. "Are you a *mohel* (one who is authorized to perform ritual circumcision)?" R' Elchonon understood this to mean that he should not travel home, and returned to his learning. He didn't go.

And since we're discussing diligence, let me tell you something else, in the name of the Chofetz Chaim's grandson, R' Hillel (descended from the Chofetz Chaim's first wife).

At the conclusion of one of the big conferences in Vilna, R' Hillel related, the Chofetz Chaim was very weary. The journey home was difficult and exhausting. As the two entered their own town and arrived at the house, the grandson relates: "My grandfather walked into the house first. By the time I, his young grandson, had a chance to take off my overcoat, the Chofetz Chaim was already leaning over his *shtender* and learning."

Oy, oy, a *shtender!* What is a *shtender?* I'll tell you another story. R' Baruch Ber, as we all know, was a great zealot. He once saw an improper scratch on a *bachur's shtender* and reacted forcefully: "A cross in the *beis midrash!*" he cried out in pain. "How can someone do something like this — to scratch a cross on the *Aron Kodesh* of the *Torah She'be'al Peh?*"

Do you hear how he expressed himself? What is a *shtender*, that lectern that yeshivah students use as they sit and learn Torah? It is a "Holy Ark of the Oral Torah"!

In that case, let me ask you something: How can a *bachur* sit in front of the *Aron Kodesh* of the Oral Torah and think about ice cream or money or other "purposeful" or "practical" things? Fool! I once heard my rebbi put it this way: "You are sitting in a sea of purpose; you are immersed in a sea of purpose — and you are seeking purpose?!"

* * *

☞ A Chicken in the Kitchen

"If you will follow My decrees and observe My commandments and perform them" — The word *"osam"* ("them") is spelled without the letter *"vav."* *Chazal* teach: *"Va'asisem osam"* ("and perform them") urges us to make something of ourselves. This is a special level that one merits through following Hashem's decrees, that is, toiling in Torah.

If *b'nei Torah* are capable of achieving this, why haven't we all achieved it?

I once heard R' Meir Chadash speak about the following verse and *Chazal's* teachings on it: "The deliberate sins of the ignorant are considered as though they were done without deliberation (that is, unknowingly or accidentally)." With regard to Torah scholars, however, "Erroneous sins are considered deliberate." This would seem astonishing. Why should ignorant boors be rewarded, in that their purposeful transgressions are considered non-purposeful, while Torah scholars lose out by having their erroneous transgressions considered purposeful?

"There are several ways to explain this Gemara," R' Meir told us. "But I will not tell them all to you. I'll will only tell you this: you will be punished! Nothing can help you escape that. 'The erroneous sin will be considered a deliberate one.' And you don't have the option of going back to being ignorant. Nothing can help us now. We've been caught. We are *b'nei Torah*! If we behave like ignorant folk now, we will be slapped down."

My rebbi, R' Elya Lopian, told a fine story in relation to this teaching of *Chazal*.

"When I was a boy of about 5 years old," he said, "I once threw a glass off the table. My mother came and smacked me a few times: I'd broken a glass. From then on, I knew: If you break a glass, you get a few slaps.

"A few days later, when my mother was not at home, I noticed that our rooster had come into the kitchen. He climbed up onto the box of glasses and threw five of them down to the floor. They shattered. I thought to myself, *Now Mama will come and smack him, too!*

"My mother came in, saw the broken glasses, and began making shushing noises to shoo the rooster out of the house. Then she took a broom and swept up the shards of glass. I asked myself, *I broke a glass, and I got smacked. The rooster broke five glasses, and nothing happened to him at all?!*

"Later, however, I thought it over. That rooster — where was he now? Out there rooting around in the rubbish in the yard, and saying 'cock-a-doodle-doo.' He's pecking around in the garbage for a few stray seeds. What will his end be? In a few weeks, we'll take him to the *shochet* and say, 'Who sanctified us with His mitzvos and commanded us with regard to shechitah.' We will eat that rooster at our table … But I — I am a person! It's worth being a person and to get smacked, rather than to be a rooster and not get smacked!"

Yes, *Rabbosai*. There are many roosters in this world. However, "*If you will follow My decrees and observe My commandments,*" then "*v'asisem osam.*" You will make something of yourselves. You will become a human being! A person can create himself, and this is the greatest joy that there is.

It is in our power to merit more and more, *b'ezras Hashem*. As Rashi says here (26:12): until we reach the tremendous bliss of "*I will stroll with you in Gan Eden.*" "*I will be a God for you!*"